JESSICA ABEL
TRISH TRASH

ROLLERGIRL OF MARS
THE COLLECTED EDITION

By Jessica Abel

Backgrounds and Design
Lydia Roberts

Colors
Walter

New York

JESSICA ABEL
TRISH TRASH
ROLLERGIRL OF MARS
THE COLLECTED EDITION

Backgrounds and design by Lydia Roberts
Colors by Walter
Wikimarz.red art and colors by Lydia Roberts

Super Genius books may be purchased for
business or promotional use. For information
on bulk purchases please contact Macmillan
Corporate and Premium Sales Department at
(800) 221-7945 x 5442

Super Genius graphic novels are also
available digitally wherever e-books are sold.

Super Genius is an imprint of Papercutz.

JayJay Jackson — Production
Jeff Whitman — Editor
Dawn Guzzo — Special Thanks
Jim Salicrup
Editor-in-Chief

PB ISBN: 978-1-5458-0167-3
HC ISBN: 978-1-5458-0166-6

Printed in India
November 2018

Distributed by Macmillan
First Super Genius Printing

TRISH TRASH # 1

TRISH TRASH # 2

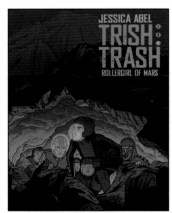

TRISH TRASH # 3

TRISH TRASH graphic novels 1 and 2 are available at booksellers everywhere for $14.99 each. Trish Trash
#3 is $15.99. Or order from us—please add $5.00 for postage and handling for the first book, add $1.00
for each additional book. Please make check payable to NBM Publishing.
Send to: SUPER GENIUS, 160 Broadway, Suite 700, East Wing, New York, NY 10038 (1-800-886-1223)
www.supergeniuscomics.com

Trish Trash has been a very, very long time coming. The list of people I am indebted to is extensive. I am thrilled to finally have the opportunity to acknowledge and thank everyone, even as I'm slightly paralyzed by fear that the tortured history of the book may mean that I've omitted someone. Matt Madden, of course, is my ever-present one-man writer's room. I can't express how much I appreciate and love him for it. Thanks, too, to all my readers over the years: Benjamin Fisch, Kim Chaloner, JP Kim, Nancy Ethiel, Jeremy Sorese, Nick Bertozzi, Jessica Hedrick, and to my agent, Bob Mecoy.

For their invaluable help in the studio, my sincere thanks to Wyeth Yates, Li-Or Zaltzman, Hilary Allison, Eric Arroyo, Kou Chen, and Justine Sarlat.

The Dargaud creative team has brought this book to a level I've never even visited before. Thank you, Fanny Soubiran, Walter, Philippe Ravon, Renaud DeChateaubourg, Nicolas Thibaudin, and Eve Bardin. My thanks also go to my attentive team at Super Genius, Jim Salicrup, Sven Larsen, Michelle Hart, and JayJay Jackson. My particular thanks to the indefatigable Jeff Whitman, who made it all happen.

The early work of Alina Urusov, Sang Jun Ohn, and Ron Wimberly in thinking about and helping me imagine the visual world of Trish Trash was enormously helpful. Thank you.

For their expertise in roller derby and their generous help in clarifying my understanding of what the hell is going on out there, I want to thank Justine Sarlat, Zoë Michaels, Anaïs Ninja, and Molly Flogger. And for their information and inspiration, I extend my deep thanks to Kim Stanley Robinson, NASA's Mars rover teams, Space X, Google Mars, MarsOne, and the Gotham Girls Roller Derby.

Finally, to my assistant Lydia Roberts—you've made this book so much more than I could have alone. Your imagination, intelligence, and determination are stamped on every page. Thank you for all you do.

For Aldara and Jasper. *Ad astra.*

-Jessica Abel

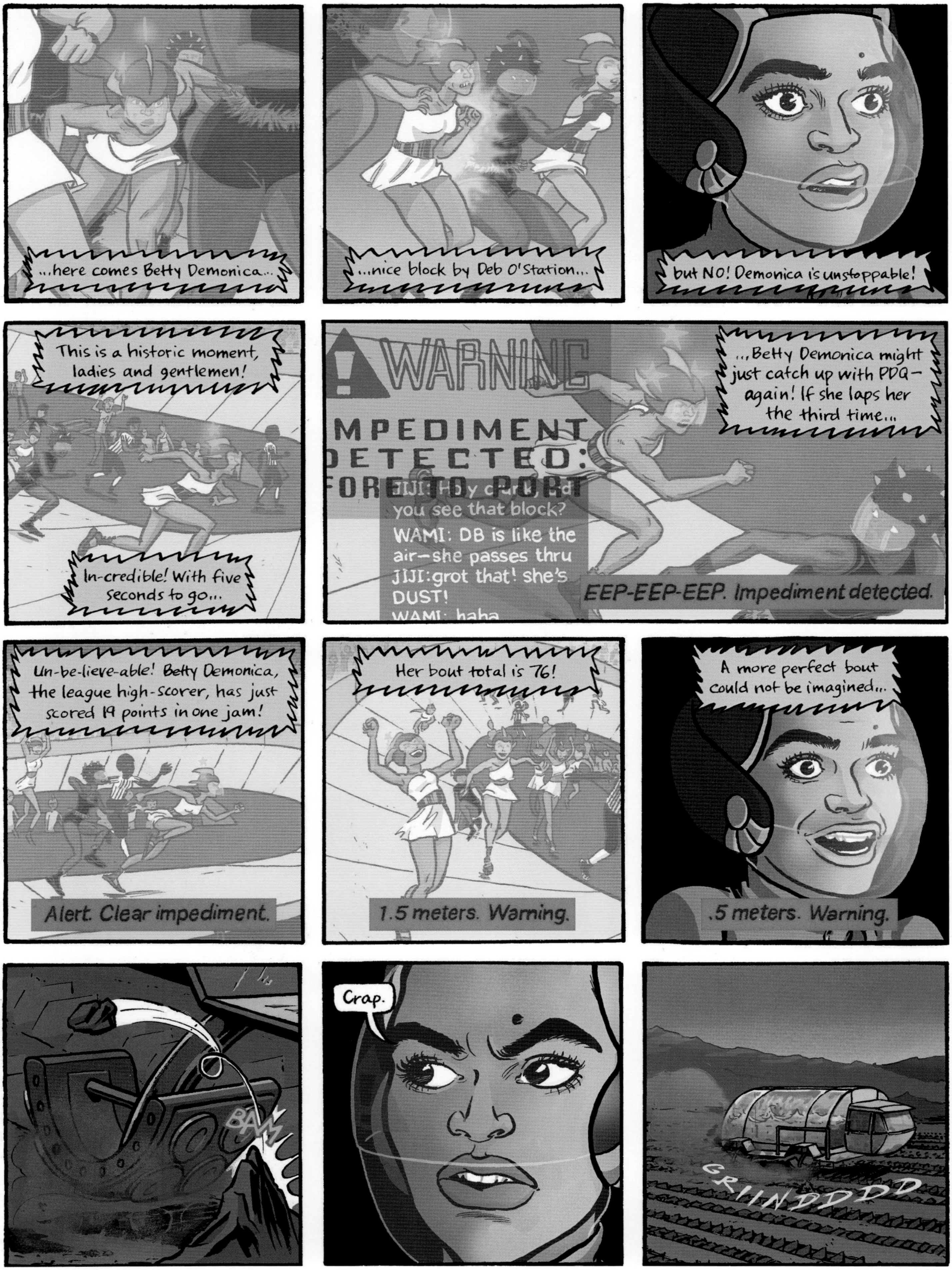
...here comes Betty Demonica...
...nice block by Deb O'Station...
but NO! Demonica is unstoppable!
This is a historic moment, ladies and gentlemen!
In-credible! With five seconds to go...
WARNING
MPEDIMENT DETECTED: FORE TO PORT
you see that block?
WAMI: DB is like the air—she passes thru
JIJI: grot that! she's DUST!
...Betty Demonica might just catch up with PDQ—again! If she laps her the third time...
EEP-EEP-EEP. Impediment detected.
Un-be-lieve-able! Betty Demonica, the league high-scorer, has just scored 19 points in one jam!
Alert. Clear impediment.
Her bout total is 76!
1.5 meters. Warning.
A more perfect bout could not be imagined...
.5 meters. Warning.
BAM
Crap.
GRIINDDDD

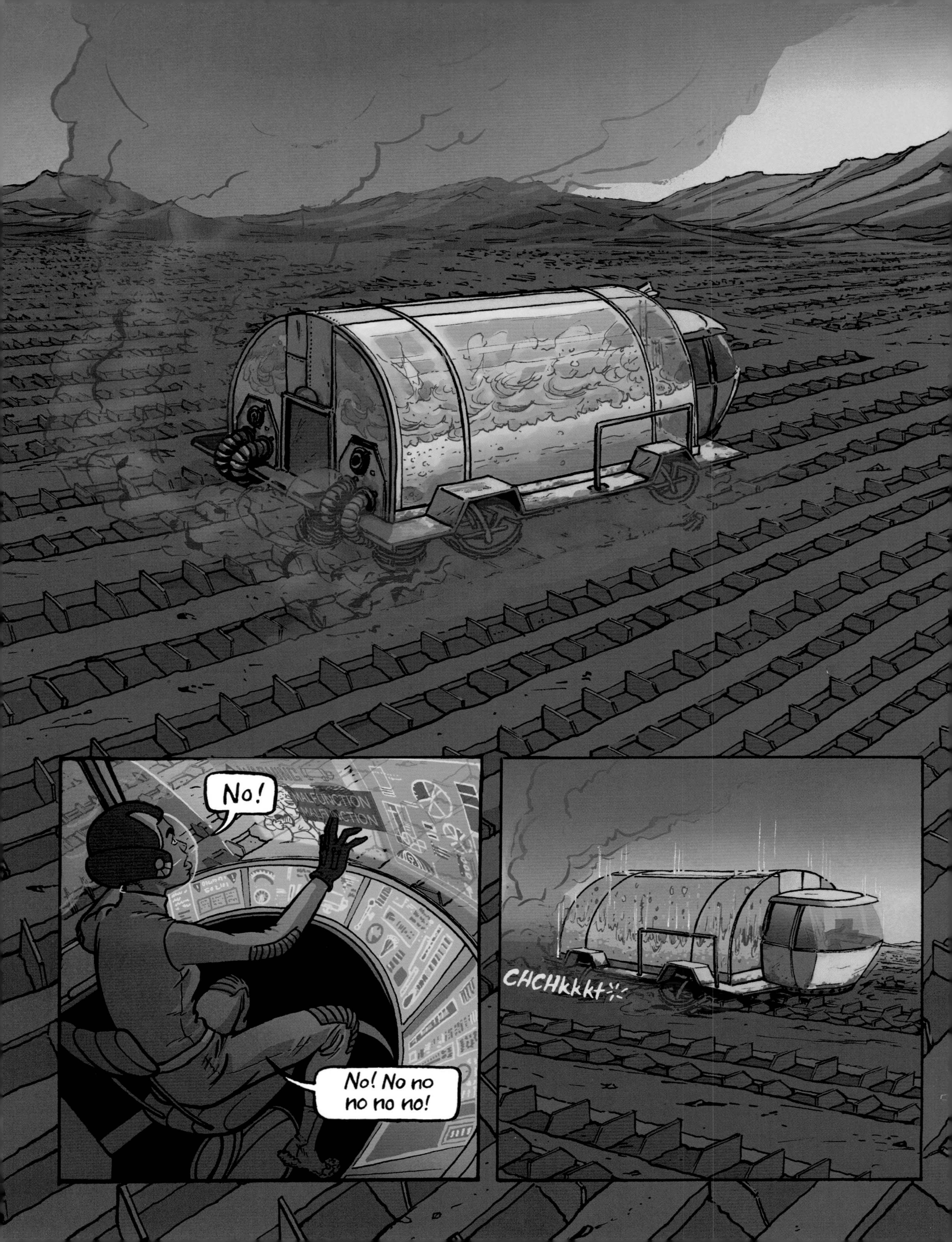
No!
MALFUNCTION
MALFUNCTION
No! No no no no no!
CHCHkkkt

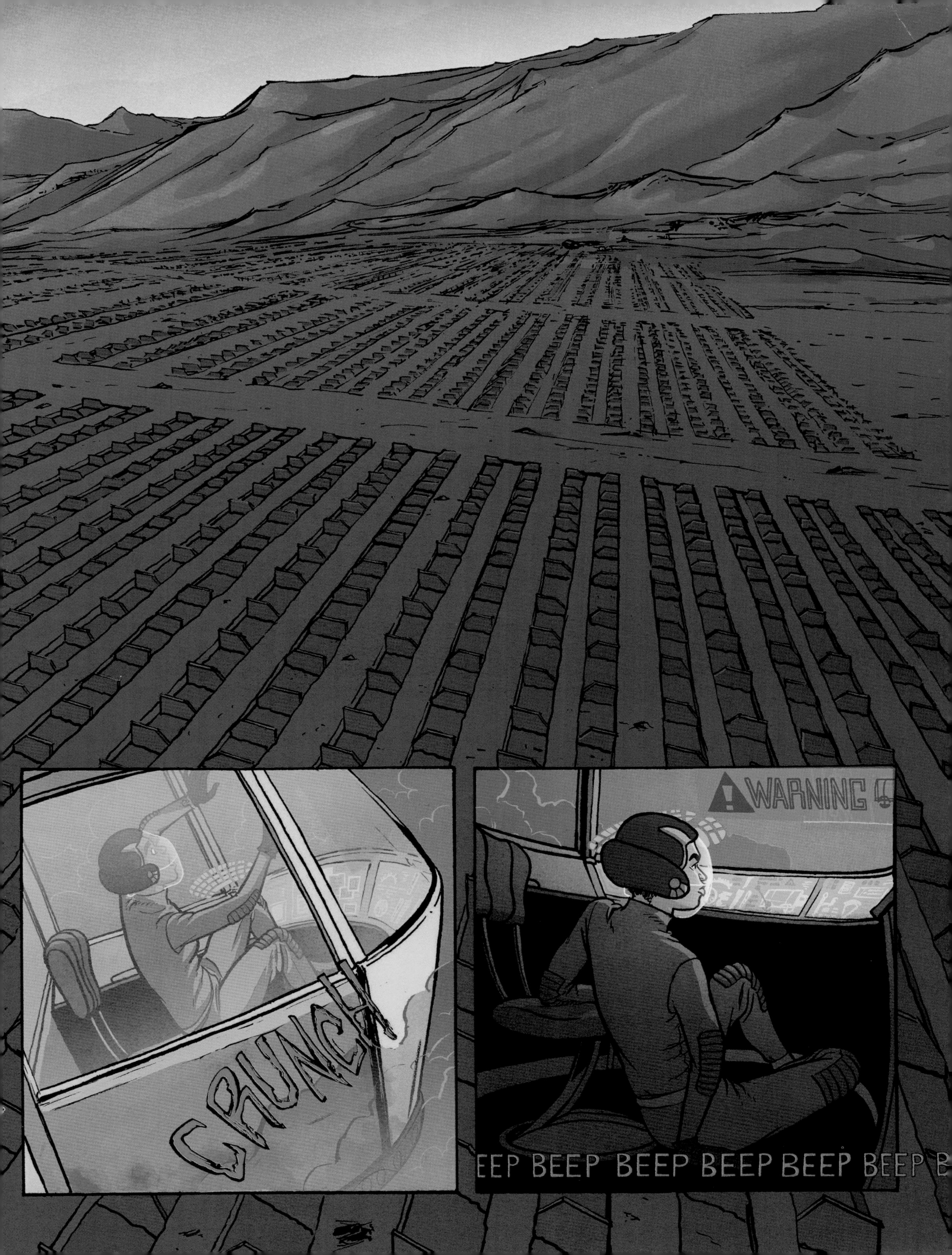
CRUNCH
WARNING
EEP BEEP BEEP BEEP BEEP BEEP B

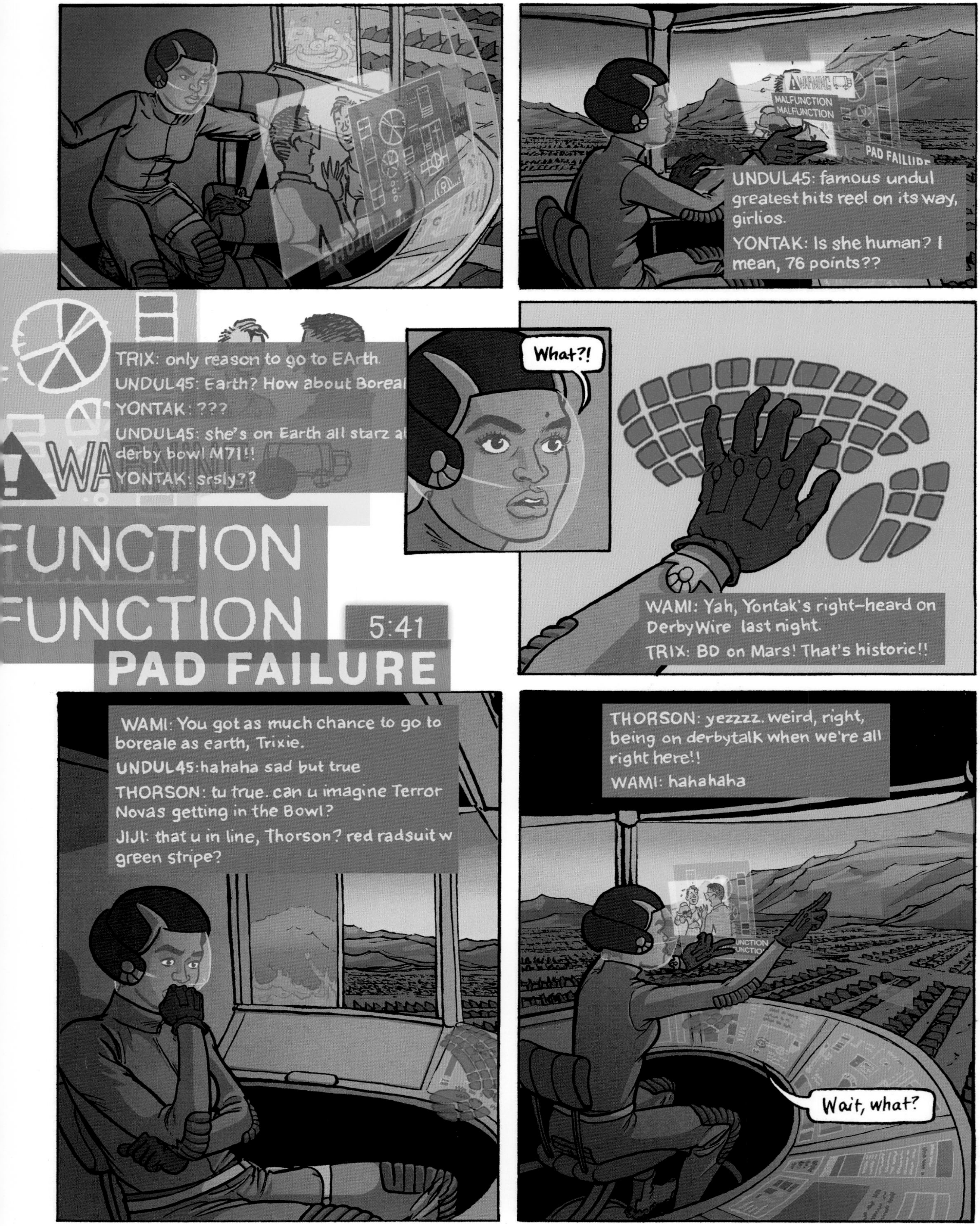

MALFUNCTION
MALFUNCTION
PAD FAILURE
UNDUL45: famous undul greatest hits reel on its way, girlios.
YONTAK: Is she human? I mean, 76 points??
TRIX: only reason to go to EArth.
UNDUL45: Earth? How about Boreal
YONTAK: ???
UNDUL45: she's on Earth all starz at derby bowl M71!!
YONTAK: srsly??
FUNCTION
FUNCTION
5:41
PAD FAILURE
What?!
WAMI: Yah, Yontak's right—heard on DerbyWire last night.
TRIX: BD on Mars! That's historic!!
WAMI: You got as much chance to go to boreale as earth, Trixie.
UNDUL45: hahaha sad but true
THORSON: tu true. can u imagine Terror Novas getting in the Bowl?
JIJI: that u in line, Thorson? red radsuit w green stripe?
THORSON: yezzzz. weird, right, being on derbytalk when we're all right here!!
WAMI: hahahaha
Wait, what?

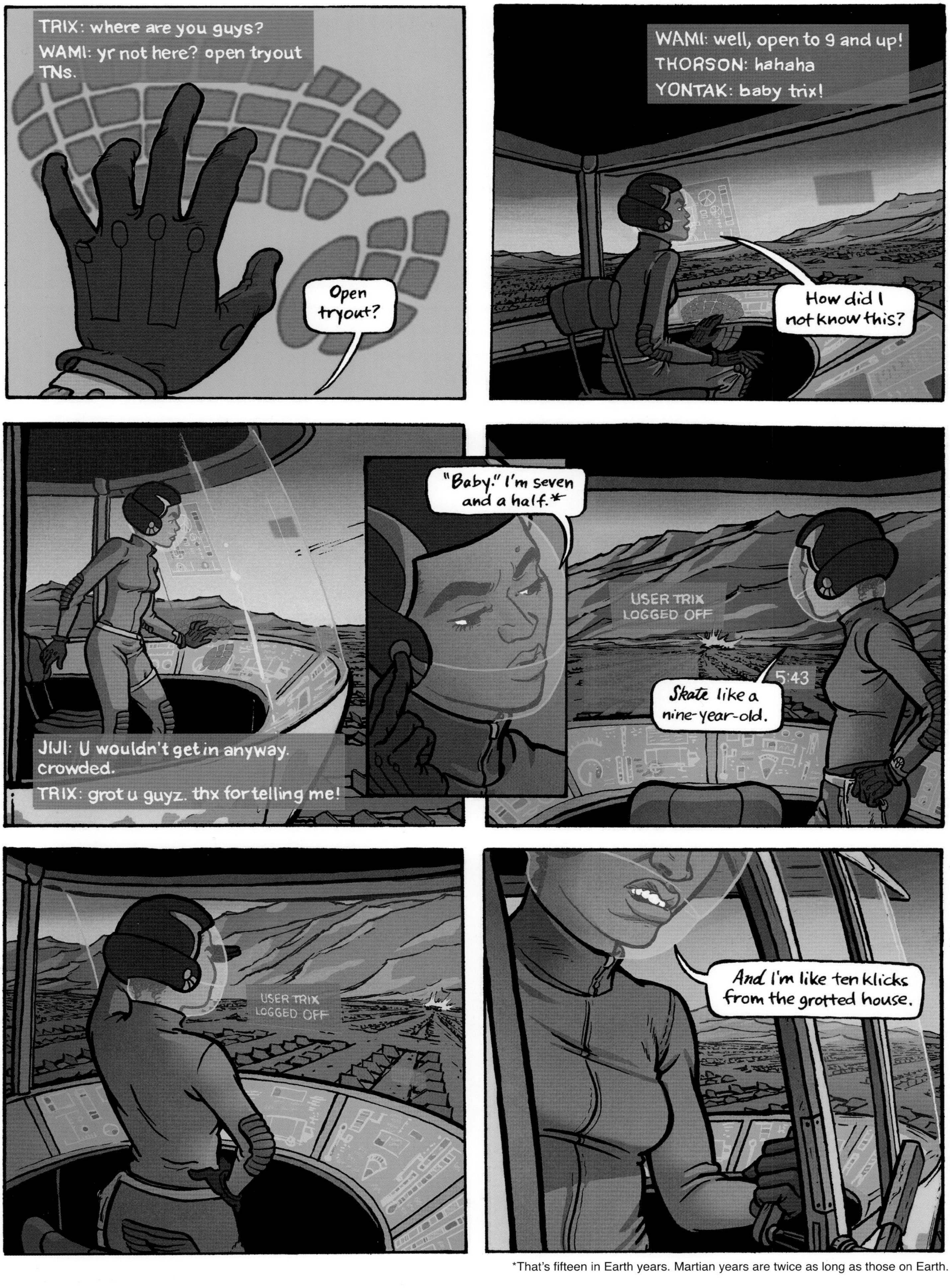
TRIX: where are you guys?
WAMI: yr not here? open tryout TNs.
Open tryout?
WAMI: well, open to 9 and up!
THORSON: hahaha
YONTAK: baby trix!
How did I not know this?
JIJI: U wouldn't get in anyway. crowded.
TRIX: grot u guyz. thx for telling me!
"Baby." I'm seven and a half.*
USER TRIX LOGGED OFF
5:43
Skate like a nine-year-old.
USER TRIX LOGGED OFF
And I'm like ten klicks from the grotted house.

*That's fifteen in Earth years. Martian years are twice as long as those on Earth.

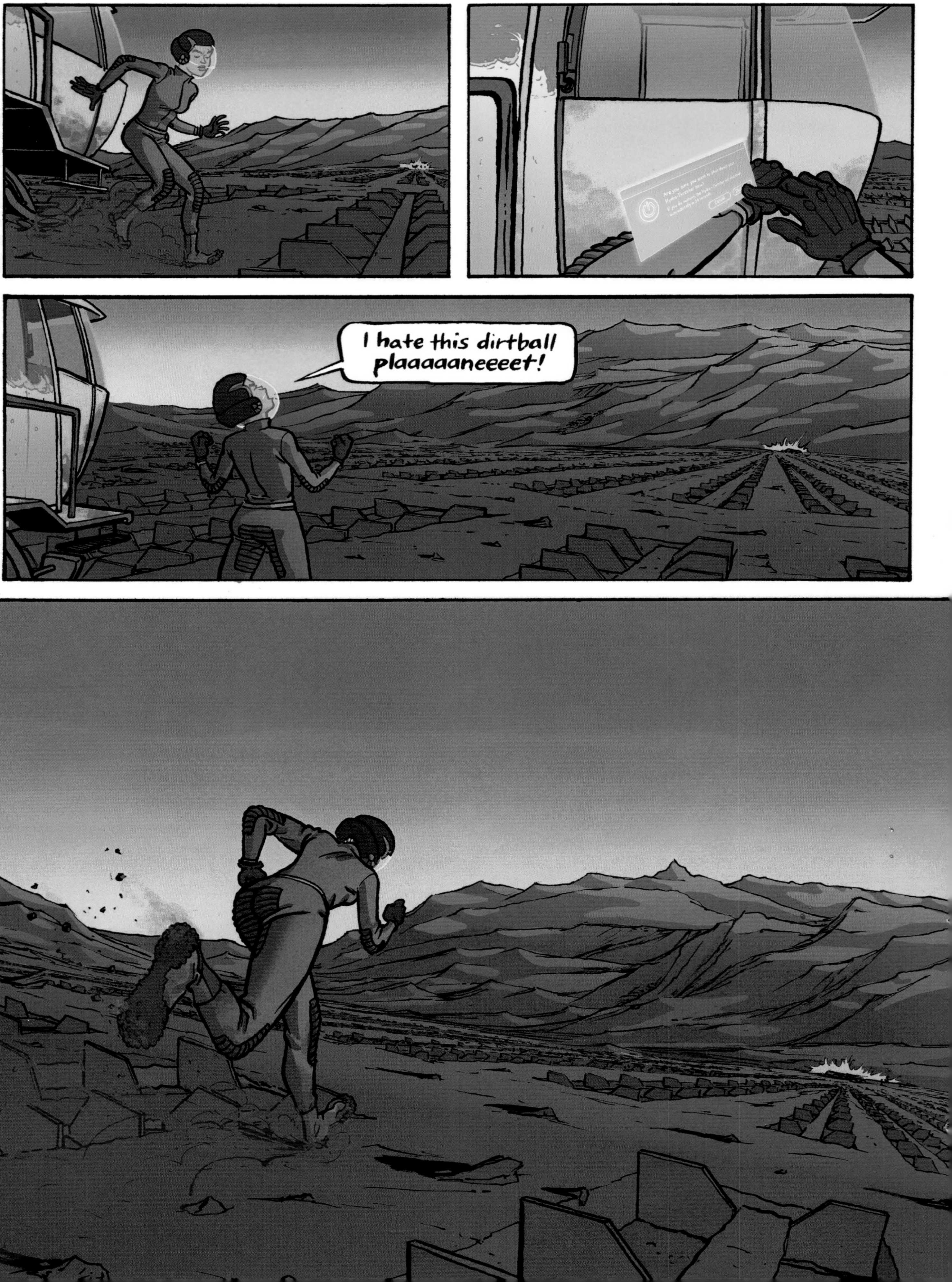
I hate this dirtball plaaaaaneeeet!

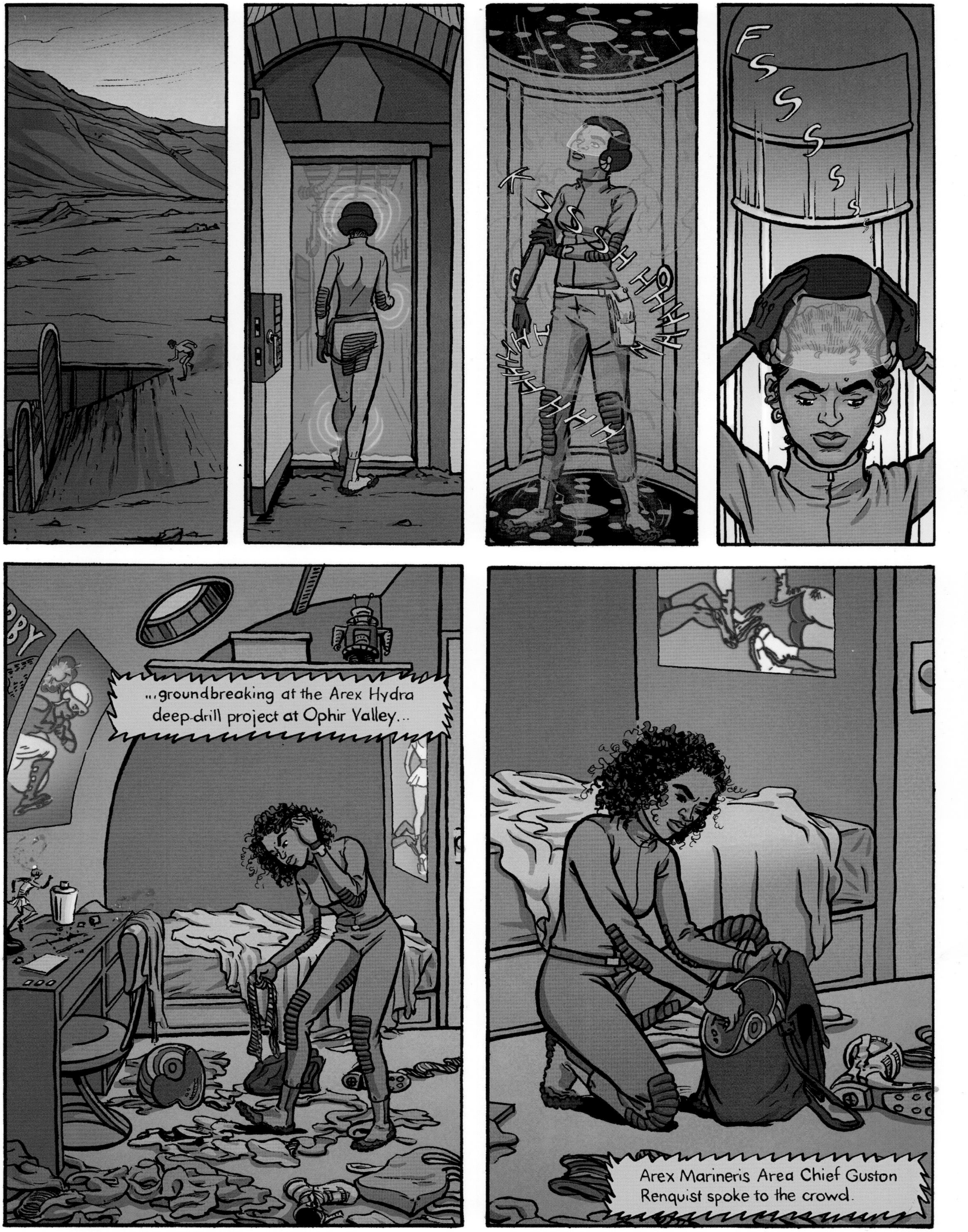
KSSSHHHHHHHHHHHHHHHHHH
FSSSSSS
...groundbreaking at the Arex Hydra deep-drill project at Ophir Valley...
Arex Marineris Area Chief Guston Renquist spoke to the crowd.

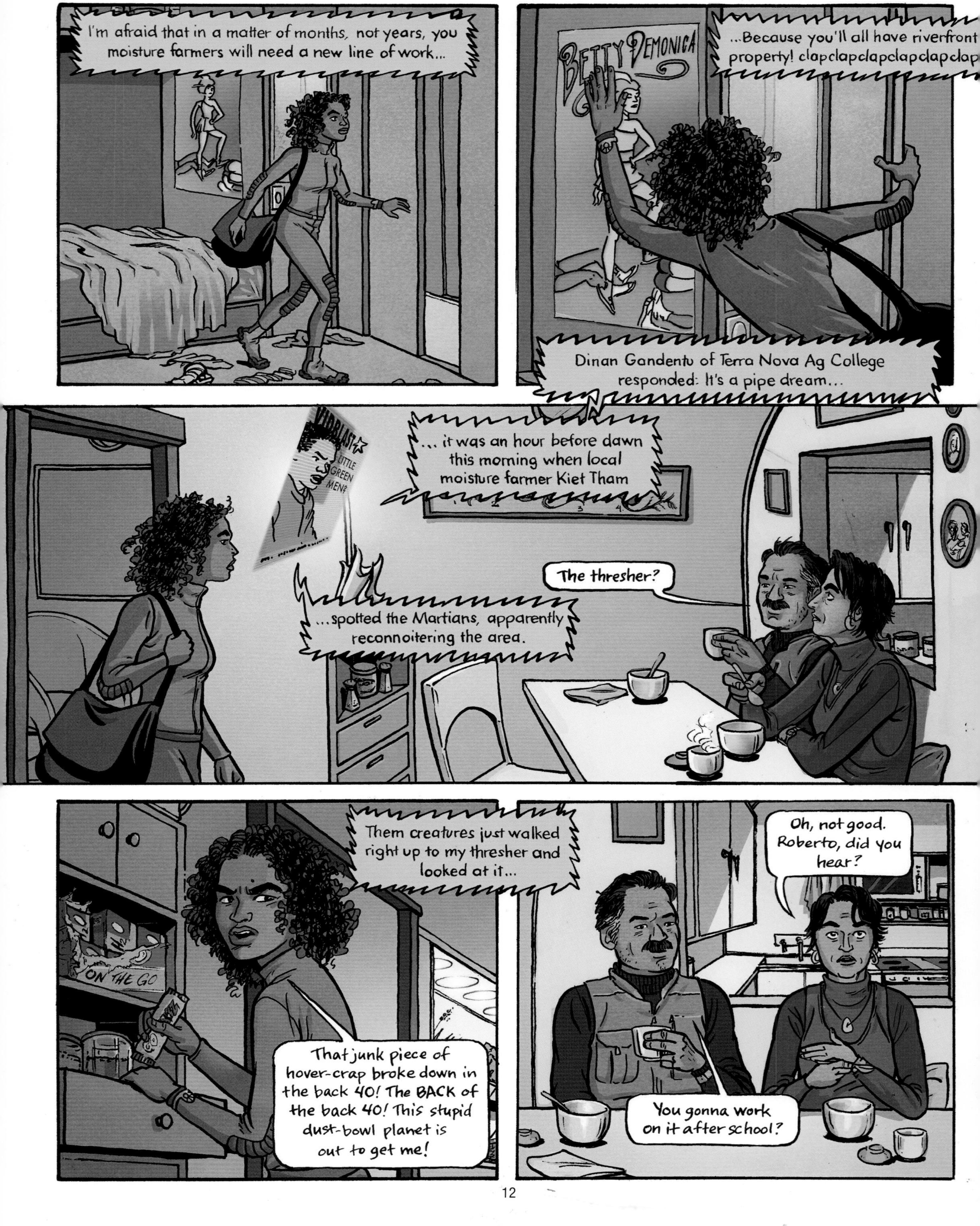
I'm afraid that in a matter of months, not years, you moisture farmers will need a new line of work...
BETTY DEMONICA
...Because you'll all have riverfront property! clapclapclapclapclapclap
Dinan Gandentu of Terra Nova Ag College responded: It's a pipe dream...
... it was an hour before dawn this morning when local moisture farmer Kiet Tham
LITTLE GREEN MEN?
The thresher?
...spotted the Martians, apparently reconnoitering the area.
Them creatures just walked right up to my thresher and looked at it...
ON THE GO
That junk piece of hover-crap broke down in the back 40! The BACK of the back 40! This stupid dust-bowl planet is out to get me!
Oh, not good. Roberto, did you hear?
You gonna work on it after school?

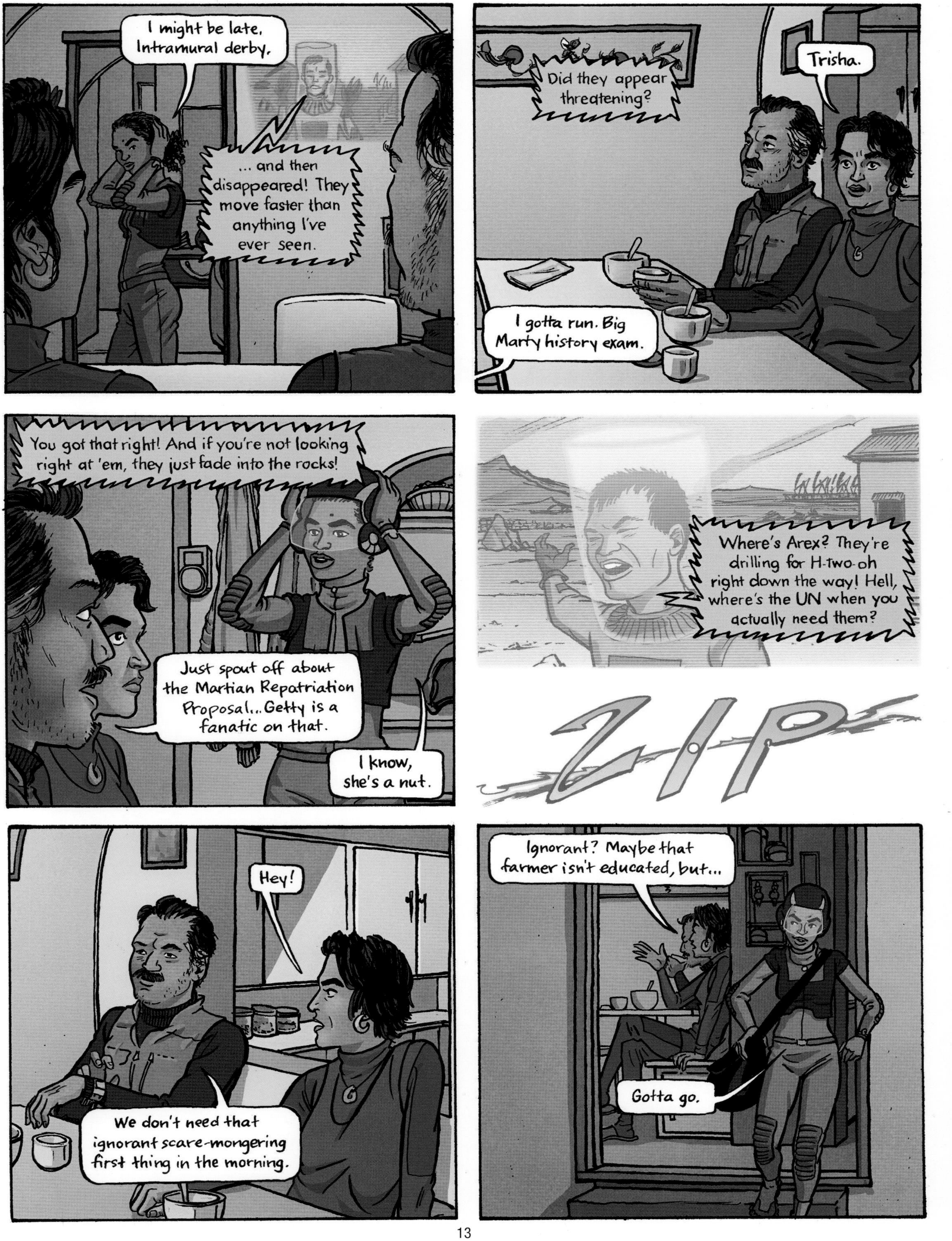
I might be late. Intramural derby.
... and then disappeared! They move faster than anything I've ever seen.
Did they appear threatening?
Trisha.
I gotta run. Big Marty history exam.
You got that right! And if you're not looking right at 'em, they just fade into the rocks!
Just spout off about the Martian Repatriation Proposal... Getty is a fanatic on that.
I know, she's a nut.
Where's Arex? They're drilling for H-two-oh right down the way! Hell, where's the UN when you actually need them?
ZIP
Hey!
We don't need that ignorant scare-mongering first thing in the morning.
Ignorant? Maybe that farmer isn't educated, but...
Gotta go.

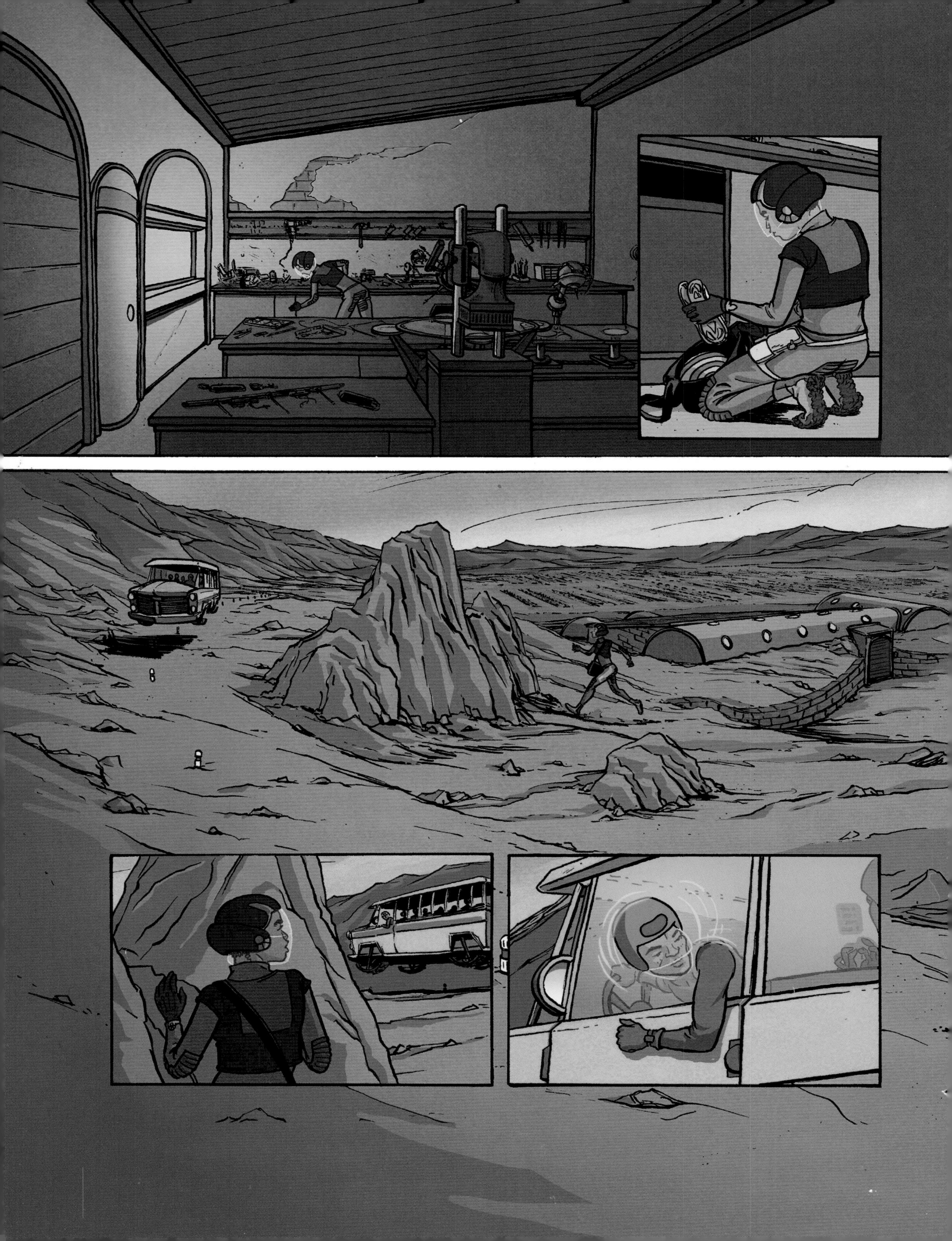

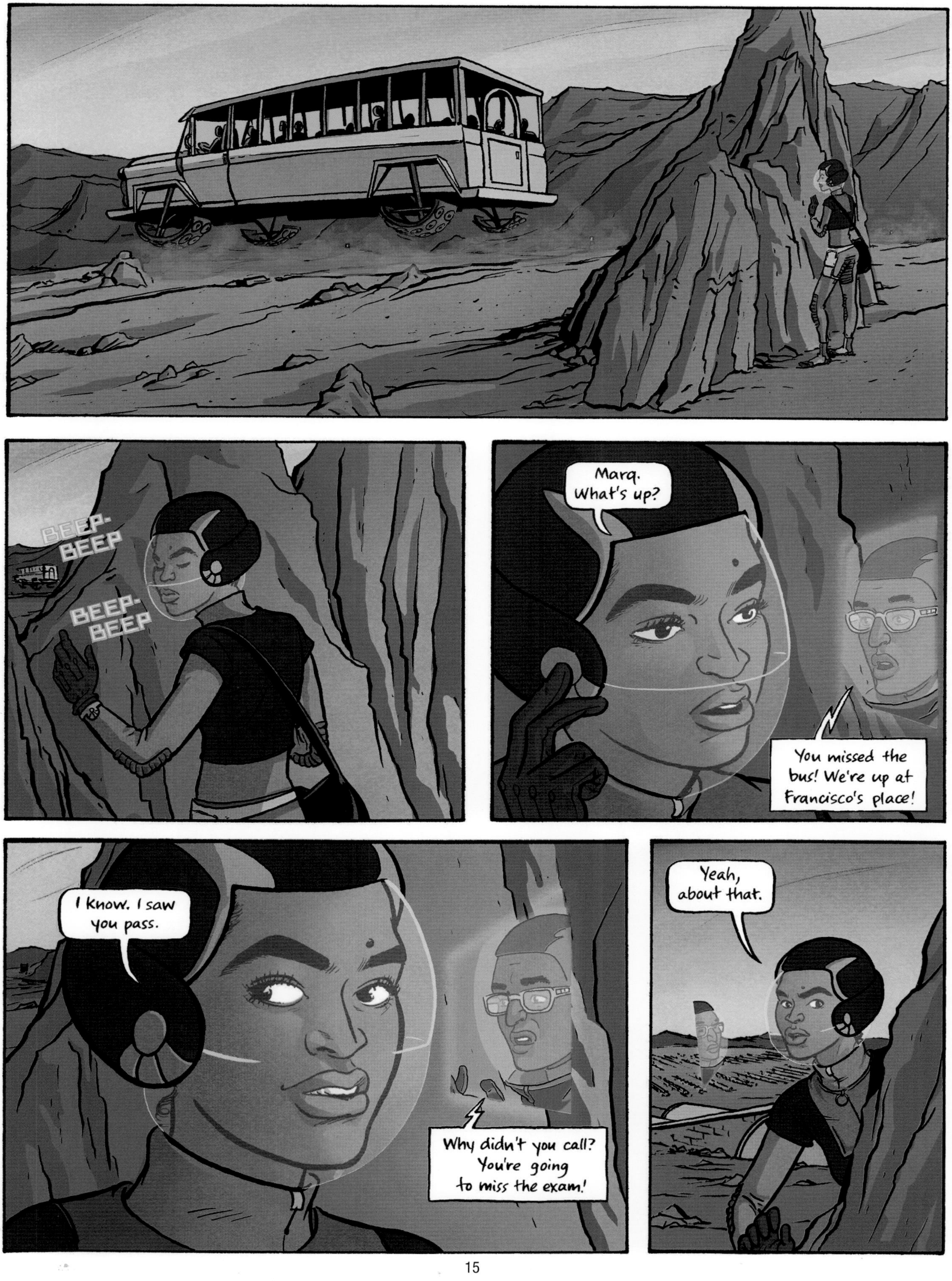
BEEP-BEEP
BEEP-BEEP
Marq. What's up?
You missed the bus! We're up at Francisco's place!
I know. I saw you pass.
Why didn't you call? You're going to miss the exam!
Yeah, about that.

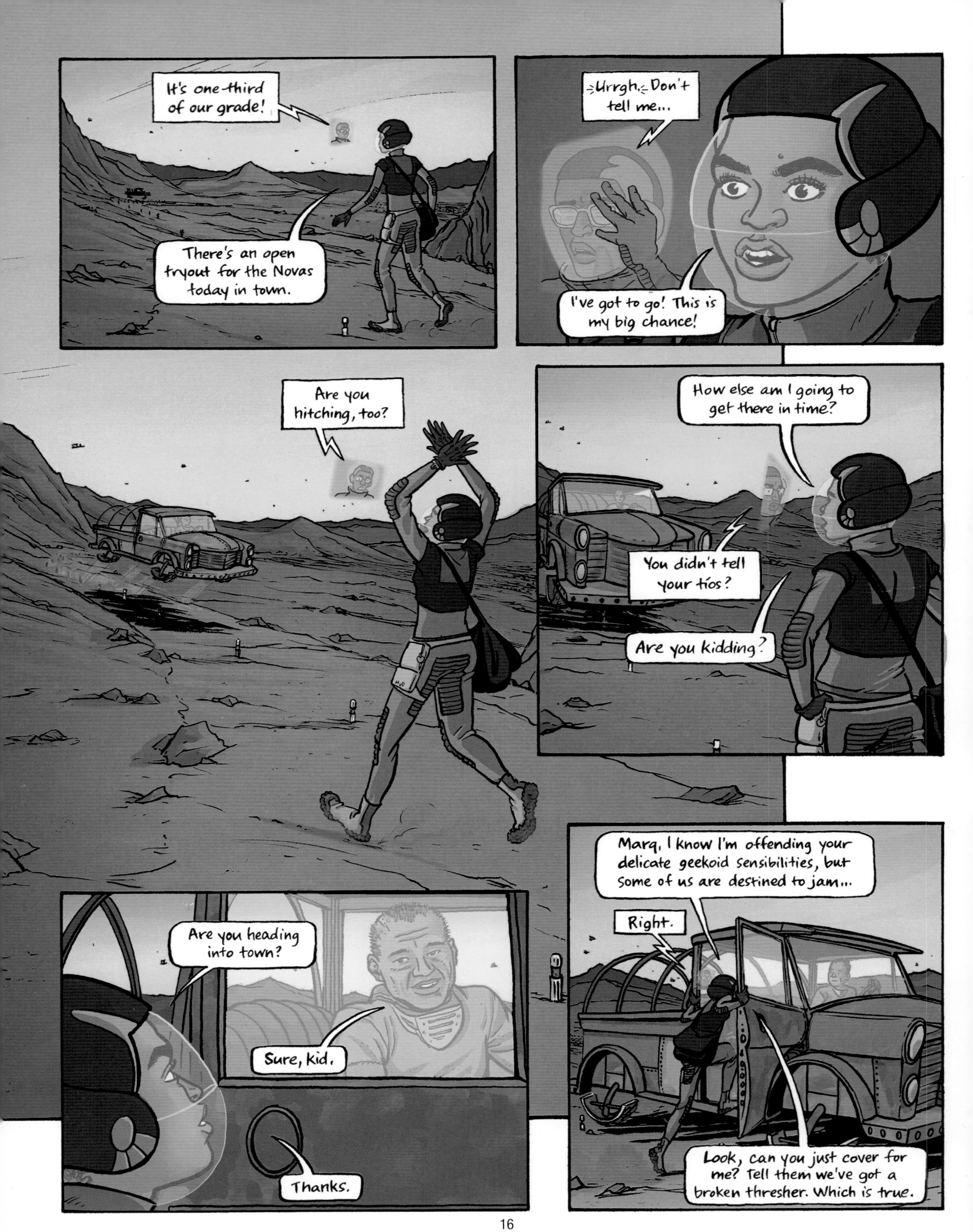
It's one-third of our grade!
There's an open tryout for the Novas today in town.
Urrgh. Don't tell me...
I've got to go! This is my big chance!
Are you hitching, too?
How else am I going to get there in time?
You didn't tell your tíos?
Are you kidding?
Are you heading into town?
Sure, kid.
Thanks.
Marq, I know I'm offending your delicate geekoid sensibilities, but some of us are destined to jam...
Right.
Look, can you just cover for me? Tell them we've got a broken thresher. Which is true.

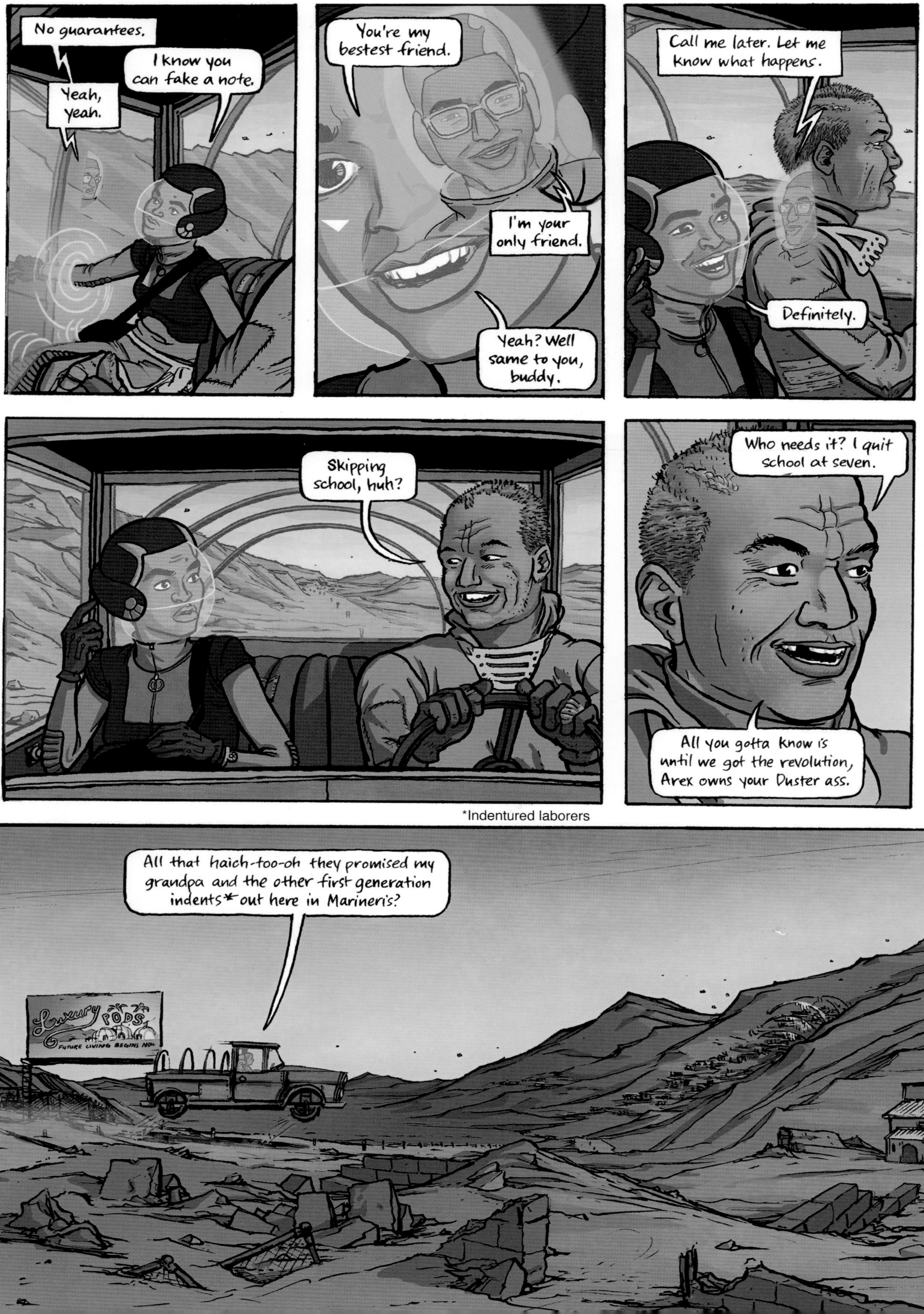
No guarantees.
I know you can fake a note.
Yeah, yeah.
You're my bestest friend.
I'm your only friend.
Yeah? Well same to you, buddy.
Call me later. Let me know what happens.
Definitely.
Skipping school, huh?
Who needs it? I quit school at seven.
All you gotta know is until we got the revolution, Arex owns your Duster ass.
All that haich-too-oh they promised my grandpa and the other first generation indents* out here in Marineris?
Luxury PODS
FUTURE LIVING BEGINS NOW

*Indentured laborers

It ain't there. It don't exist.

See those drills?

Those big drills are strictly for show.

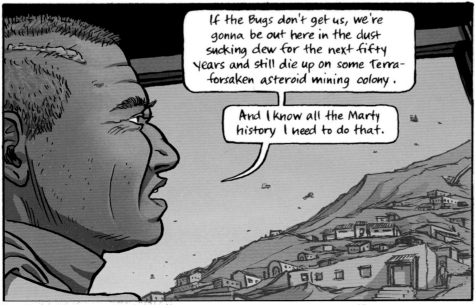

If the Bugs don't get us, we're gonna be out here in the dust sucking dew for the next fifty years and still die up on some Terra-forsaken asteroid mining colony.

And I know all the Marty history I need to do that.

Yeah.

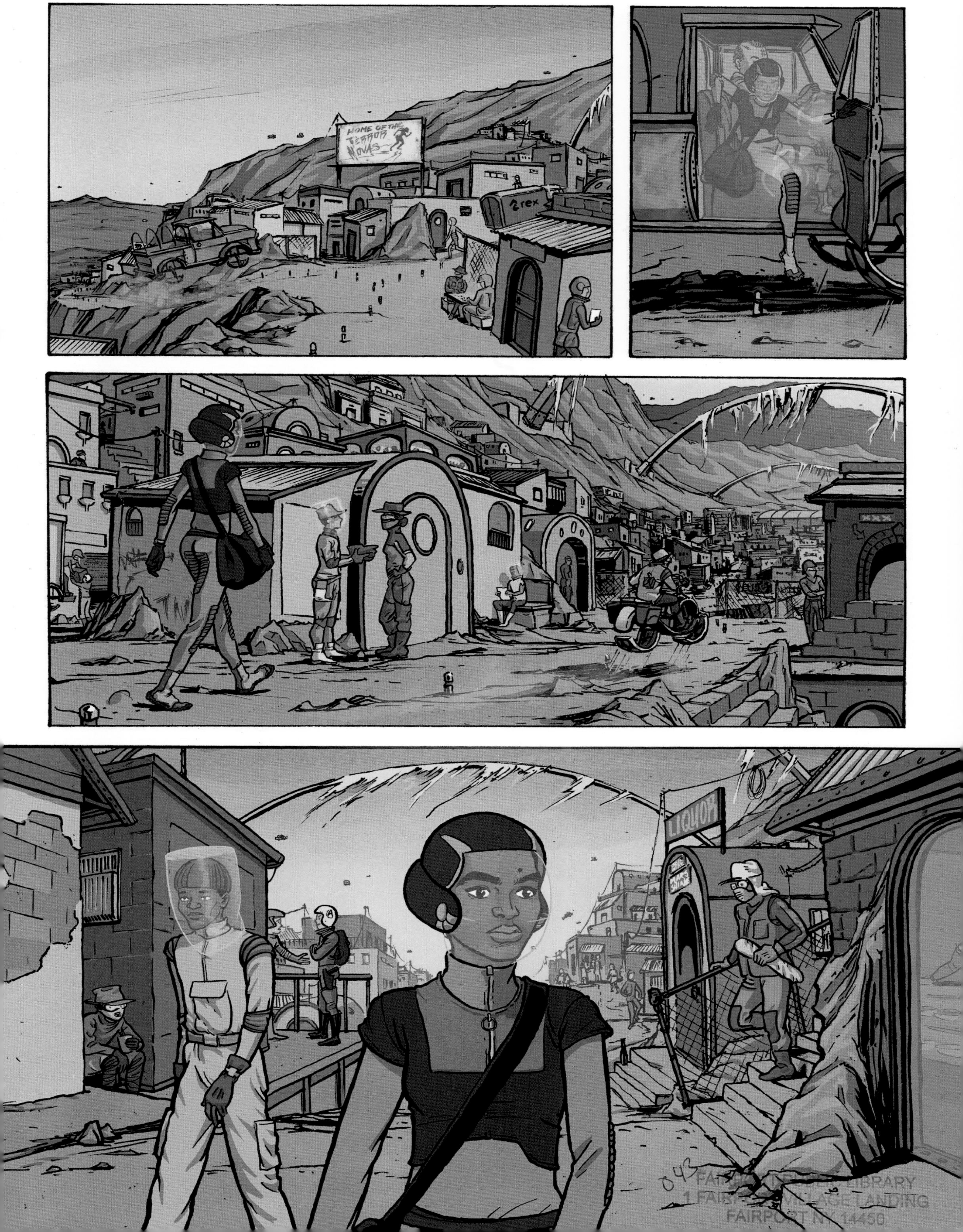
HOME OF THE TERROR NOVAS
rex
LIQUOR

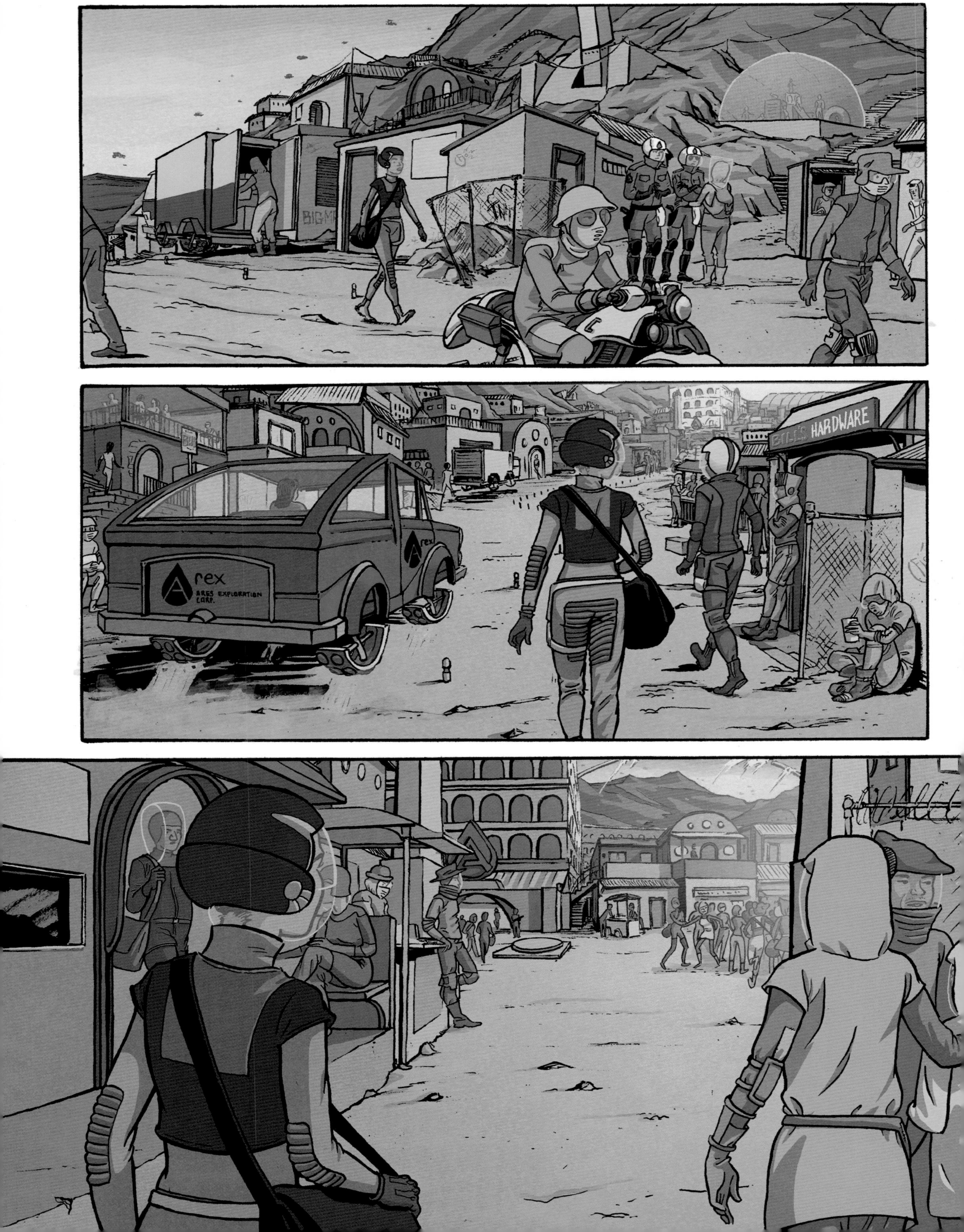

rex
ARES EXPLORATION CORP.
BILL'S HARDWARE

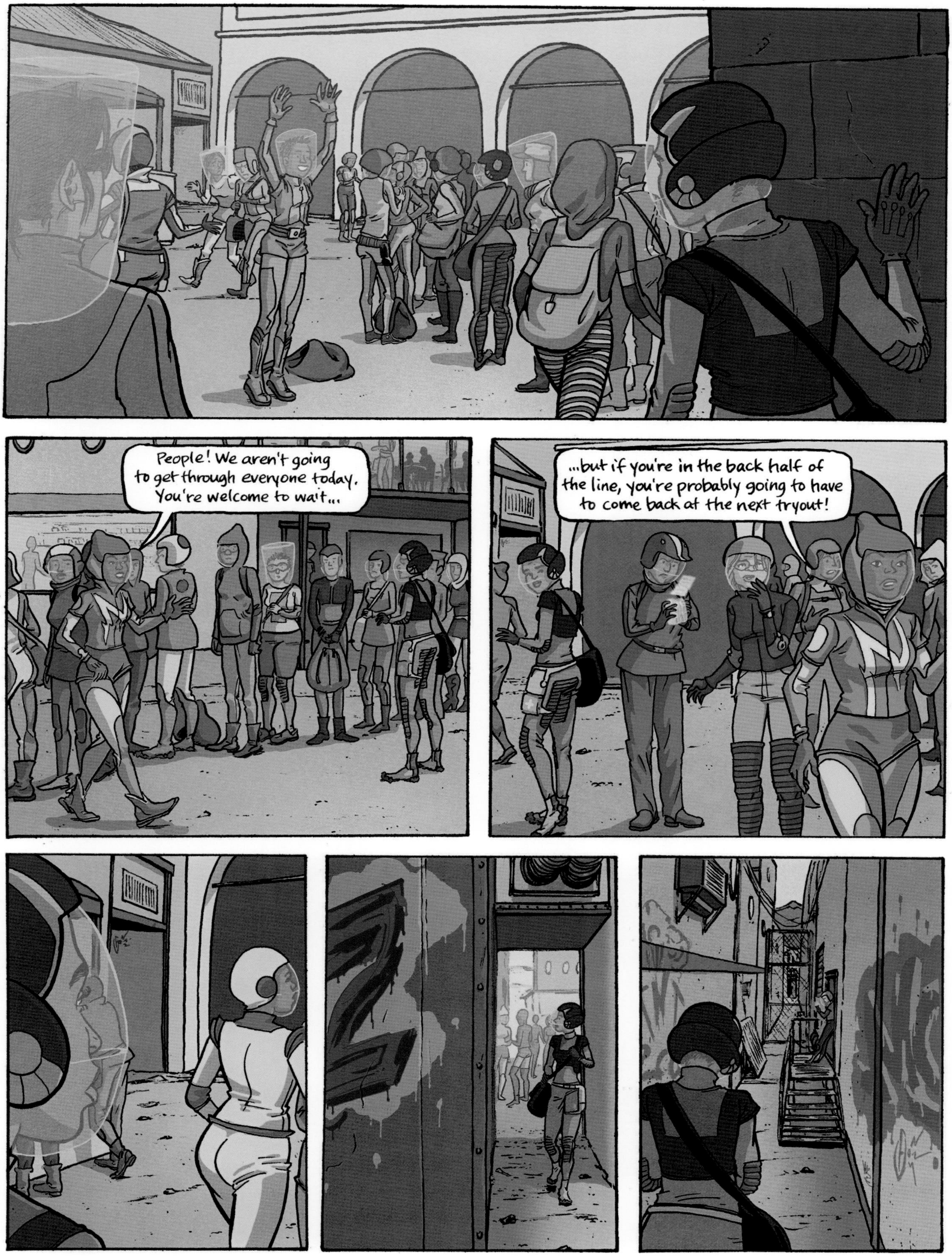
People! We aren't going to get through everyone today. You're welcome to wait...
...but if you're in the back half of the line, you're probably going to have to come back at the next tryout!

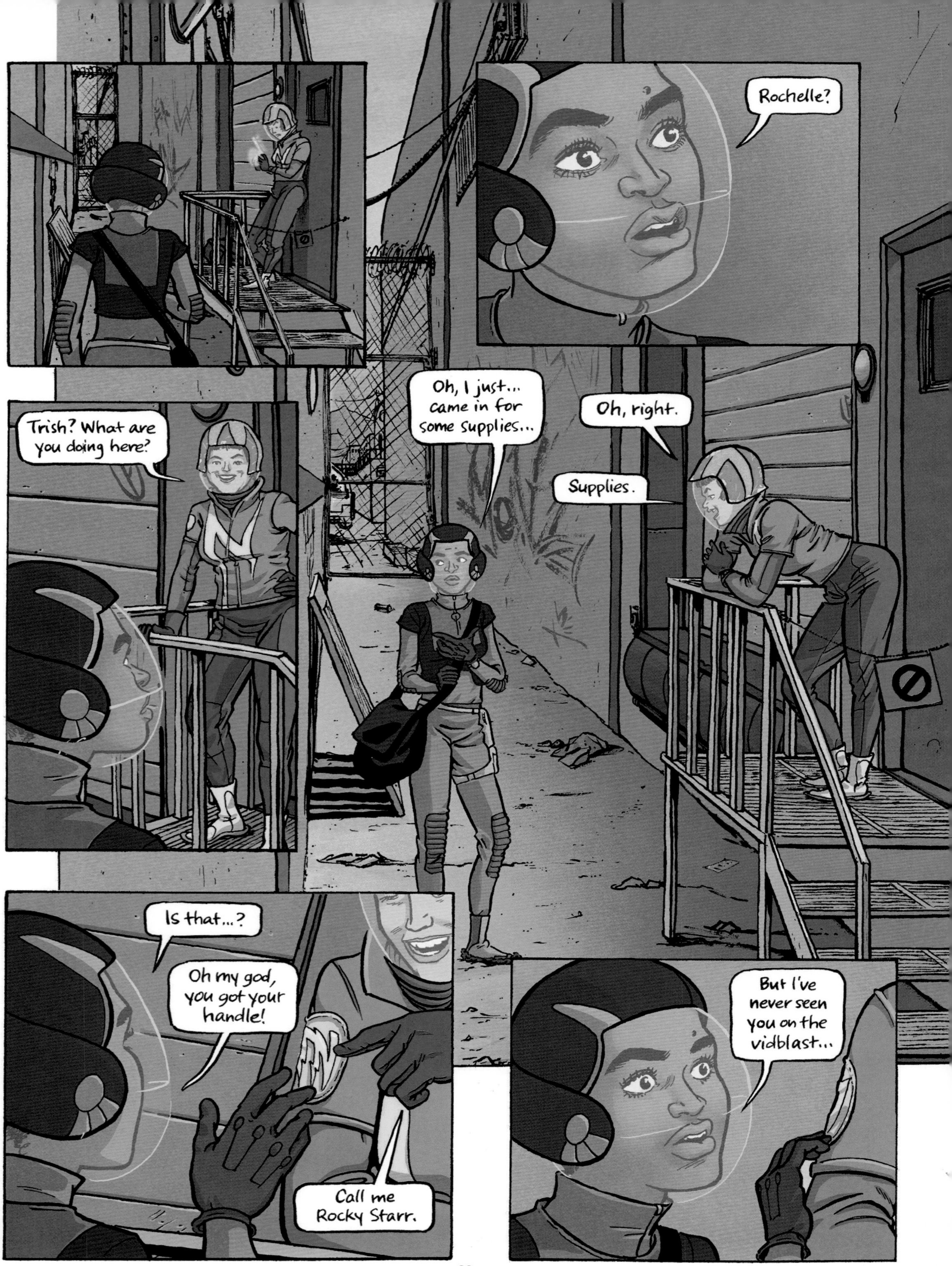

Rochelle?
Trish? What are you doing here?
Oh, I just... came in for some supplies...
Oh, right.
Supplies.
Is that...?
Oh my god, you got your handle!
Call me Rocky Starr.
But I've never seen you on the vidblast...

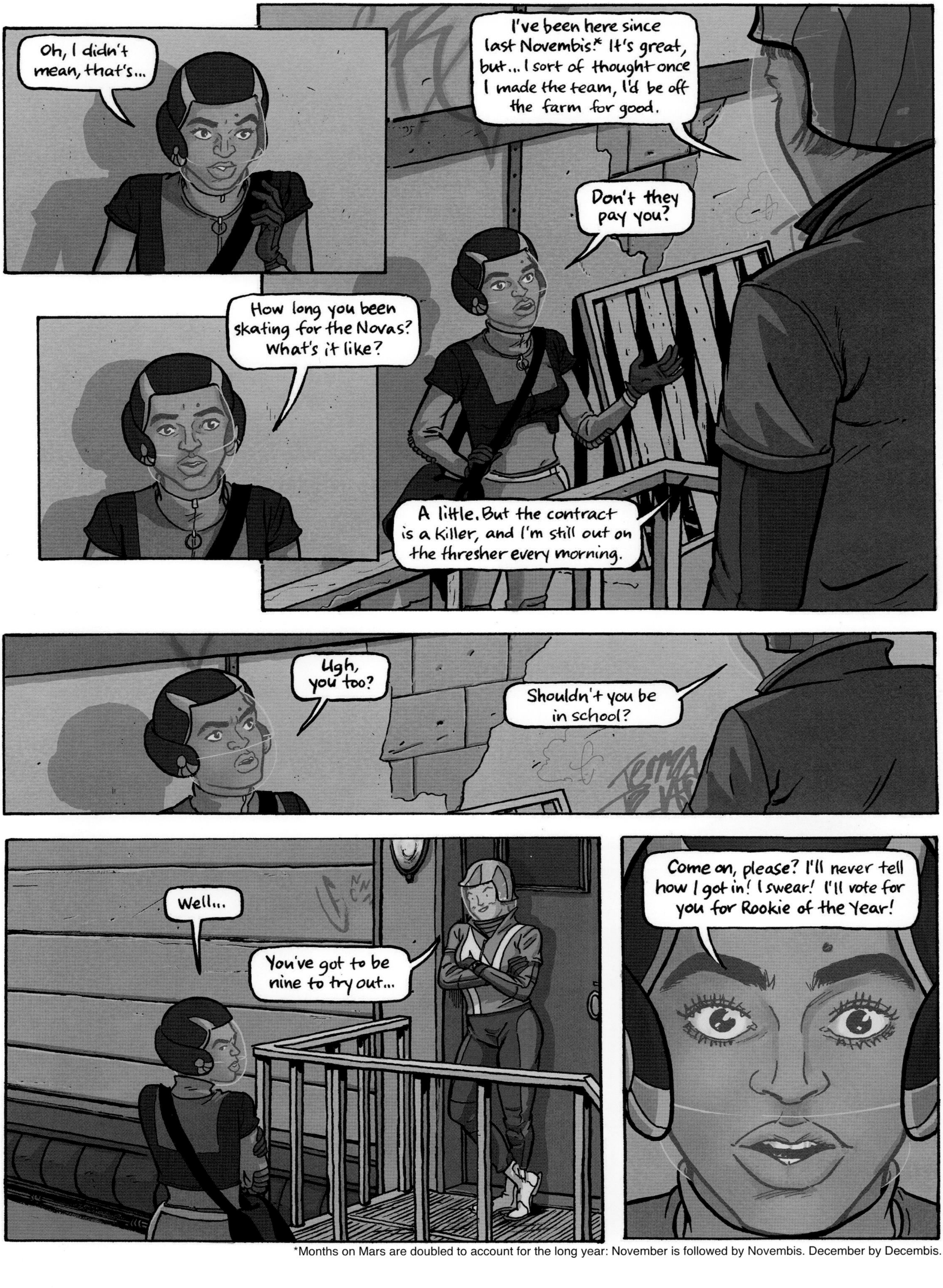
Oh, I didn't mean, that's...
I've been here since last Novembis.* It's great, but... I sort of thought once I made the team, I'd be off the farm for good.
How long you been skating for the Novas? What's it like?
Don't they pay you?
A little. But the contract is a killer, and I'm still out on the thresher every morning.
Ugh, you too?
Shouldn't you be in school?
Well...
You've got to be nine to try out...
Come on, please? I'll never tell how I got in! I swear! I'll vote for you for Rookie of the Year!

*Months on Mars are doubled to account for the long year: November is followed by Novembis. December by Decembis.

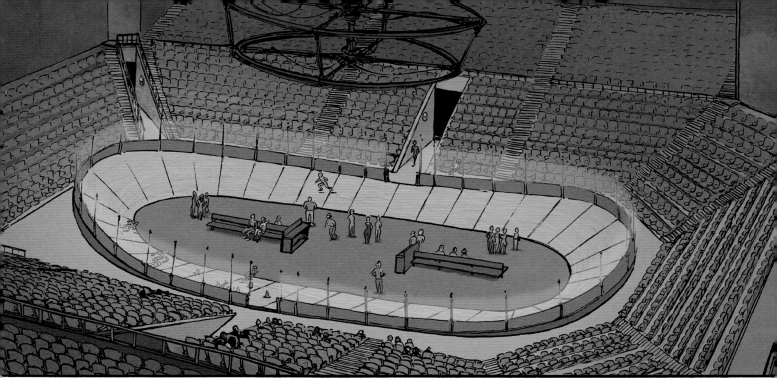

Look, there's Hanna Barbarian!

We're ready for the next group here—group four, get lined up!

OK, ladies, we're going to run a couple of drills to see what you can do.

Get set!

24

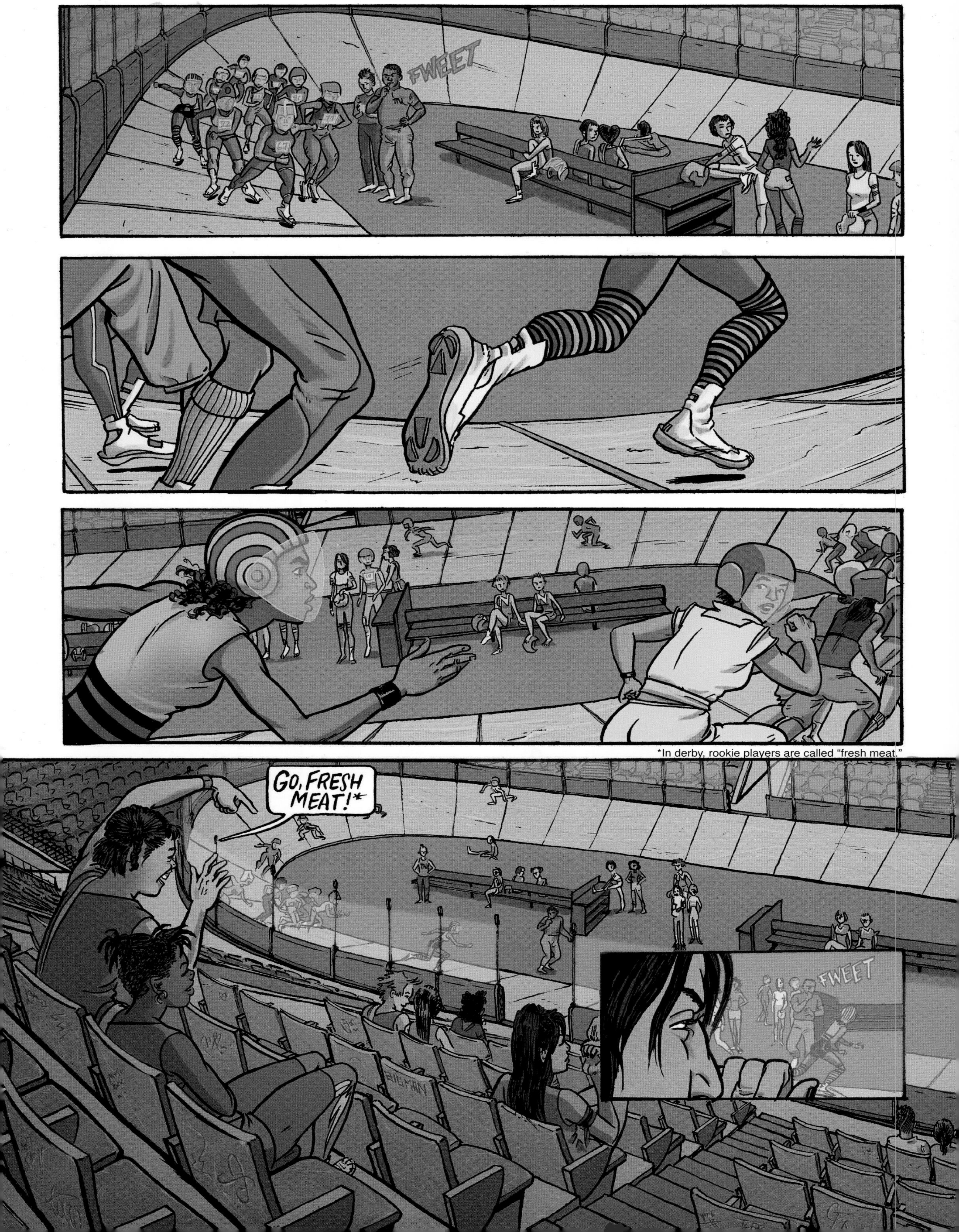
FWEET
GO, FRESH MEAT!*
FWEET
*In derby, rookie players are called "fresh meat."

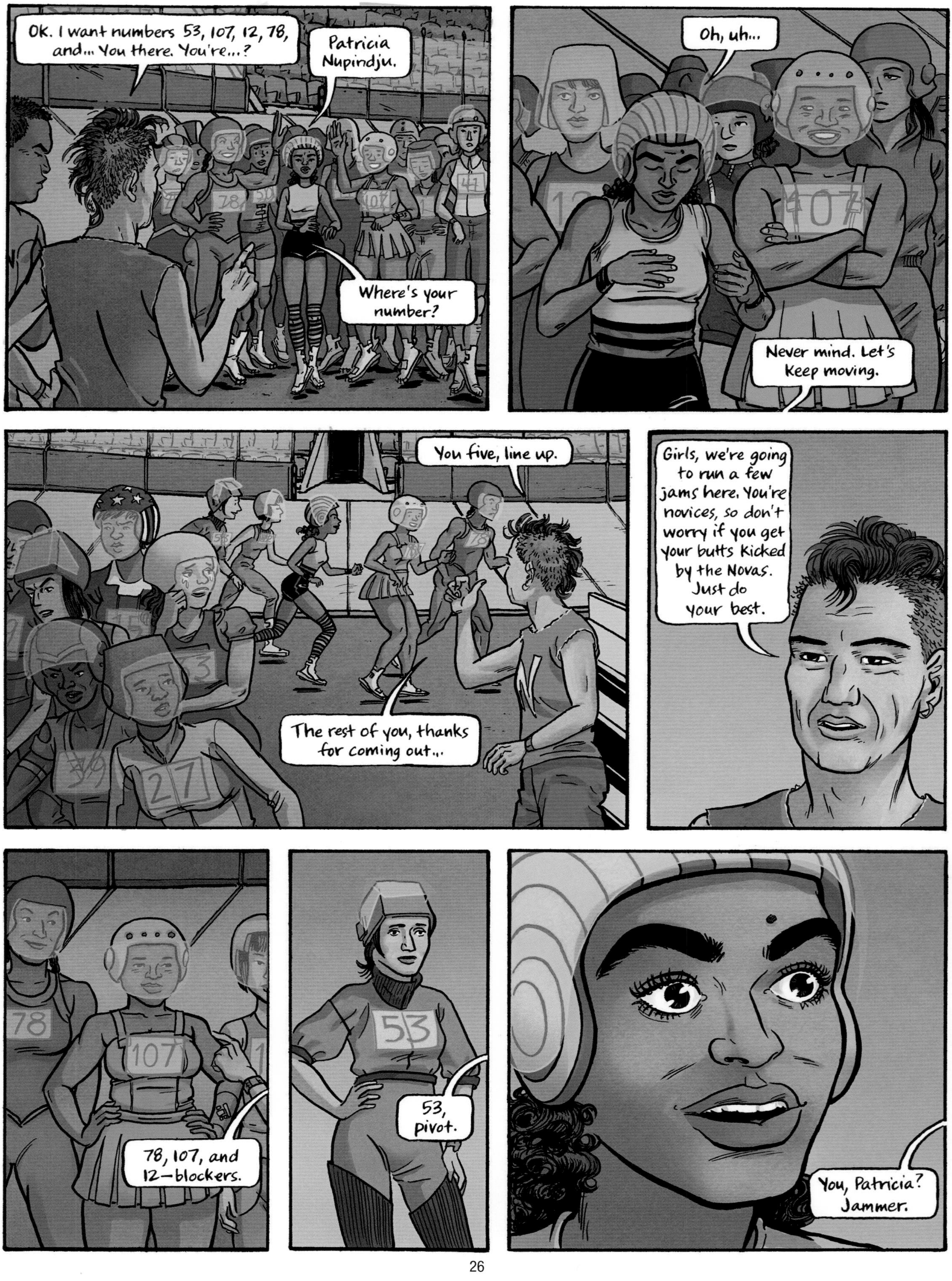
Ok. I want numbers 53, 107, 12, 78, and... You there. You're...?
Patricia Nupindju.
Where's your number?
Oh, uh...
Never mind. Let's keep moving.
You five, line up.
The rest of you, thanks for coming out...
Girls, we're going to run a few jams here. You're novices, so don't worry if you get your butts kicked by the Novas. Just do your best.
78, 107, and 12—blockers.
53, pivot.
You, Patricia? Jammer.

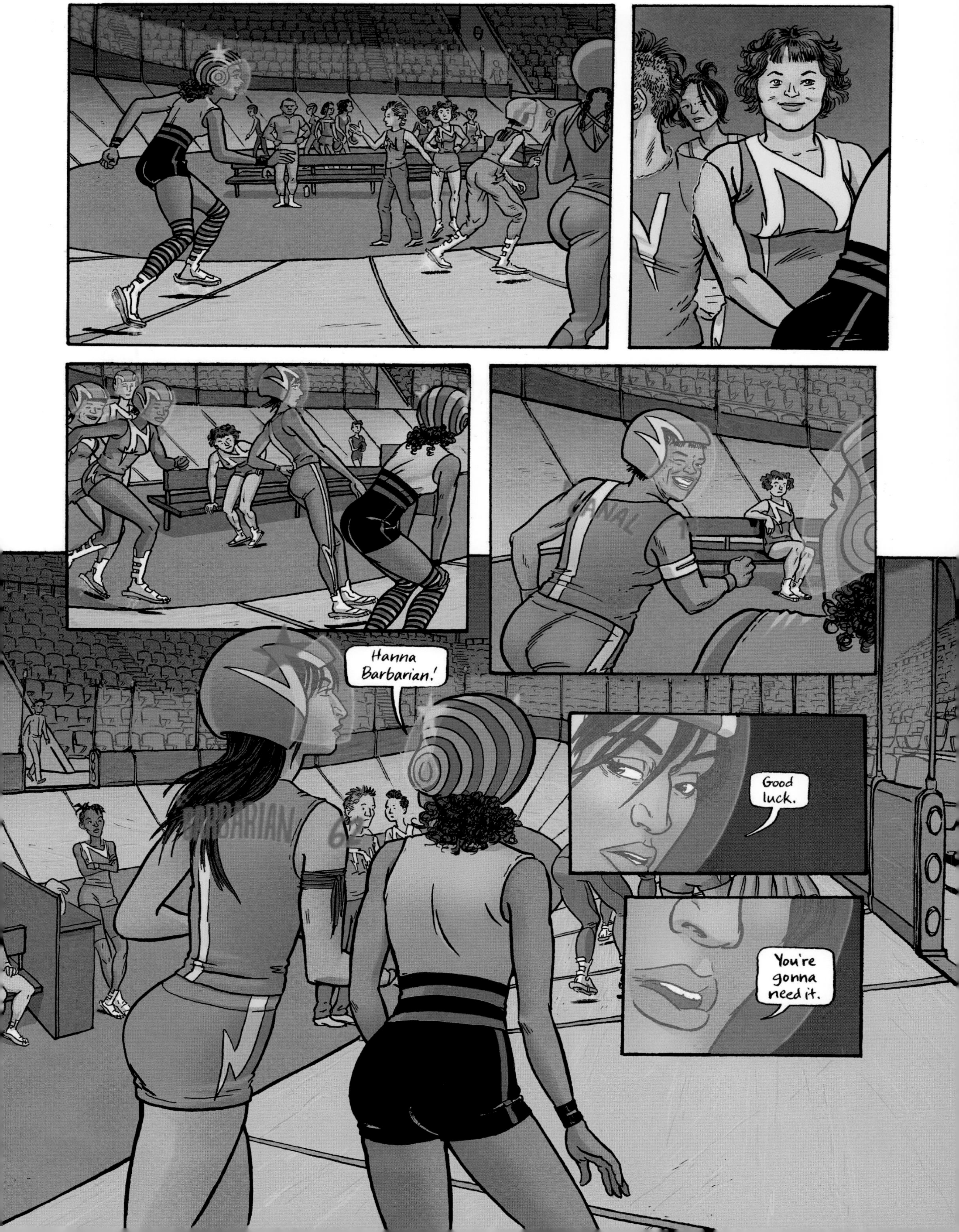
Hanna Barbarian!
Good luck.
You're gonna need it.

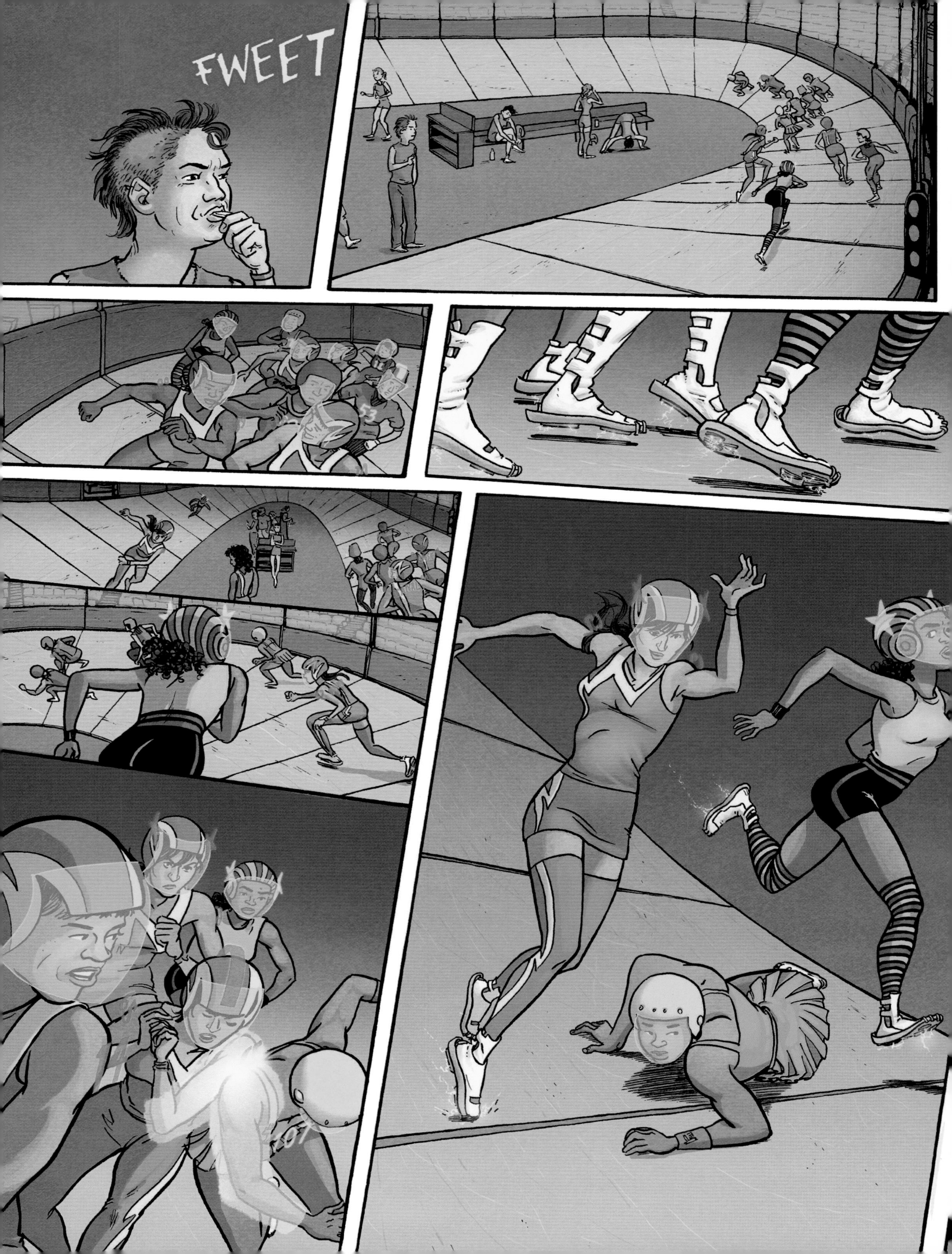
FWEET

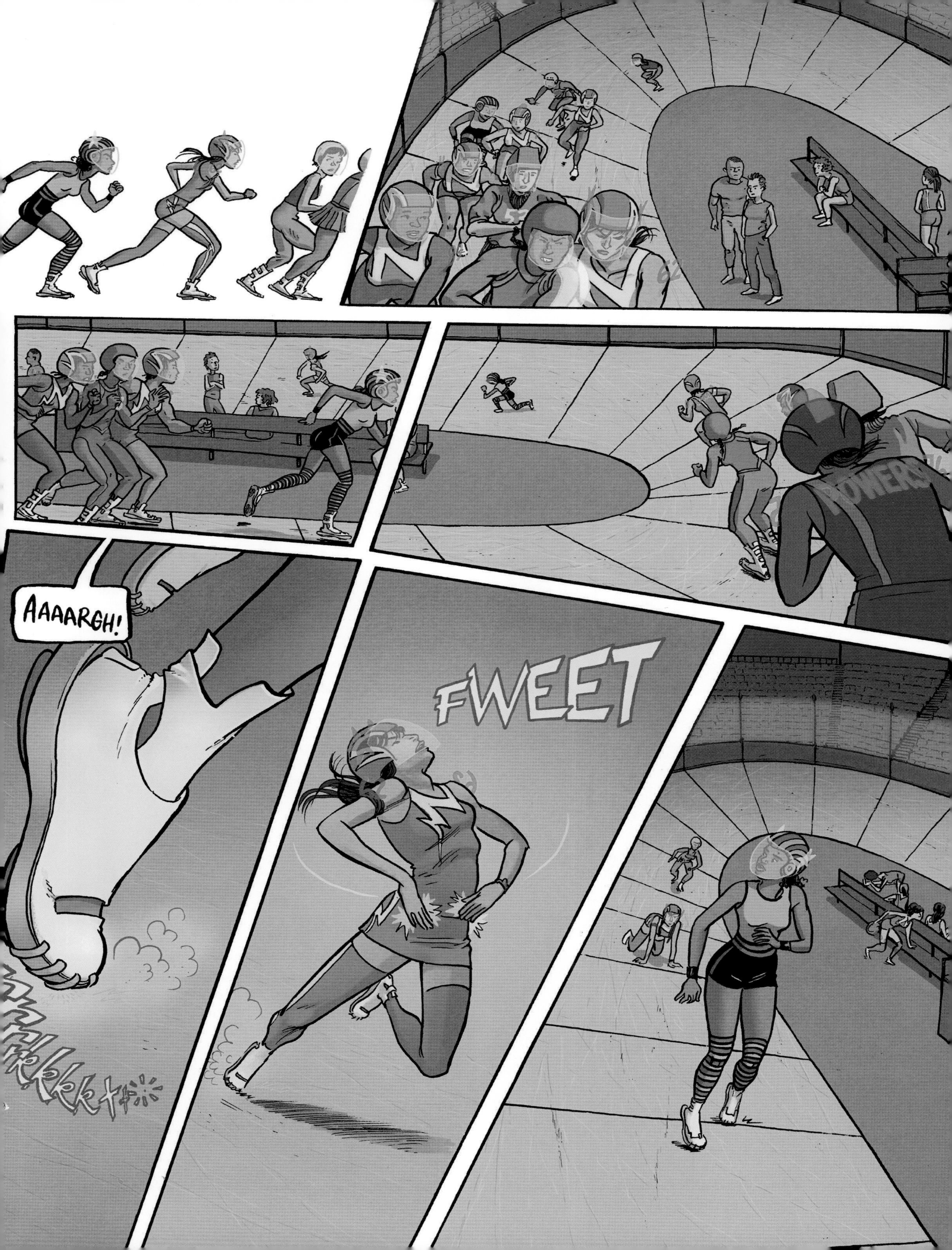

AAAARGH!
FWEET

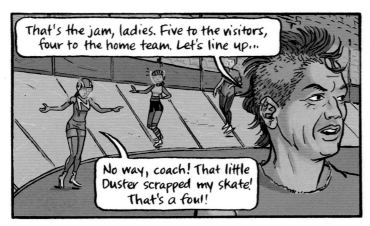

That's the jam, ladies. Five to the visitors, four to the home team. Let's line up...

No way, coach! That little Duster scrapped my skate! That's a foul!

Hanna, come on. We all dust-up.

She did it! She knew she'd never win a jam against me without sabotage!

Hanna...

I'm not jamming with trash like that. Thinks she's tough, right?

You just skate your grotty little Duster butt out of here. You're not making this team...

Hanna!

I didn't mean...

Now wait a second...

I can fix it! I can fix the skate! Here, give it to me! I can...

I'm going to give you my skate. Right. How old are you, anyway?

I'm seven, OK? Seven! I snuck in! I just... But I can fix skates! Just give me a chance!

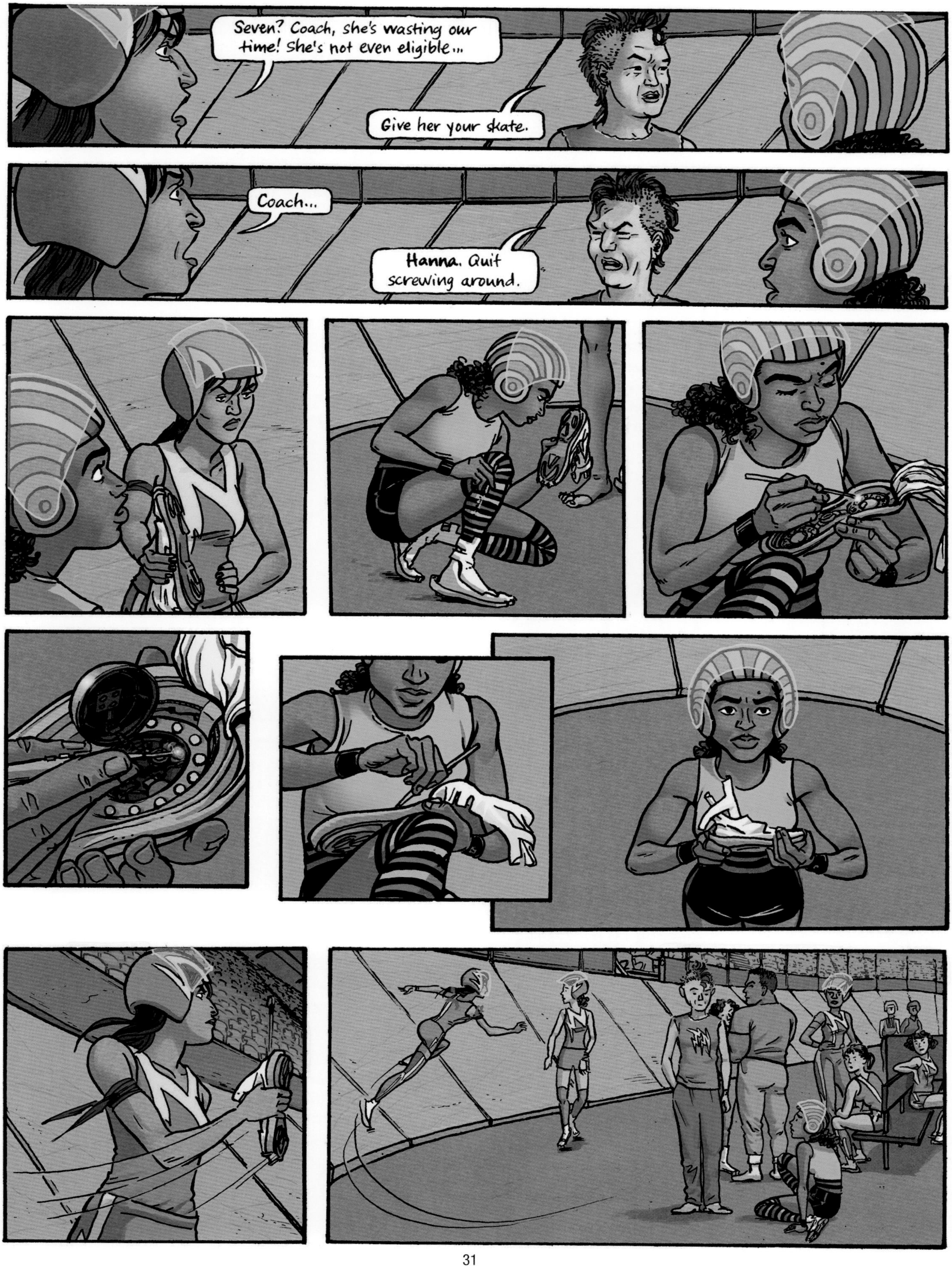
Seven? Coach, she's wasting our time! She's not even eligible...
Give her your skate.
Coach...
Hanna. Quit screwing around.

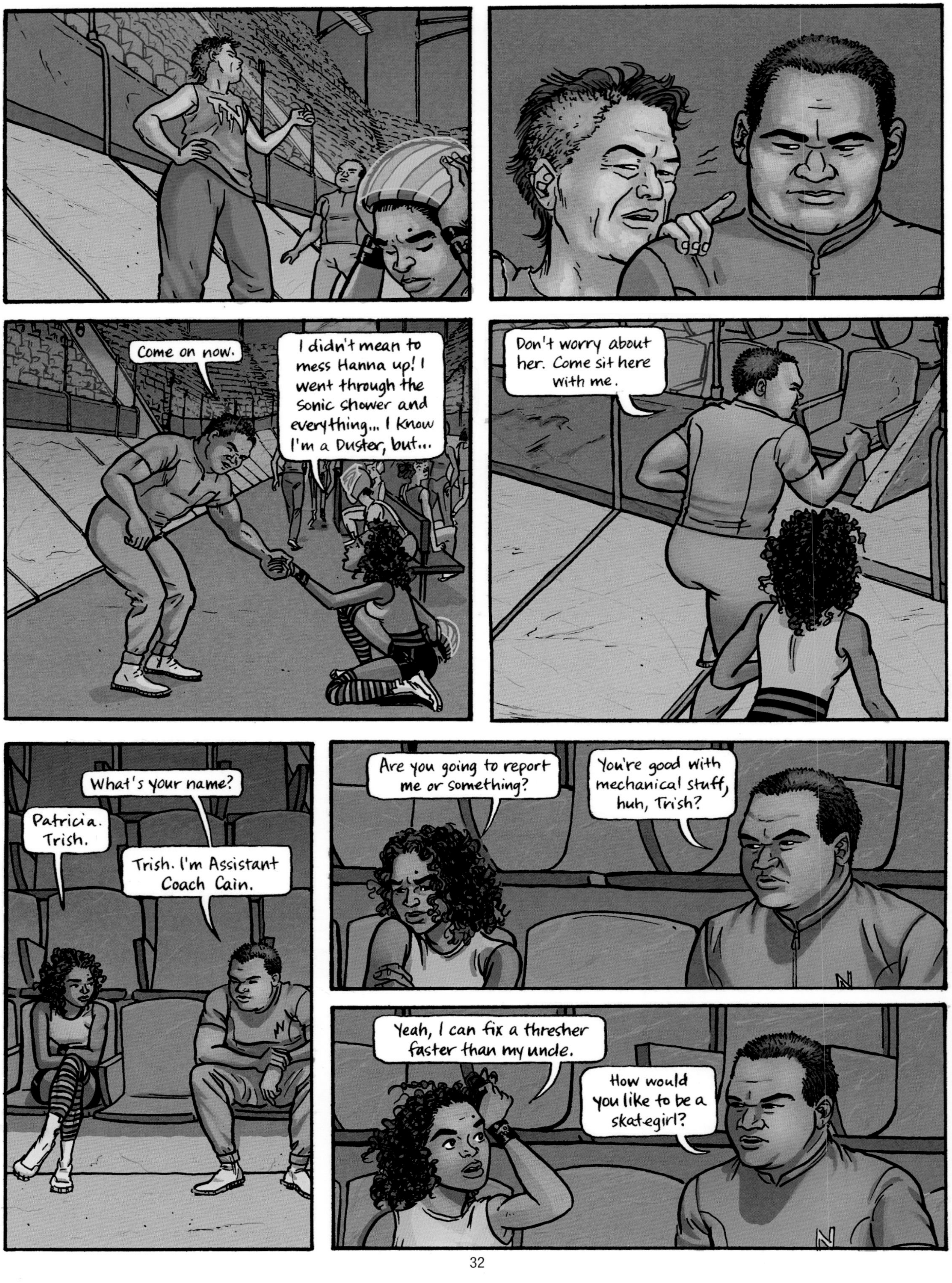
Come on now.
I didn't mean to mess Hanna up! I went through the sonic shower and everything... I know I'm a Duster, but...
Don't worry about her. Come sit here with me.
What's your name?
Patricia. Trish.
Trish. I'm Assistant Coach Cain.
Are you going to report me or something?
You're good with mechanical stuff, huh, Trish?
Yeah, I can fix a thresher faster than my uncle.
How would you like to be a skategirl?

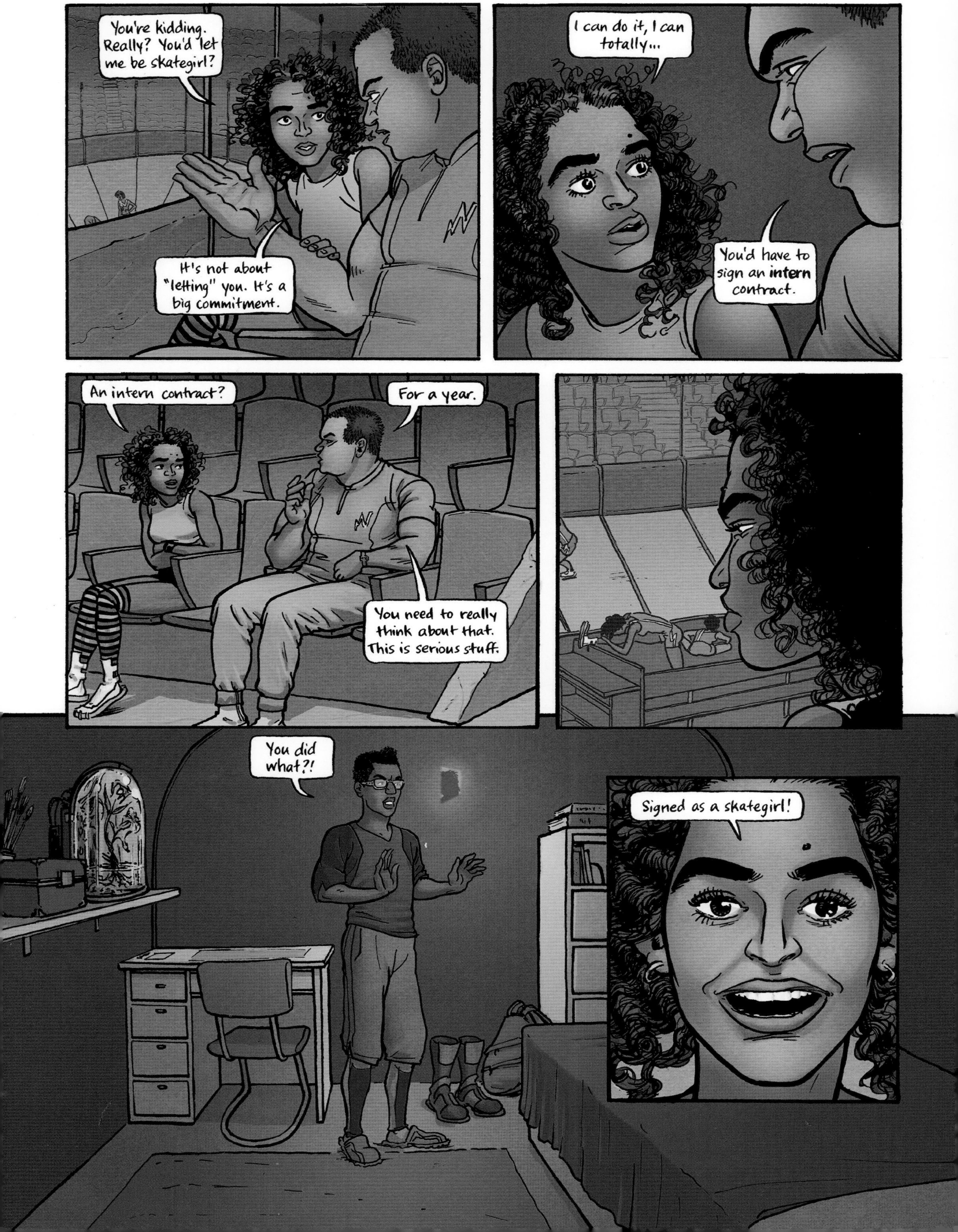
You're kidding. Really? You'd let me be skategirl?
It's not about "letting" you. It's a big commitment.
I can do it, I can totally...
You'd have to sign an **intern** contract.
An intern contract?
For a year.
You need to really think about that. This is serious stuff.
You did what?!
Signed as a skategirl!

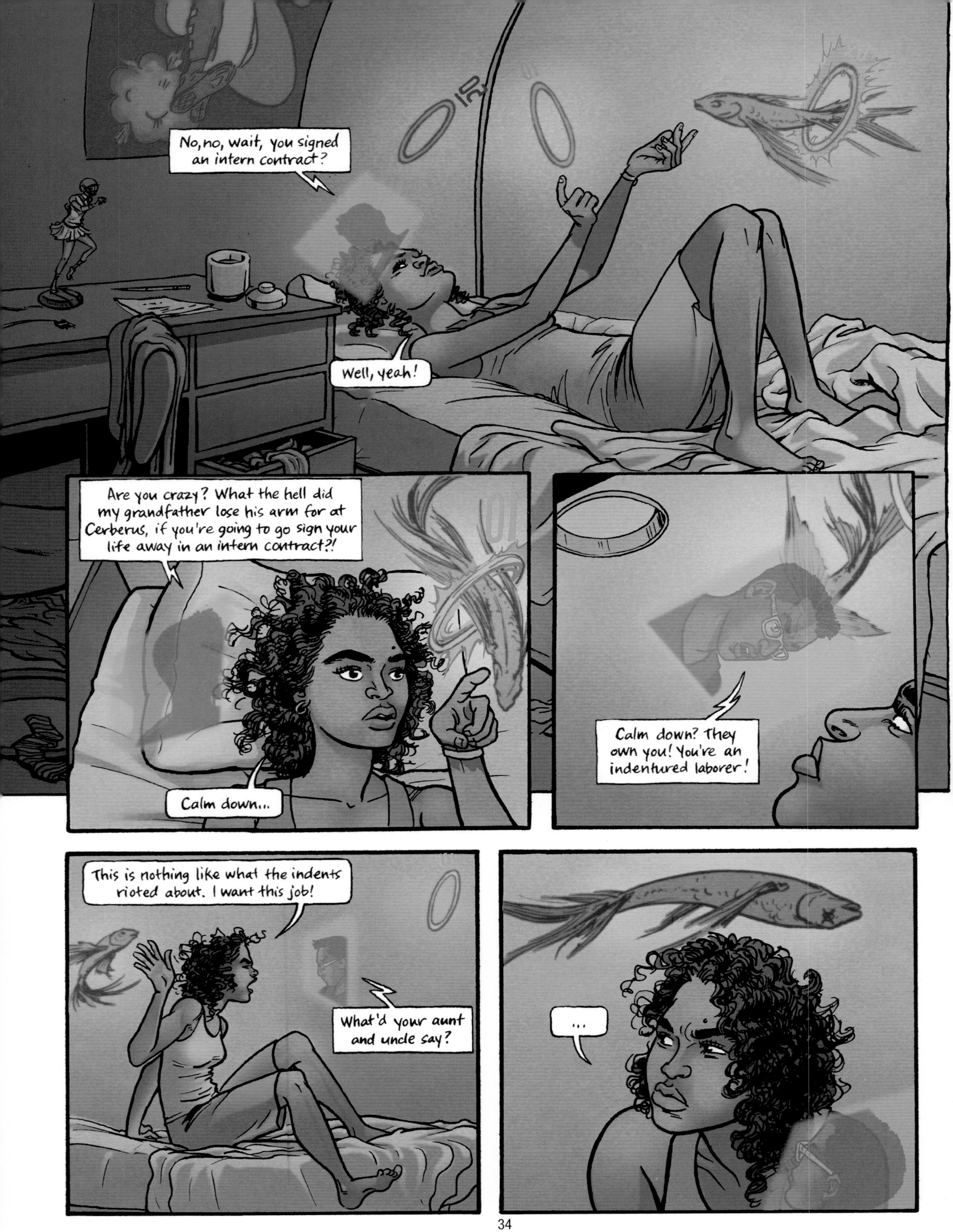
No, no, wait, you signed an intern contract?
Well, yeah!
Are you crazy? What the hell did my grandfather lose his arm for at Cerberus, if you're going to go sign your life away in an intern contract?!
Calm down...
Calm down? They own you! You're an indentured laborer!
This is nothing like what the indents rioted about. I want this job!
What'd your aunt and uncle say?
...

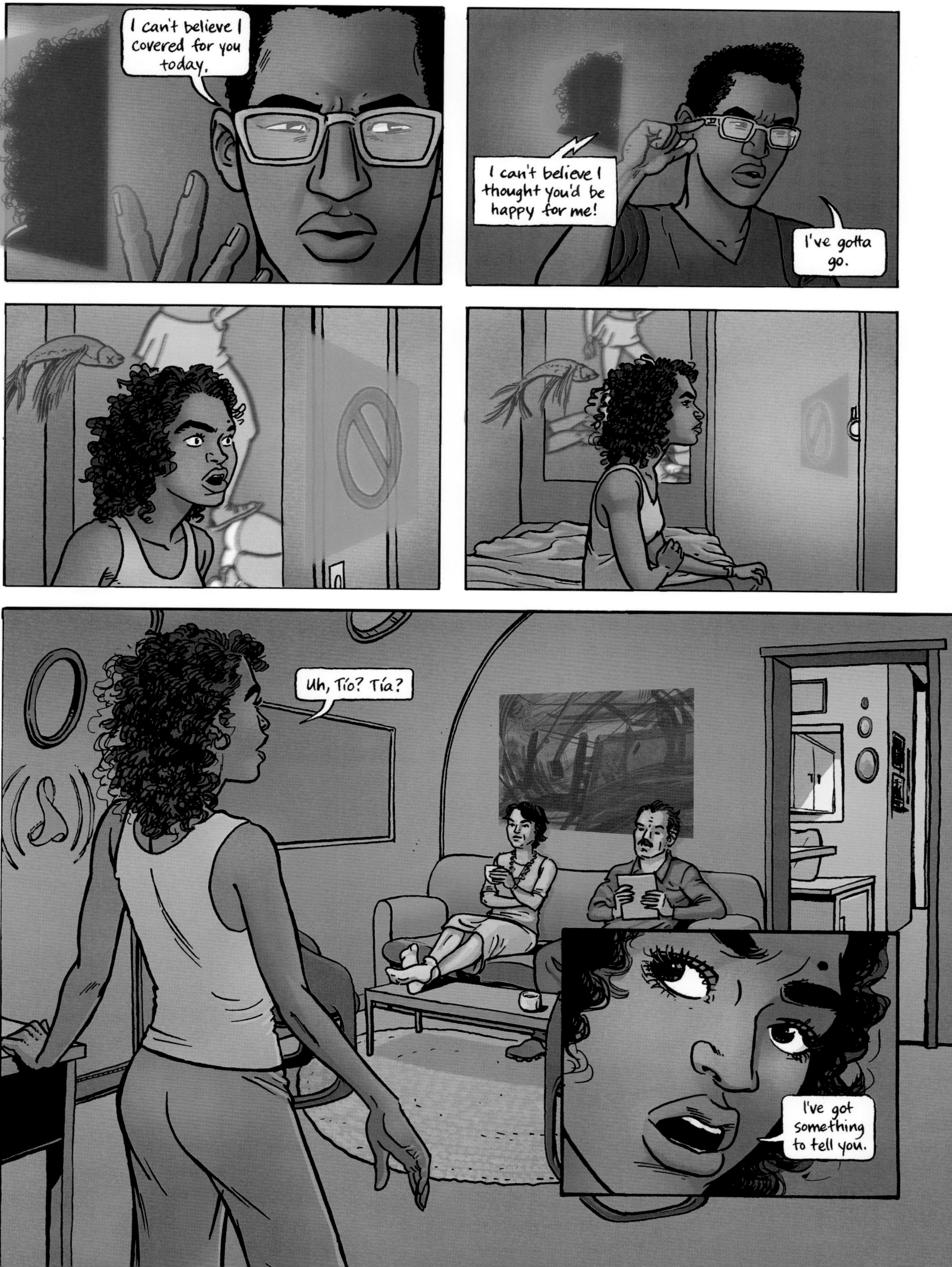
I can't believe I covered for you today.
I can't believe I thought you'd be happy for me!
I've gotta go.
Uh, Tío? Tía?
I've got something to tell you.

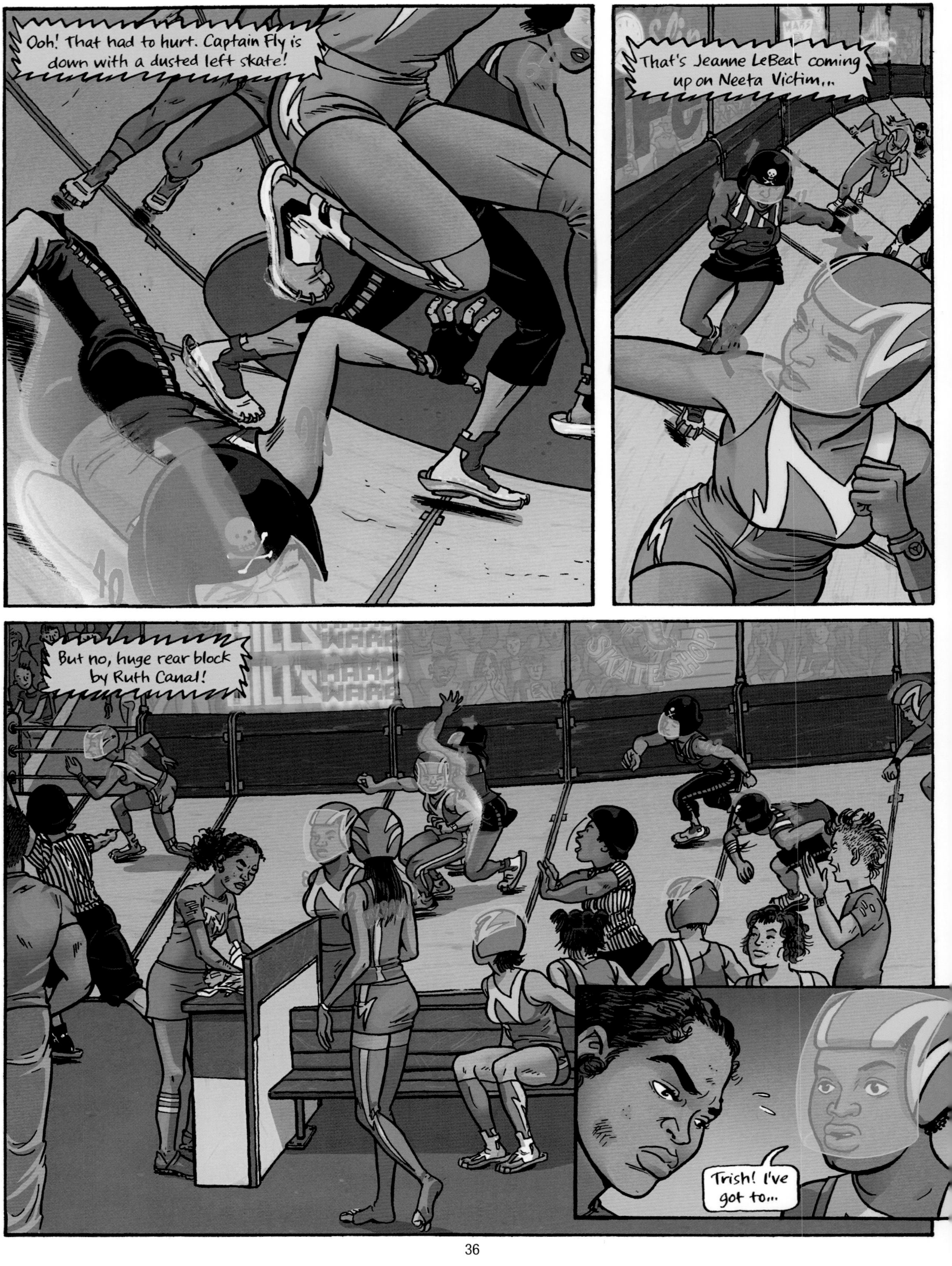
Ooh! That had to hurt. Captain Fly is down with a dusted left skate!
That's Jeanne LeBeat coming up on Neeta Victim...
But no, huge rear block by Ruth Canal!
Trish! I've got to...

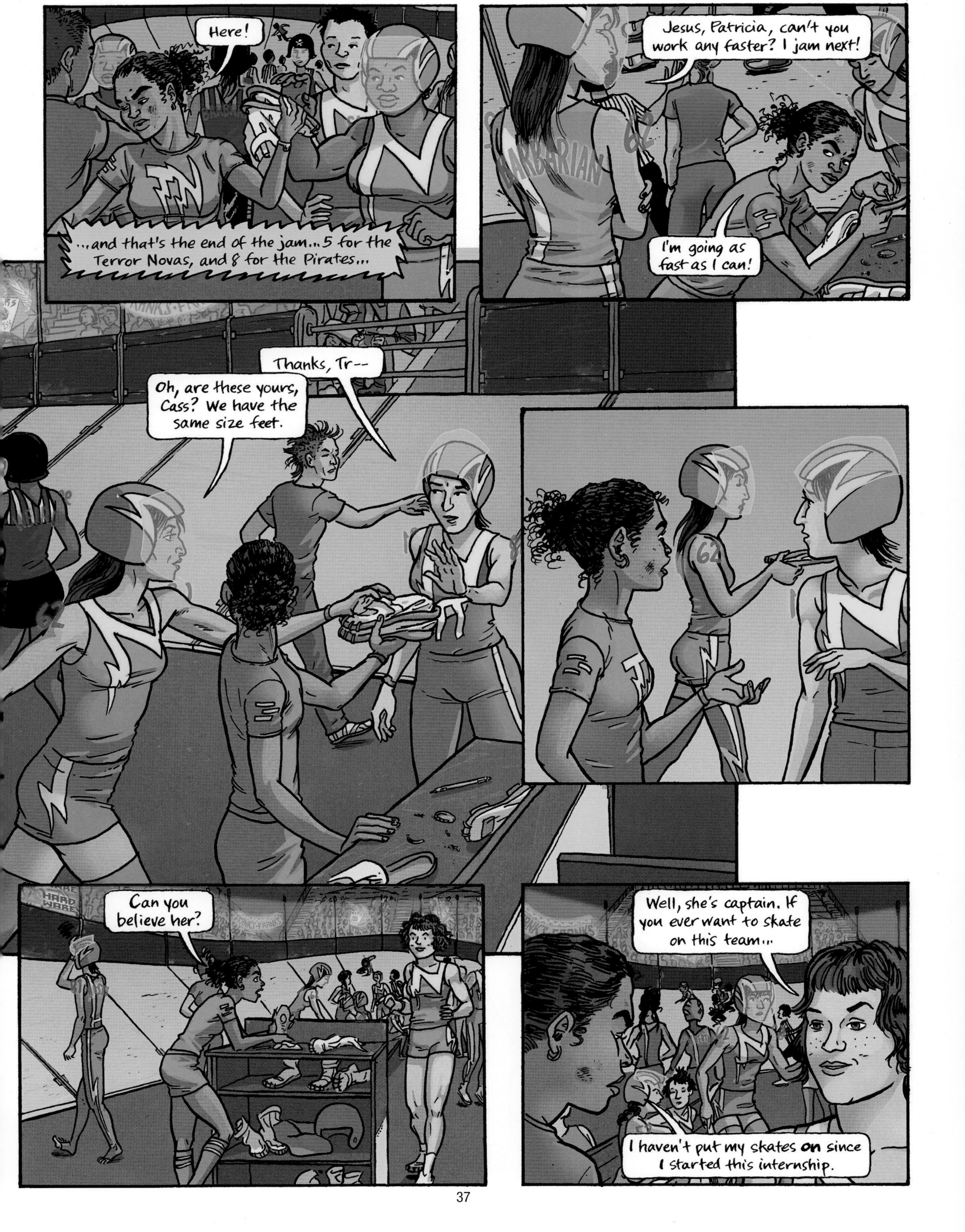
Here!
...and that's the end of the jam...5 for the Terror Novas, and 8 for the Pirates...
Jesus, Patricia, can't you work any faster? I jam next!
I'm going as fast as I can!
Oh, are these yours, Cass? We have the same size feet.
Thanks, Tr--
Can you believe her?
Well, she's captain. If you ever want to skate on this team...
I haven't put my skates **on** since I started this internship.

I could have told you that. But at least you're not **supposed** to be out there.

Wow, what a crack-up! Looks like Cora Sair took out a barrier-generator!

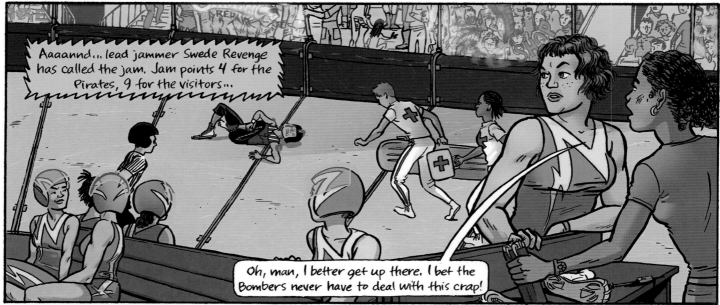

Aaaannd... lead jammer Swede Revenge has called the jam. Jam points 4 for the Pirates, 9 for the visitors...

Oh, man, I better get up there. I bet the Bombers never have to deal with this crap!

Have you ever seen their stadium?

Only on the holo.

If we make it to playoffs, you'll see it for real. You are going to be amazed, it's so... clean.

Not after we're through with it!

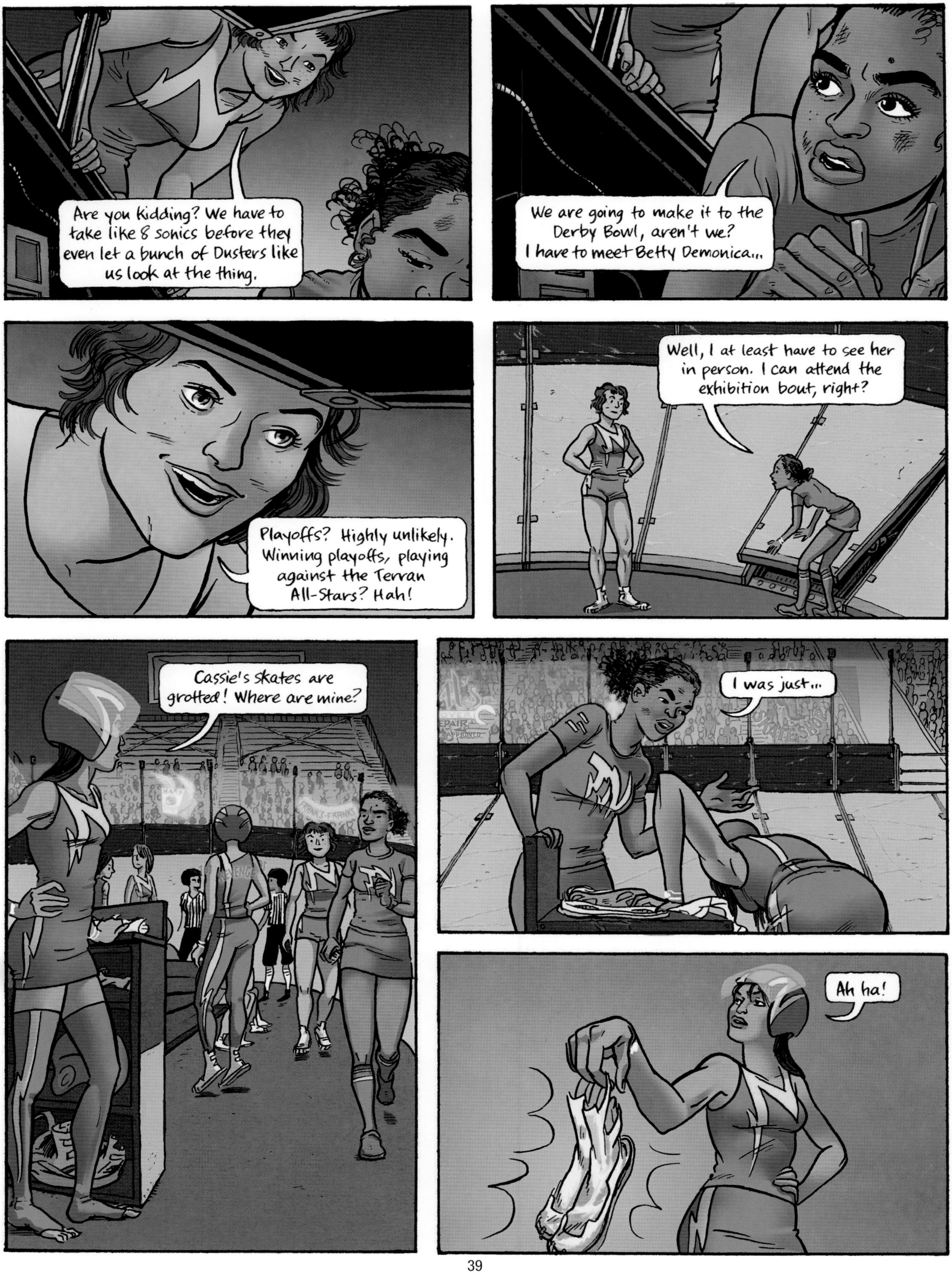
Are you kidding? We have to take like 8 sonics before they even let a bunch of Dusters like us look at the thing.
We are going to make it to the Derby Bowl, aren't we? I have to meet Betty Demonica...
Playoffs? Highly unlikely. Winning playoffs, playing against the Terran All-Stars? Hah!
Well, I at least have to see her in person. I can attend the exhibition bout, right?
Cassie's skates are grotted! Where are mine?
I was just...
Ah ha!

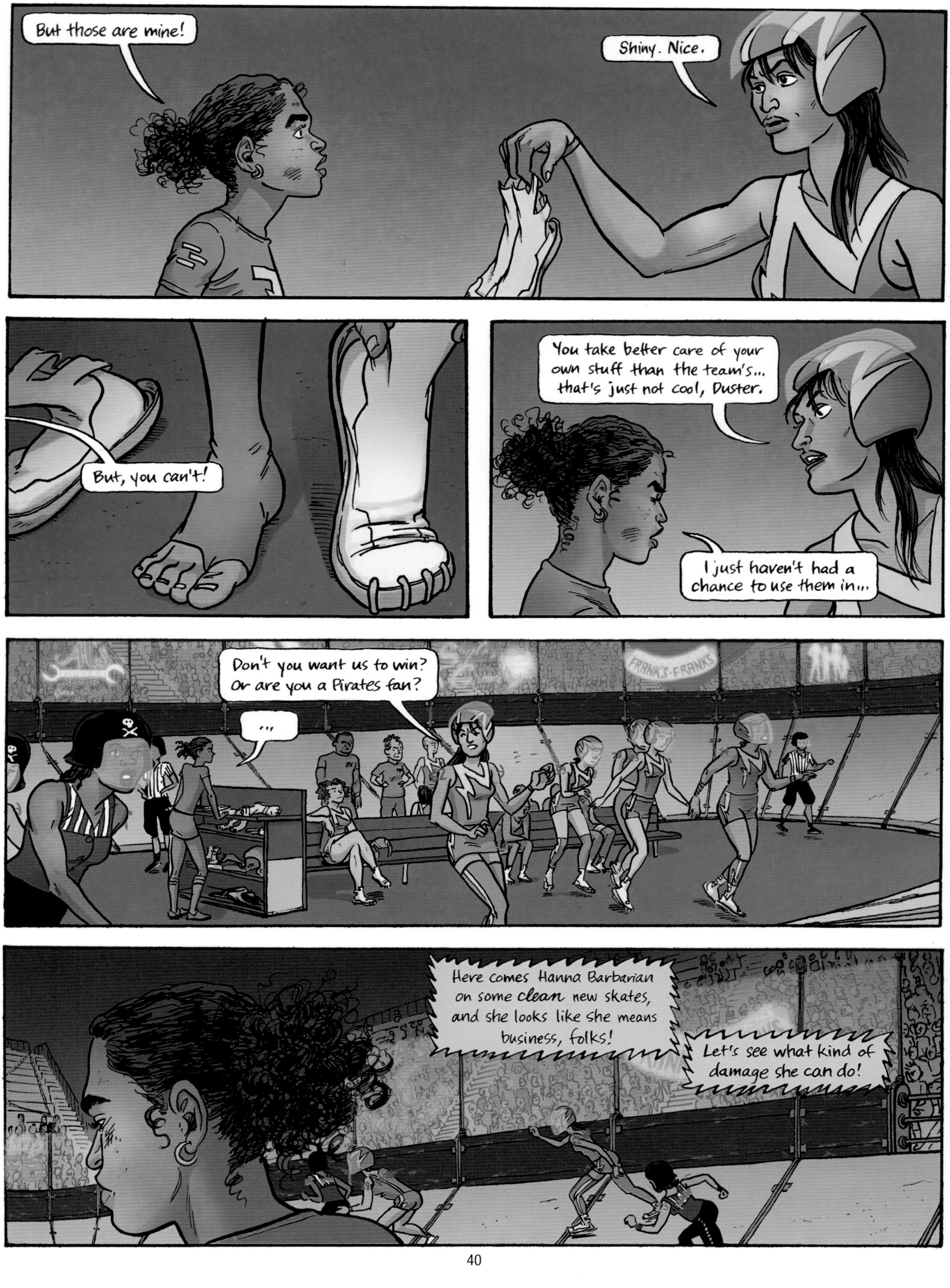
But those are mine!
Shiny. Nice.
But, you can't!
You take better care of your own stuff than the team's... that's just not cool, Duster.
I just haven't had a chance to use them in...
FRANK'S FRANKS
Don't you want us to win? Or are you a Pirates fan?
...
Here comes Hanna Barbarian on some clean new skates, and she looks like she means business, folks!
Let's see what kind of damage she can do!

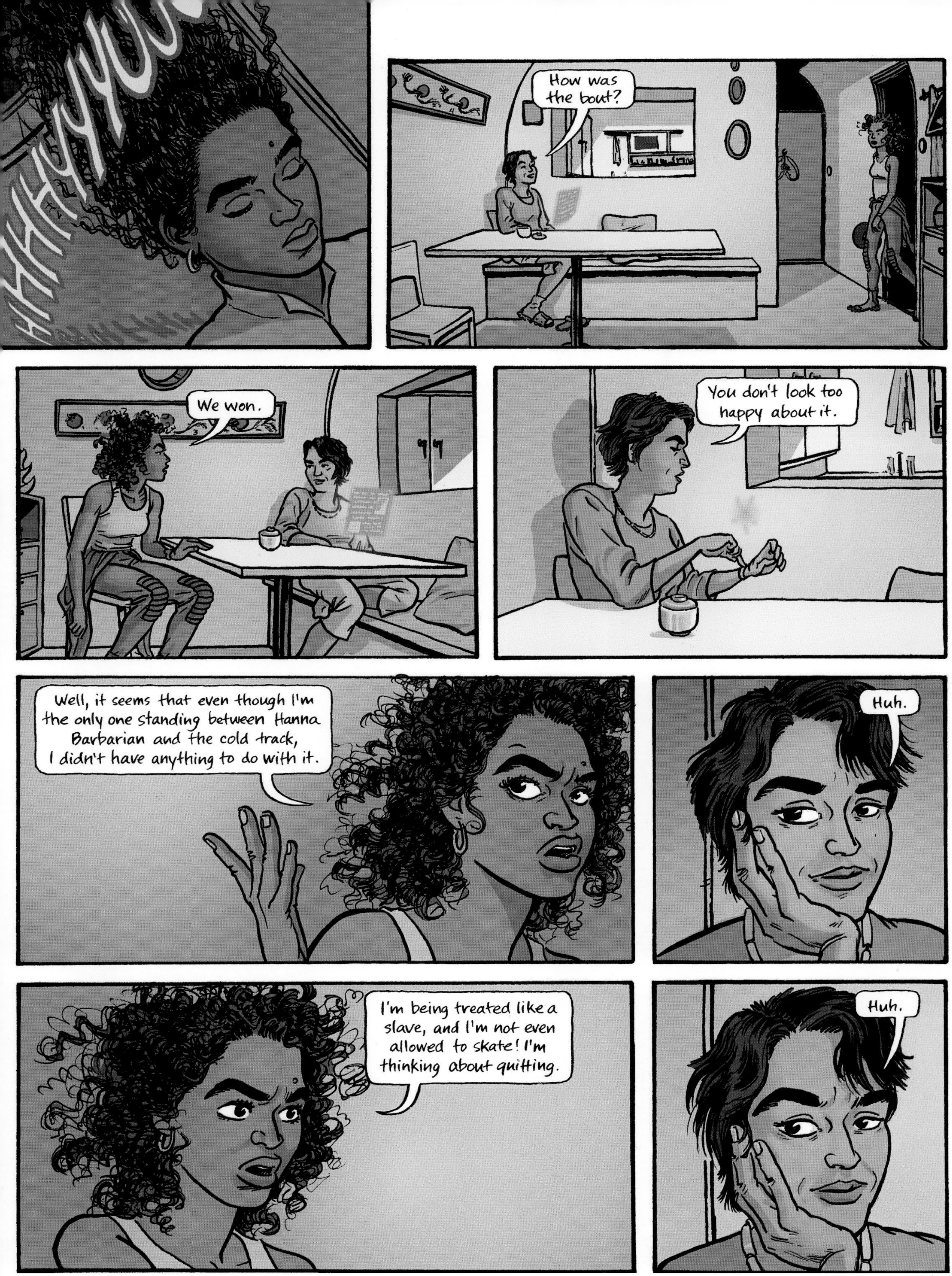
HHHYYYOU
How was the bout?
We won.
You don't look too happy about it.
Well, it seems that even though I'm the only one standing between Hanna Barbarian and the cold track, I didn't have anything to do with it.
Huh.
I'm being treated like a slave, and I'm not even allowed to skate! I'm thinking about quitting.
Huh.

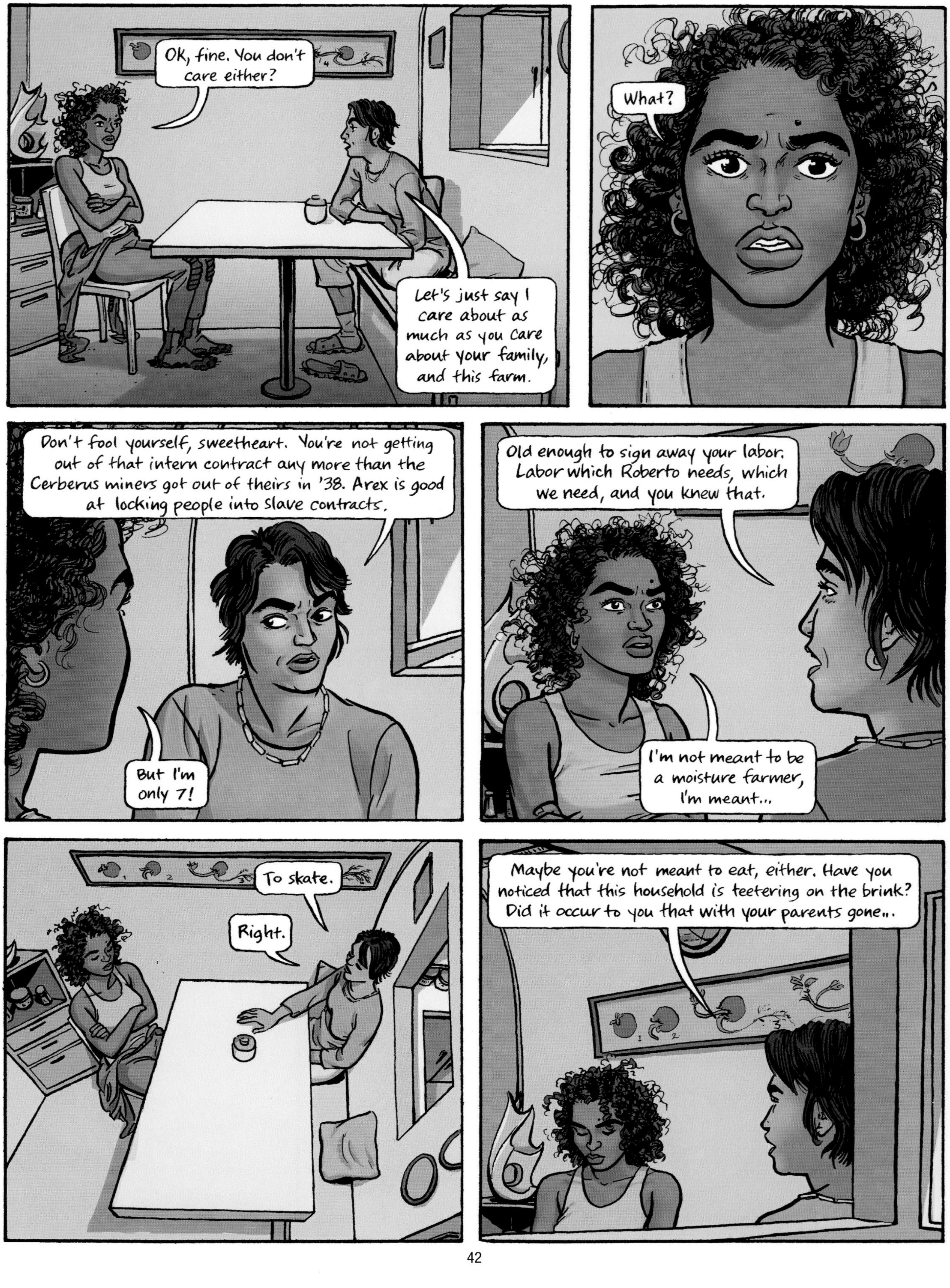
Ok, fine. You don't care either?
Let's just say I care about as much as you care about your family, and this farm.
What?
Don't fool yourself, sweetheart. You're not getting out of that intern contract any more than the Cerberus miners got out of theirs in '38. Arex is good at locking people into slave contracts.
But I'm only 7!
Old enough to sign away your labor. Labor which Roberto needs, which we need, and you knew that.
I'm not meant to be a moisture farmer, I'm meant...
To skate.
Right.
Maybe you're not meant to eat, either. Have you noticed that this household is teetering on the brink? Did it occur to you that with your parents gone...

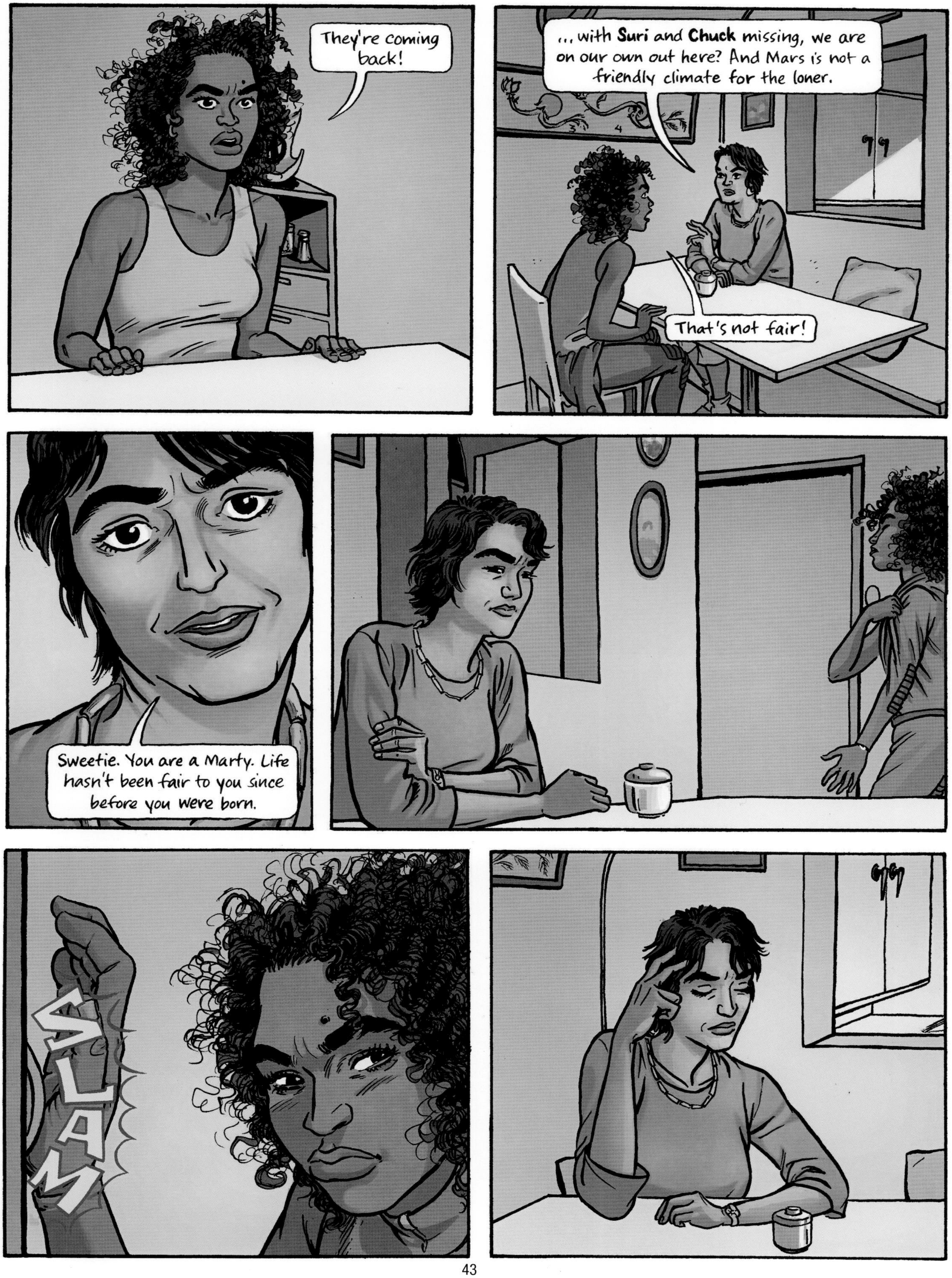
They're coming back!
...with Suri and Chuck missing, we are on our own out here? And Mars is not a friendly climate for the loner.
That's not fair!
Sweetie. You are a Marty. Life hasn't been fair to you since before you were born.
SLAM

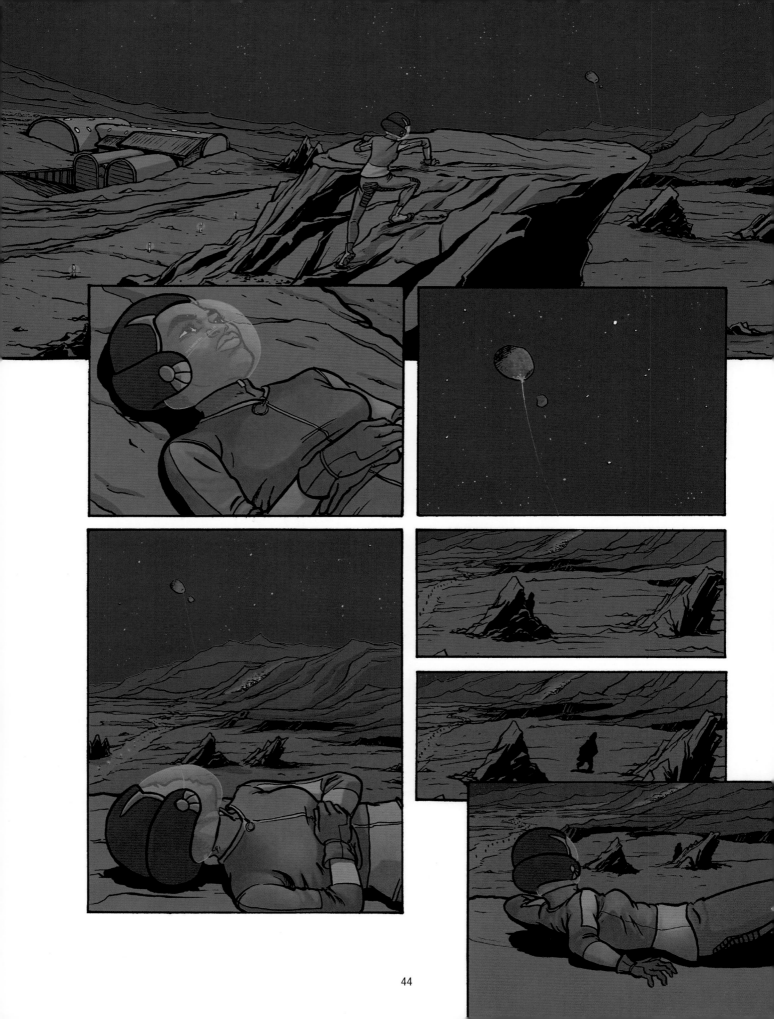

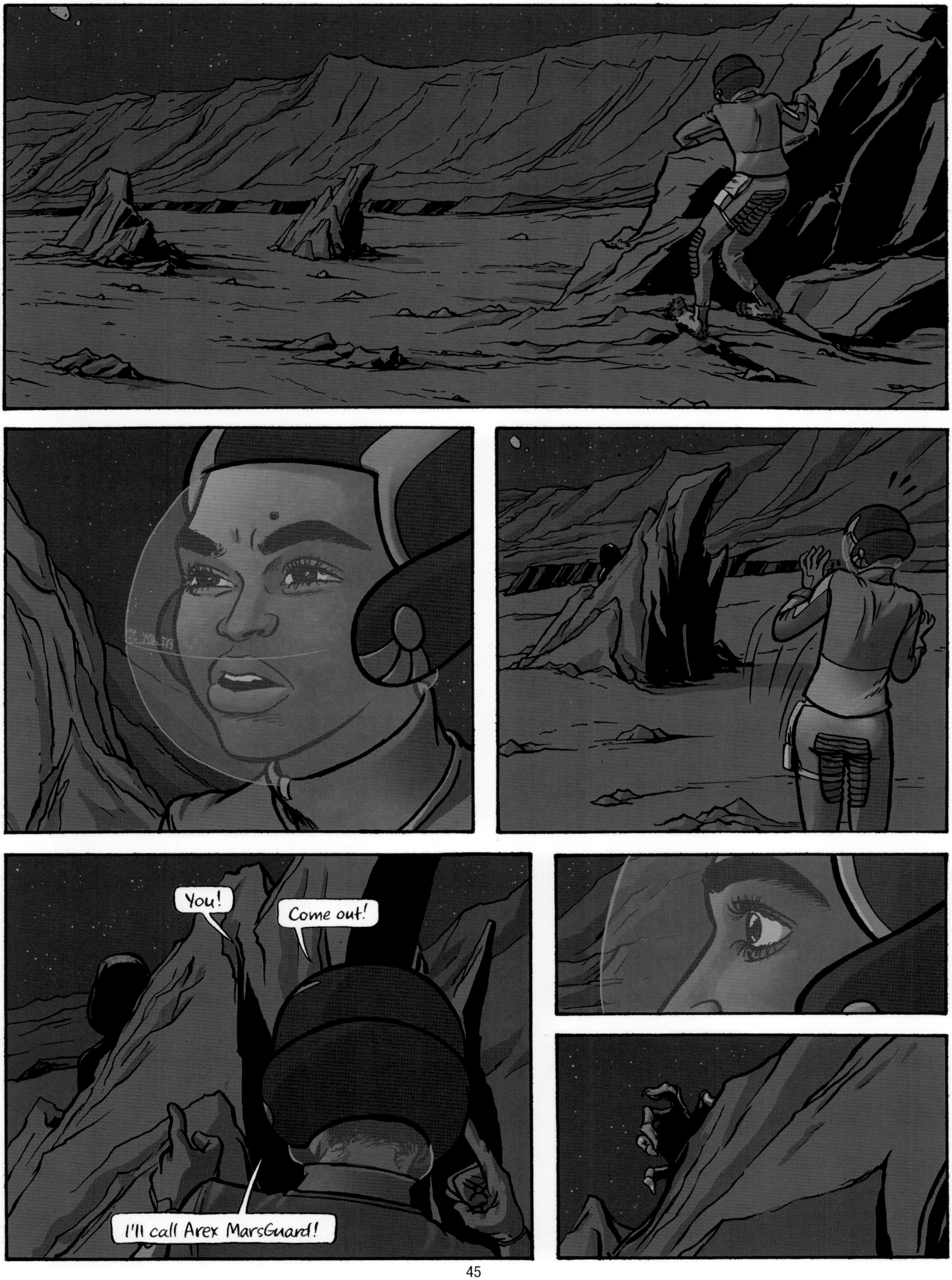
You!
Come out!
I'll call Arex MarsGuard!

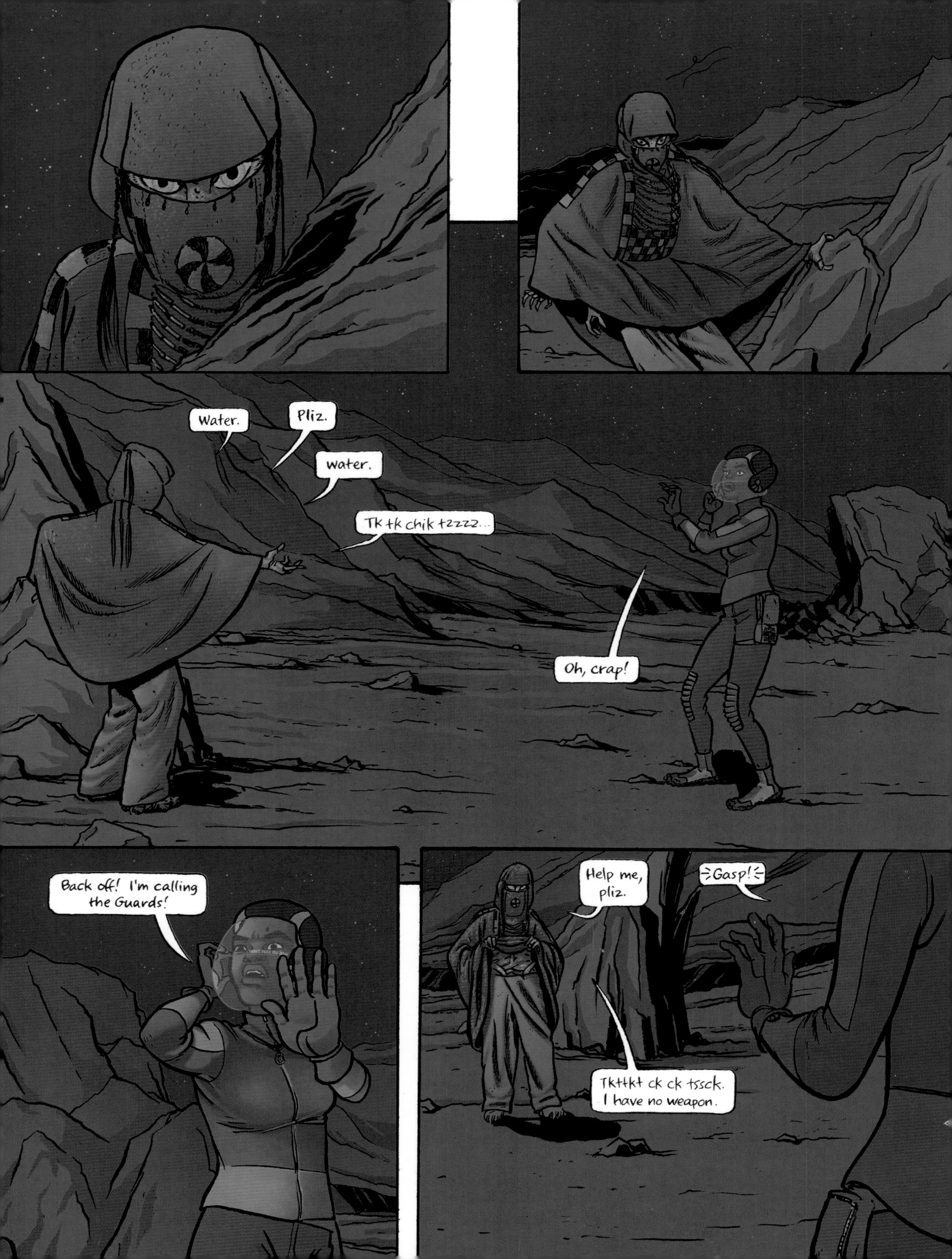
Water.
Pliz.
water.
Tk tk chik tzzzz...
Oh, crap!
Back off! I'm calling the Guards!
Help me, pliz.
Gasp!
Tktktkt ck ck tssck. I have no weapon.

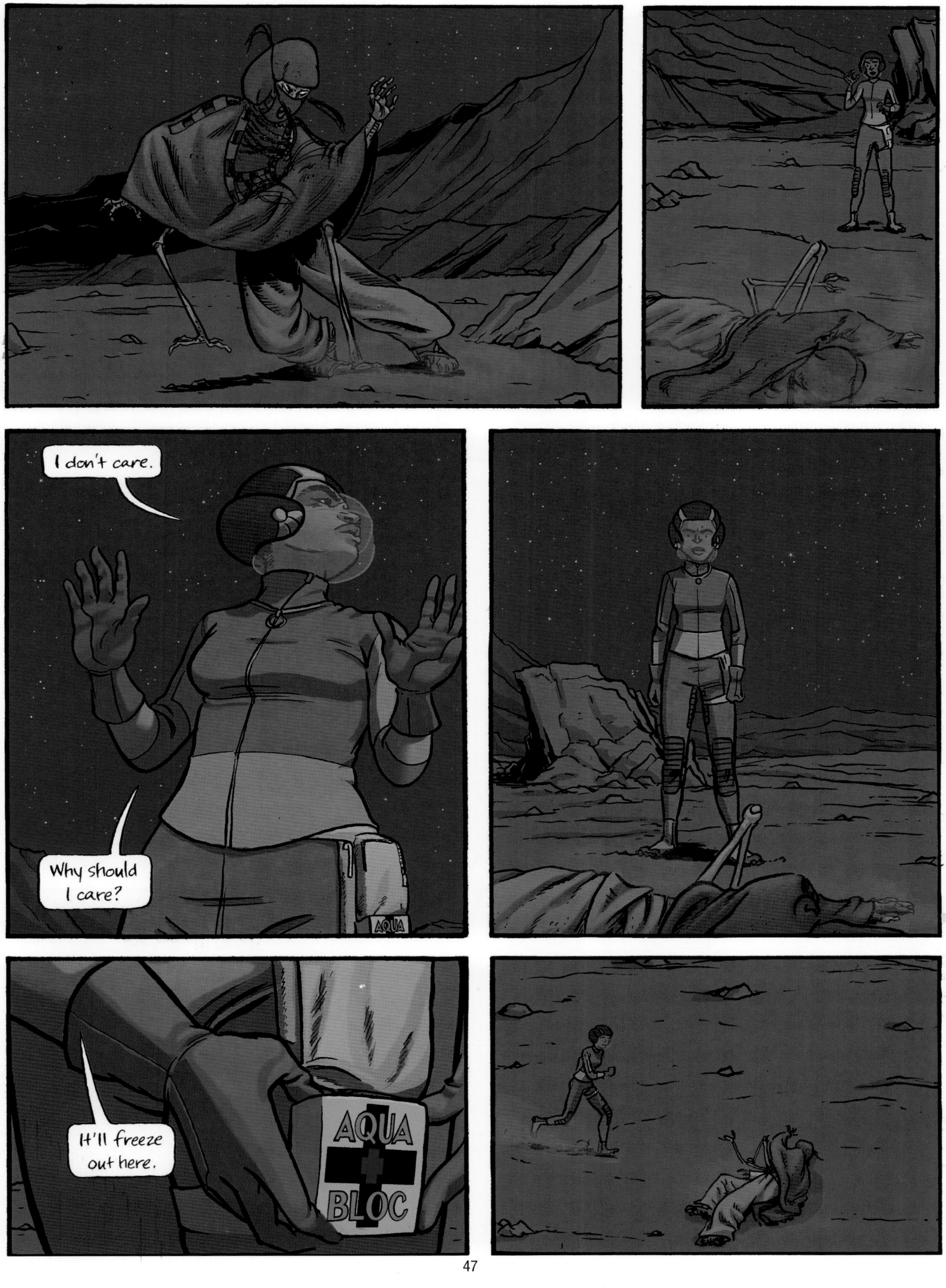
I don't care.
Why should I care?
AQUA
It'll freeze out here.
AQUA BLOC

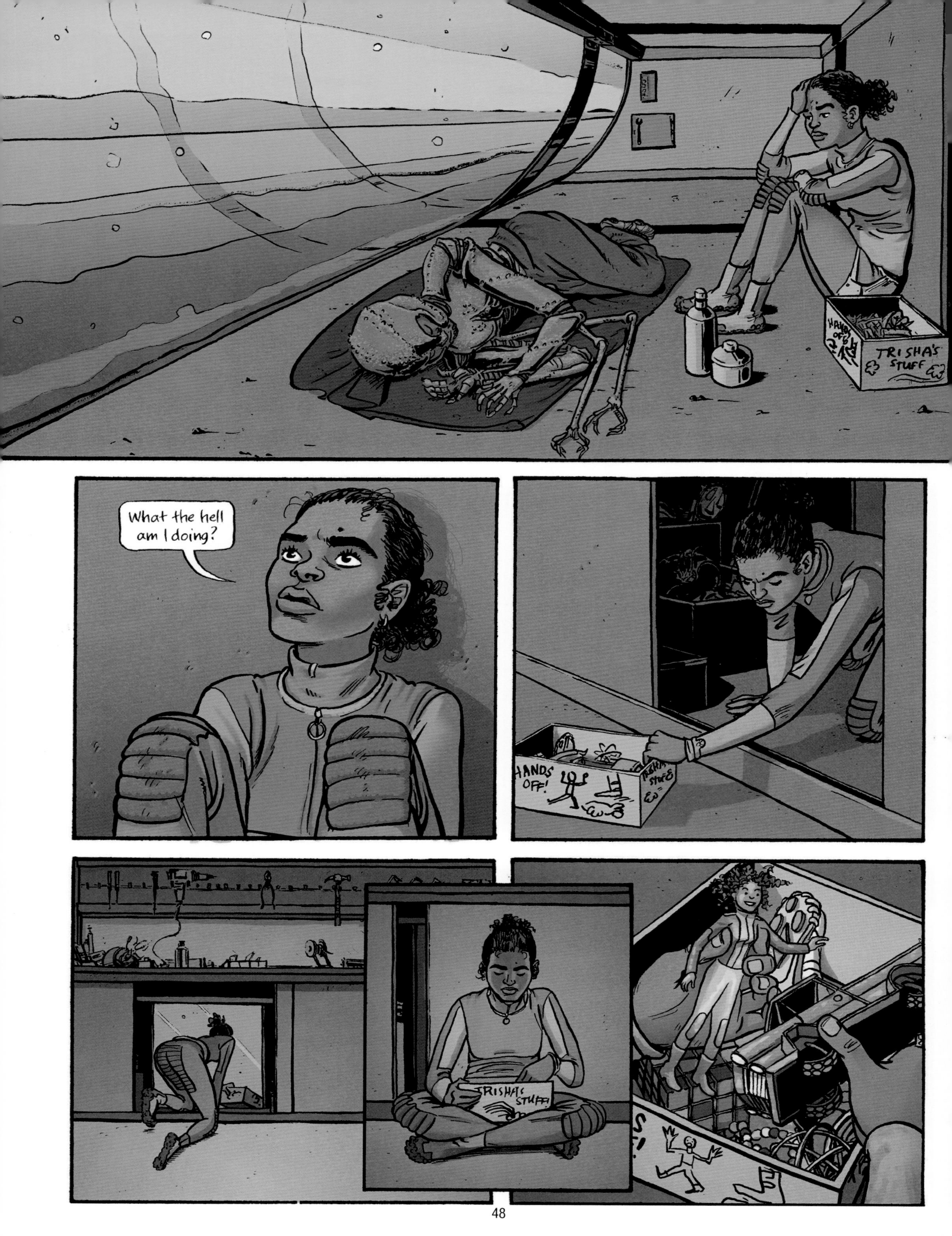
TRISHA'S STUFF
What the hell am I doing?
HANDS OFF!
TRISHA'S STUFF

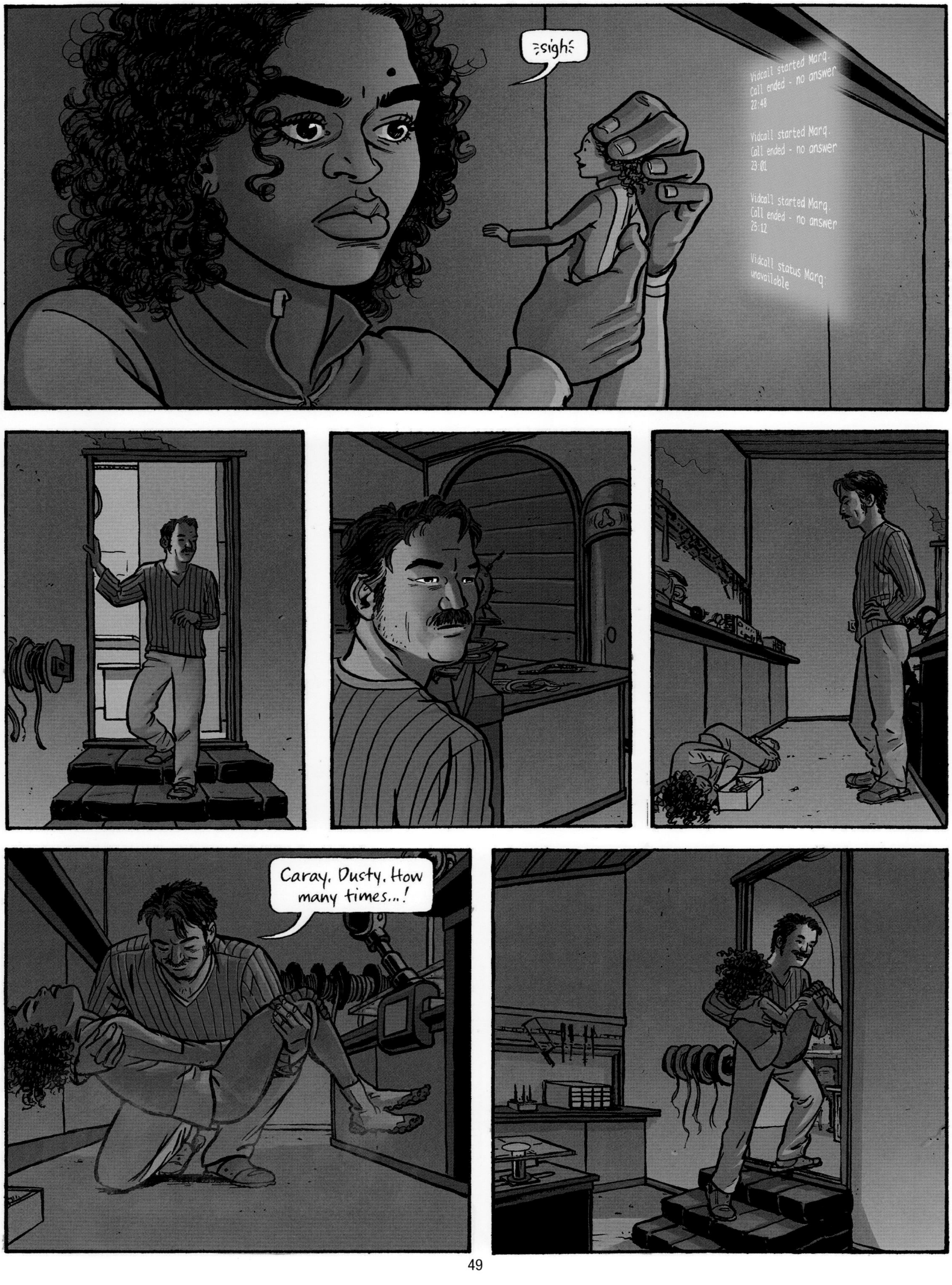
sigh
Vidcall started Marq.
Call ended - no answer
22:48
Vidcall started Marq.
Call ended - no answer
23:01
Vidcall started Marq.
Call ended - no answer
25:12
Vidcall status Marq:
unavailable
Caray, Dusty. How many times...!

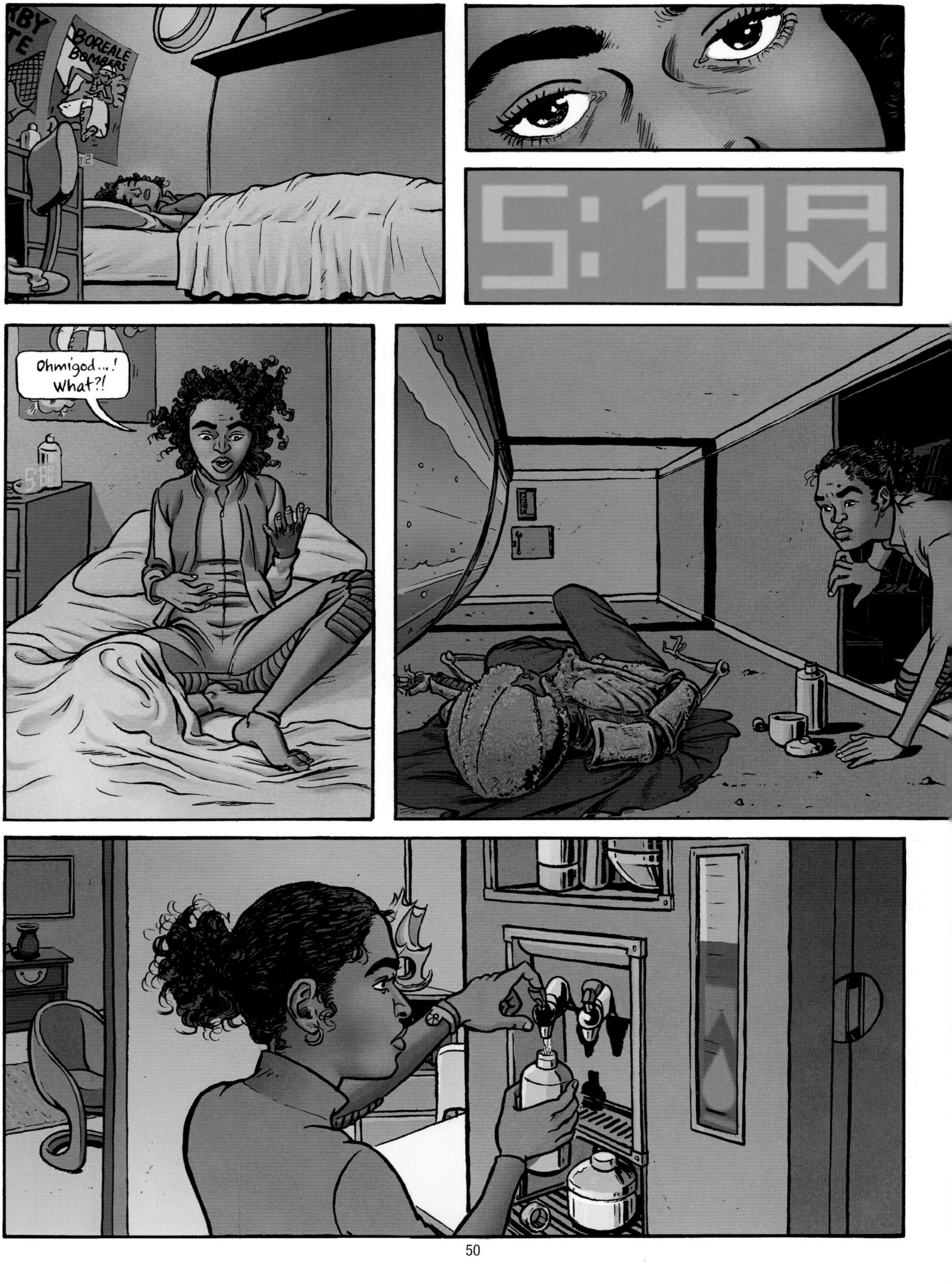
BOREALE BOMBERS
5:13 AM
Ohmigod...! What?!

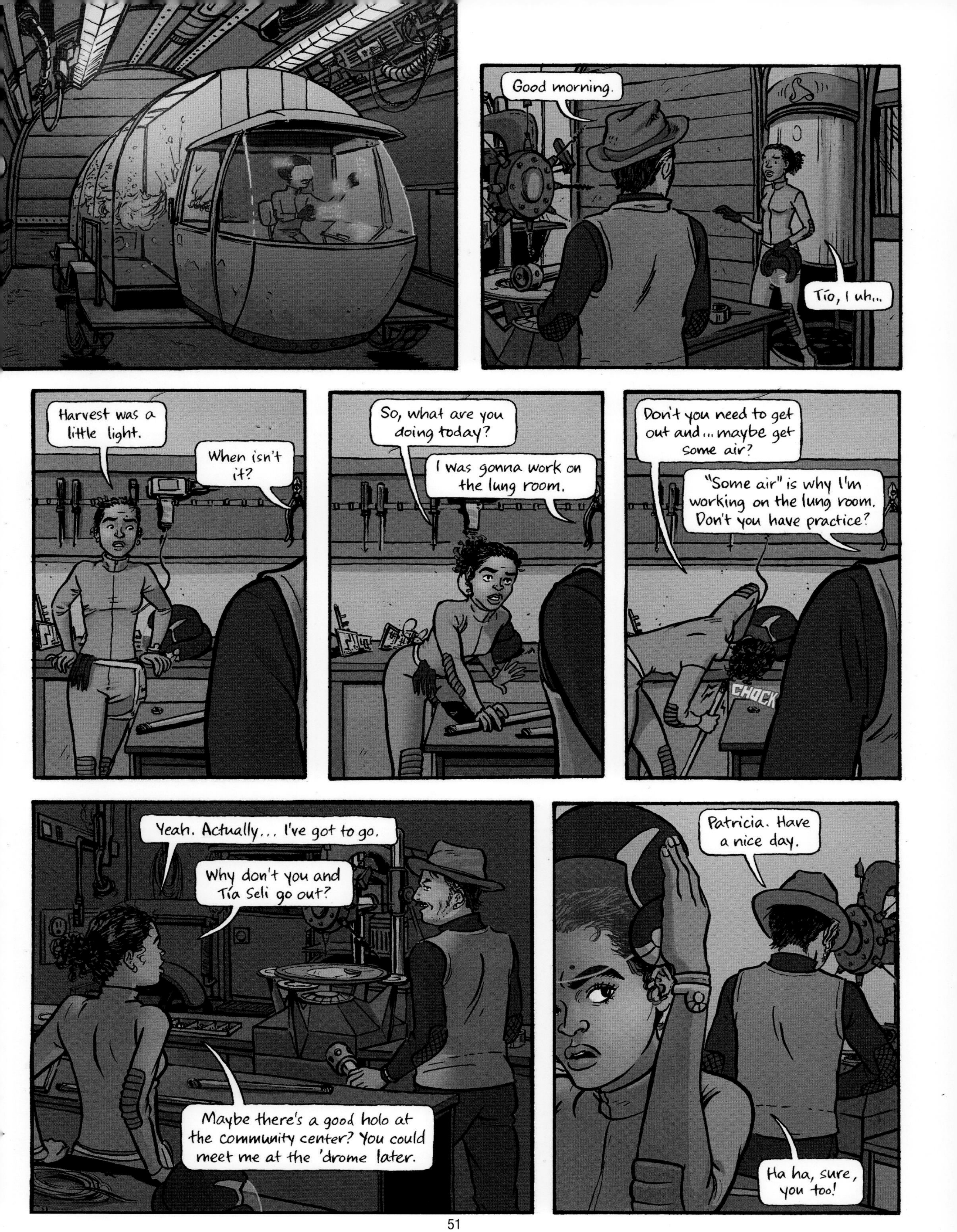
Good morning.
Tío, I uh...
Harvest was a little light.
When isn't it?
So, what are you doing today?
I was gonna work on the lung room.
Don't you need to get out and... maybe get some air?
"Some air" is why I'm working on the lung room. Don't you have practice?
CHOCK
Yeah. Actually... I've got to go.
Why don't you and Tía Seli go out?
Maybe there's a good holo at the community center? You could meet me at the 'drome later.
Patricia. Have a nice day.
Ha ha, sure, you too!

Marq! Pick up, you...

VIDCALL STATUS MARQ:

UNAVAILABLE

Come on man, you've lived for this day...

MARQ:

UNAVAILABLE

TXT STATUS MARQ: AVAILABLE

TRIX: Can you come over?

STATUS MARQ: ABLE

X: Can you e over?

achX: What, now?

TRIX: no...im @ prctice

MachX: ...right yr SLAVE cntrct. Sry. Moms needs me. Since haven't signed life away, cn help. L8r

You jerk!

What now?

Uh, nothing. Just...

...stuff.

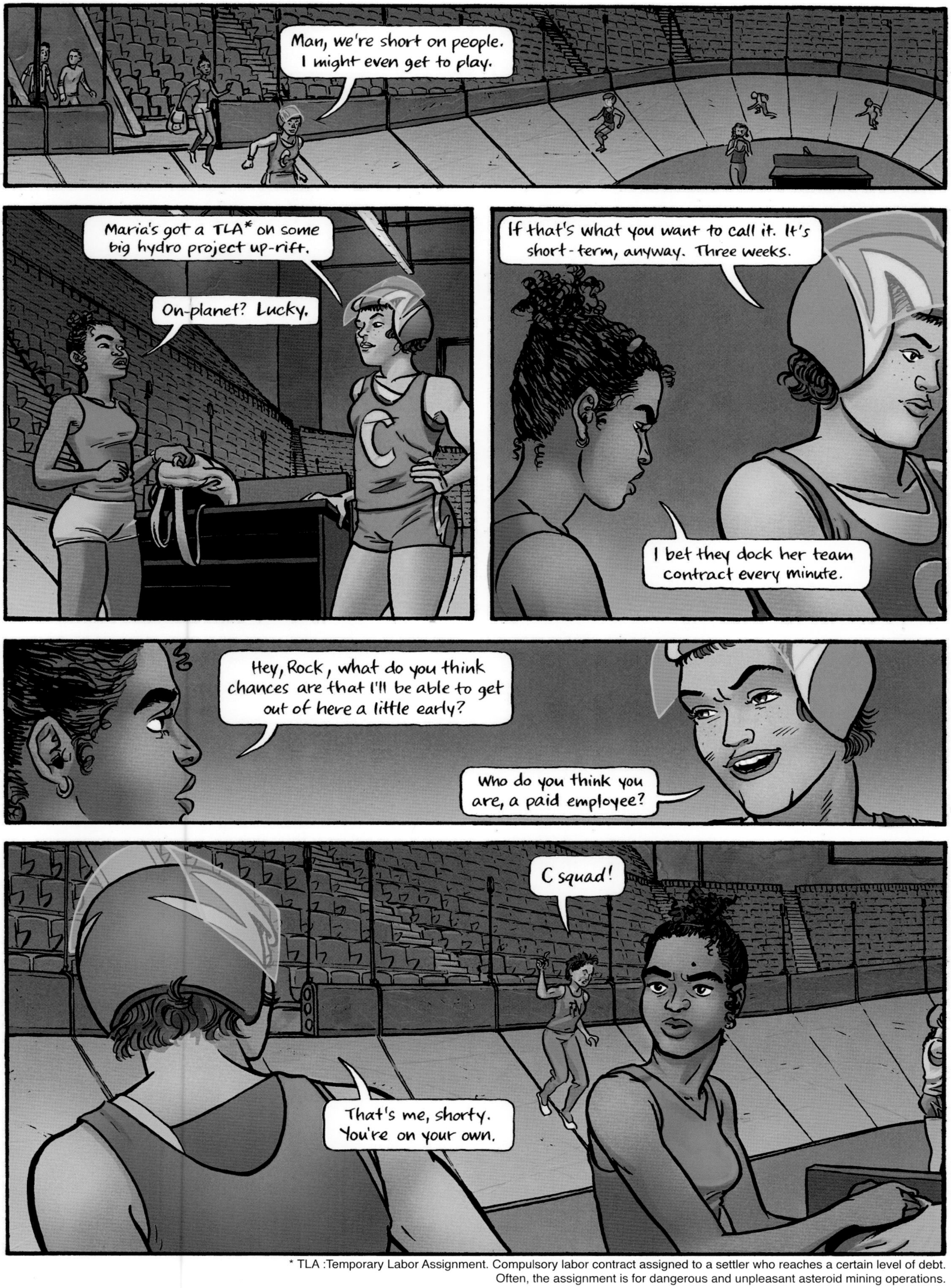
Man, we're short on people. I might even get to play.
Maria's got a TLA* on some big hydro project up-rift.
On-planet? Lucky.
If that's what you want to call it. It's short-term, anyway. Three weeks.
I bet they dock her team contract every minute.
Hey, Rock, what do you think chances are that I'll be able to get out of here a little early?
Who do you think you are, a paid employee?
C squad!
That's me, shorty. You're on your own.

* TLA :Temporary Labor Assignment. Compulsory labor contract assigned to a settler who reaches a certain level of debt. Often, the assignment is for dangerous and unpleasant asteroid mining operations.

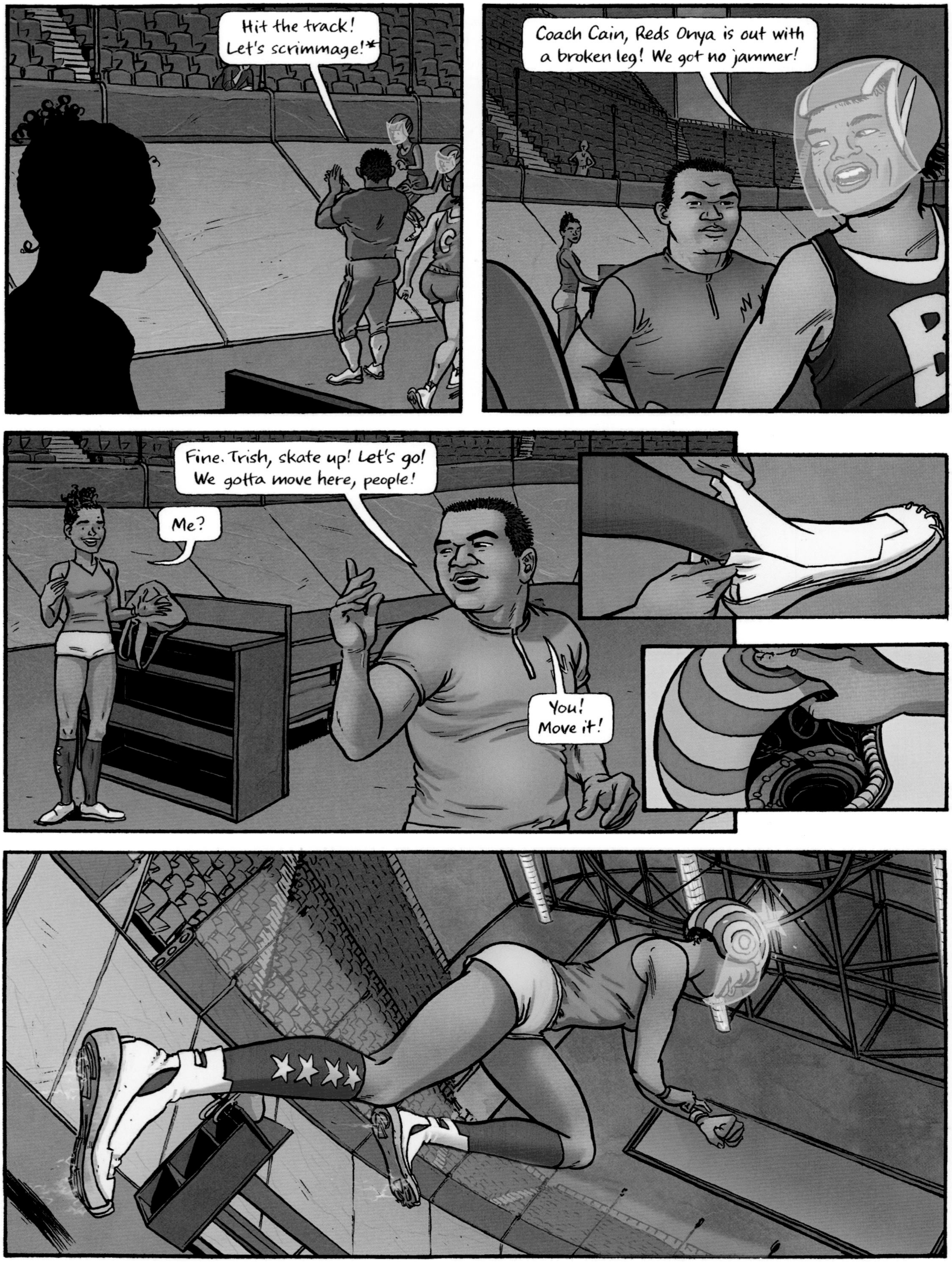
Hit the track! Let's scrimmage!*
Coach Cain, Reds Onya is out with a broken leg! We got no jammer!
Fine. Trish, skate up! Let's go! We gotta move here, people!
Me?
You! Move it!

*A scrimmage is an unofficial match between members of the same team to practice strategy.

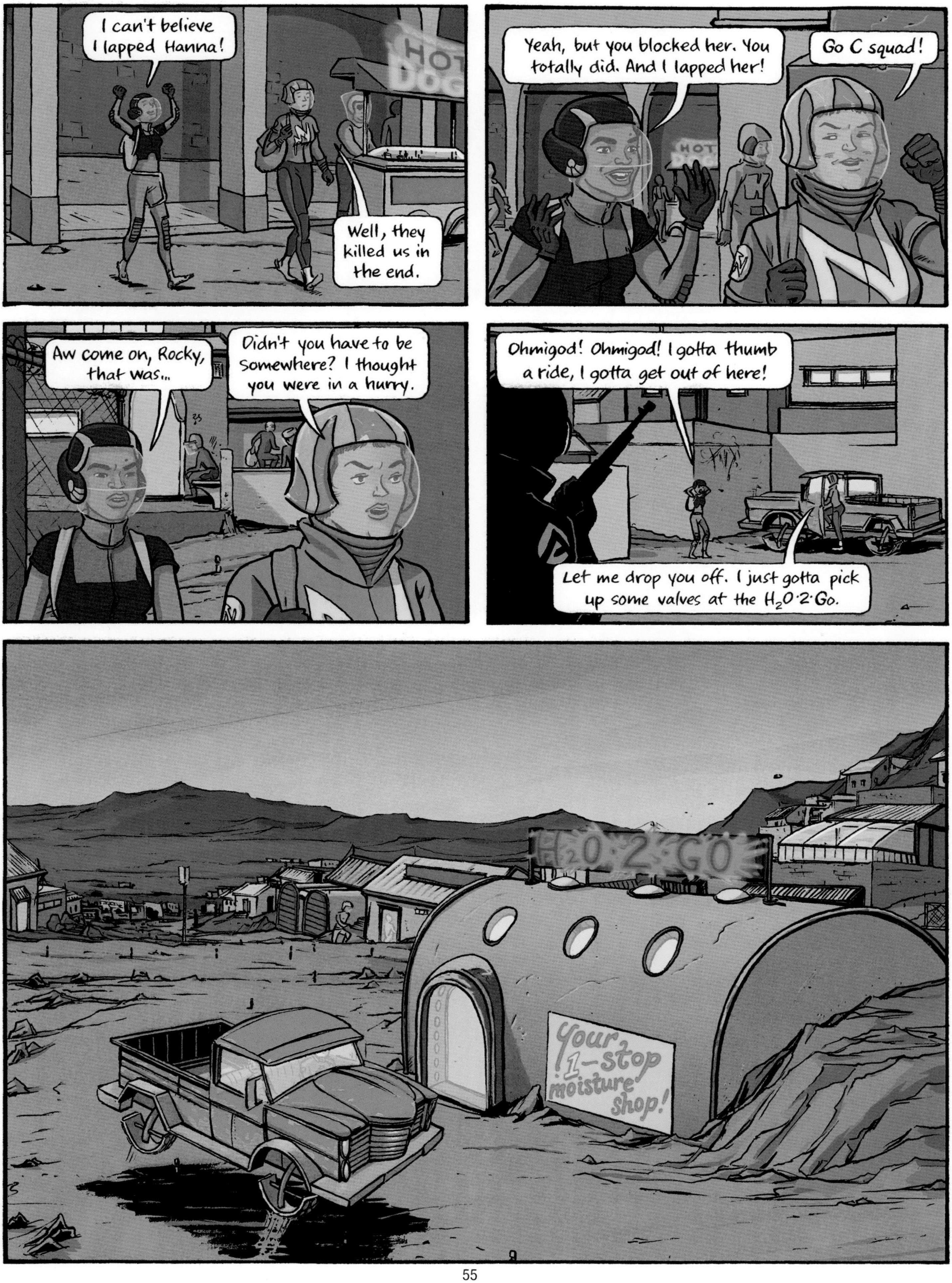

I can't believe I lapped Hanna!
HOT DOG
Well, they killed us in the end.
Yeah, but you blocked her. You totally did. And I lapped her!
Go C squad!
Aw come on, Rocky, that was...
Didn't you have to be somewhere? I thought you were in a hurry.
Ohmigod! Ohmigod! I gotta thumb a ride, I gotta get out of here!
Let me drop you off. I just gotta pick up some valves at the H2O·2·Go.
H2O·2·GO
Your 1-stop moisture shop!

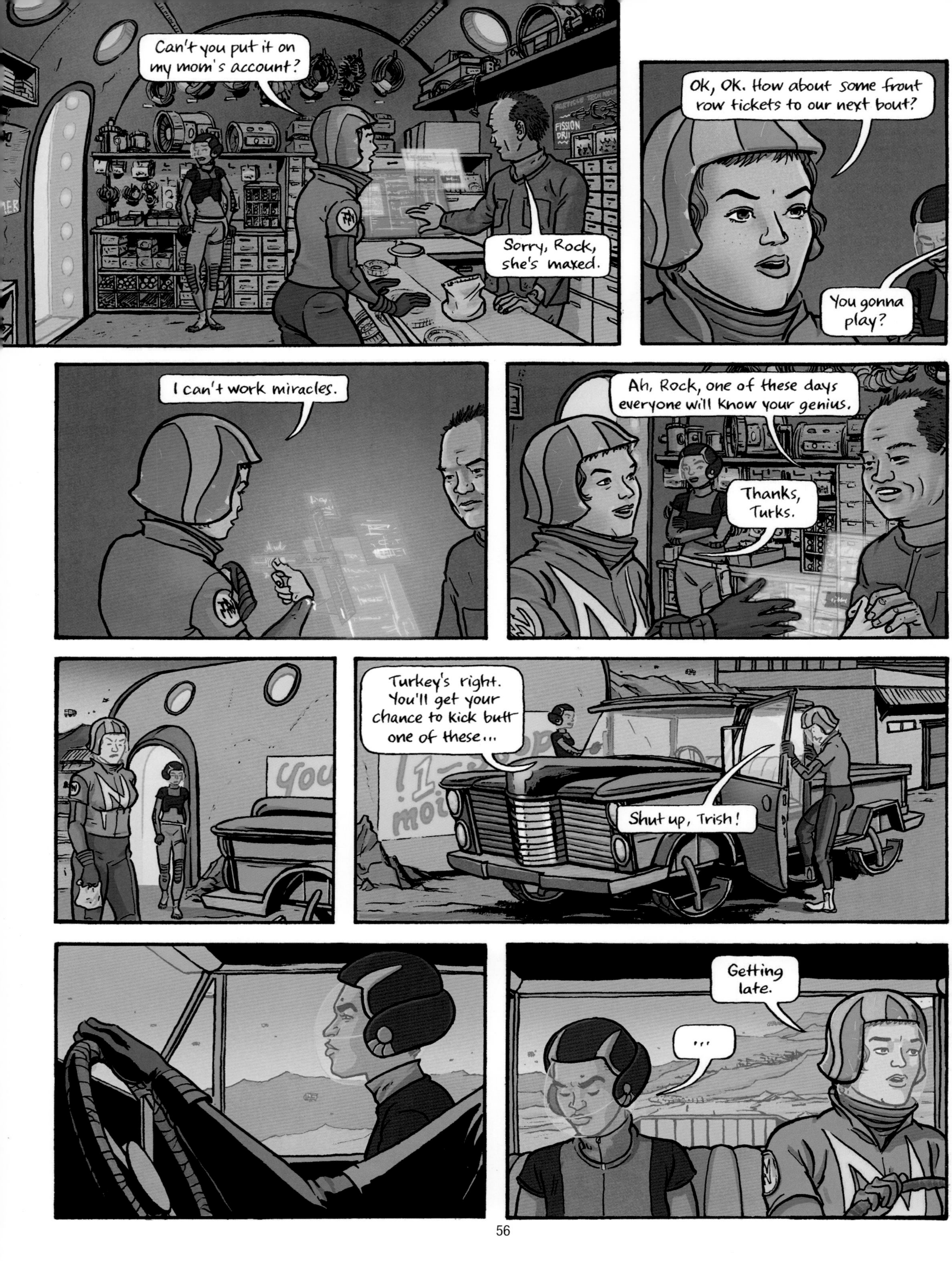
Can't you put it on my mom's account?
Sorry, Rock, she's maxed.
Ok, OK. How about some front row tickets to our next bout?
You gonna play?
I can't work miracles.
Ah, Rock, one of these days everyone will know your genius.
Thanks, Turks.
Turkey's right. You'll get your chance to kick butt one of these...
Shut up, Trish!
Getting late.
...

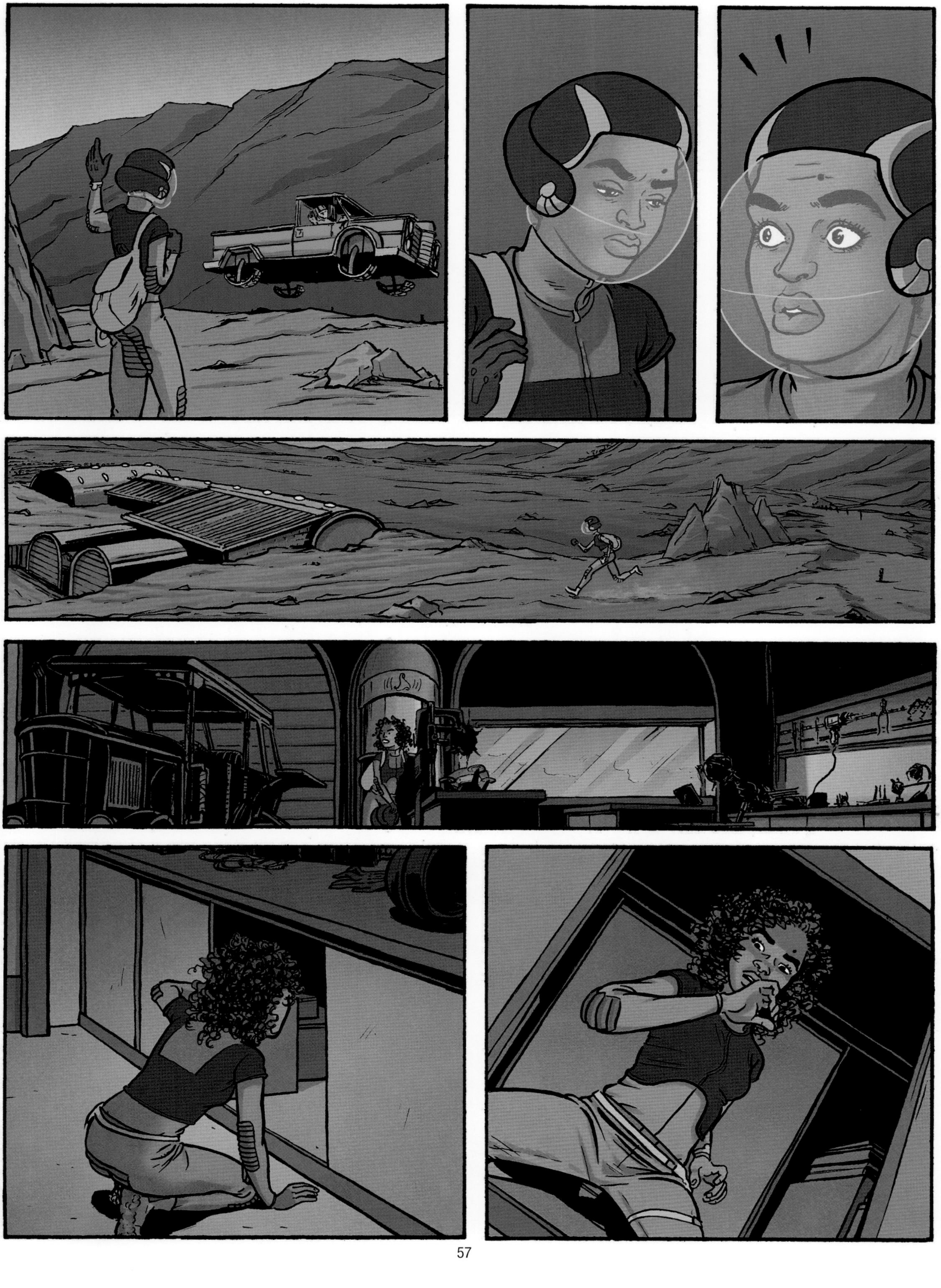

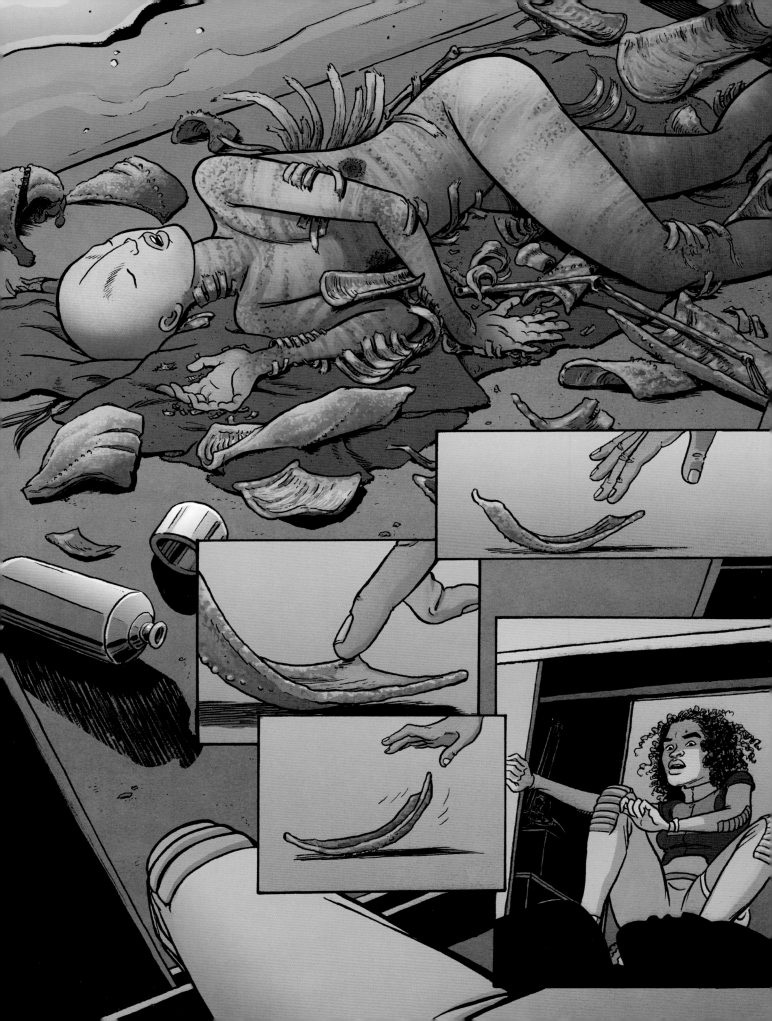

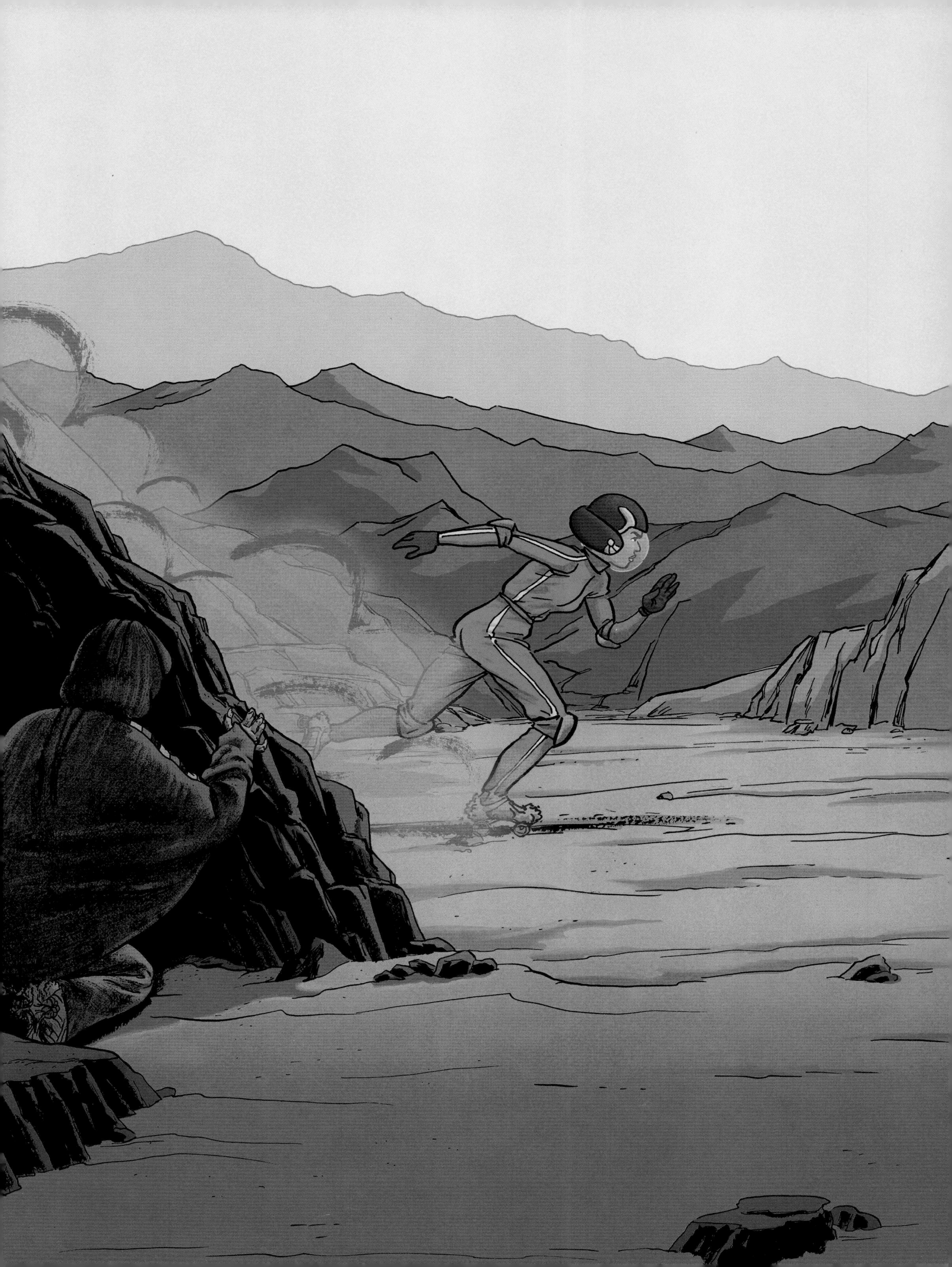

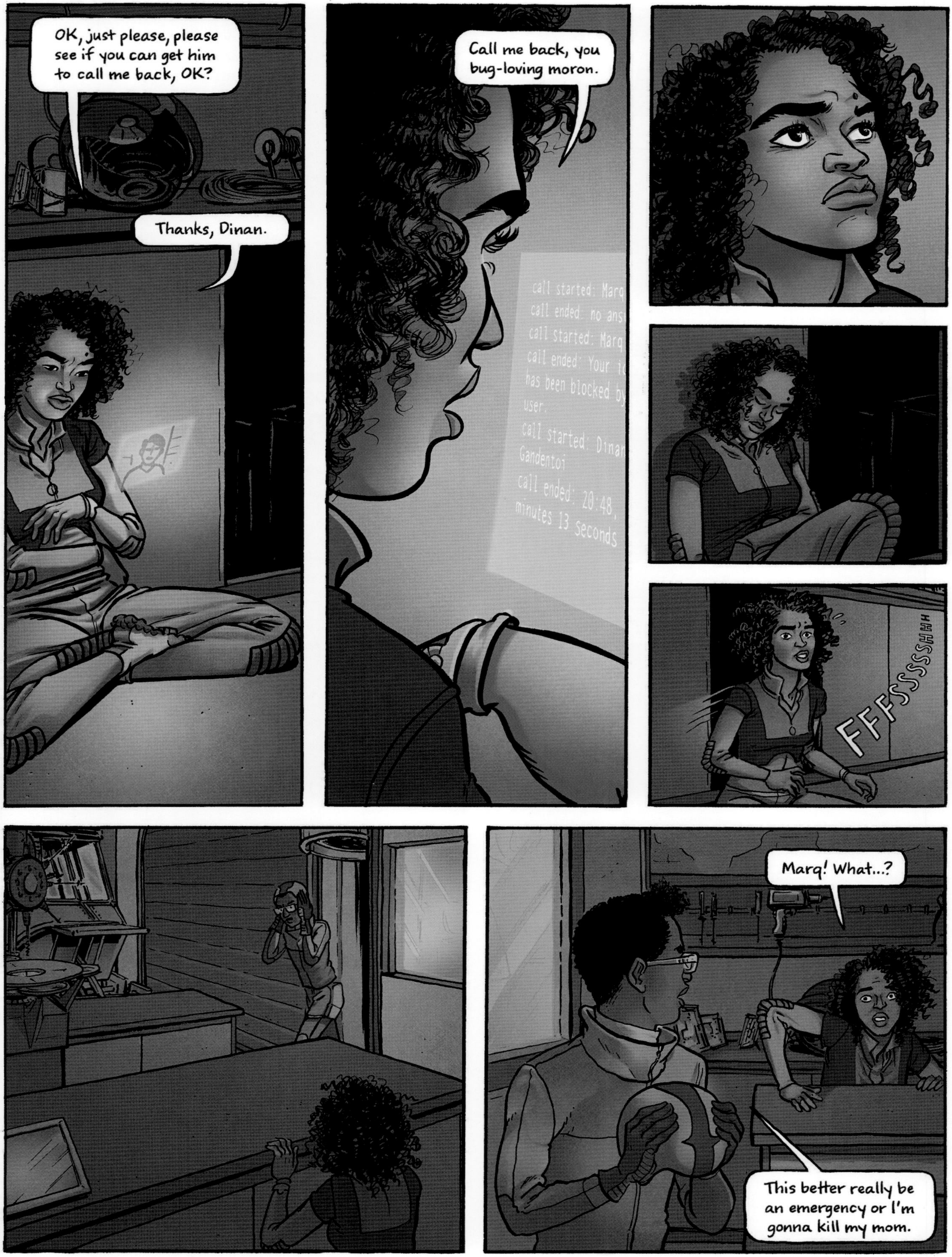
OK, just please, please see if you can get him to call me back, OK?
Thanks, Dinan.
Call me back, you bug-loving moron.
call started: Marq
call ended: no ans
call started: Marq
call ended: Your ic
has been blocked by
user.
call started: Dinan
Gandentoi
call ended: 20:48,
minutes 13 seconds
FFFSSSSSHHH
Marq! What...?
This better really be an emergency or I'm gonna kill my mom.

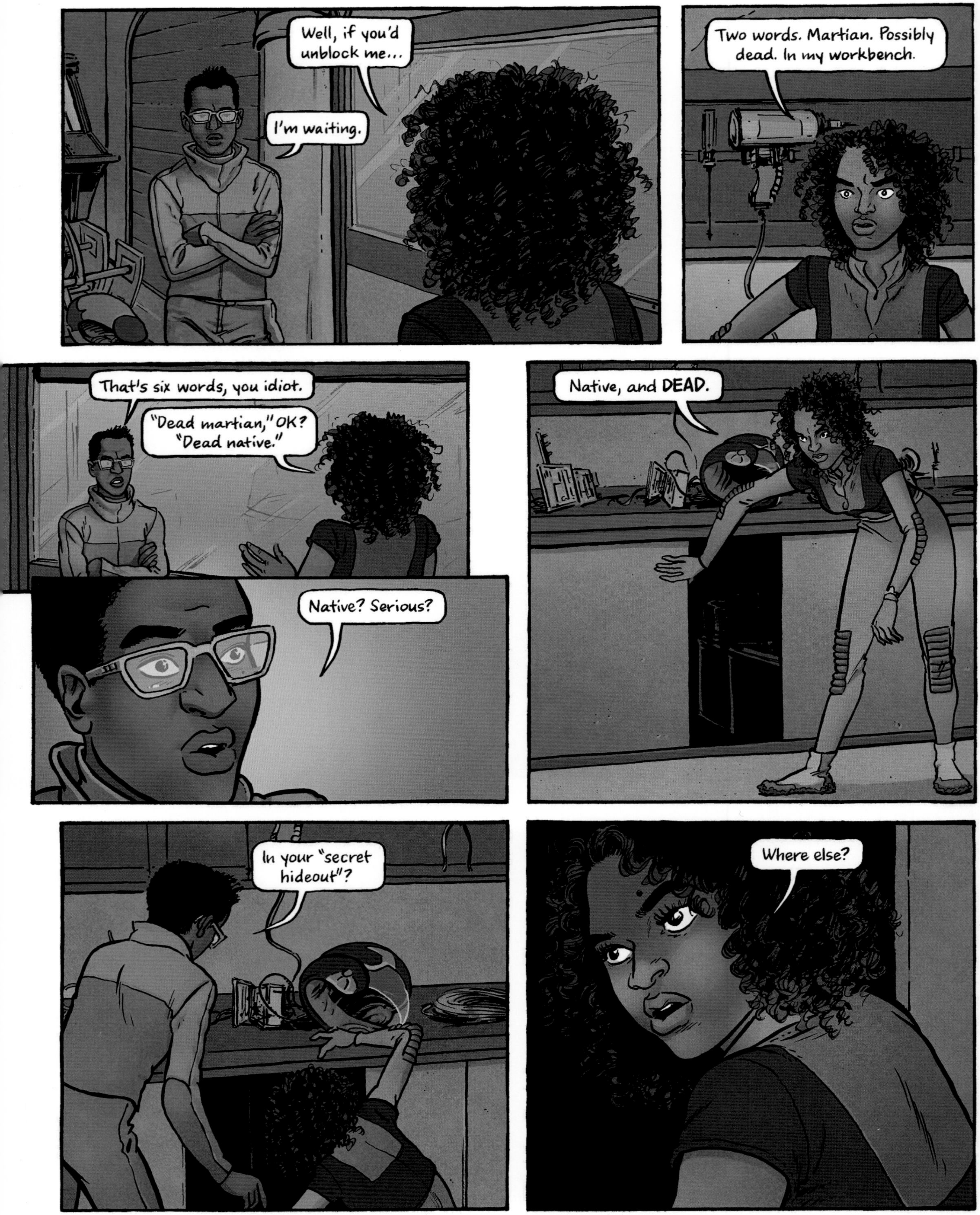
Well, if you'd unblock me...
I'm waiting.
Two words. Martian. Possibly dead. In my workbench.
That's six words, you idiot.
"Dead martian," OK? "Dead native."
Native? Serious?
Native, and **DEAD.**
In your "secret hideout"?
Where else?

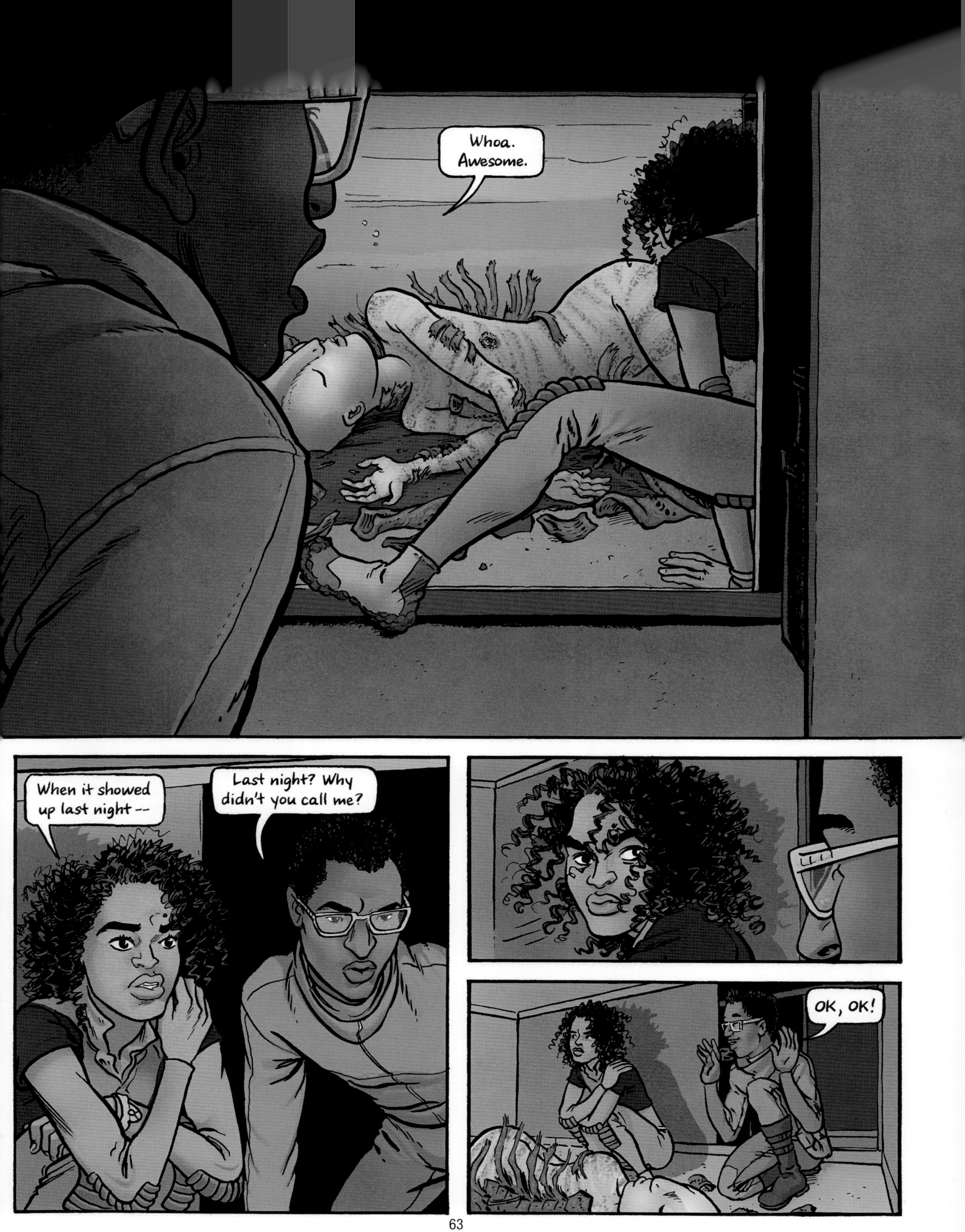
Whoa. Awesome.
When it showed up last night --
Last night? Why didn't you call me?
OK, OK!

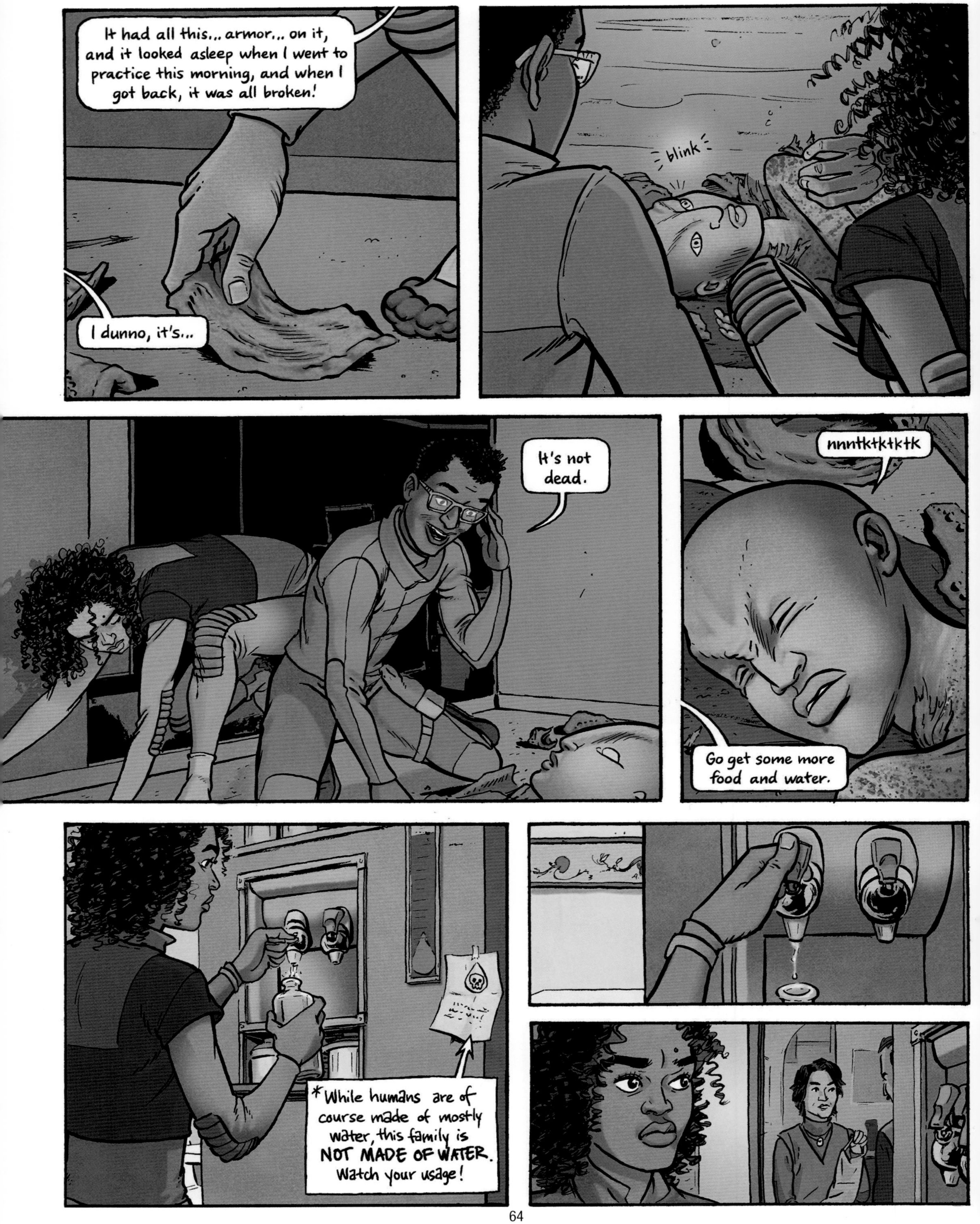
It had all this... armor... on it, and it looked asleep when I went to practice this morning, and when I got back, it was all broken!
I dunno, it's...
blink
It's not dead.
nnntktktktk
Go get some more food and water.
*While humans are of course made of mostly water, this family is NOT MADE OF WATER. Watch your usage!

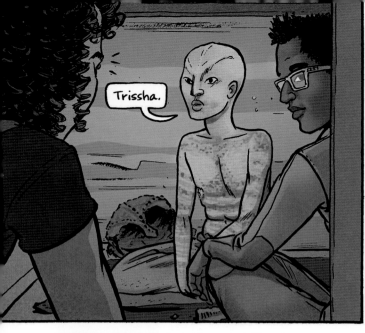

Trissha.

Ohmigod. You told it my name?

Her. I told *her* your name.

Her name is... what is it?

Tkqiqisspkdggrrr. But easszier to say Qiqi.

Uh, OK.

What happened to its—her—arms?

What?

Didn't you have... more arms?

Secondary limbssz part of carapassze. Will grow again.

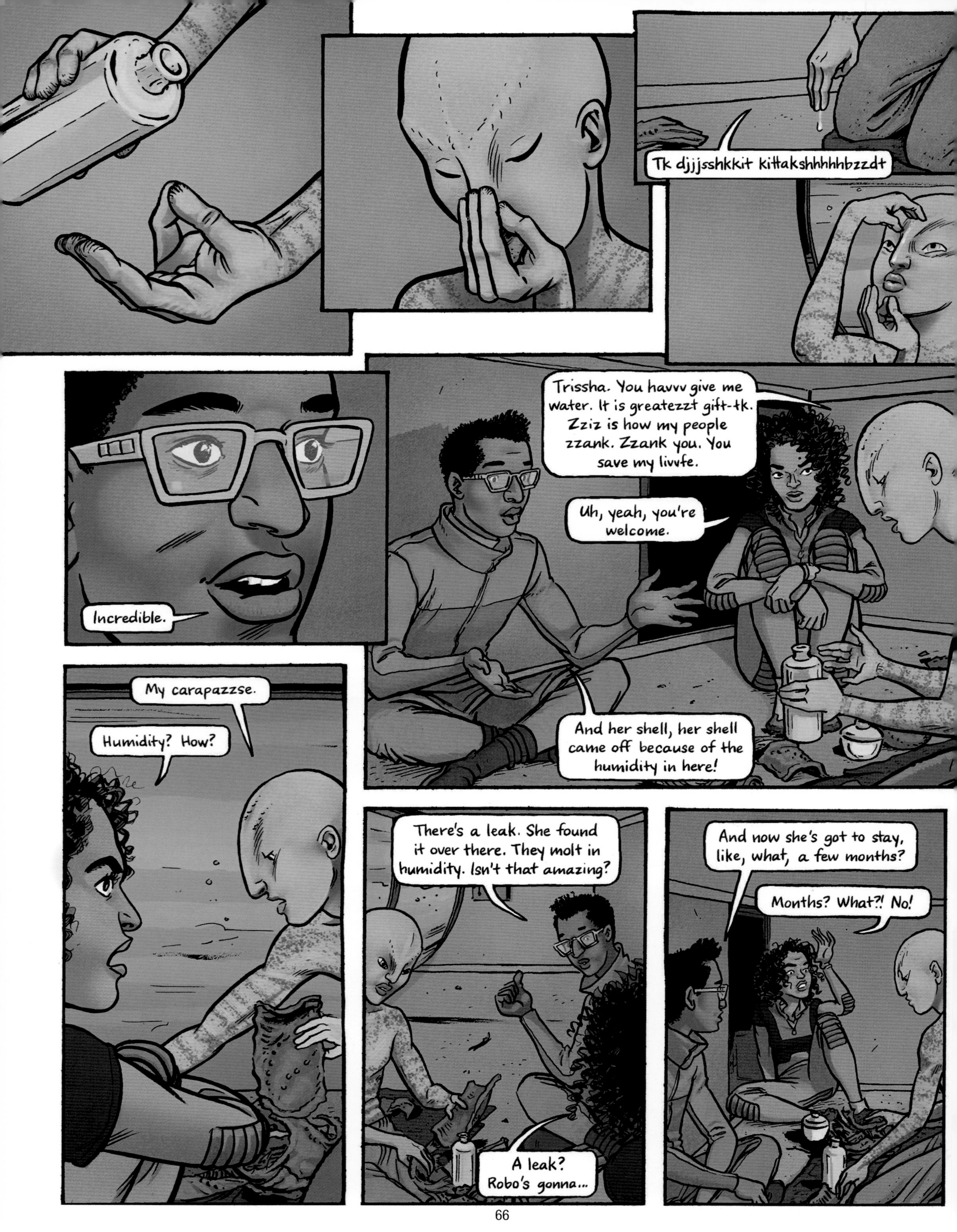
Tk djjjsshkkit kittakshhhhhbzzdt
Incredible.
Trissha. You havvv give me water. It is greatezzt gift-tk. Zziz is how my people zzank. Zzank you. You save my livvfe.
Uh, yeah, you're welcome.
And her shell, her shell came off because of the humidity in here!
My carapazzse.
Humidity? How?
There's a leak. She found it over there. They molt in humidity. Isn't that amazing?
A leak? Robo's gonna...
And now she's got to stay, like, what, a few months?
Months? What?! No!

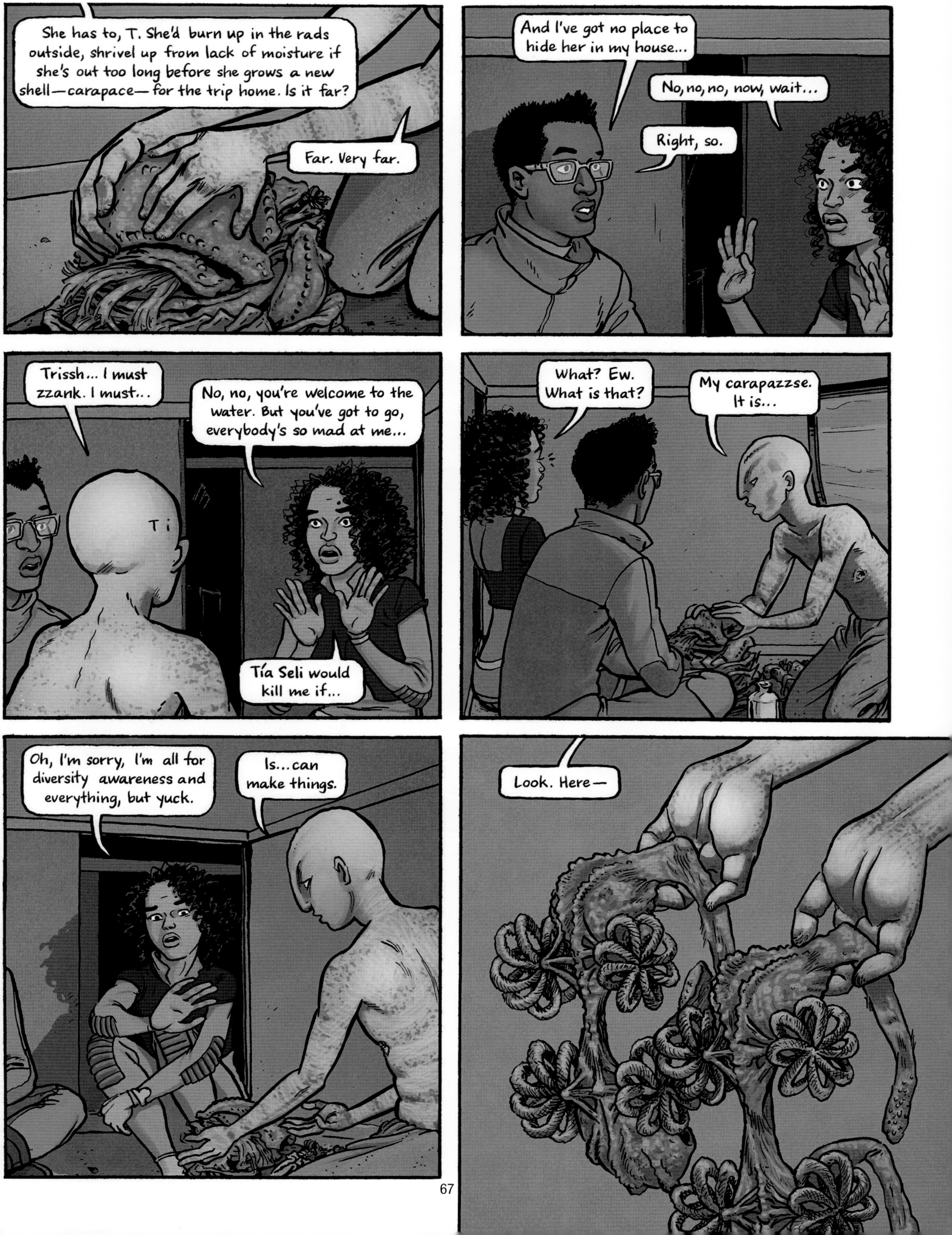
She has to, T. She'd burn up in the rads outside, shrivel up from lack of moisture if she's out too long before she grows a new shell—carapace—for the trip home. Is it far?
Far. Very far.
And I've got no place to hide her in my house...
No, no, no, now, wait...
Right, so.
Trissh... I must zzank. I must...
No, no, you're welcome to the water. But you've got to go, everybody's so mad at me...
Tía Seli would kill me if...
What? Ew. What is that?
My carapazzse. It is...
Oh, I'm sorry, I'm all for diversity awareness and everything, but yuck.
Is...can make things.
Look. Here—

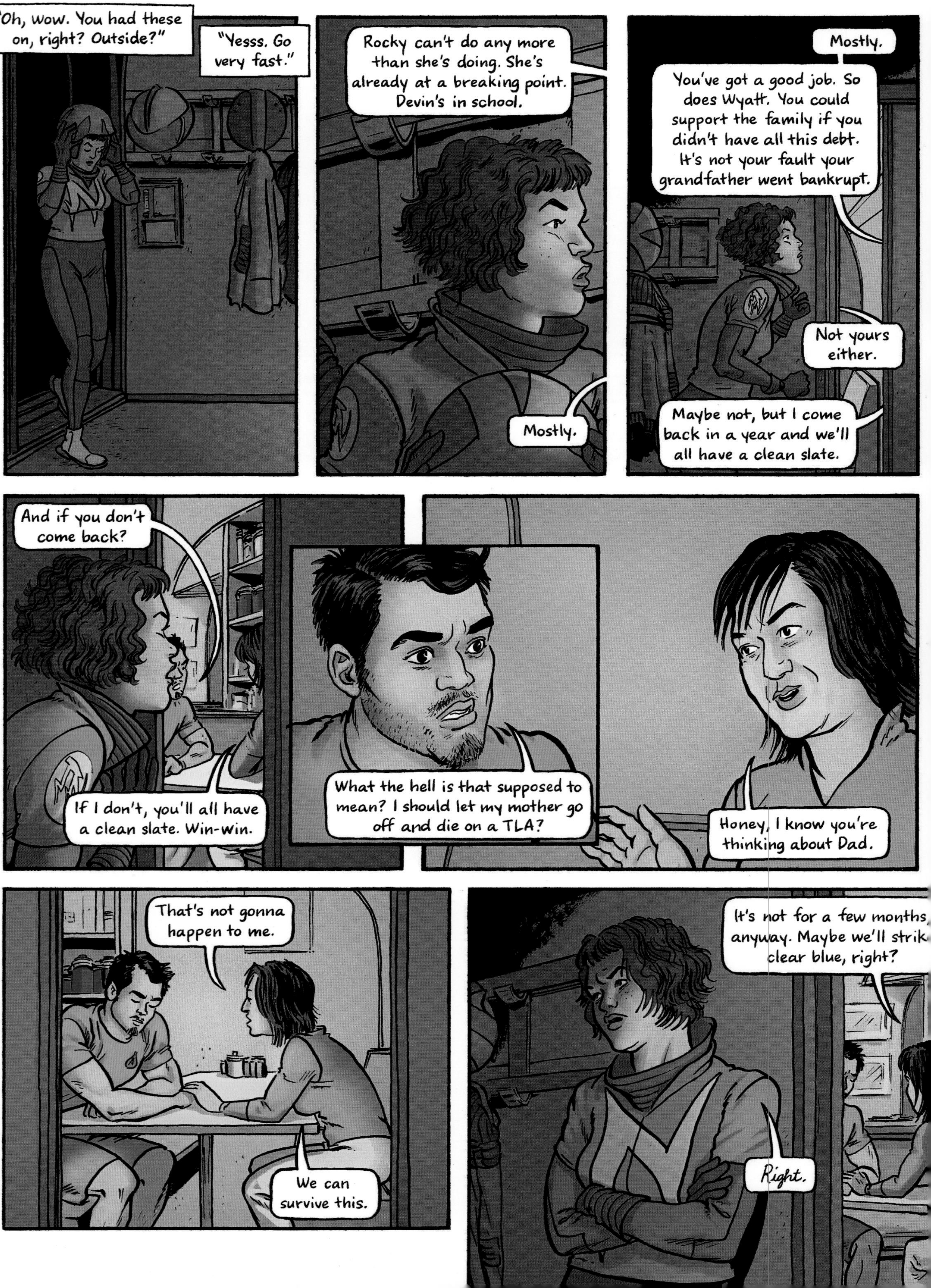
"Oh, wow. You had these on, right? Outside?"
"Yesss. Go very fast."
Rocky can't do any more than she's doing. She's already at a breaking point. Devin's in school.
Mostly.
Mostly.
You've got a good job. So does Wyatt. You could support the family if you didn't have all this debt. It's not your fault your grandfather went bankrupt.
Not yours either.
Maybe not, but I come back in a year and we'll all have a clean slate.
And if you don't come back?
If I don't, you'll all have a clean slate. Win-win.
What the hell is that supposed to mean? I should let my mother go off and die on a TLA?
Honey, I know you're thinking about Dad.
That's not gonna happen to me.
We can survive this.
It's not for a few months, anyway. Maybe we'll strik clear blue, right?
Right.

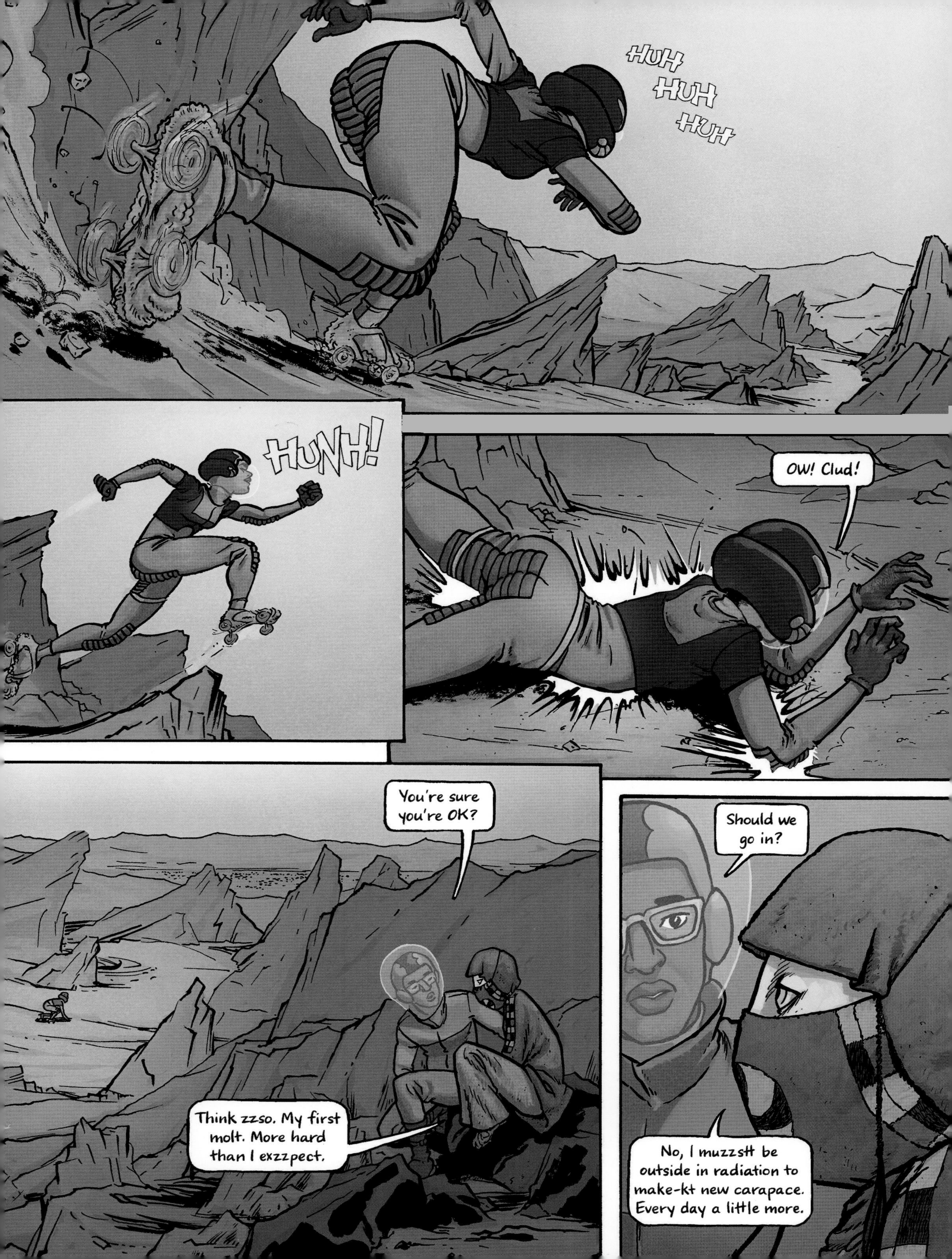
HUH
HUH
HUH
HUNH!
OW! Clud!
You're sure you're OK?
Think zzso. My first molt. More hard than I exzzpect.
Should we go in?
No, I muzzsH be outside in radiation to make-kt new carapace. Every day a little more.

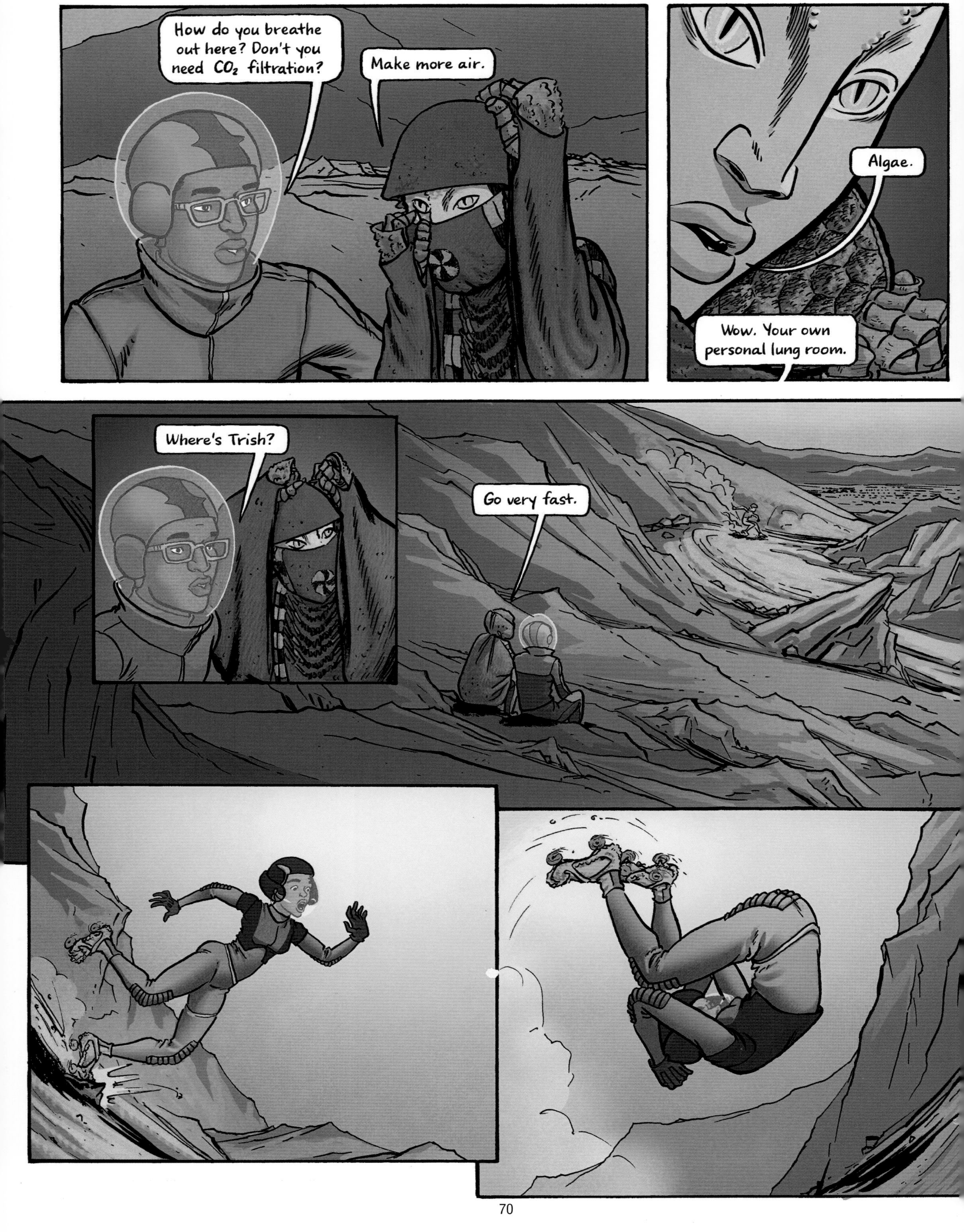
How do you breathe out here? Don't you need CO_2 filtration?
Make more air.
Algae.
Wow. Your own personal lung room.
Where's Trish?
Go very fast.

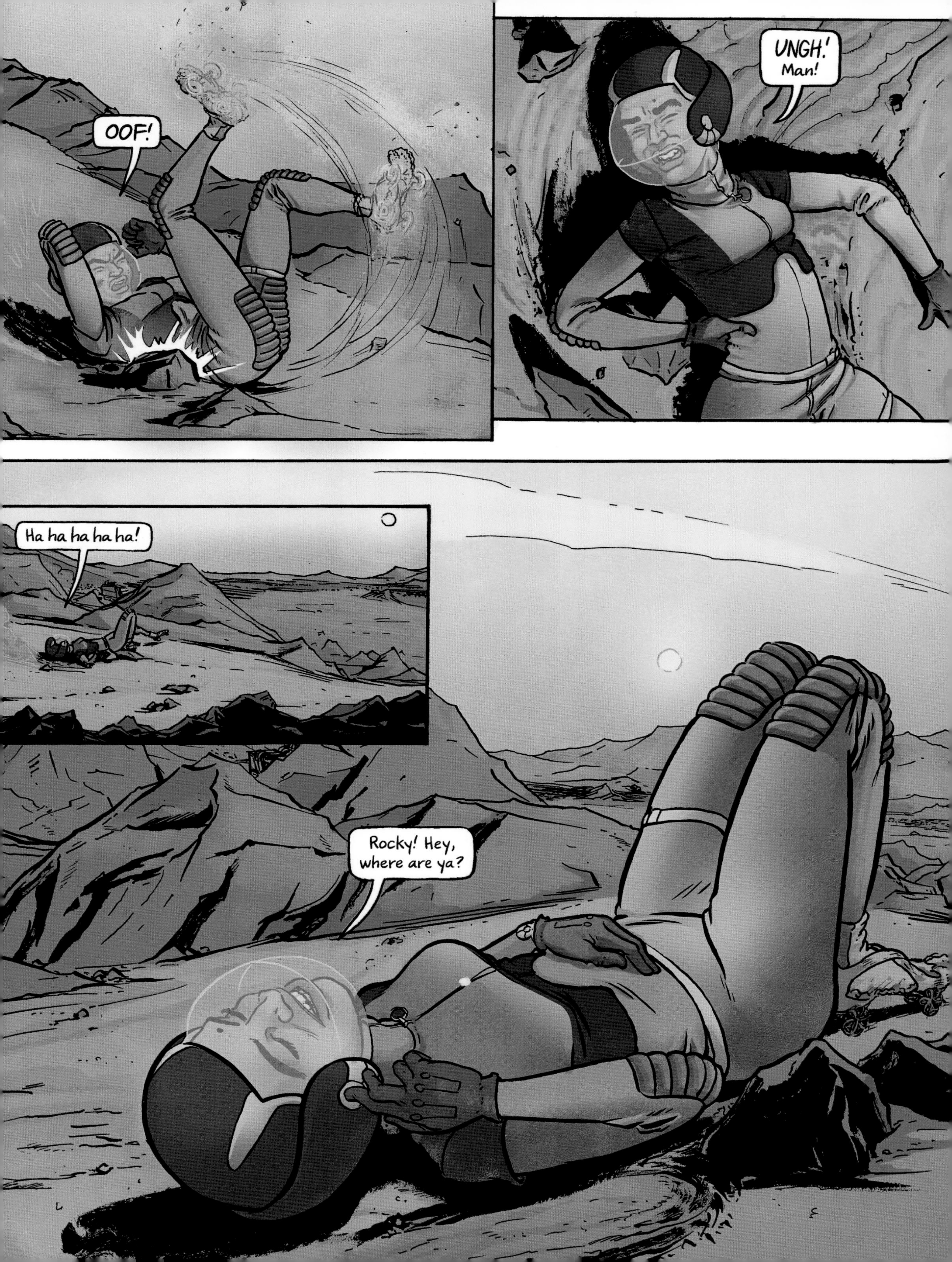
OOF!
UNGH! Man!
Ha ha ha ha ha!
Rocky! Hey, where are ya?

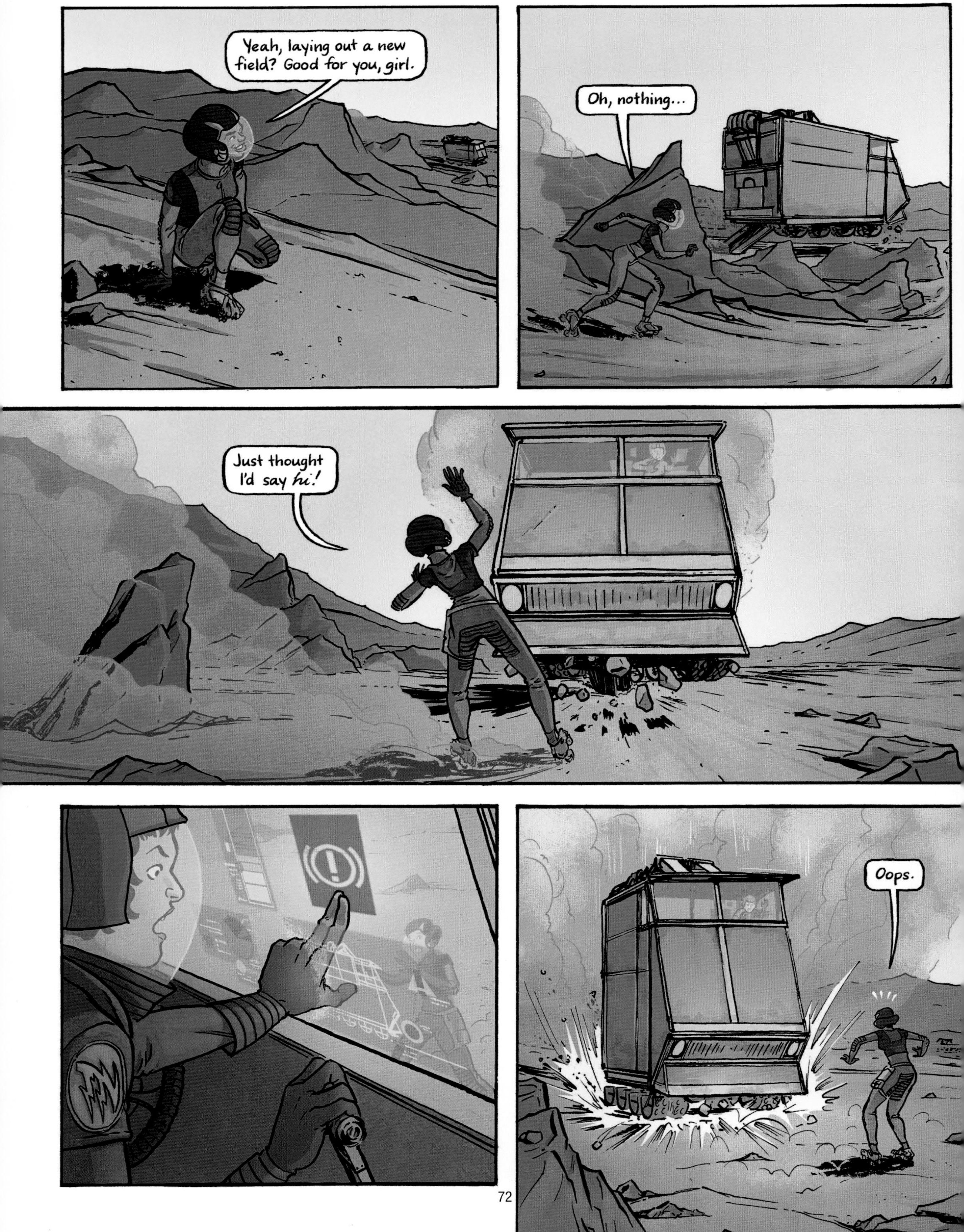
Yeah, laying out a new field? Good for you, girl.
Oh, nothing...
Just thought I'd say *hi*!
Oops.

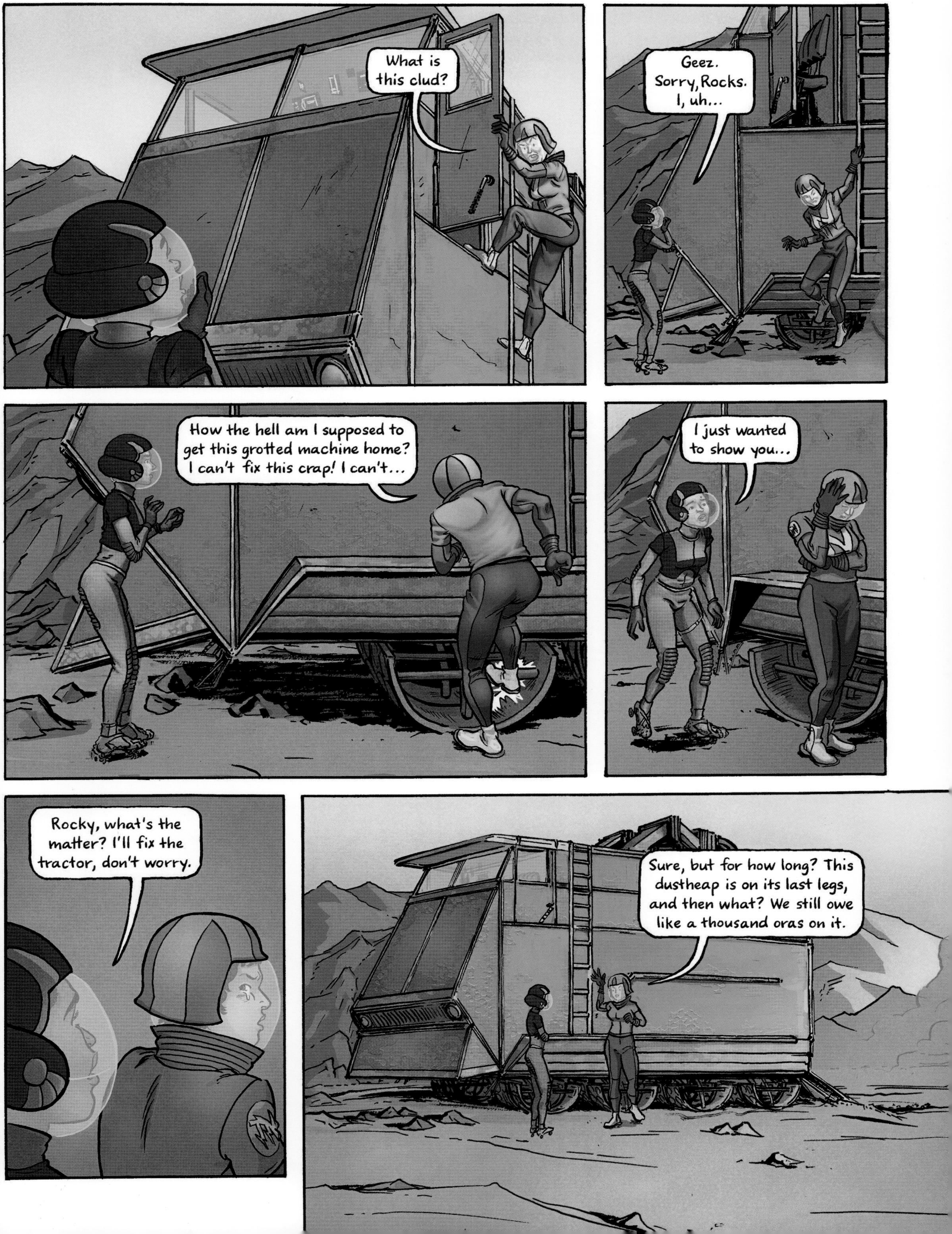
What is this clud?
Geez. Sorry, Rocks. I, uh...
How the hell am I supposed to get this grotted machine home? I can't fix this crap! I can't...
I just wanted to show you...
Rocky, what's the matter? I'll fix the tractor, don't worry.
Sure, but for how long? This dustheap is on its last legs, and then what? We still owe like a thousand oras on it.

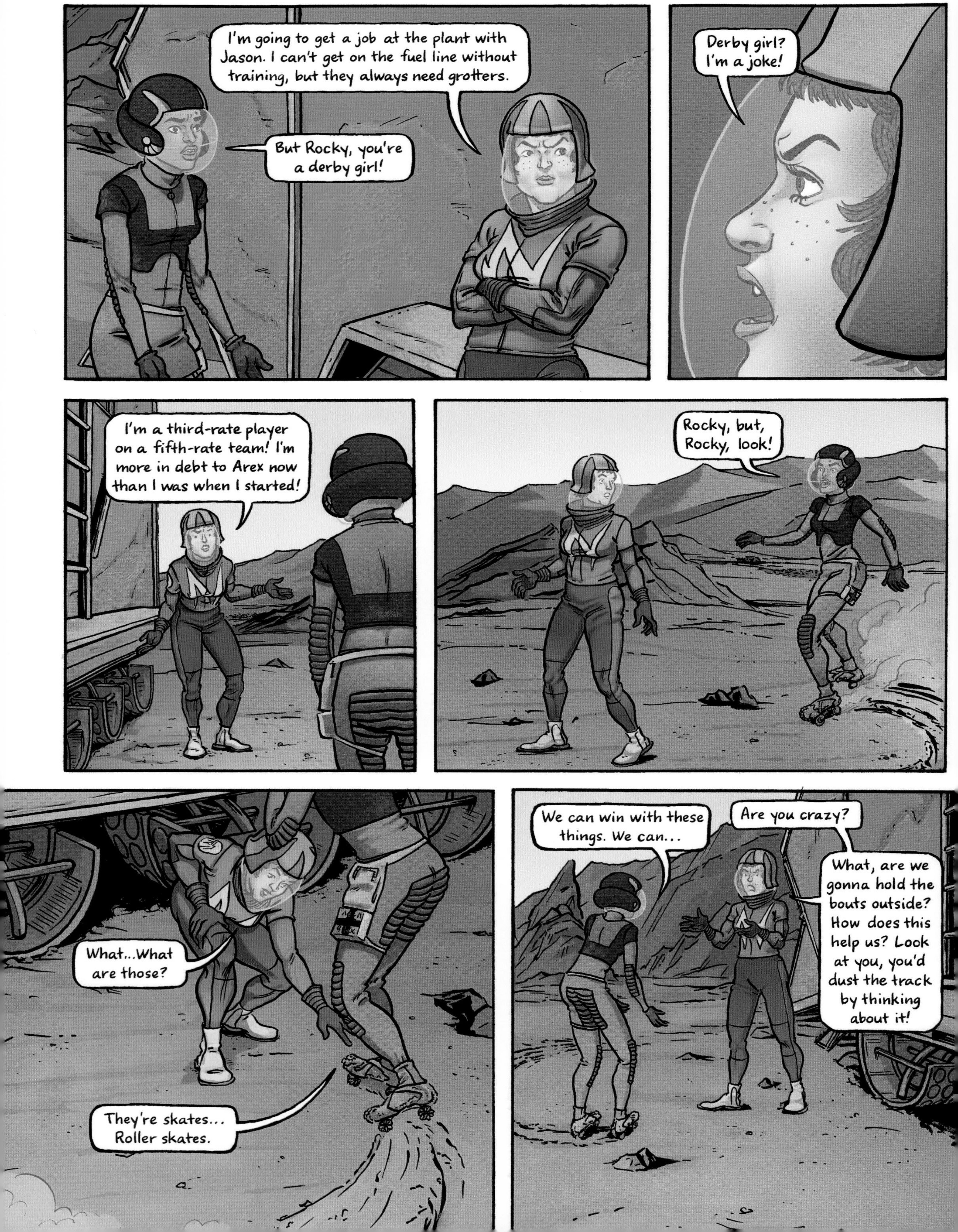
I'm going to get a job at the plant with Jason. I can't get on the fuel line without training, but they always need grotters.
But Rocky, you're a derby girl!
Derby girl? I'm a joke!
I'm a third-rate player on a fifth-rate team! I'm more in debt to Arex now than I was when I started!
Rocky, but, Rocky, look!
What...What are those?
They're skates... Roller skates.
We can win with these things. We can...
Are you crazy?
What, are we gonna hold the bouts outside? How does this help us? Look at you, you'd dust the track by thinking about it!

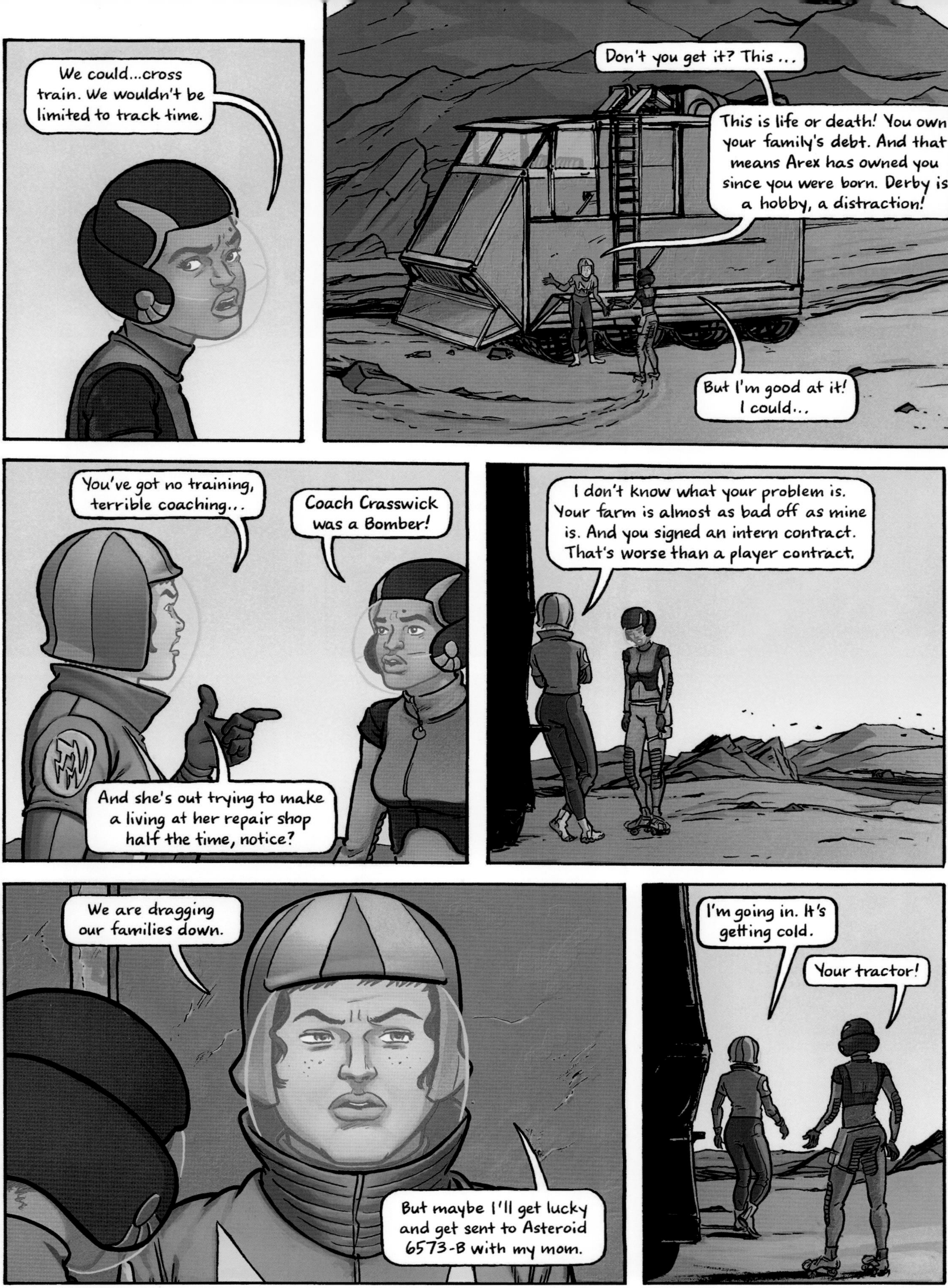
We could...cross train. We wouldn't be limited to track time.
Don't you get it? This ...
This is life or death! You own your family's debt. And that means Arex has owned you since you were born. Derby is a hobby, a distraction!
But I'm good at it! I could...
You've got no training, terrible coaching...
Coach Crasswick was a Bomber!
And she's out trying to make a living at her repair shop half the time, notice?
I don't know what your problem is. Your farm is almost as bad off as mine is. And you signed an intern contract. That's worse than a player contract.
We are dragging our families down.
But maybe I'll get lucky and get sent to Asteroid 6573-B with my mom.
I'm going in. It's getting cold.
Your tractor!

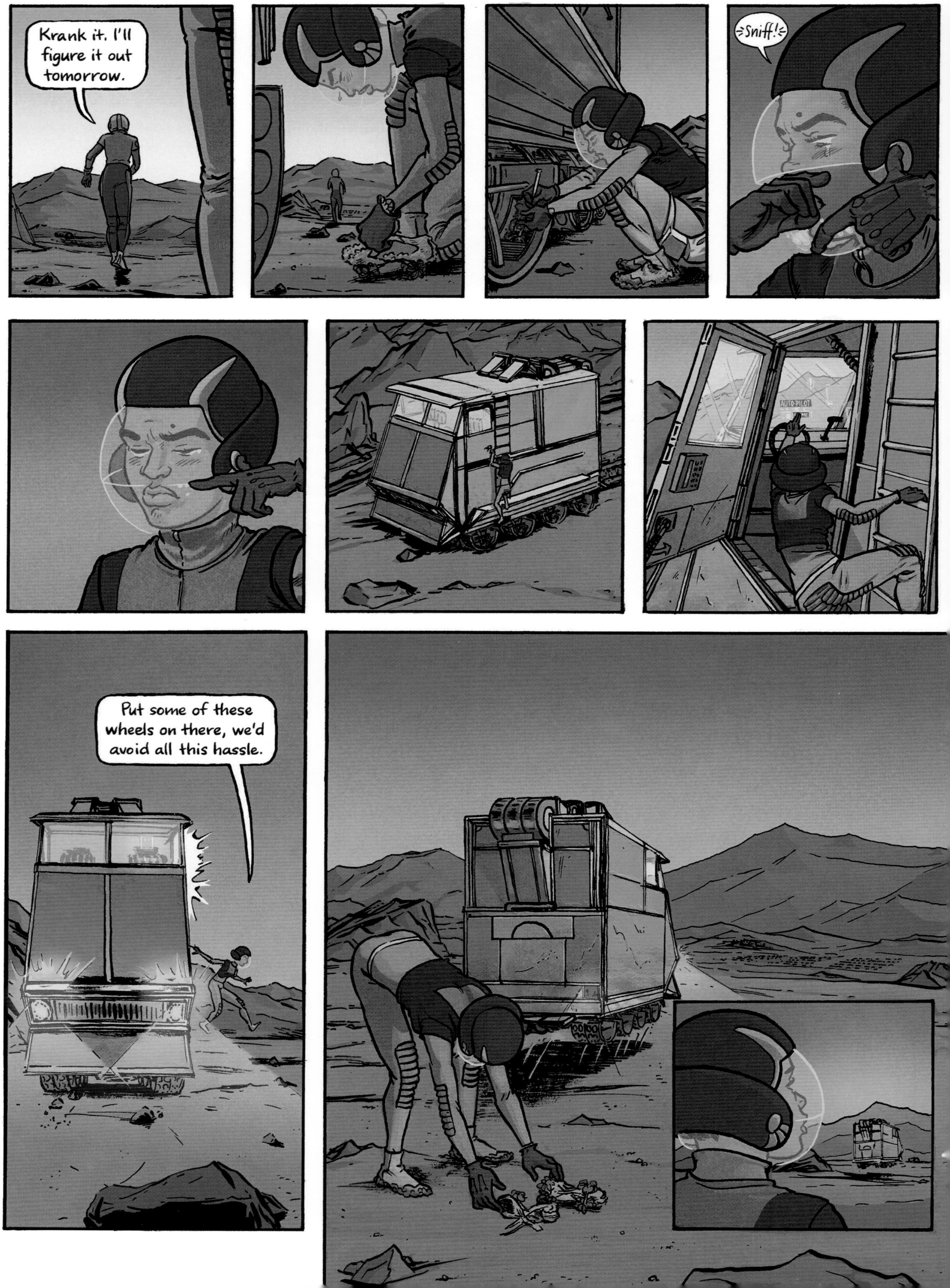
Krank it. I'll figure it out tomorrow.
Sniff!
AUTO-PILOT
Put some of these wheels on there, we'd avoid all this hassle.

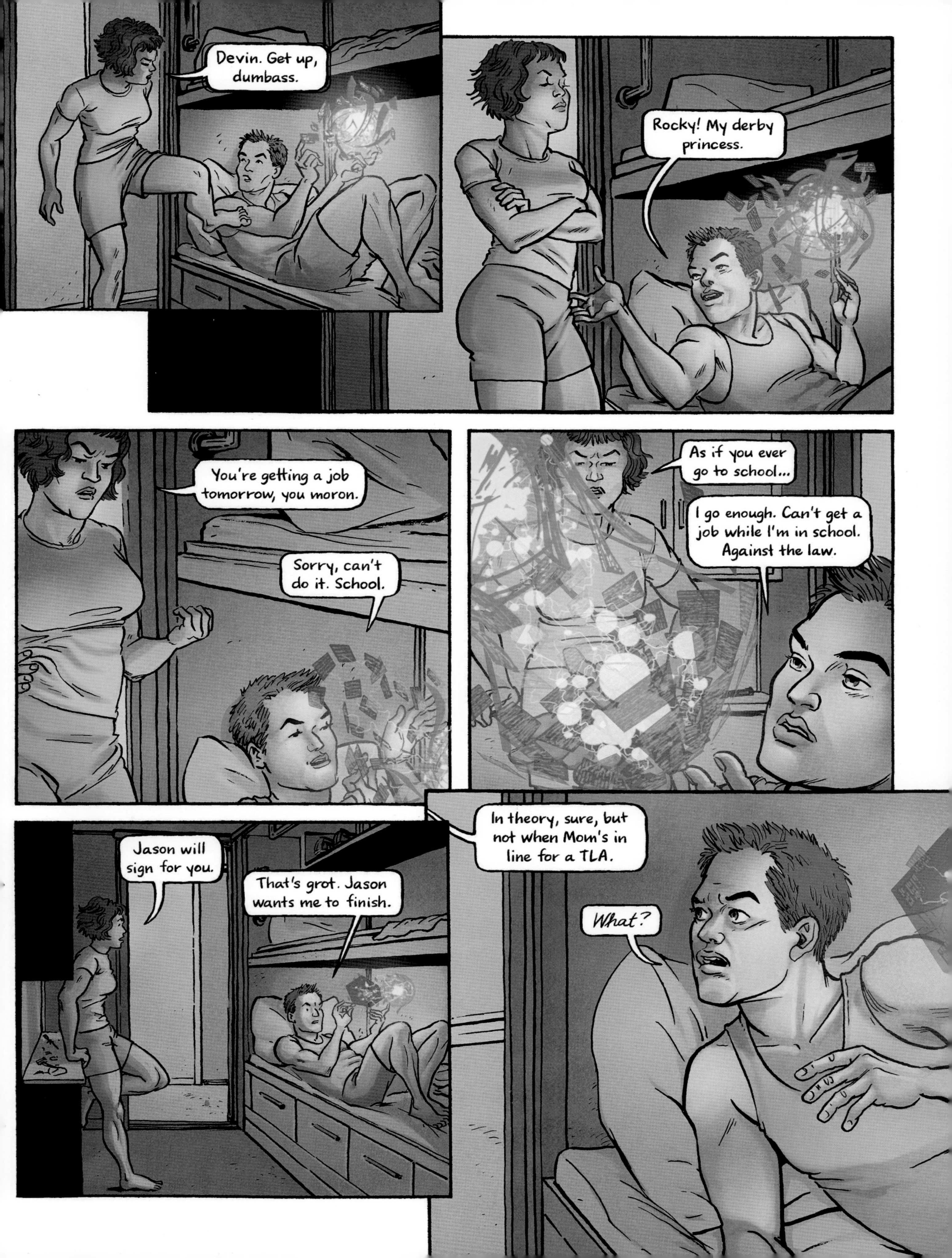
Devin. Get up, dumbass.
Rocky! My derby princess.
You're getting a job tomorrow, you moron.
Sorry, can't do it. School.
As if you ever go to school...
I go enough. Can't get a job while I'm in school. Against the law.
Jason will sign for you.
That's grot. Jason wants me to finish.
In theory, sure, but not when Mom's in line for a TLA.
What?

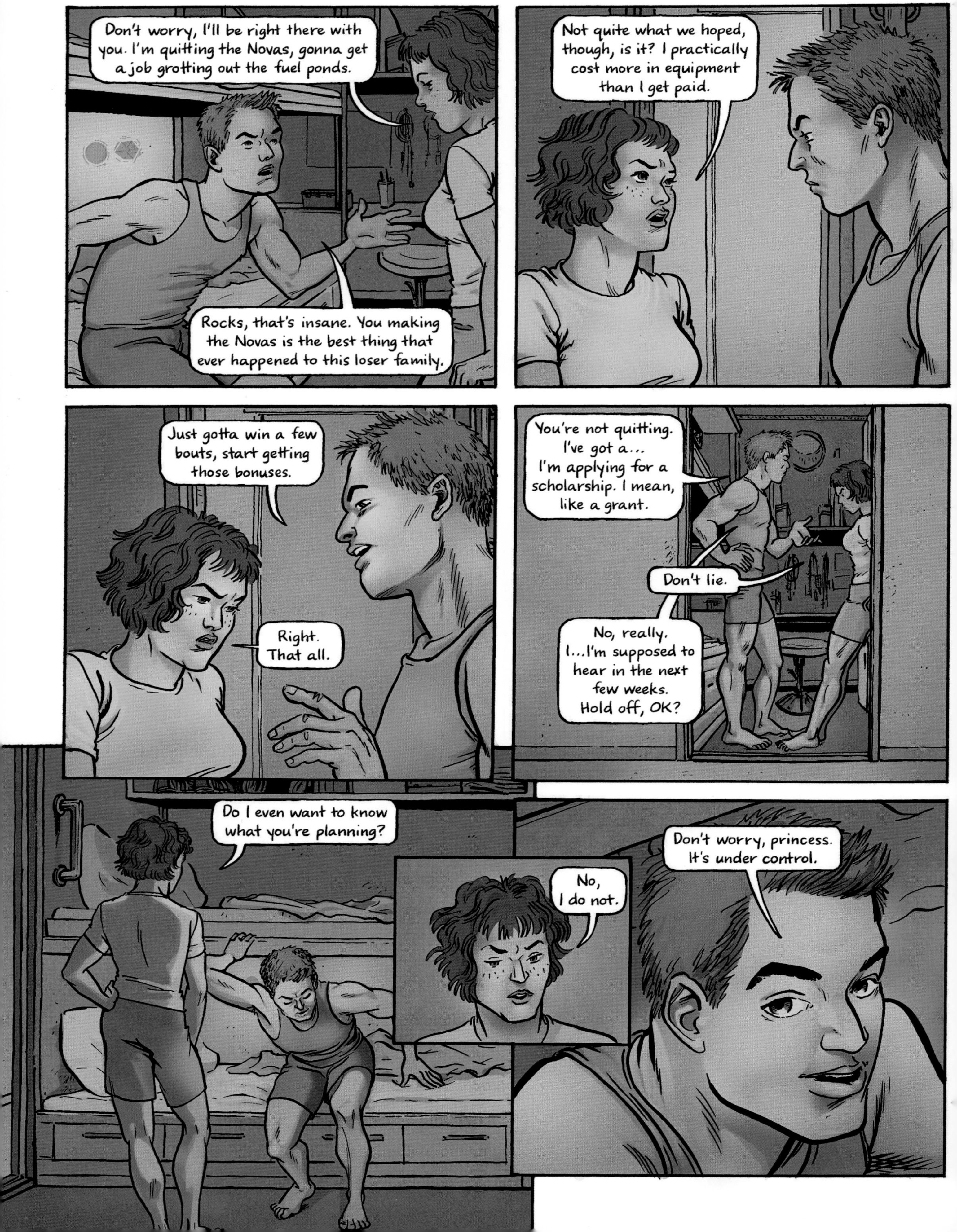
Don't worry, I'll be right there with you. I'm quitting the Novas, gonna get a job grotting out the fuel ponds.
Rocks, that's insane. You making the Novas is the best thing that ever happened to this loser family.
Not quite what we hoped, though, is it? I practically cost more in equipment than I get paid.
Just gotta win a few bouts, start getting those bonuses.
Right. That all.
You're not quitting. I've got a... I'm applying for a scholarship. I mean, like a grant.
Don't lie.
No, really. I...I'm supposed to hear in the next few weeks. Hold off, OK?
Do I even want to know what you're planning?
No, I do not.
Don't worry, princess. It's under control.

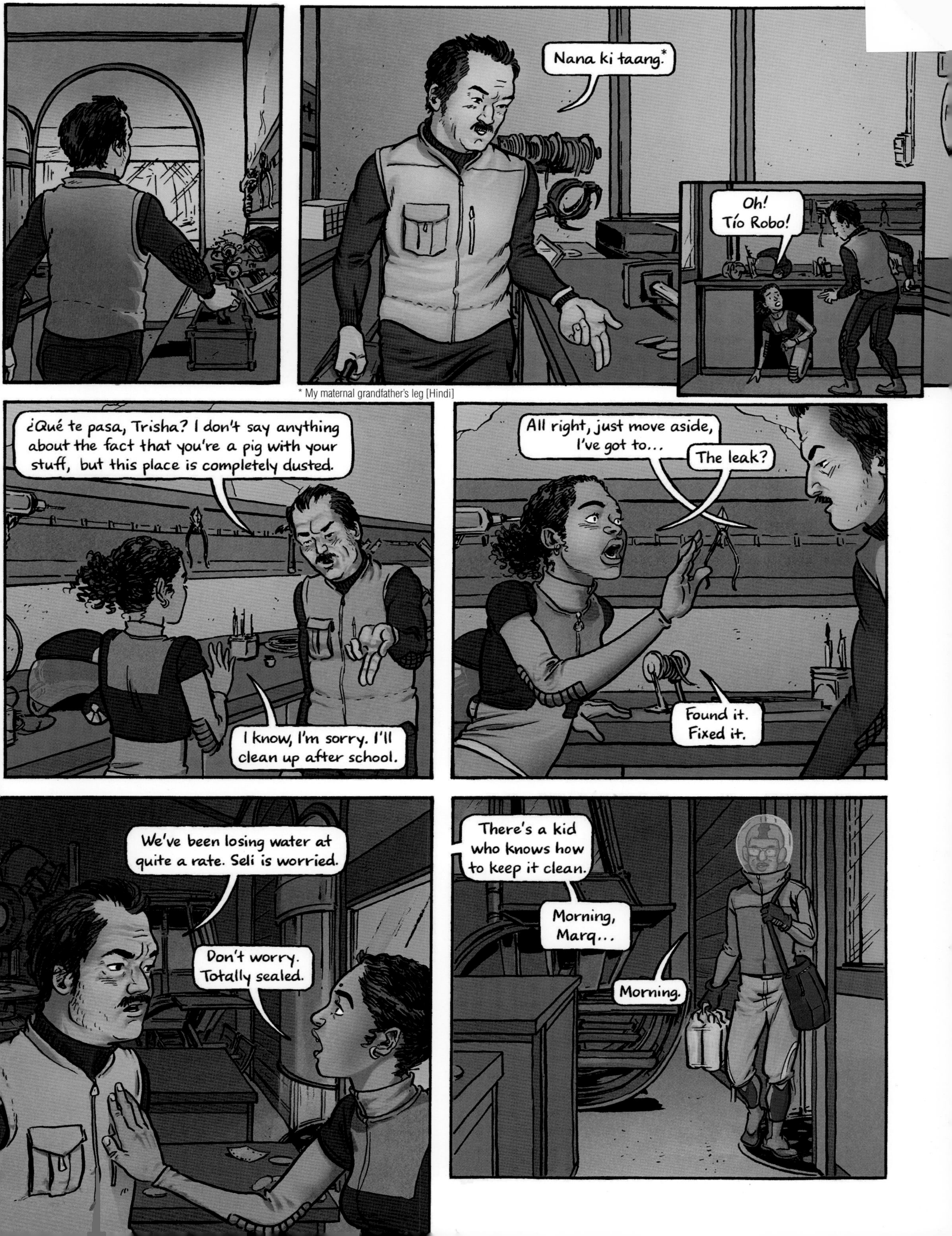
Nana ki taang.*
Oh!
Tío Robo!
¿Qué te pasa, Trisha? I don't say anything about the fact that you're a pig with your stuff, but this place is completely dusted.
I know, I'm sorry. I'll clean up after school.
All right, just move aside, I've got to...
The leak?
Found it. Fixed it.
We've been losing water at quite a rate. Seli is worried.
Don't worry. Totally sealed.
There's a kid who knows how to keep it clean.
Morning, Marq...
Morning.

* My maternal grandfather's leg [Hindi]

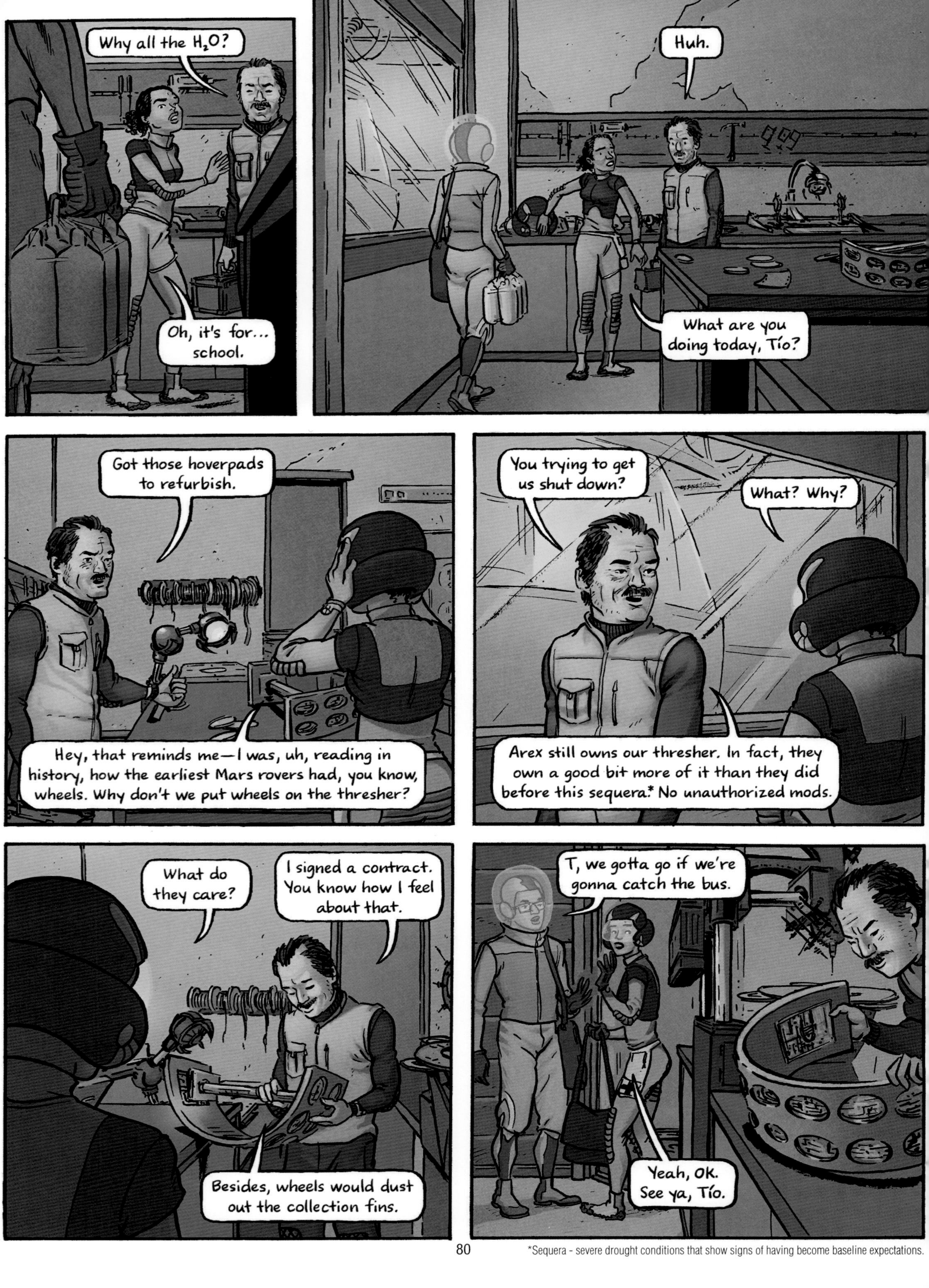
Why all the H_2O?
Oh, it's for... school.
Huh.
What are you doing today, Tío?
Got those hoverpads to refurbish.
Hey, that reminds me—I was, uh, reading in history, how the earliest Mars rovers had, you know, wheels. Why don't we put wheels on the thresher?
You trying to get us shut down?
What? Why?
Arex still owns our thresher. In fact, they own a good bit more of it than they did before this sequera.* No unauthorized mods.
What do they care?
I signed a contract. You know how I feel about that.
Besides, wheels would dust out the collection fins.
T, we gotta go if we're gonna catch the bus.
Yeah, OK. See ya, Tío.

*Sequera - severe drought conditions that show signs of having become baseline expectations.

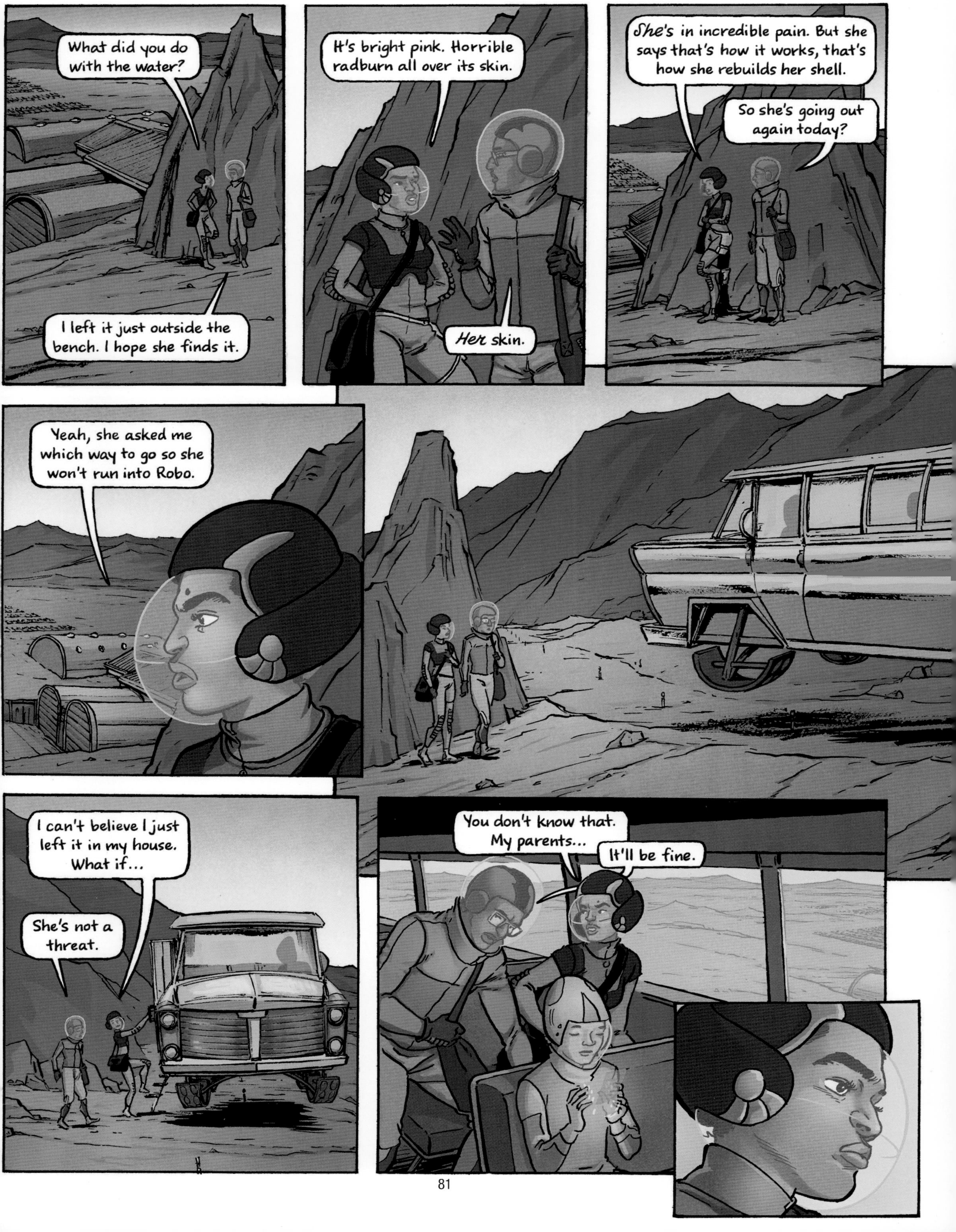
What did you do with the water?
I left it just outside the bench. I hope she finds it.
It's bright pink. Horrible radburn all over its skin.
Her skin.
She's in incredible pain. But she says that's how it works, that's how she rebuilds her shell.
So she's going out again today?
Yeah, she asked me which way to go so she won't run into Robo.
I can't believe I just left it in my house. What if...
She's not a threat.
You don't know that. My parents...
It'll be fine.

Doing your real job for once, slave?

...Thought my job was scoring on you.

I heard that. You think you're cool because Cain puts you in for a few scrimmages? We'll see how cool you feel when the Arex overlords come by for a spot check.

Interns don't skate.

SQUAD ROSTER
A
B

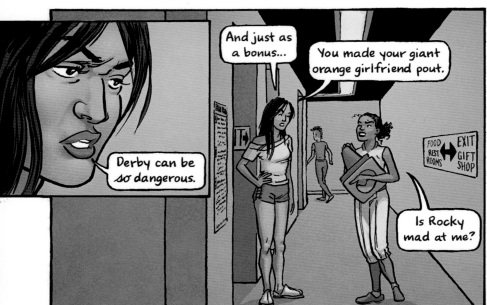

And just as a bonus...

You made your giant orange girlfriend pout.

Derby can be so dangerous.

FOOD
REST
ROOMS

EXIT
GIFT
SHOP

Is Rocky mad at me?

Because you played and she didn't? Why should she be mad?

I should have said no.

Why? I'm not even a jammer. How could I fill in?

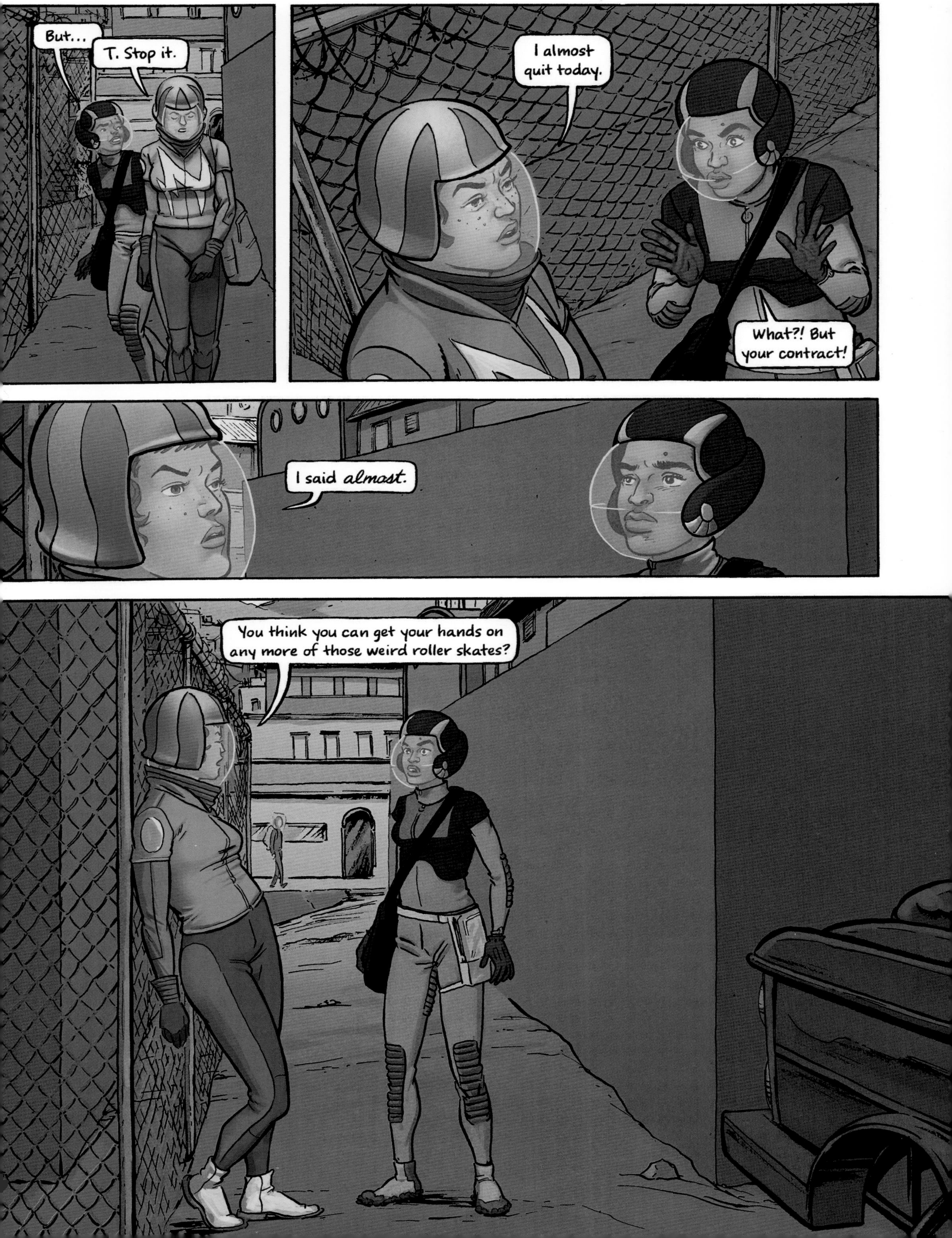

But...
T. Stop it.
I almost quit today.
What?! But your contract!
I said *almost*.
You think you can get your hands on any more of those weird roller skates?

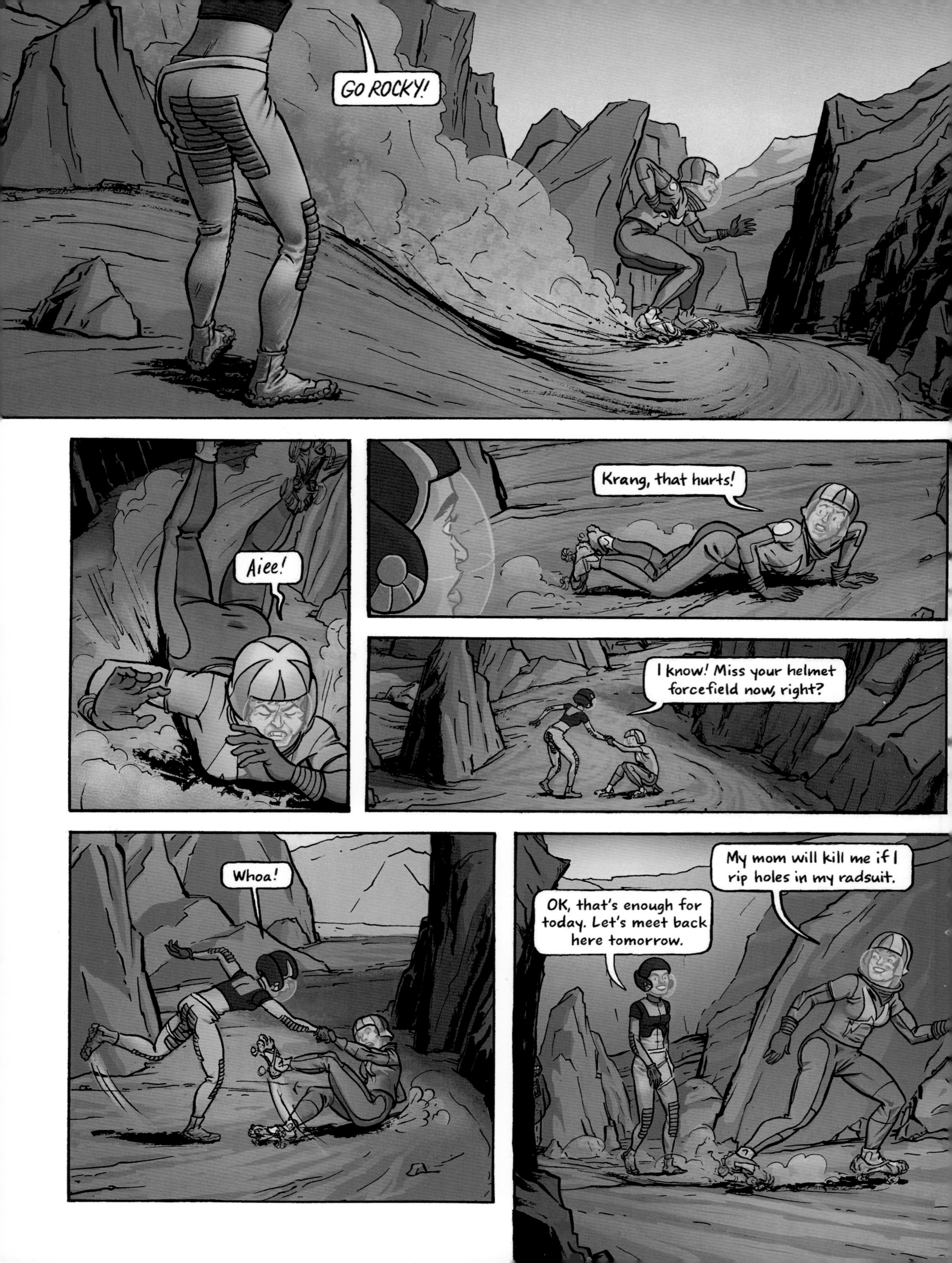
GO ROCKY!
Aiee!
Krang, that hurts!
I know! Miss your helmet forcefield now, right?
Whoa!
My mom will kill me if I rip holes in my radsuit.
OK, that's enough for today. Let's meet back here tomorrow.

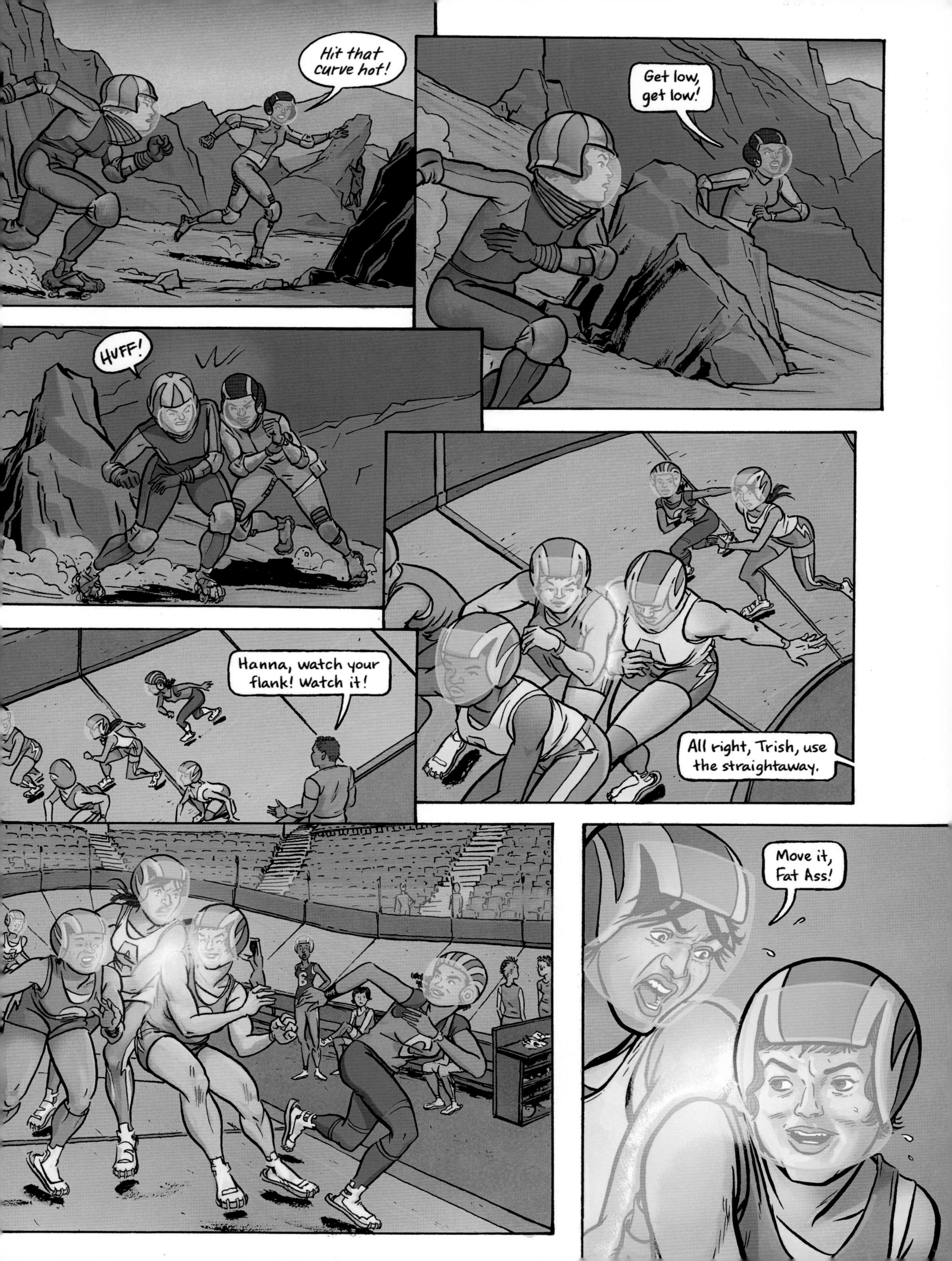
Hit that curve hot!
Get low, get low!
HUFF!
Hanna, watch your flank! Watch it!
All right, Trish, use the straightaway.
Move it, Fat Ass!

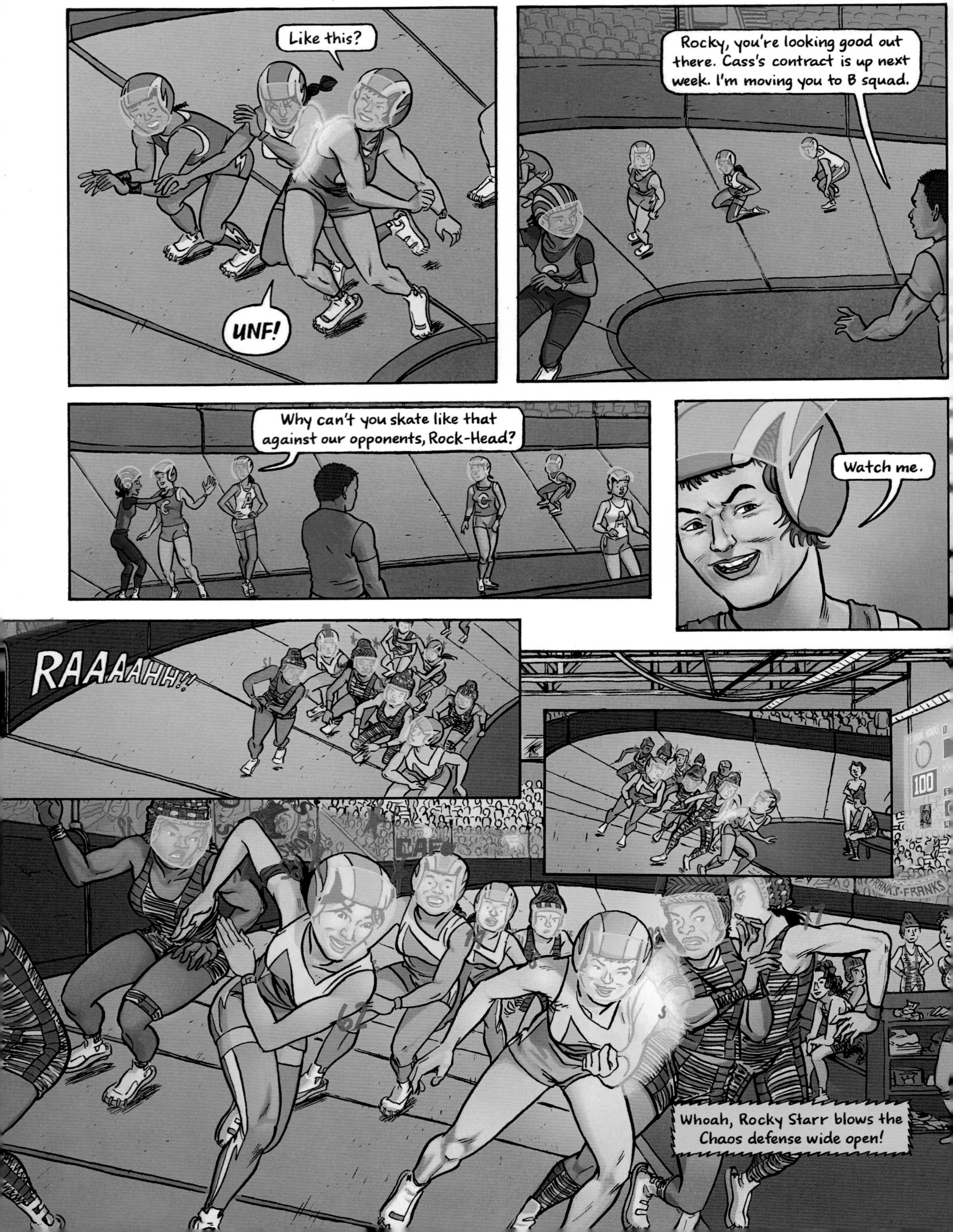
Like this?
UNF!
Rocky, you're looking good out there. Cass's contract is up next week. I'm moving you to B squad.
Why can't you skate like that against our opponents, Rock-Head?
Watch me.
RAAAAHH!!
100
FRANKS FRANKS
Whoah, Rocky Starr blows the Chaos defense wide open!

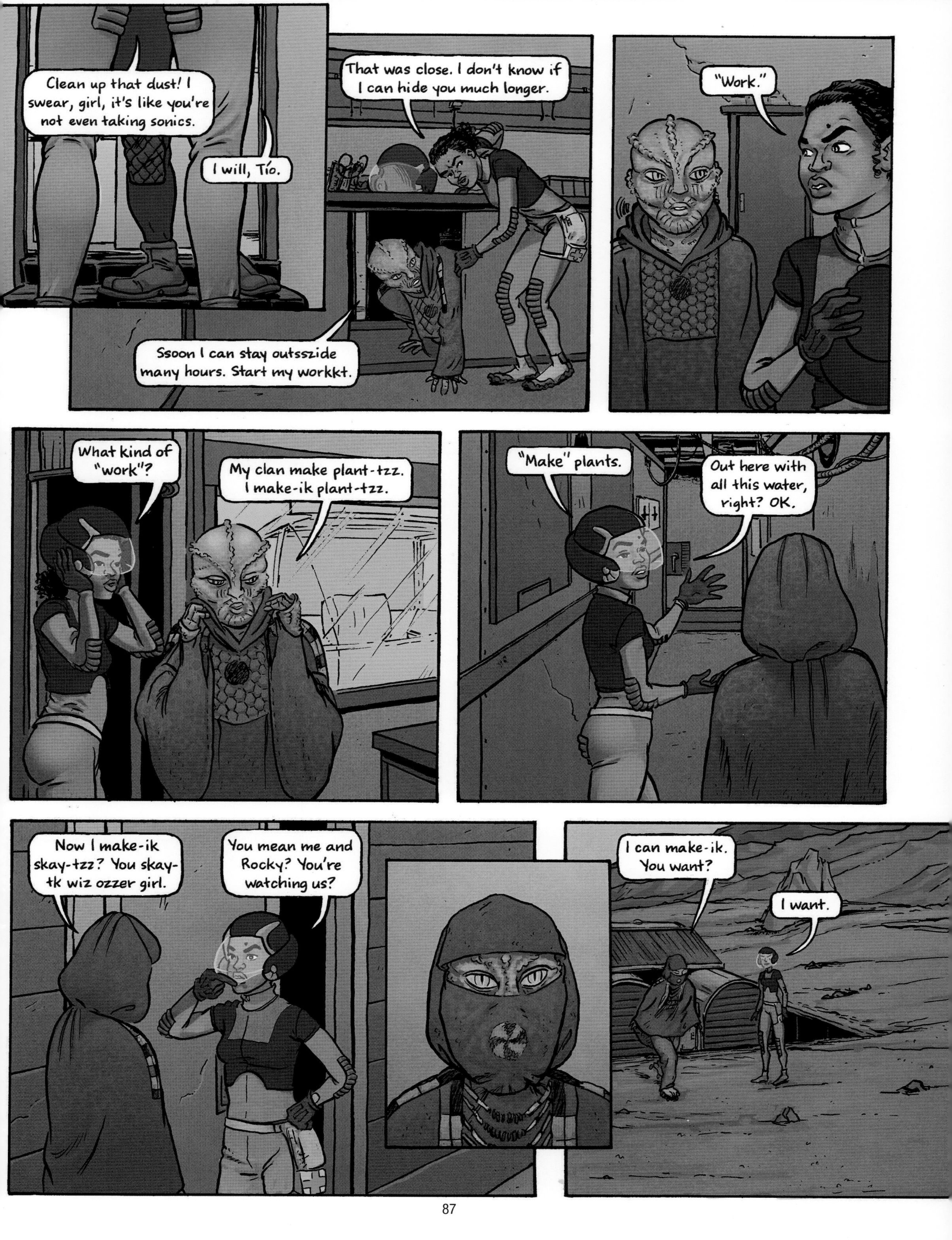
Clean up that dust! I swear, girl, it's like you're not even taking sonics.
I will, Tío.
That was close. I don't know if I can hide you much longer.
Ssoon I can stay outsszide many hours. Start my workkt.
"Work."
What kind of "work"?
My clan make plant-tzz. I make-ik plant-tzz.
"Make" plants.
Out here with all this water, right? OK.
Now I make-ik skay-tzz? You skay-tk wiz ozzer girl.
You mean me and Rocky? You're watching us?
I can make-ik. You want?
I want.

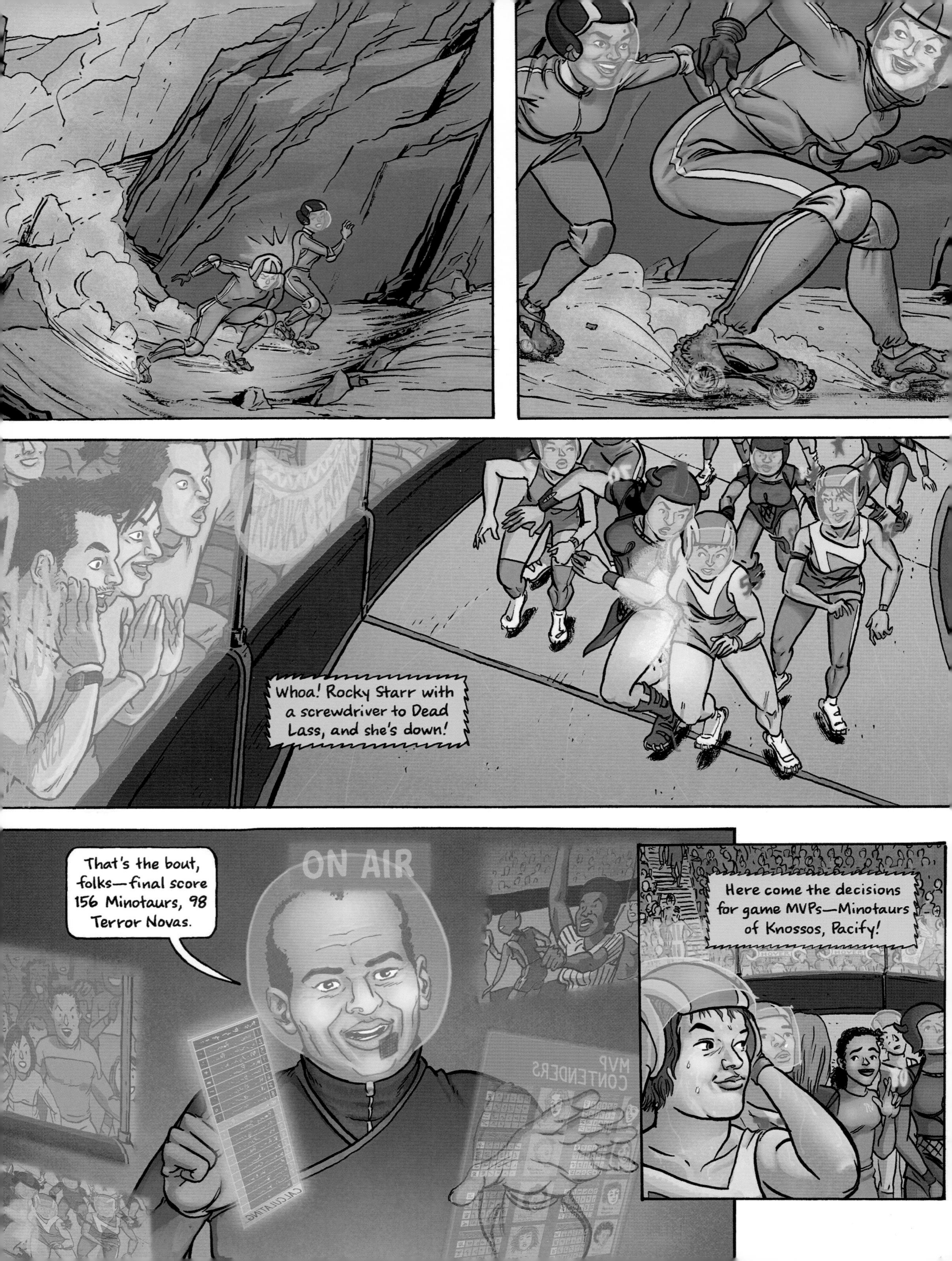

Whoa! Rocky Starr with a screwdriver to Dead Lass, and she's down!
ON AIR
That's the bout, folks—final score 156 Minotaurs, 98 Terror Novas.
MVP CONTENDERS
CALCULATING
Here come the decisions for game MVPs—Minotaurs of Knossos, Pacify!

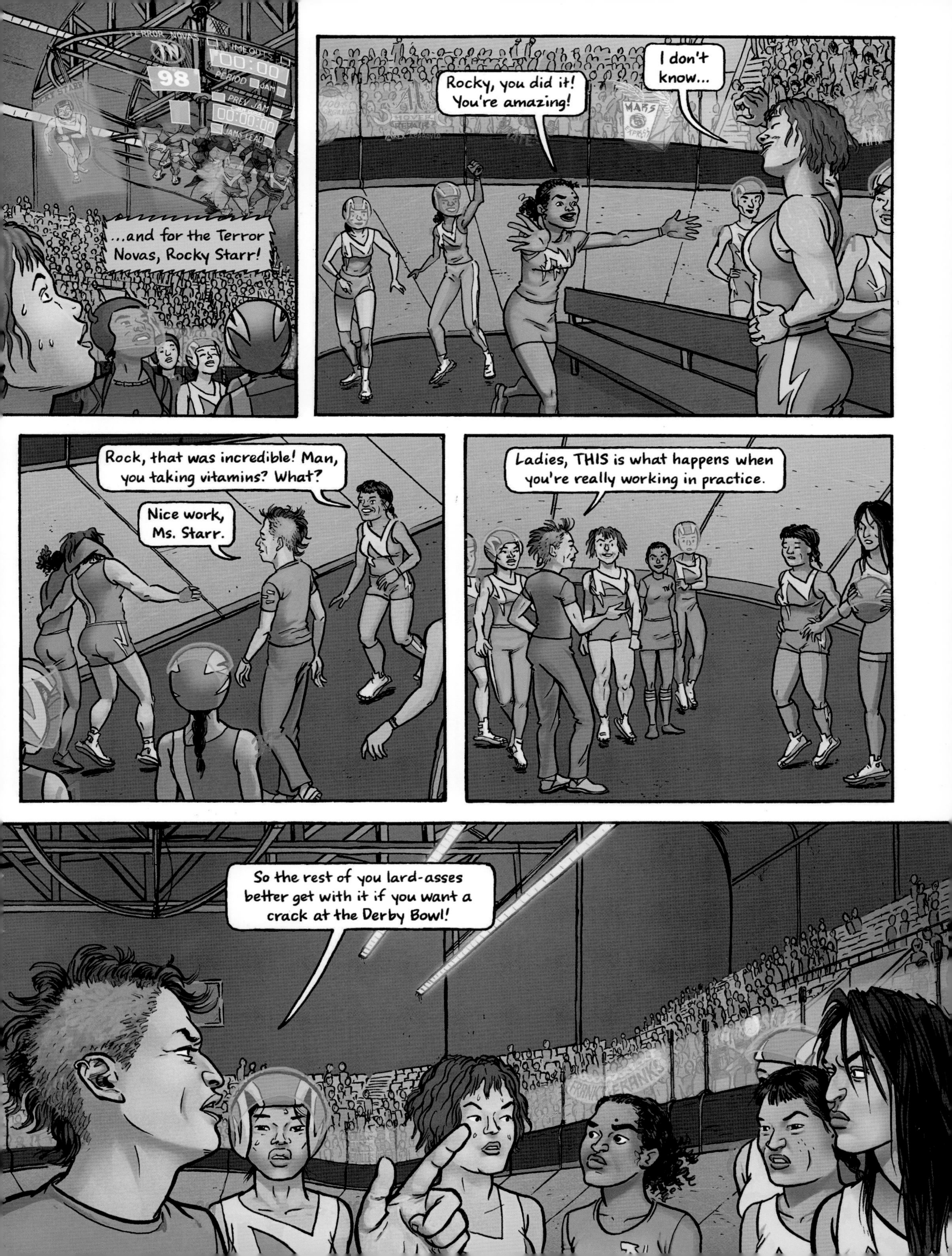
TERROR NOVAS
TIMEOUTS
98
PERIOD
JAM
PREV JAM
JAMS LEAD
ROCKY STARR
...and for the Terror Novas, Rocky Starr!
Rocky, you did it! You're amazing!
I don't know...
MARS EXPRESS
Rock, that was incredible! Man, you taking vitamins? What?
Nice work, Ms. Starr.
Ladies, THIS is what happens when you're really working in practice.
So the rest of you lard-asses better get with it if you want a crack at the Derby Bowl!

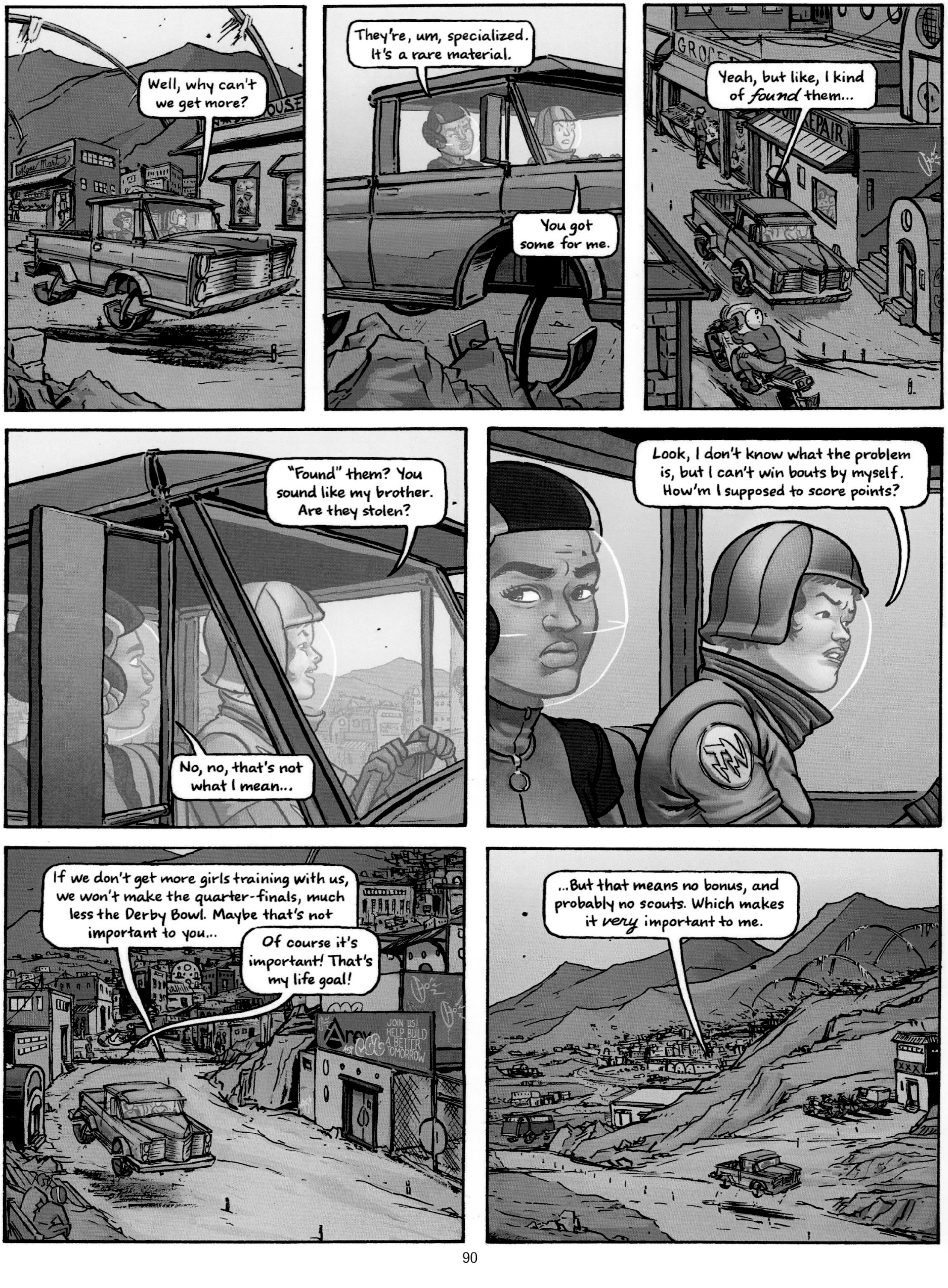
Well, why can't we get more?
HOUSE
Algae Mart
They're, um, specialized. It's a rare material.
You got some for me.
GROCE
REPAIR
Yeah, but like, I kind of *found* them...
"Found" them? You sound like my brother. Are they stolen?
No, no, that's not what I mean...
Look, I don't know what the problem is, but I can't win bouts by myself. How'm I supposed to score points?
If we don't get more girls training with us, we won't make the quarter-finals, much less the Derby Bowl. Maybe that's not important to you...
Of course it's important! That's my life goal!
Arex
JOIN US! HELP BUILD A BETTER TOMORROW
...But that means no bonus, and probably no scouts. Which makes it *very* important to me.
XXX

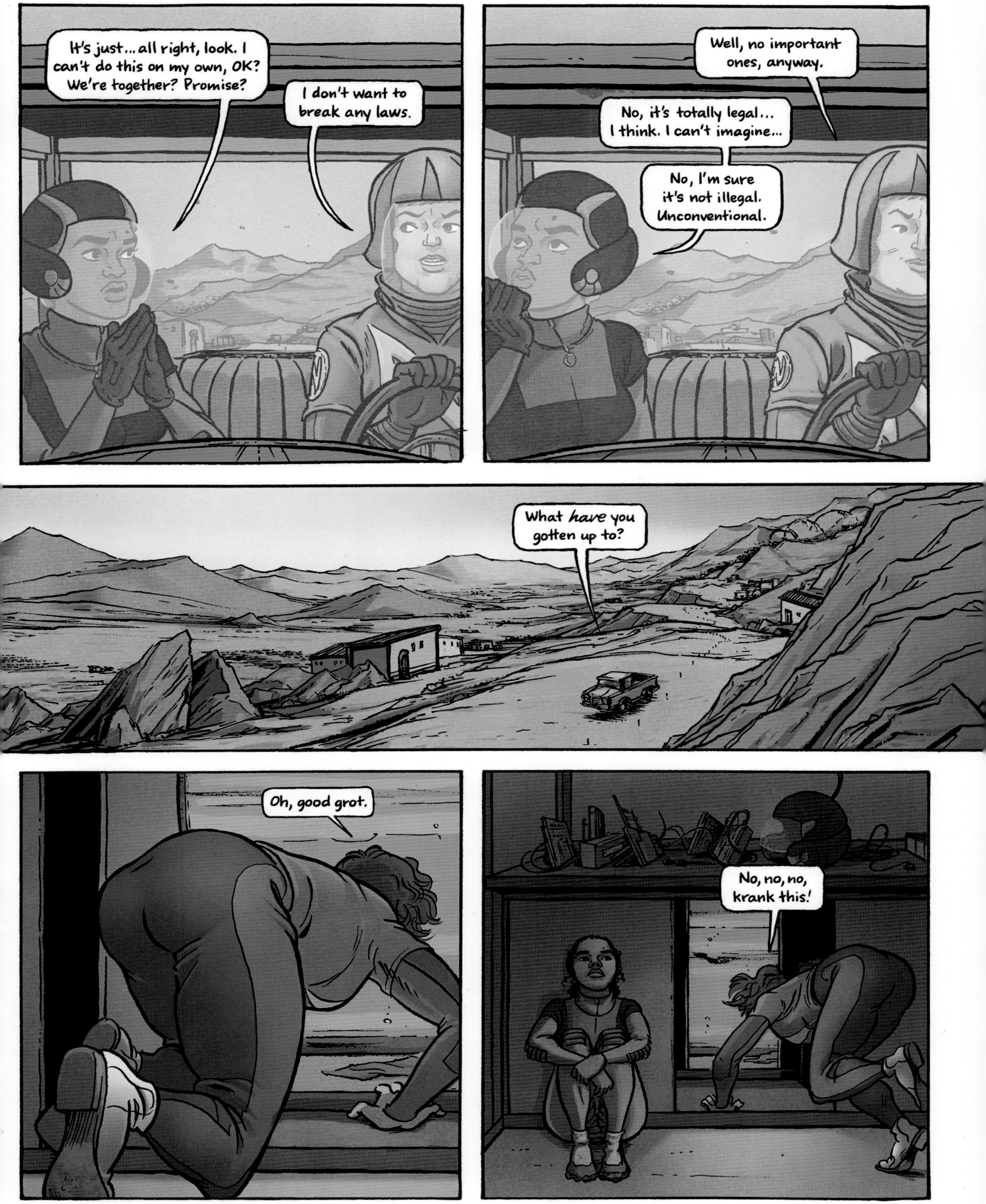
It's just... all right, look. I can't do this on my own, OK? We're together? Promise?
I don't want to break any laws.
Well, no important ones, anyway.
No, it's totally legal... I think. I can't imagine...
No, I'm sure it's not illegal. Unconventional.
What *have* you gotten up to?
Oh, good grot.
No, no, no, krank this!

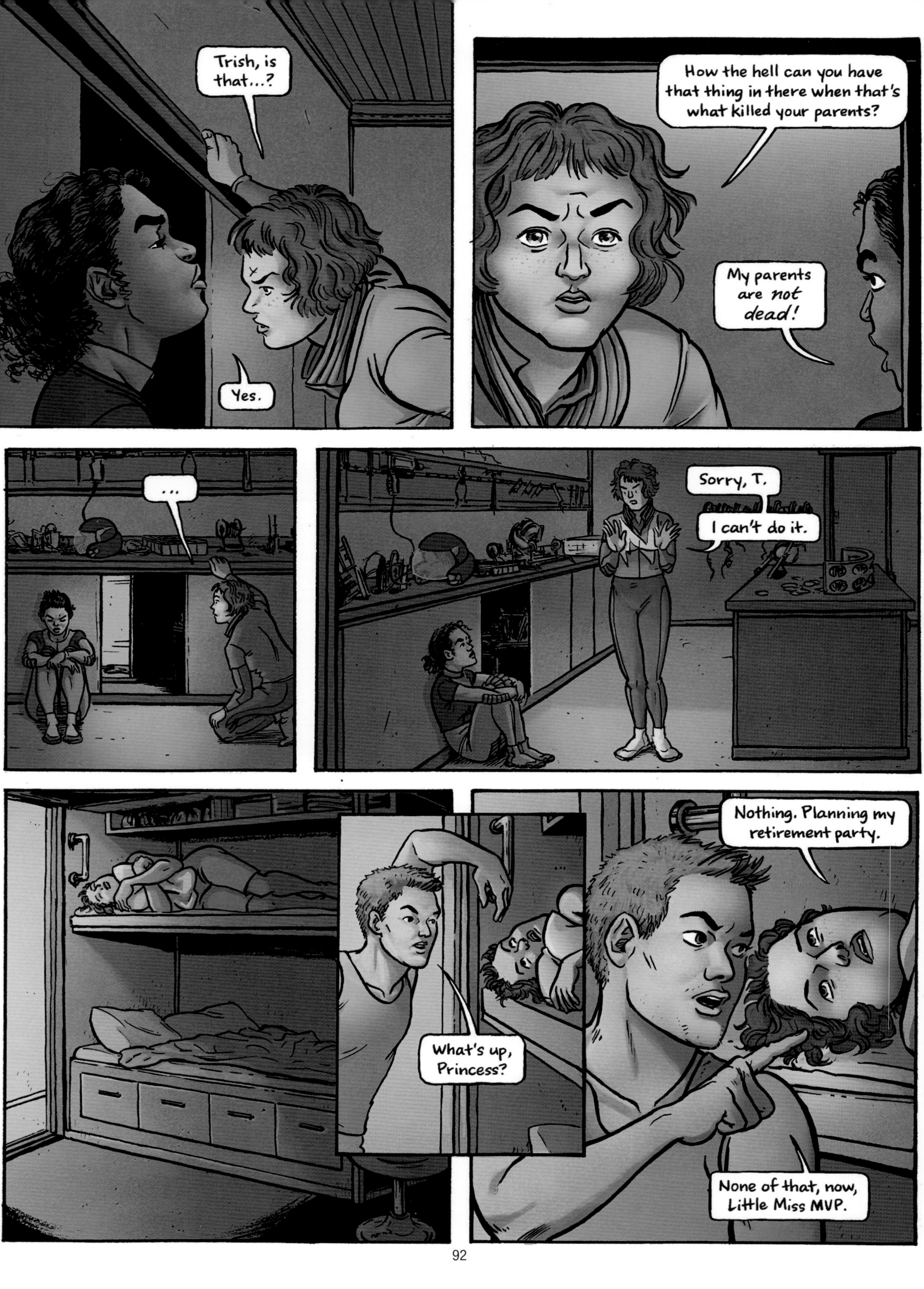
Trish, is that...?
Yes.
How the hell can you have that thing in there when that's what killed your parents?
My parents are *not* dead!
...
Sorry, T.
I can't do it.
What's up, Princess?
Nothing. Planning my retirement party.
None of that, now, Little Miss MVP.

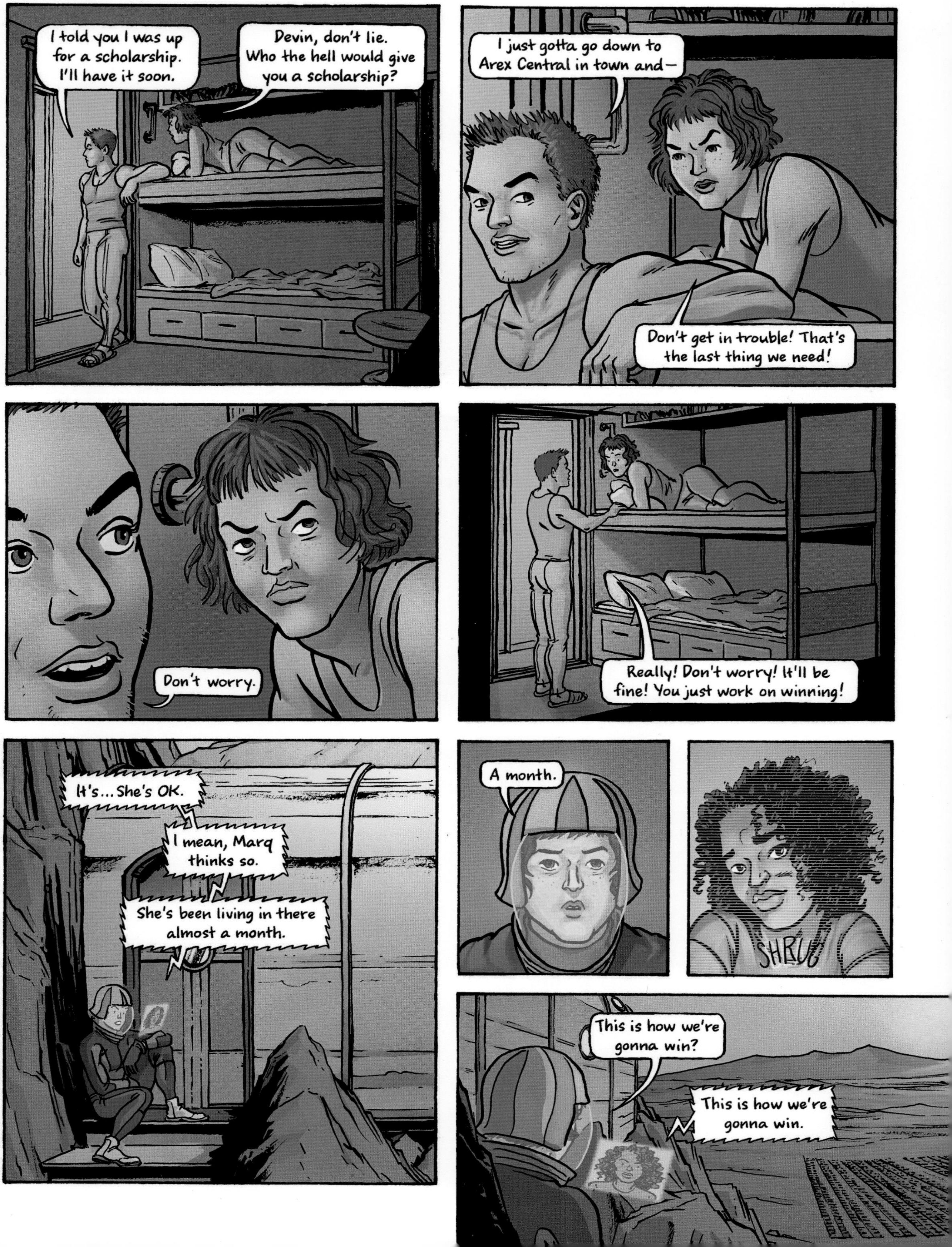
I told you I was up for a scholarship. I'll have it soon.
Devin, don't lie. Who the hell would give you a scholarship?
I just gotta go down to Arex Central in town and—
Don't get in trouble! That's the last thing we need!
Don't worry.
Really! Don't worry! It'll be fine! You just work on winning!
It's... She's OK.
I mean, Marq thinks so.
She's been living in there almost a month.
A month.
SHRUG
This is how we're gonna win?
This is how we're gonna win.

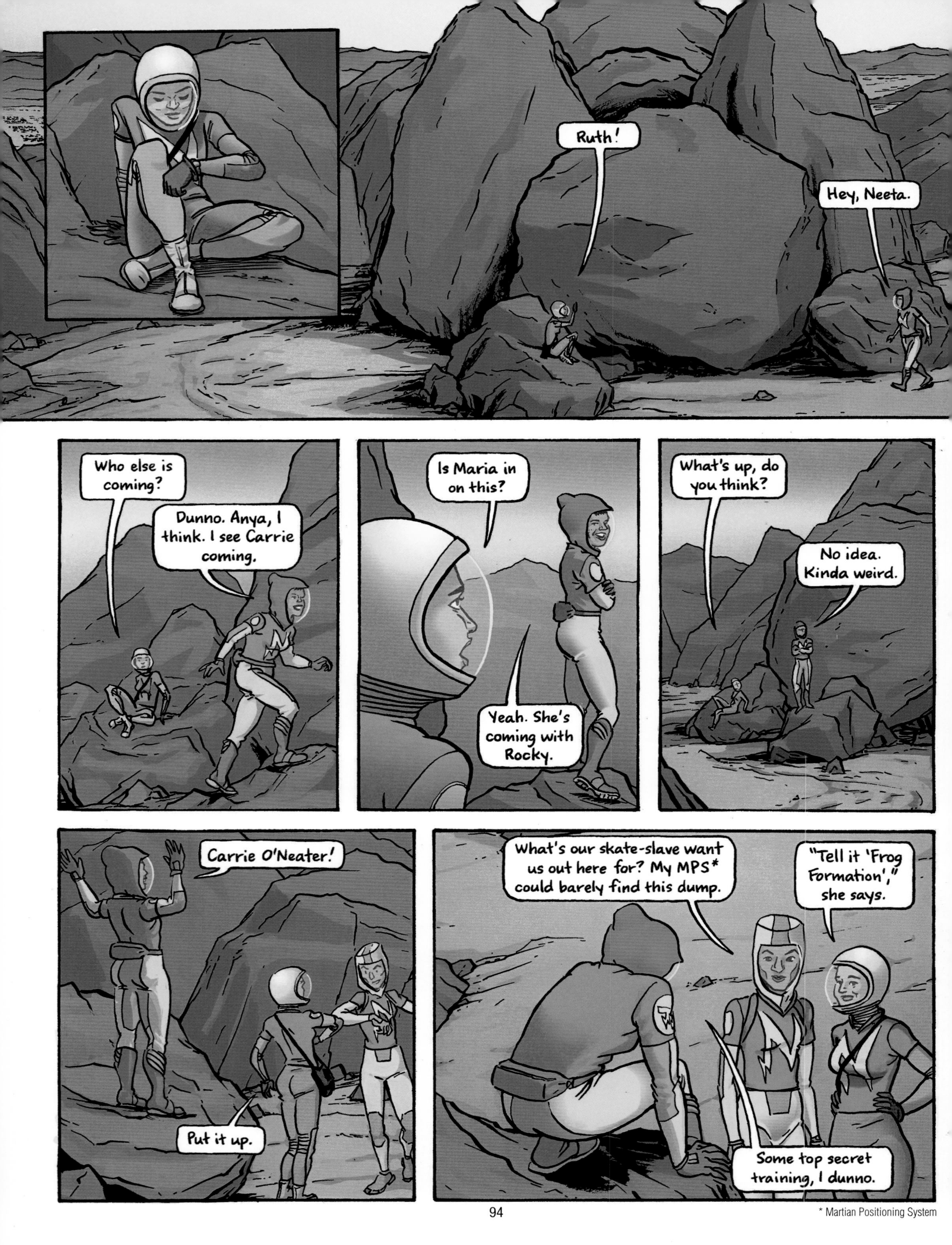

Ruth!
Hey, Neeta.
Who else is coming?
Dunno. Anya, I think. I see Carrie coming.
Is Maria in on this?
Yeah. She's coming with Rocky.
What's up, do you think?
No idea. Kinda weird.
Carrie O'Neater!
Put it up.
What's our skate-slave want us out here for? My MPS* could barely find this dump.
"Tell it 'Frog Formation'," she says.
Some top secret training, I dunno.

* Martian Positioning System

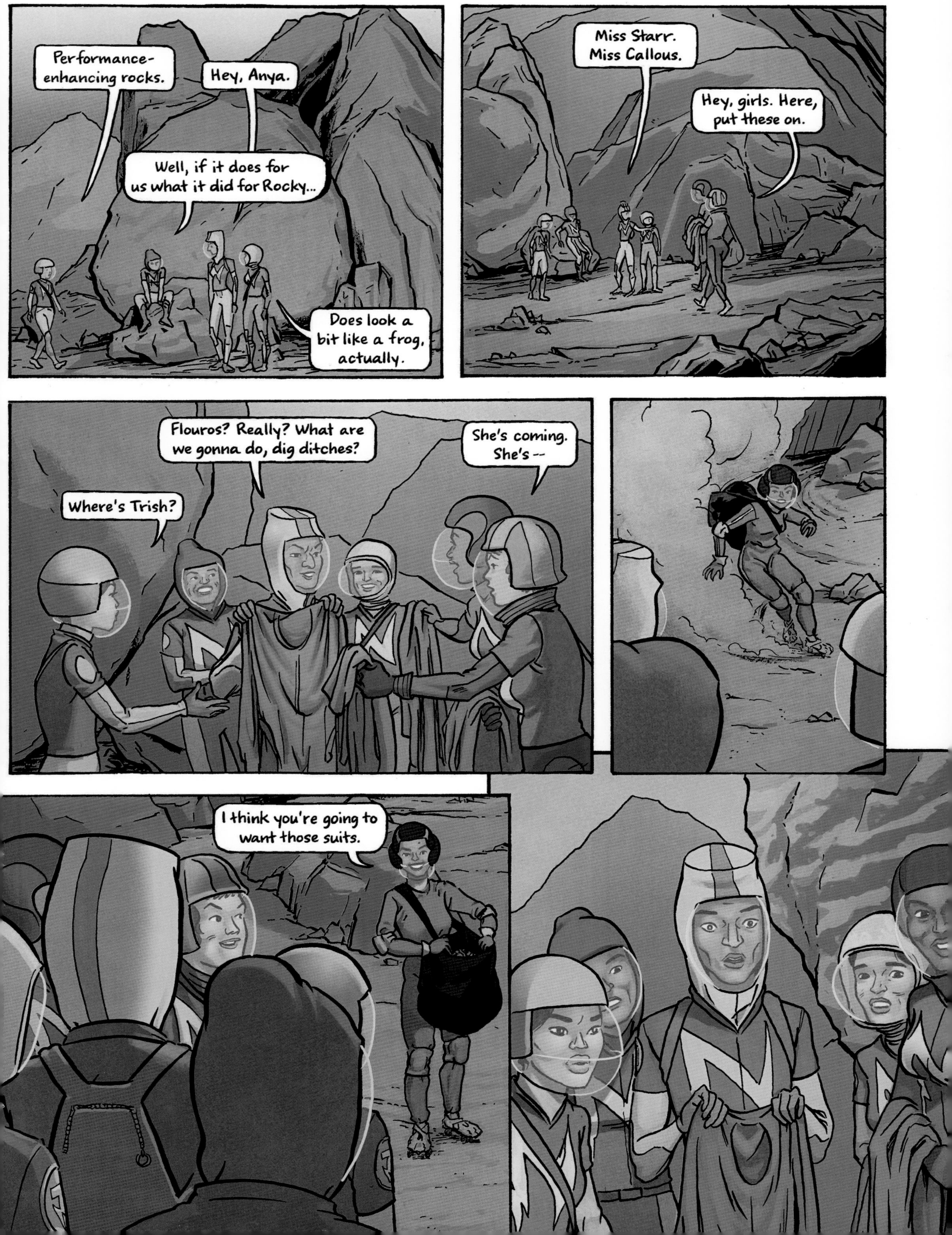
Performance-enhancing rocks.
Hey, Anya.
Well, if it does for us what it did for Rocky...
Does look a bit like a frog, actually.
Miss Starr. Miss Callous.
Hey, girls. Here, put these on.
Where's Trish?
Flouros? Really? What are we gonna do, dig ditches?
She's coming. She's --
I think you're going to want those suits.

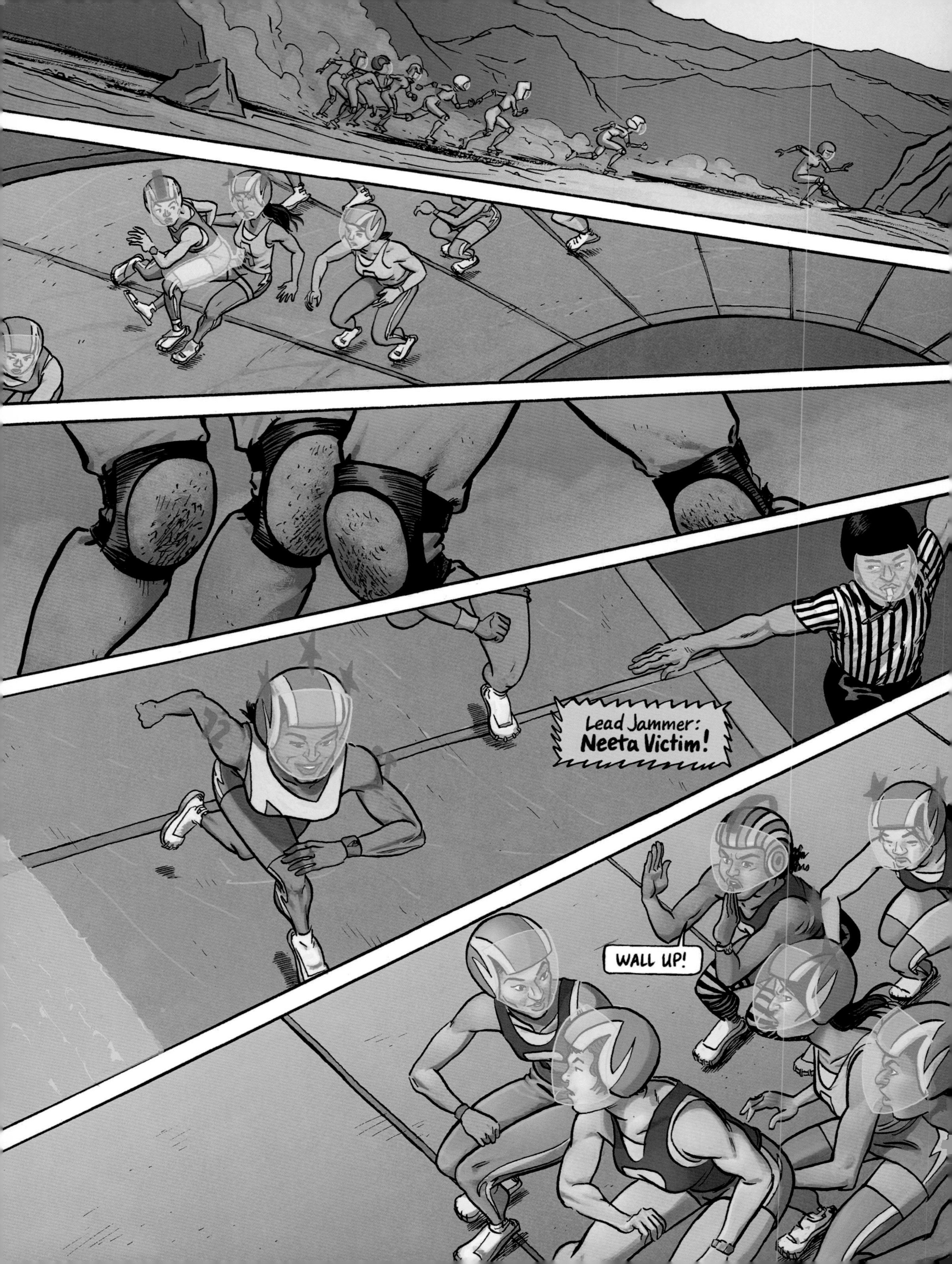
Lead Jammer: Neeta Victim!
WALL UP!

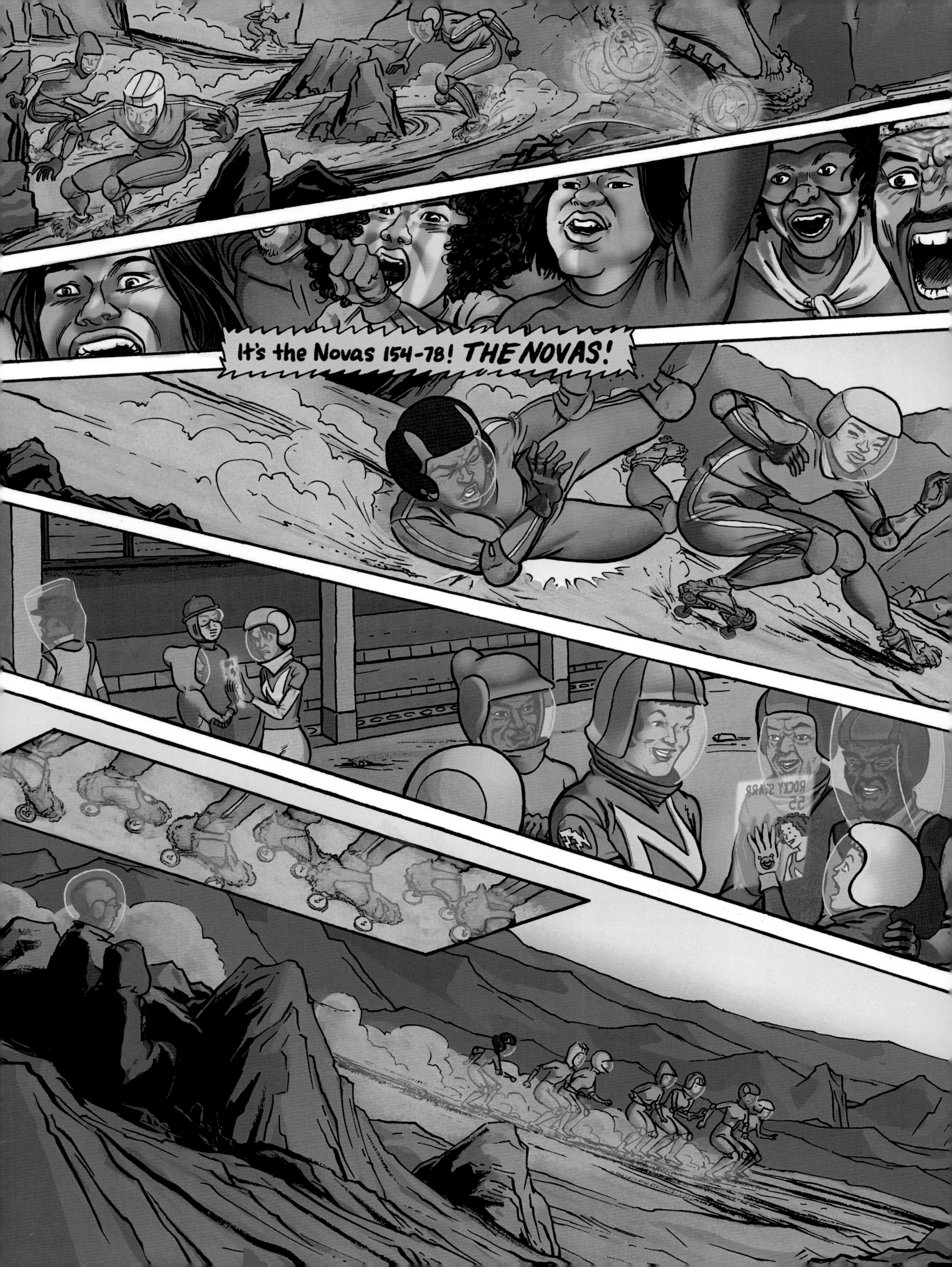
It's the Novas 154-78! THE NOVAS!
ROCKY STARR 55

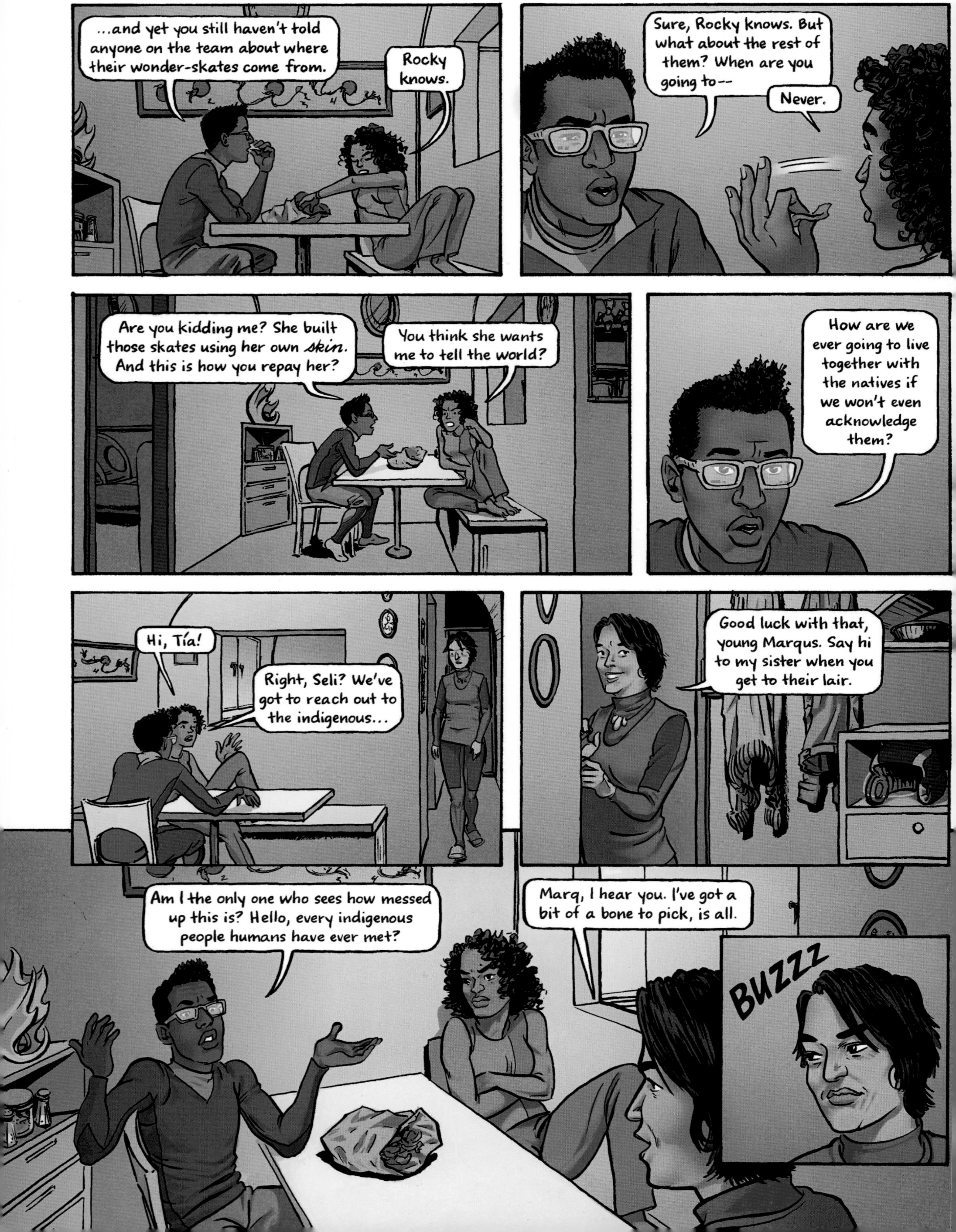
...and yet you still haven't told anyone on the team about where their wonder-skates come from.
Rocky knows.
Sure, Rocky knows. But what about the rest of them? When are you going to--
Never.
Are you kidding me? She built those skates using her own *skin*. And this is how you repay her?
You think she wants me to tell the world?
How are we ever going to live together with the natives if we won't even acknowledge them?
Hi, Tía!
Right, Seli? We've got to reach out to the indigenous...
Good luck with that, young Marqus. Say hi to my sister when you get to their lair.
Am I the only one who sees how messed up this is? Hello, every indigenous people humans have ever met?
Marq, I hear you. I've got a bit of a bone to pick, is all.
BUZZZ

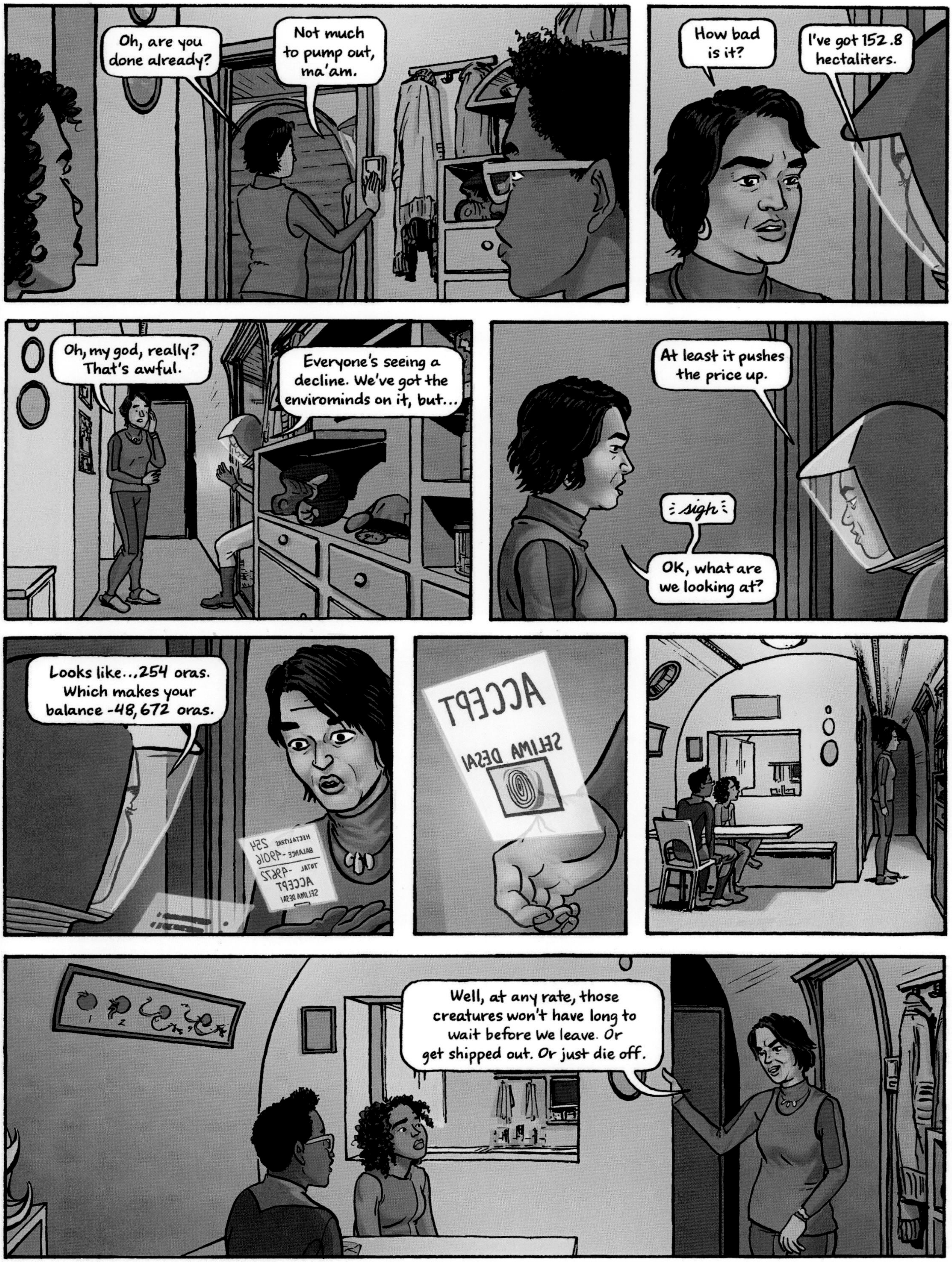

Oh, are you done already?
Not much to pump out, ma'am.
How bad is it?
I've got 152.8 hectaliters.
Oh, my god, really? That's awful.
Everyone's seeing a decline. We've got the enirominds on it, but...
At least it pushes the price up.
sigh
OK, what are we looking at?
Looks like...254 oras. Which makes your balance -48,672 oras.
ACCEPT
SELIMA DESAI
Well, at any rate, those creatures won't have long to wait before we leave. Or get shipped out. Or just die off.

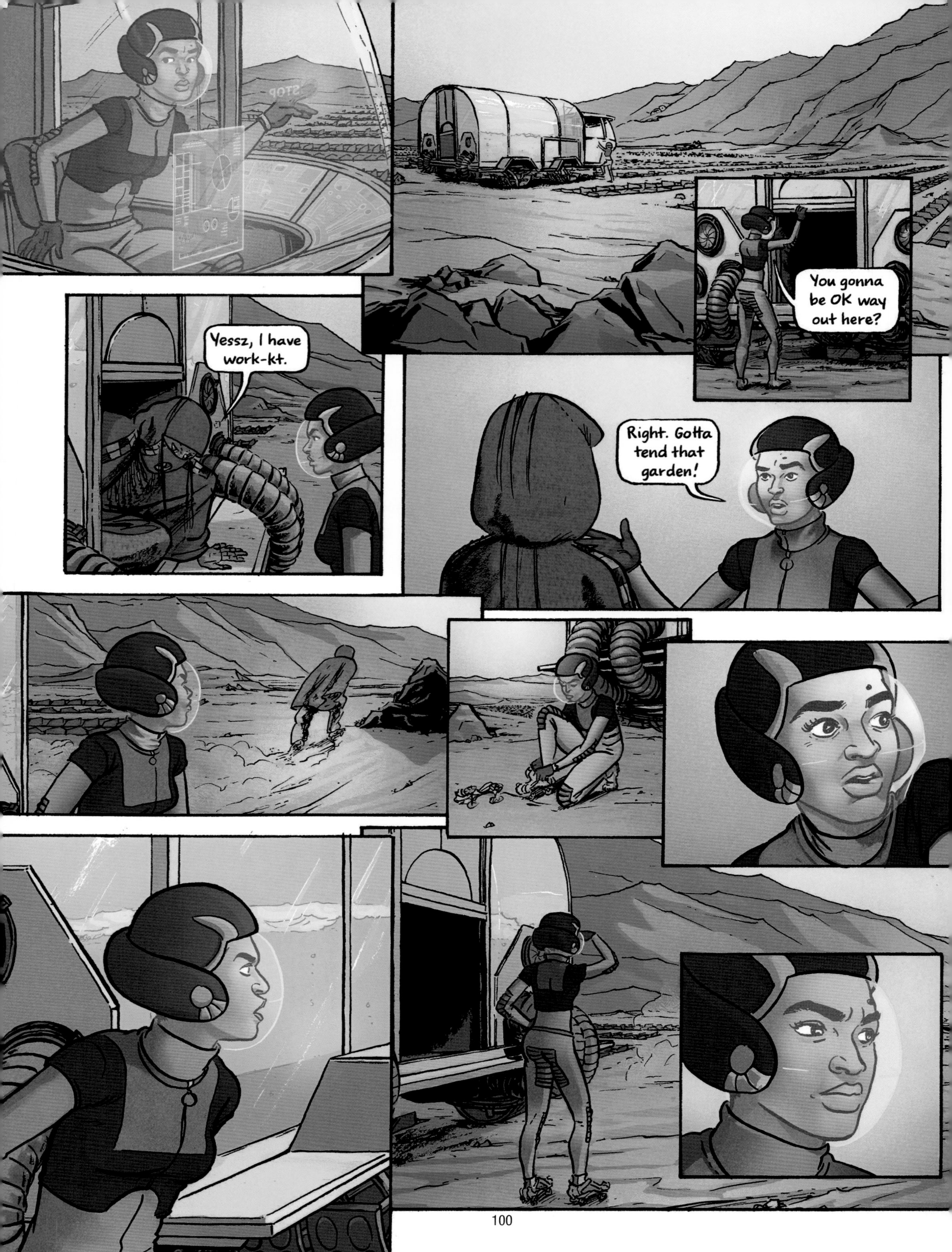
STOP
You gonna be OK way out here?
Yessz, I have work-kt.
Right. Gotta tend that garden!

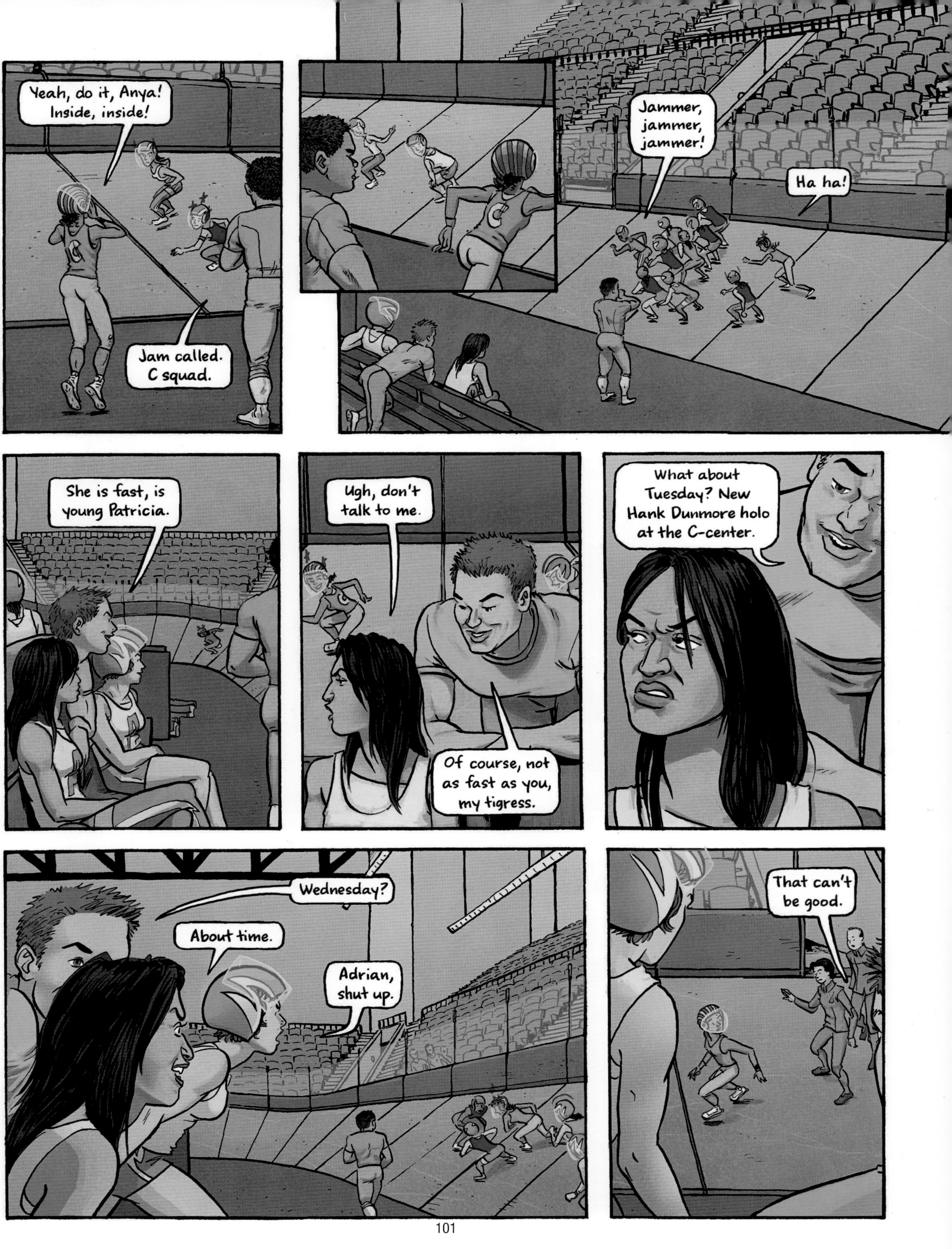
Yeah, do it, Anya! Inside, inside!
Jam called. C squad.
Jammer, jammer, jammer!
Ha ha!
She is fast, is young Patricia.
Ugh, don't talk to me.
Of course, not as fast as you, my tigress.
What about Tuesday? New Hank Dunmore holo at the C-center.
Wednesday?
About time.
Adrian, shut up.
That can't be good.

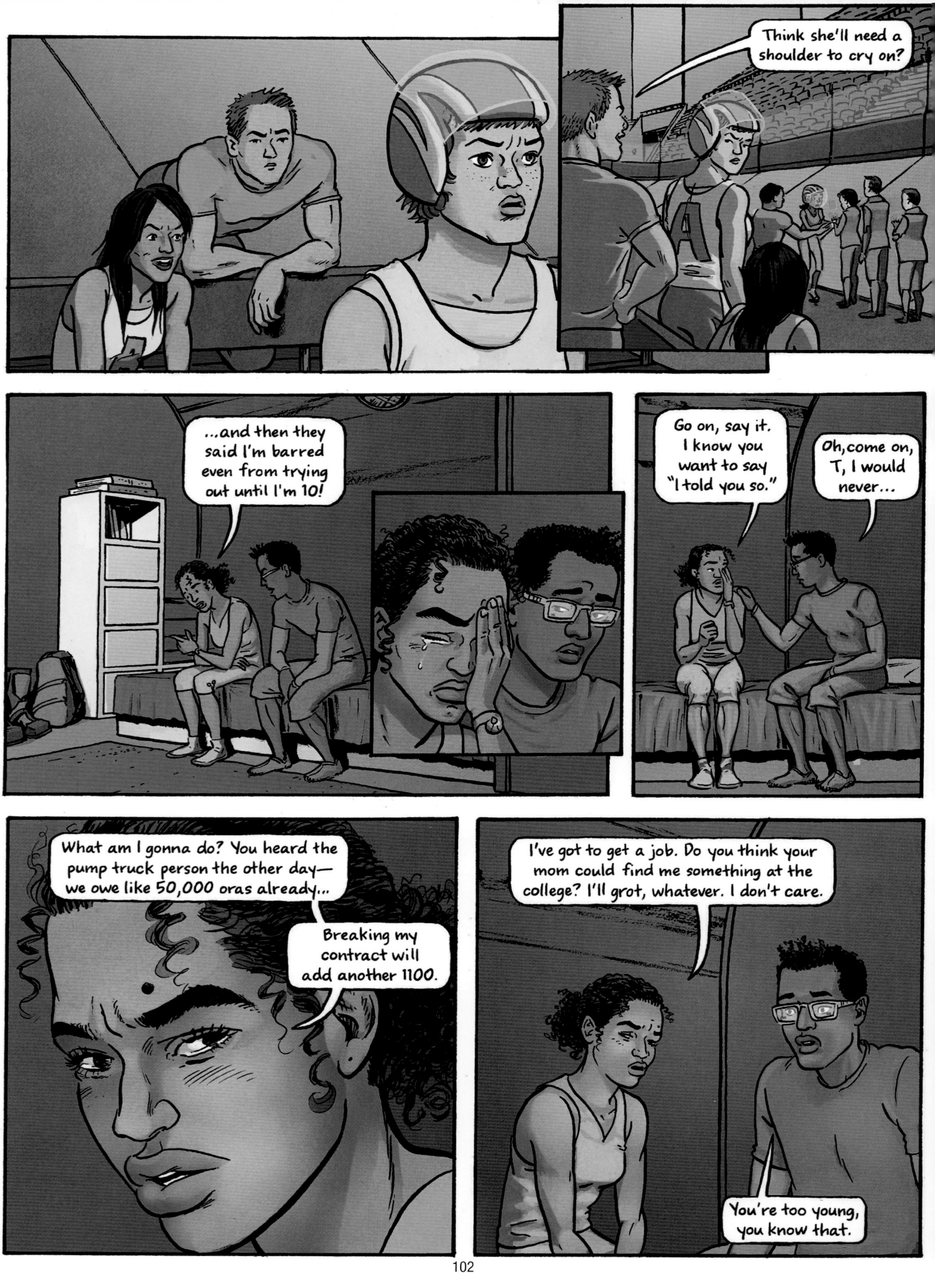
Think she'll need a shoulder to cry on?
...and then they said I'm barred even from trying out until I'm 10!
Go on, say it. I know you want to say "I told you so."
Oh, come on, T, I would never...
What am I gonna do? You heard the pump truck person the other day—we owe like 50,000 oras already...
Breaking my contract will add another 1100.
I've got to get a job. Do you think your mom could find me something at the college? I'll grot, whatever. I don't care.
You're too young, you know that.

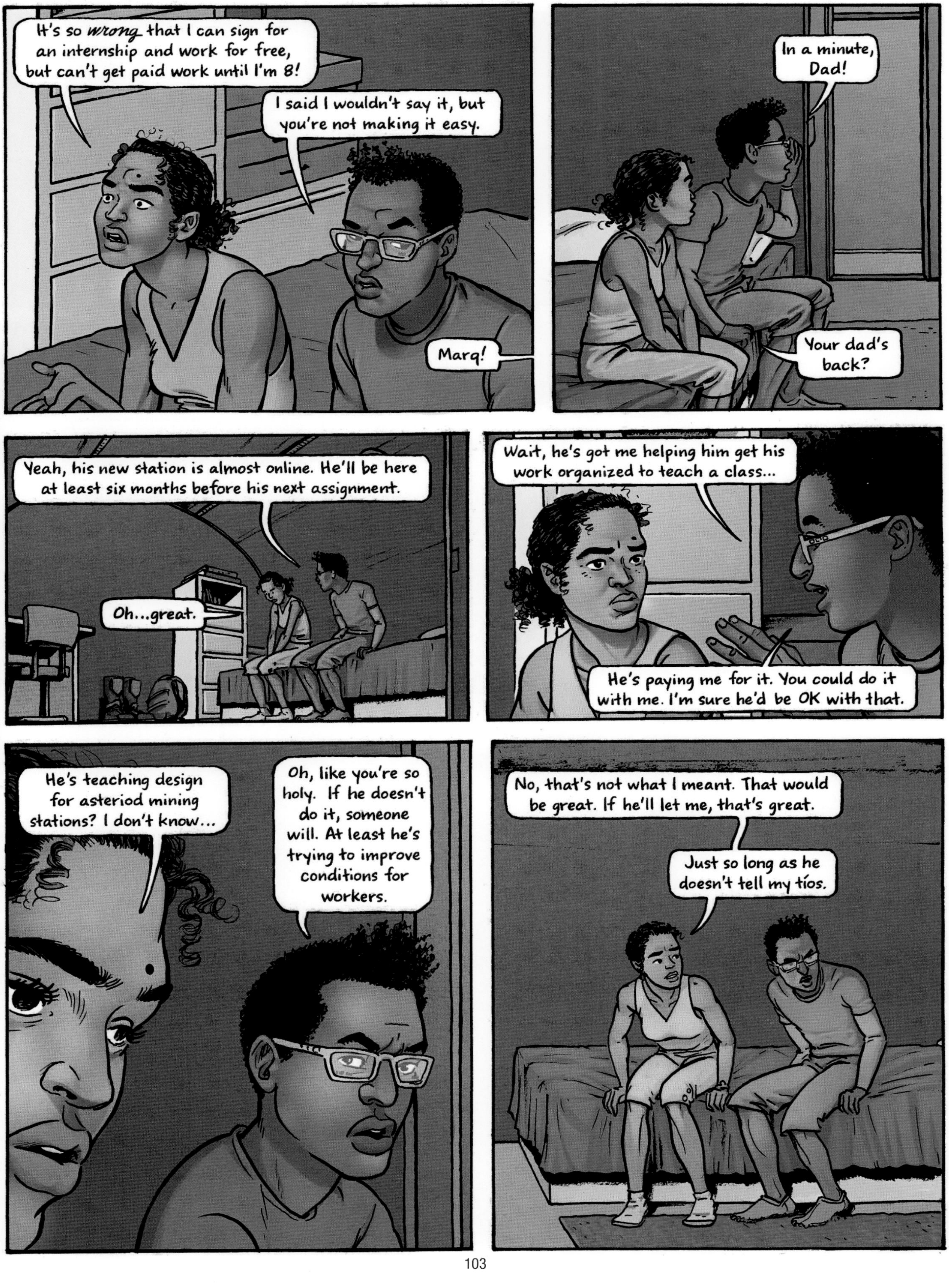
It's so *wrong* that I can sign for an internship and work for free, but can't get paid work until I'm 8!
I said I wouldn't say it, but you're not making it easy.
Marq!
In a minute, Dad!
Your dad's back?
Yeah, his new station is almost online. He'll be here at least six months before his next assignment.
Oh...great.
Wait, he's got me helping him get his work organized to teach a class...
He's paying me for it. You could do it with me. I'm sure he'd be OK with that.
He's teaching design for asteriod mining stations? I don't know...
Oh, like you're so holy. If he doesn't do it, someone will. At least he's trying to improve conditions for workers.
No, that's not what I meant. That would be great. If he'll let me, that's great.
Just so long as he doesn't tell my tíos.

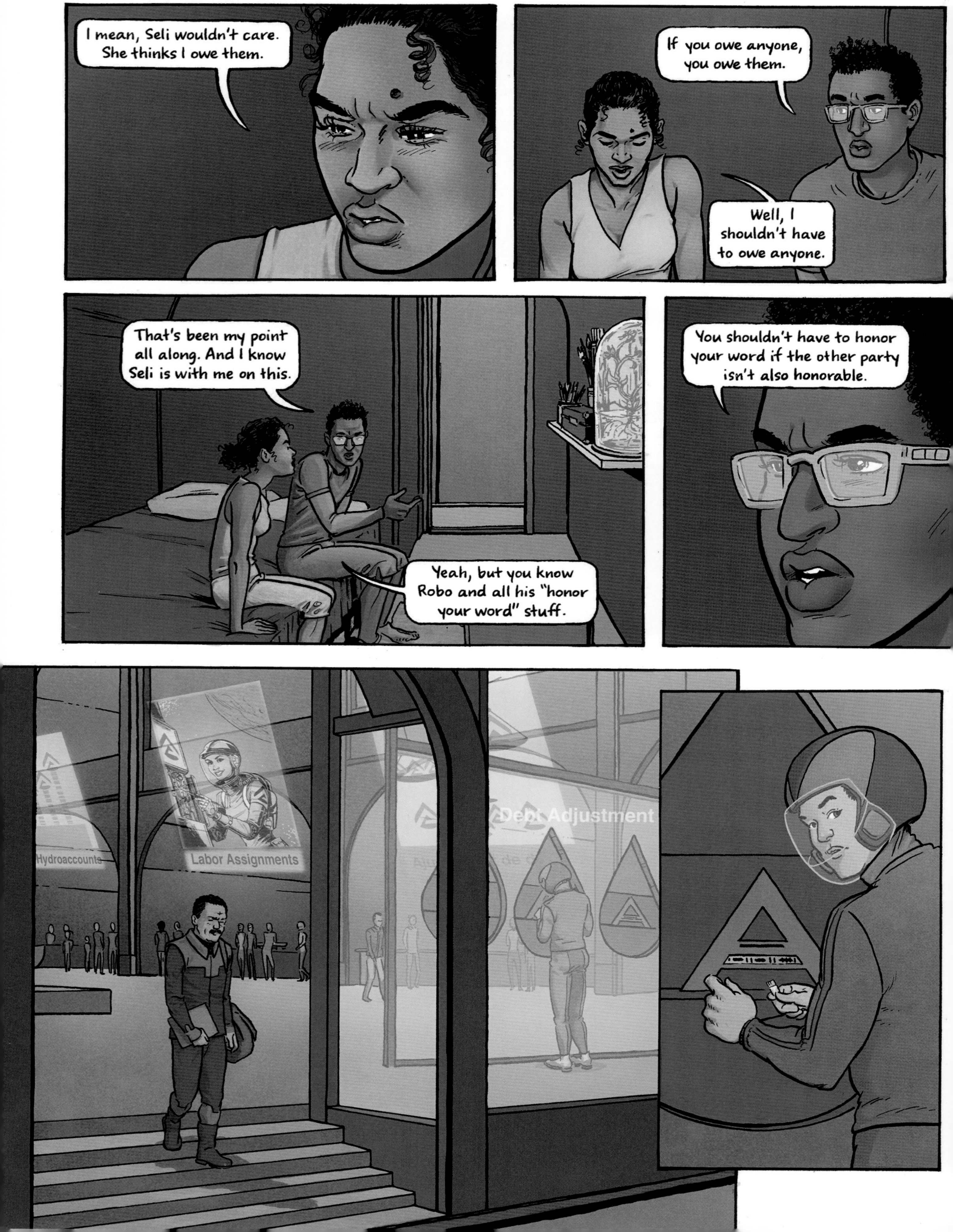
I mean, Seli wouldn't care. She thinks I owe them.
If you owe anyone, you owe them.
Well, I shouldn't have to owe anyone.
That's been my point all along. And I know Seli is with me on this.
Yeah, but you know Robo and all his "honor your word" stuff.
You shouldn't have to honor your word if the other party isn't also honorable.
Hydroaccounts
Labor Assignments
Debt Adjustment

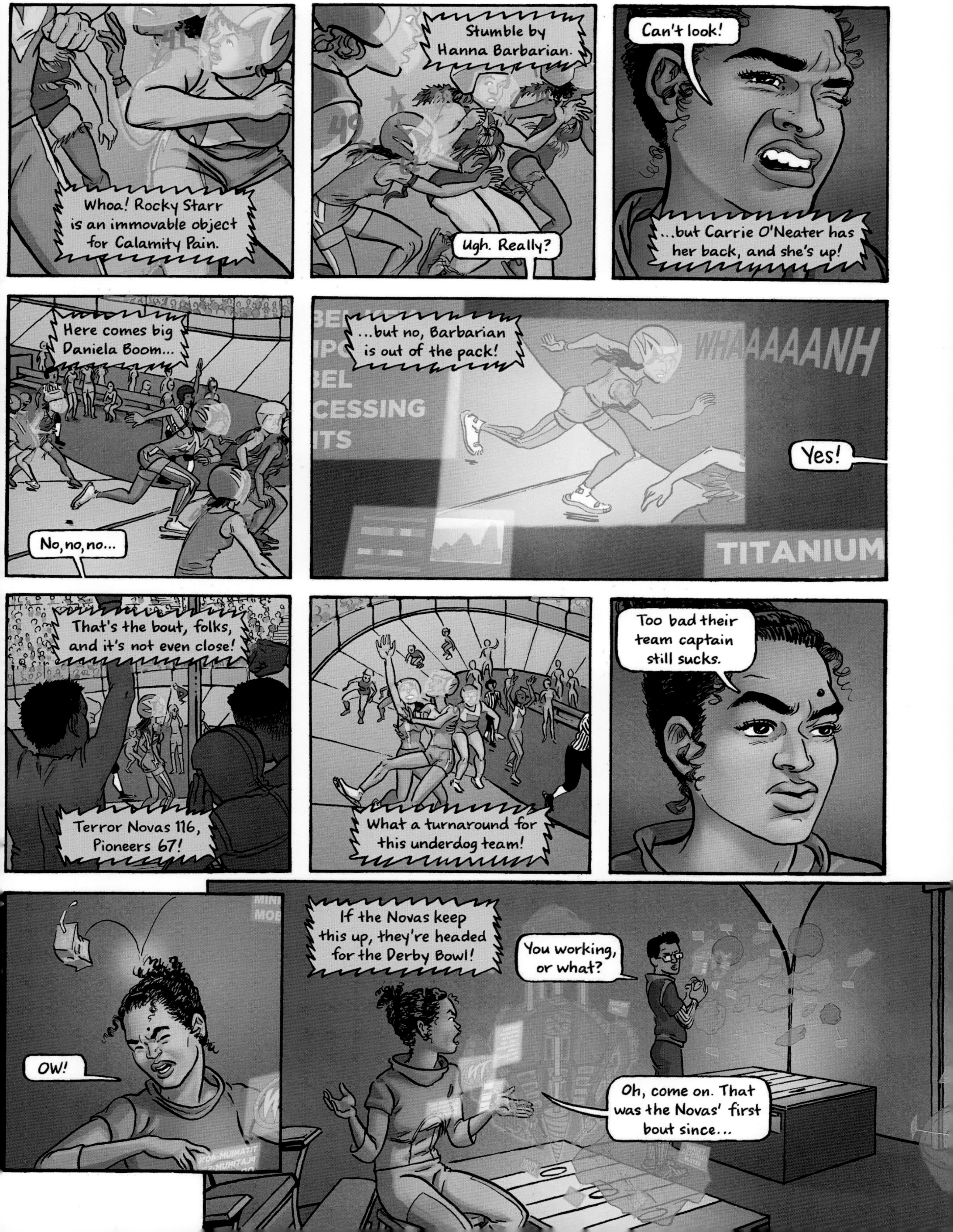

Whoa! Rocky Starr is an immovable object for Calamity Pain.
Stumble by Hanna Barbarian.
Ugh. Really?
Can't look!
...but Carrie O'Neater has her back, and she's up!
Here comes big Daniela Boom...
No, no, no...
...but no, Barbarian is out of the pack!
WHAAAAANH
Yes!
TITANIUM
That's the bout, folks, and it's not even close!
Terror Novas 116, Pioneers 67!
What a turnaround for this underdog team!
Too bad their team captain still sucks.
OW!
If the Novas keep this up, they're headed for the Derby Bowl!
You working, or what?
Oh, come on. That was the Novas' first bout since...

How can you even watch after what happened?

Are you kidding? Those are my girls!

But Hanna is a problem.

Yeah, obviously.

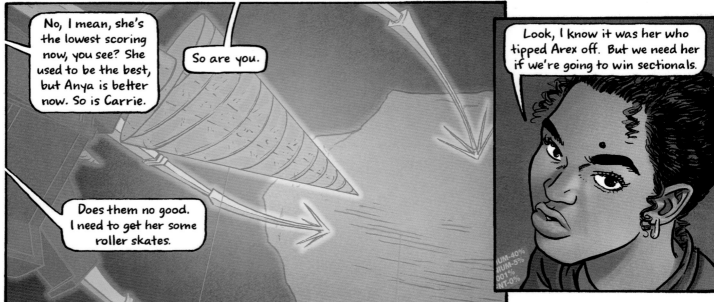

No, I mean, she's the lowest scoring now, you see? She used to be the best, but Anya is better now. So is Carrie.

So are you.

Does them no good. I need to get her some roller skates.

Look, I know it was her who tipped Arex off. But we need her if we're going to win sectionals.

Who's this "we"?

You are not on that team anymore!

Rocky is. They've gotta win this for Rocky.

So you're going to ask Qiqi to give the last bits of her own SKIN to that sack of grot?

Yeah, I am.

106

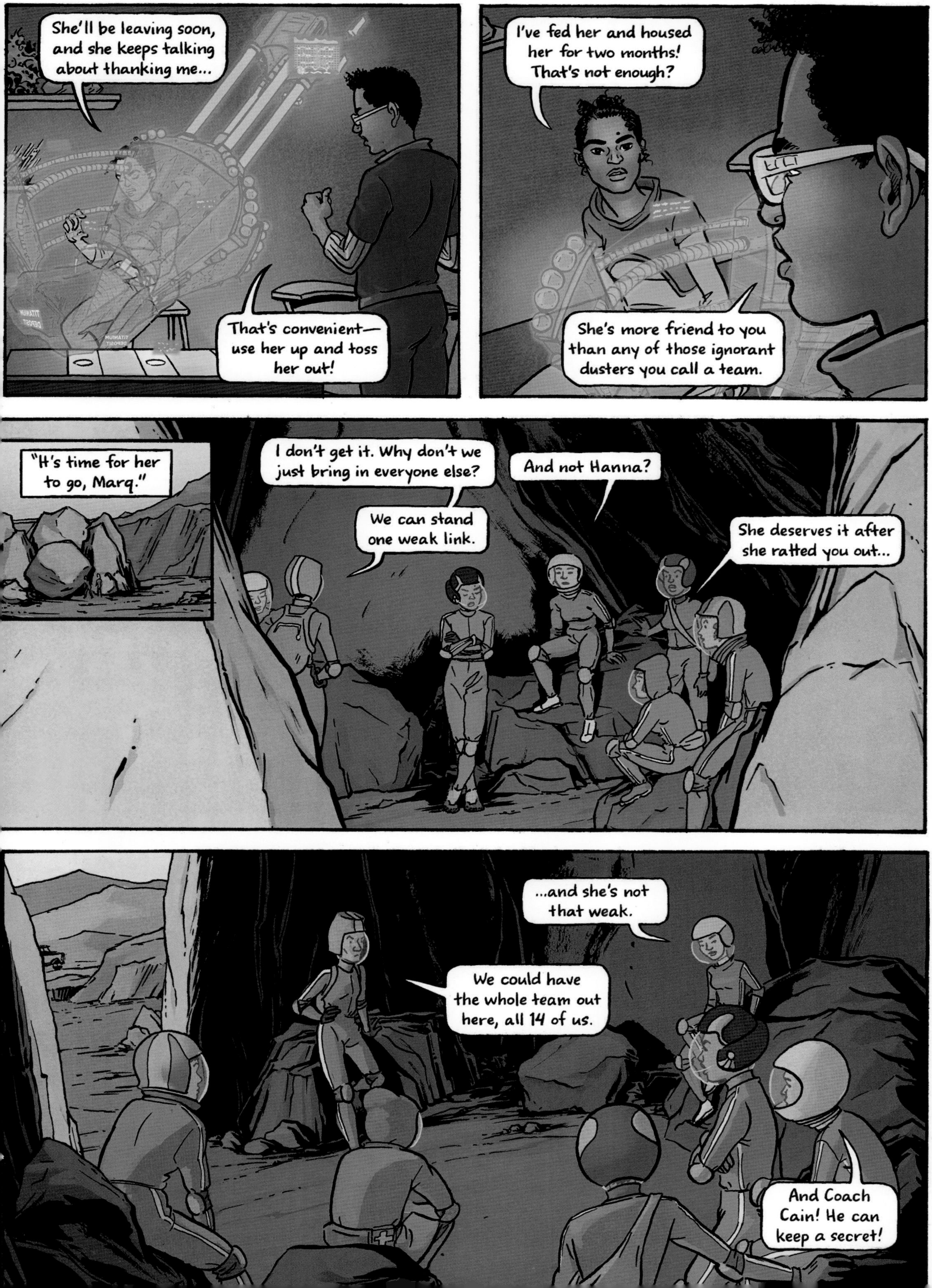
She'll be leaving soon, and she keeps talking about thanking me...
That's convenient—use her up and toss her out!
I've fed her and housed her for two months! That's not enough?
She's more friend to you than any of those ignorant dusters you call a team.
"It's time for her to go, Marq."
I don't get it. Why don't we just bring in everyone else?
We can stand one weak link.
And not Hanna?
She deserves it after she ratted you out...
...and she's not that weak.
We could have the whole team out here, all 14 of us.
And Coach Cain! He can keep a secret!

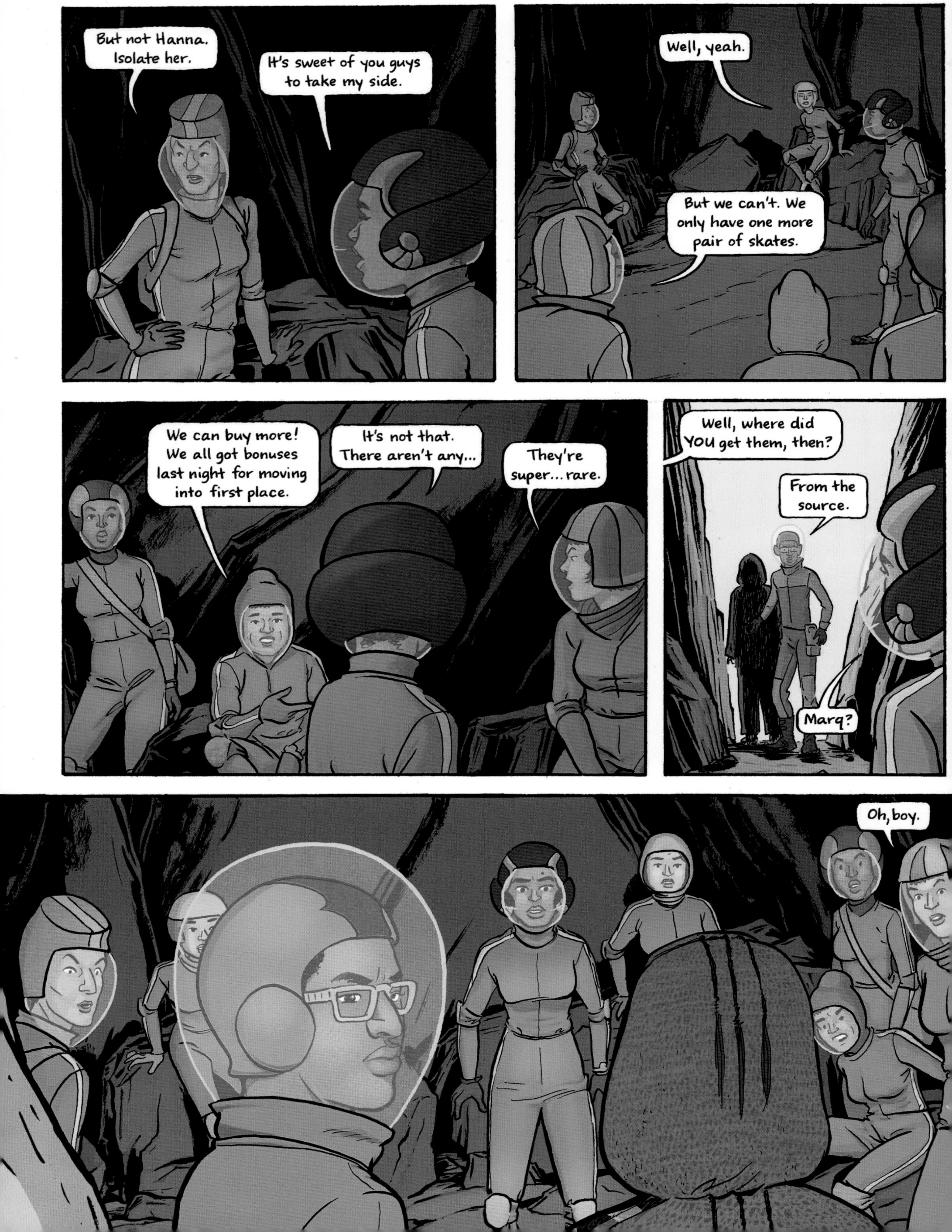
But not Hanna. Isolate her.
It's sweet of you guys to take my side.
Well, yeah.
But we can't. We only have one more pair of skates.
We can buy more! We all got bonuses last night for moving into first place.
It's not that. There aren't any...
They're super... rare.
Well, where did YOU get them, then?
From the source.
Marq?
Oh, boy.

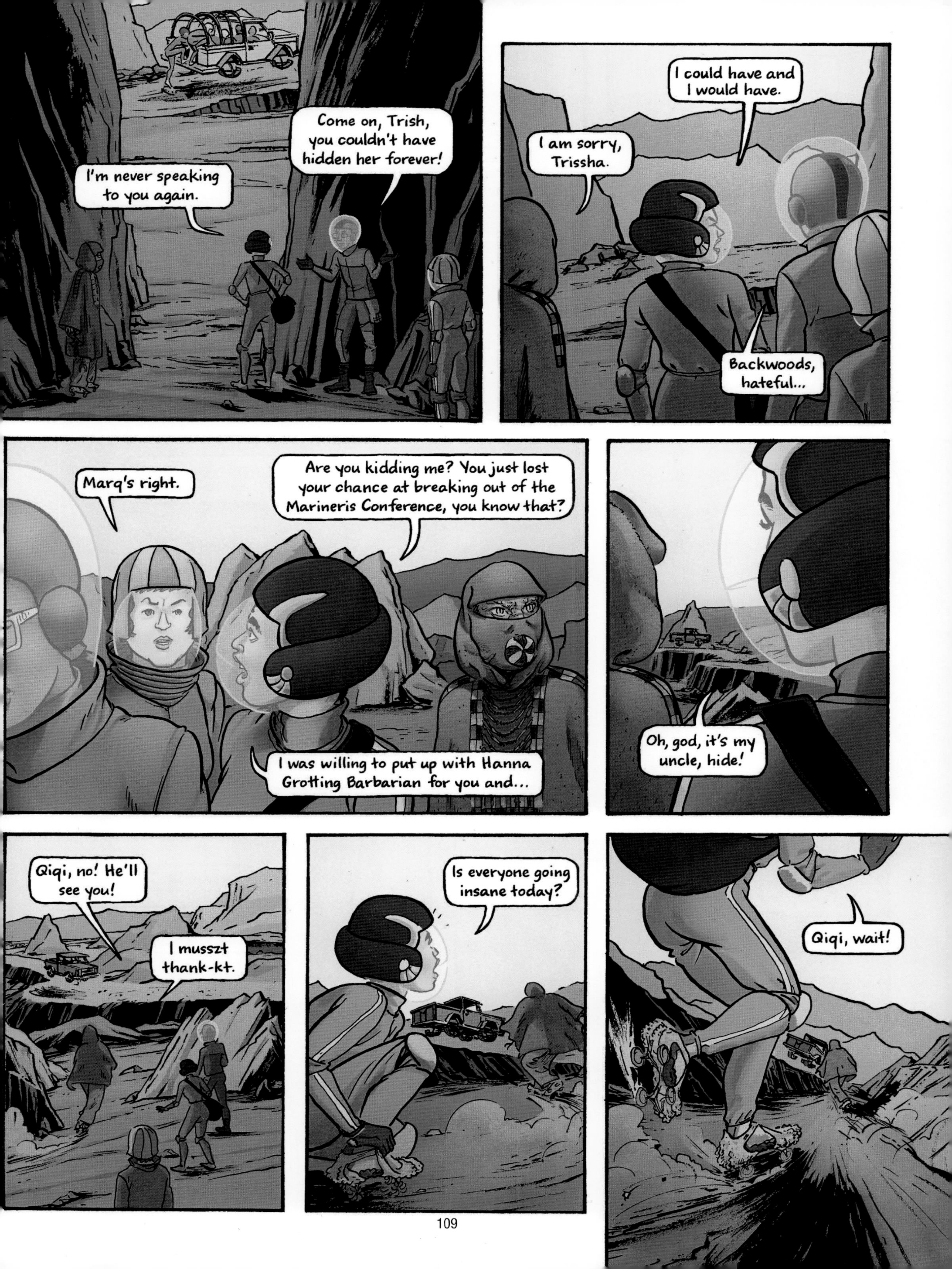
I'm never speaking to you again.
Come on, Trish, you couldn't have hidden her forever!
I am sorry, Trissha.
I could have and I would have.
Backwoods, hateful...
Marq's right.
Are you kidding me? You just lost your chance at breaking out of the Marineris Conference, you know that?
I was willing to put up with Hanna Grotting Barbarian for you and...
Oh, god, it's my uncle, hide!
Qiqi, no! He'll see you!
I musszt thank-kt.
Is everyone going insane today?
Qiqi, wait!

There you are.

Ha ha, Tío, I...

I was looking for you. Listen, I need to talk to you before Seli gets home.

Marq, can you give us a--

Who're you?

Anak ka nang puta*! Is that a native?

Oh, uh, Tío Robo...Uh, I mean Roberto...this is Qiqi. She's a *friend*...

*Tagalog for "son of a bitch"

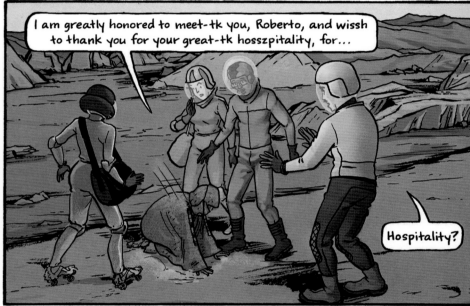

I am greatly honored to meet-tk you, Roberto, and wissh to thank you for your great-tk hosszpitality, for...

Hospitality?

She was going to die! I didn't want to hide her, but Seli is so...

I mean, I...

Roberto, I am sorry if I bring you trk-trouble.

How long?

110

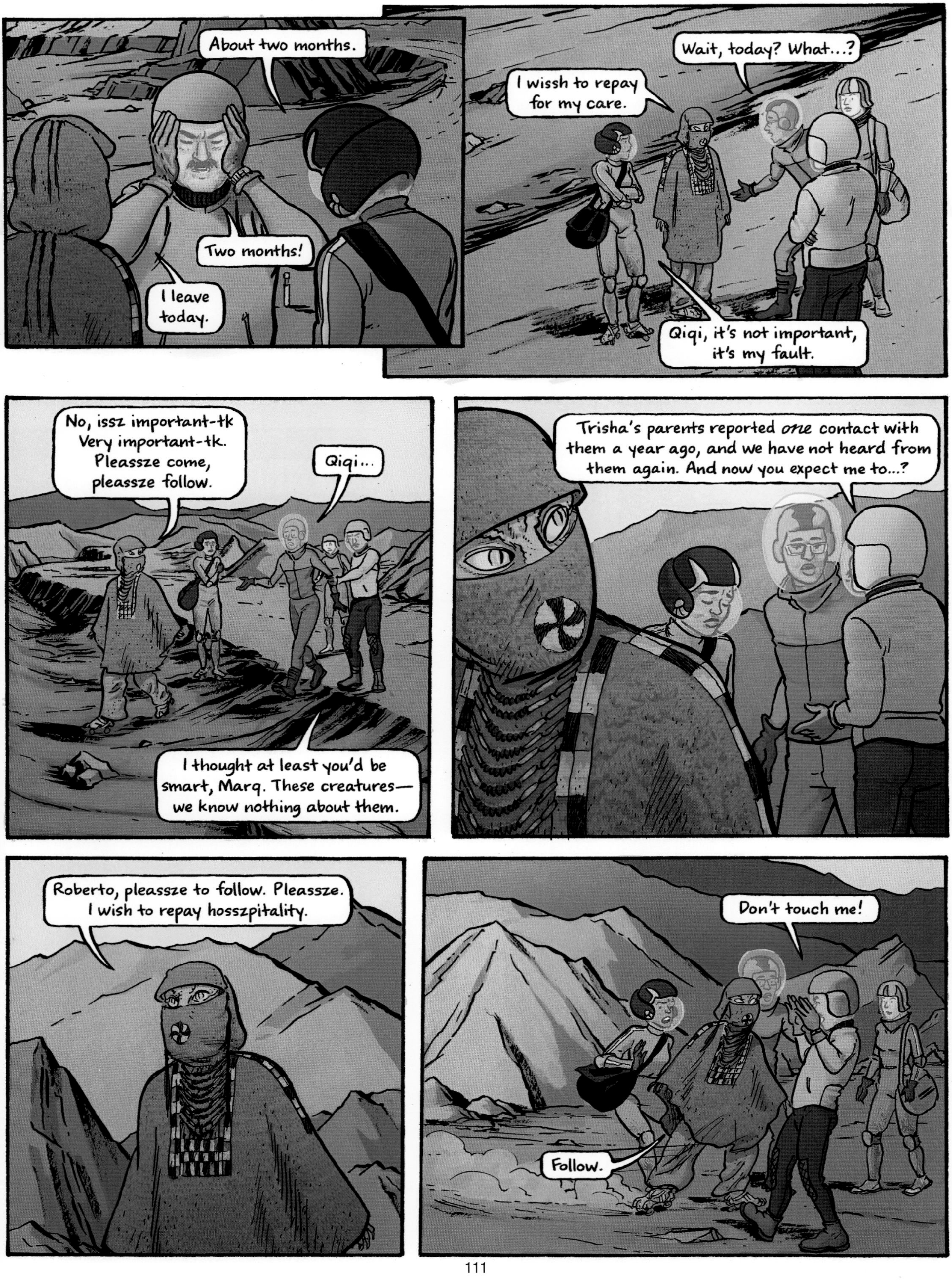
About two months.
Two months!
I leave today.
I wissh to repay for my care.
Wait, today? What...?
Qiqi, it's not important, it's my fault.
No, issz important-tk Very important-tk. Pleassze come, pleassze follow.
Qiqi...
I thought at least you'd be smart, Marq. These creatures— we know nothing about them.
Trisha's parents reported *one* contact with them a year ago, and we have not heard from them again. And now you expect me to...?
Roberto, pleassze to follow. Pleassze. I wish to repay hosszpitality.
Don't touch me!
Follow.

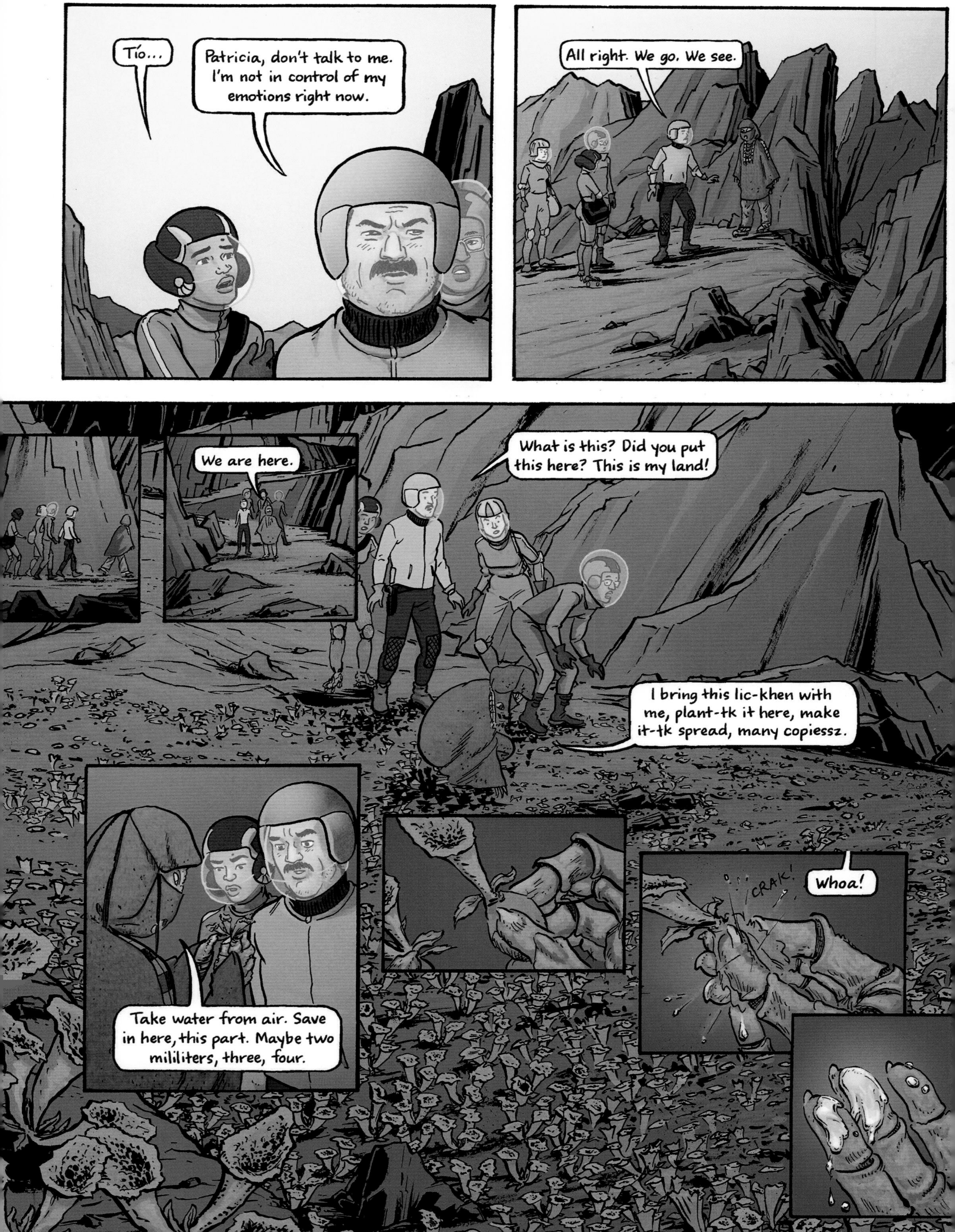
Tío...
Patricia, don't talk to me. I'm not in control of my emotions right now.
All right. We go. We see.
We are here.
What is this? Did you put this here? This is my land!
I bring this lic-khen with me, plant-tk it here, make it-tk spread, many copiessz.
Take water from air. Save in here, this part. Maybe two mililiters, three, four.
CRAK!
Whoa!

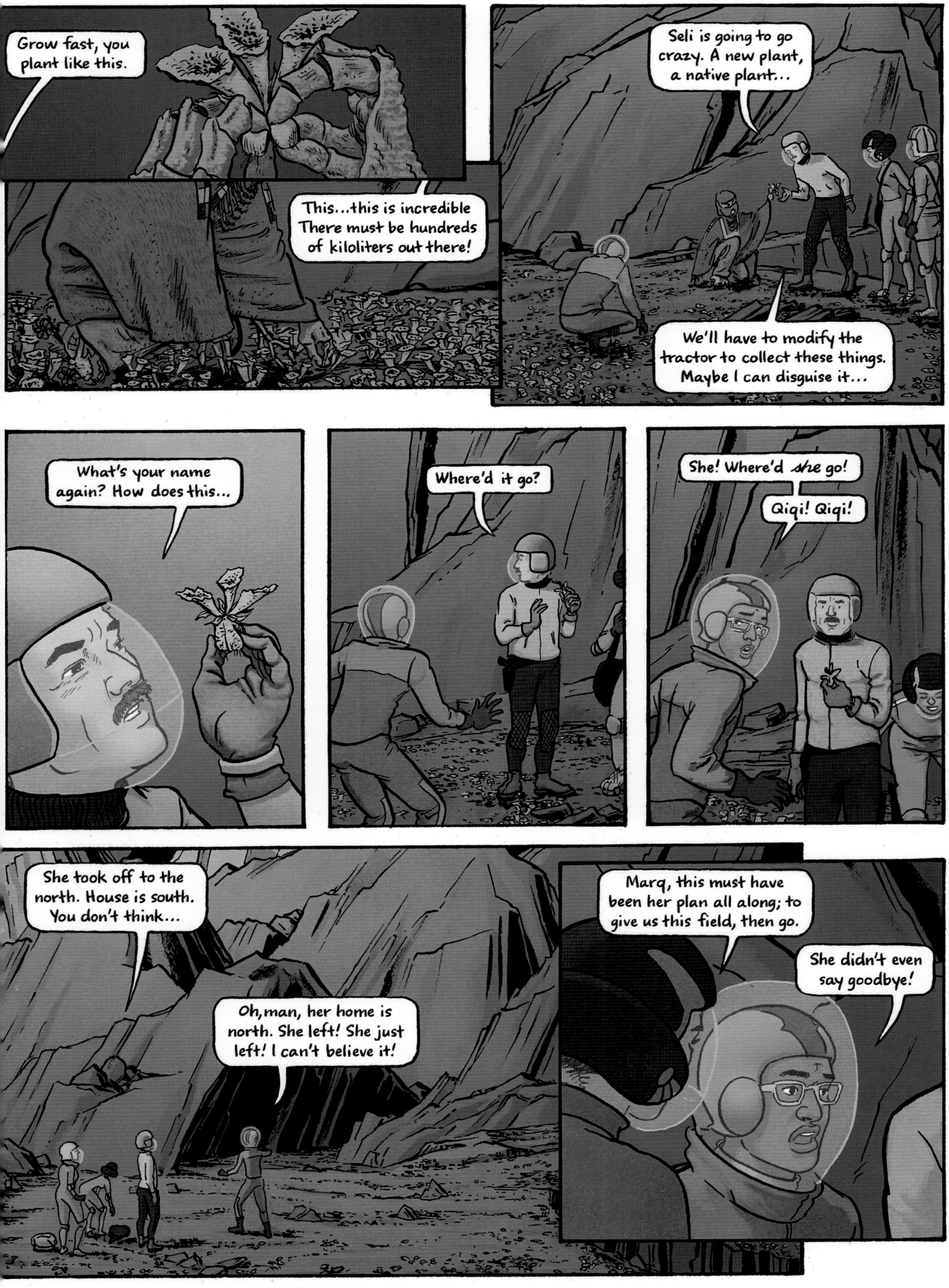

Grow fast, you plant like this.
This...this is incredible There must be hundreds of kiloliters out there!
Seli is going to go crazy. A new plant, a native plant...
We'll have to modify the tractor to collect these things. Maybe I can disguise it...
What's your name again? How does this...
Where'd it go?
She! Where'd *she* go!
Qiqi! Qiqi!
She took off to the north. House is south. You don't think...
Oh, man, her home is north. She left! She just left! I can't believe it!
Marq, this must have been her plan all along; to give us this field, then go.
She didn't even say goodbye!

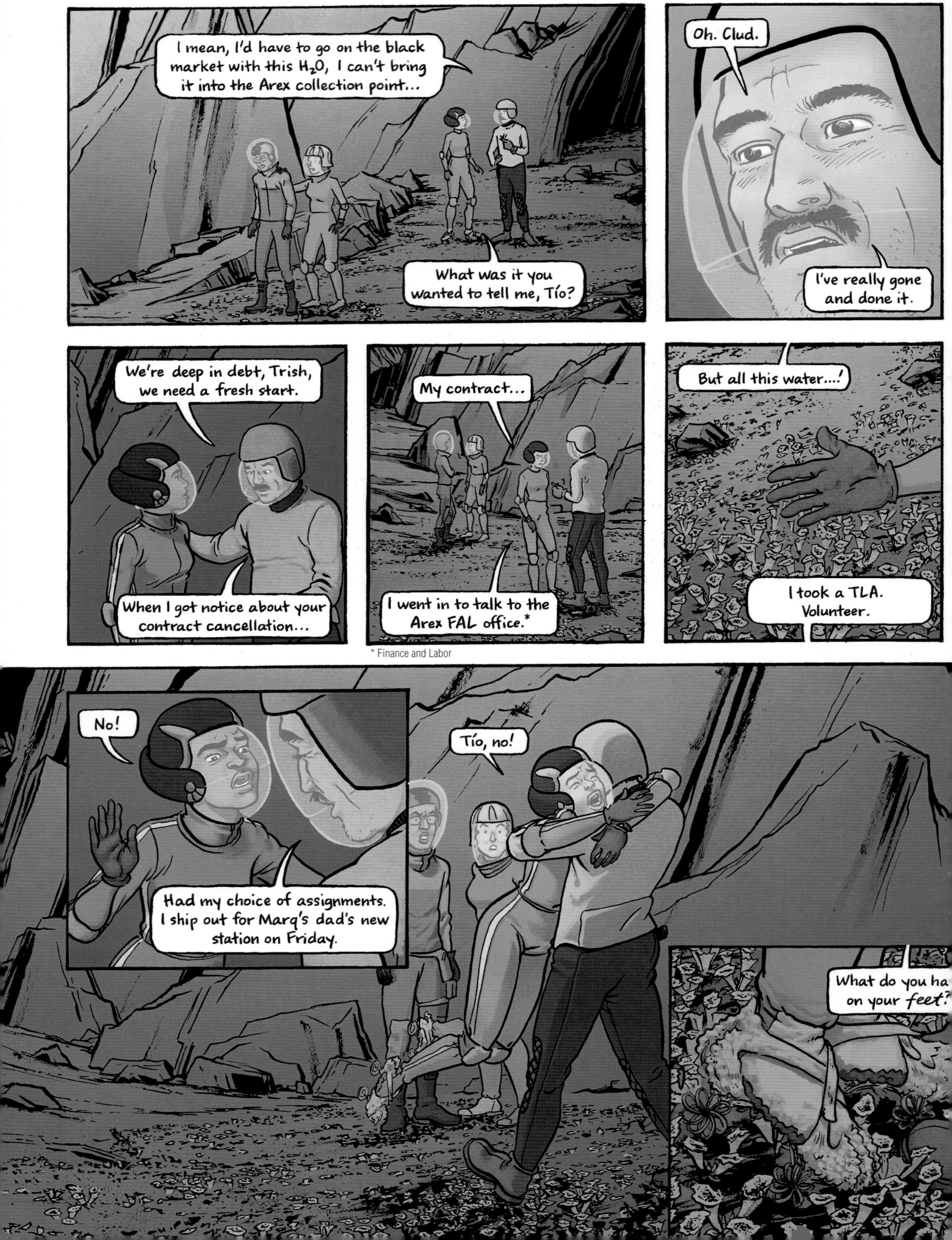
I mean, I'd have to go on the black market with this H_2O, I can't bring it into the Arex collection point...
What was it you wanted to tell me, Tío?
Oh. Clud.
I've really gone and done it.
We're deep in debt, Trish, we need a fresh start.
When I got notice about your contract cancellation...
My contract...
I went in to talk to the Arex FAL office.*
But all this water....!
I took a TLA. Volunteer.
No!
Had my choice of assignments. I ship out for Marq's dad's new station on Friday.
Tío, no!
What do you ha
on your feet?

* Finance and Labor

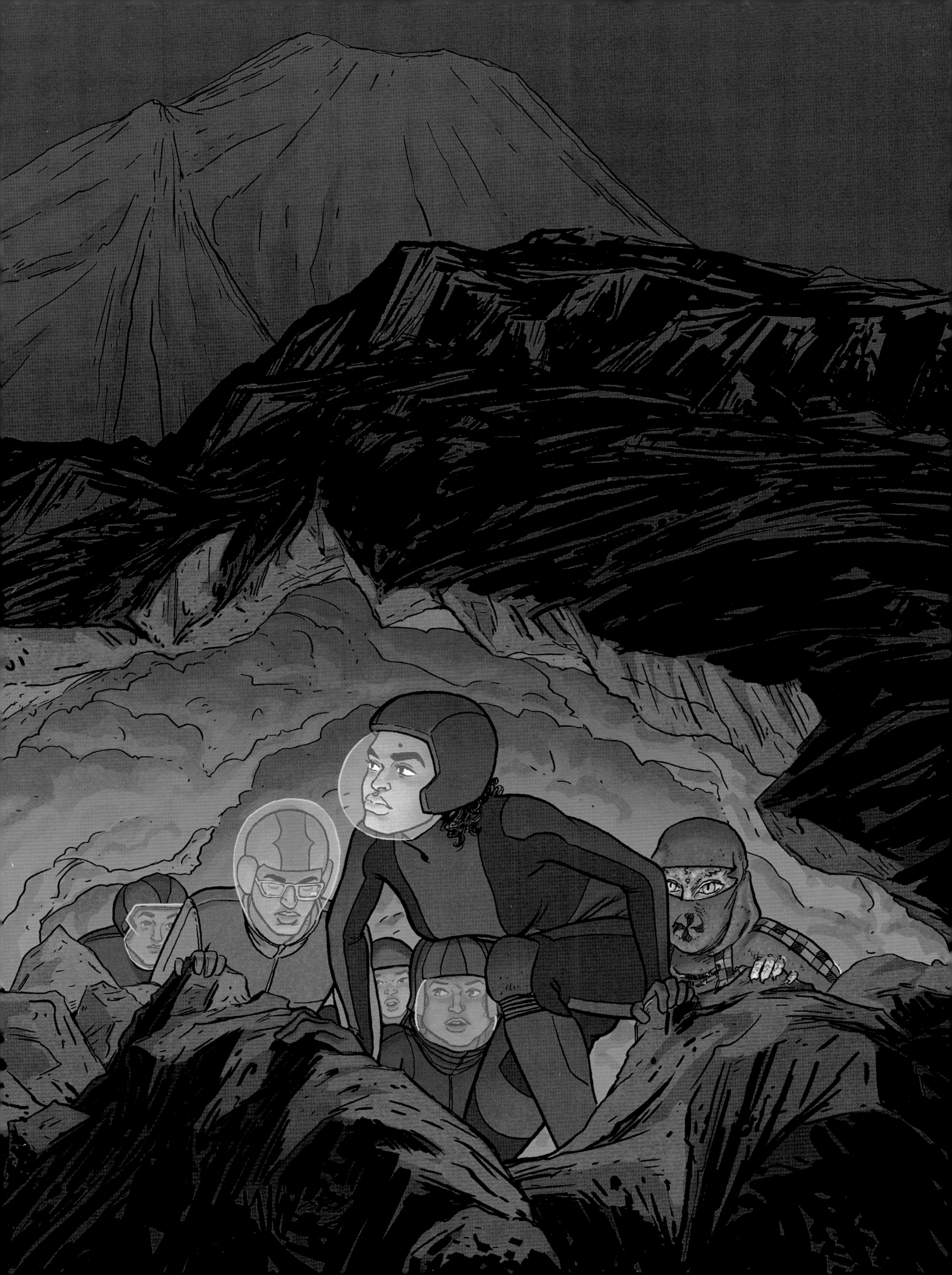

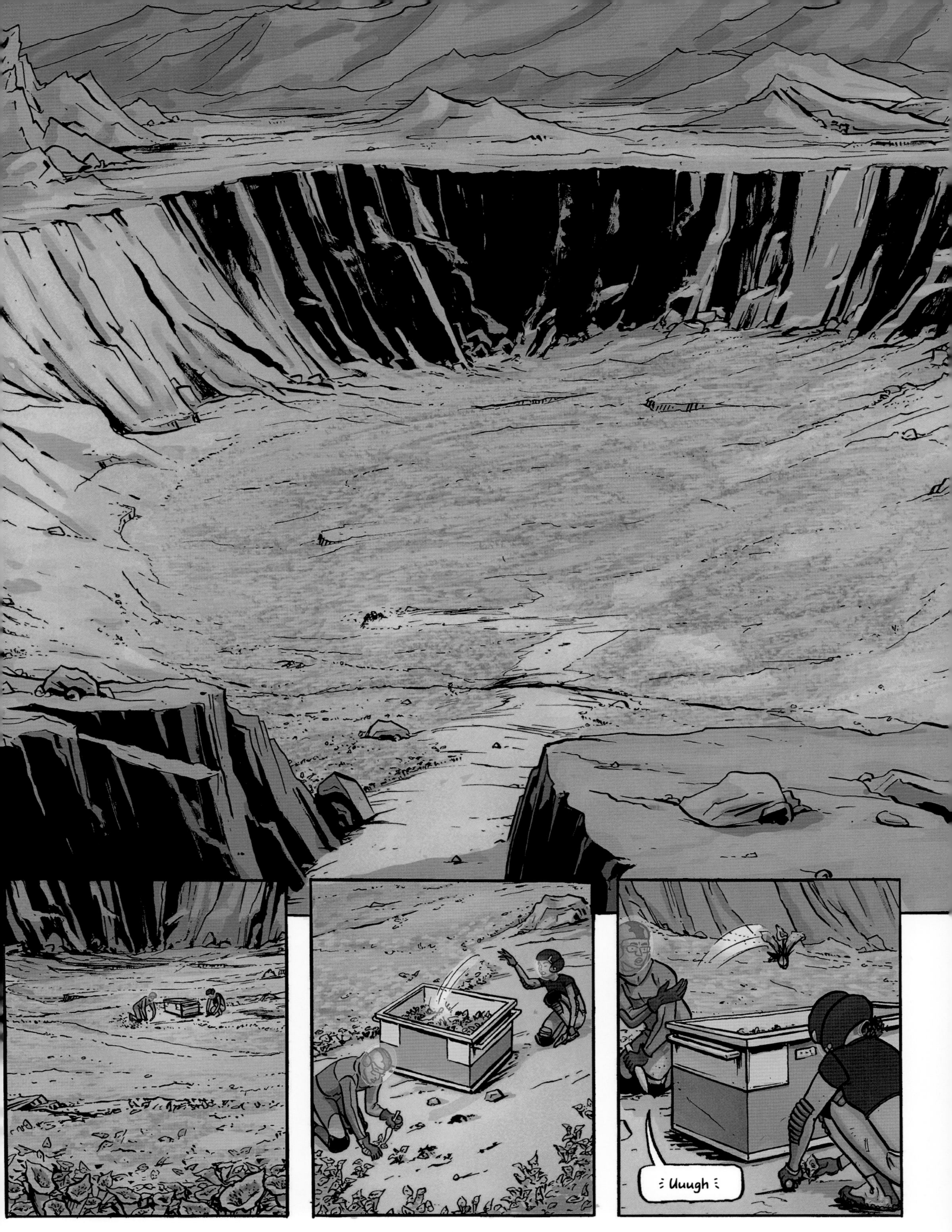
Uuugh

Oh, my back.

Hey, help me with this side. The forward hoverpad is dusted, but I don't have time to fix it.

Where is Rocky today?

She's got an early practice. Team is slipping.

Well, that's obviously a good use of her time.

Lay off, Marq. They've got a shot at the Derby Bowl if they get back on track.

Which will definitely change her life more than having a whole bunch of water.

FWOOMF

Let me put this in terms you'll understand: she's under contract.

Pff

Hey, young moisture farmers of Mars! It's your old pal Marquis Marq with a cheerful message of motivation!

Are you doing your stupid political holog again?

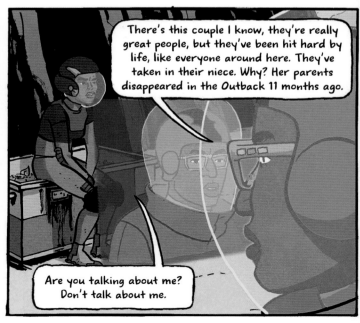

There's this couple I know, they're really great people, but they've been hit hard by life, like everyone around here. They've taken in their niece. Why? Her parents disappeared in the Outback 11 months ago.

Are you talking about me? Don't talk about me.

118

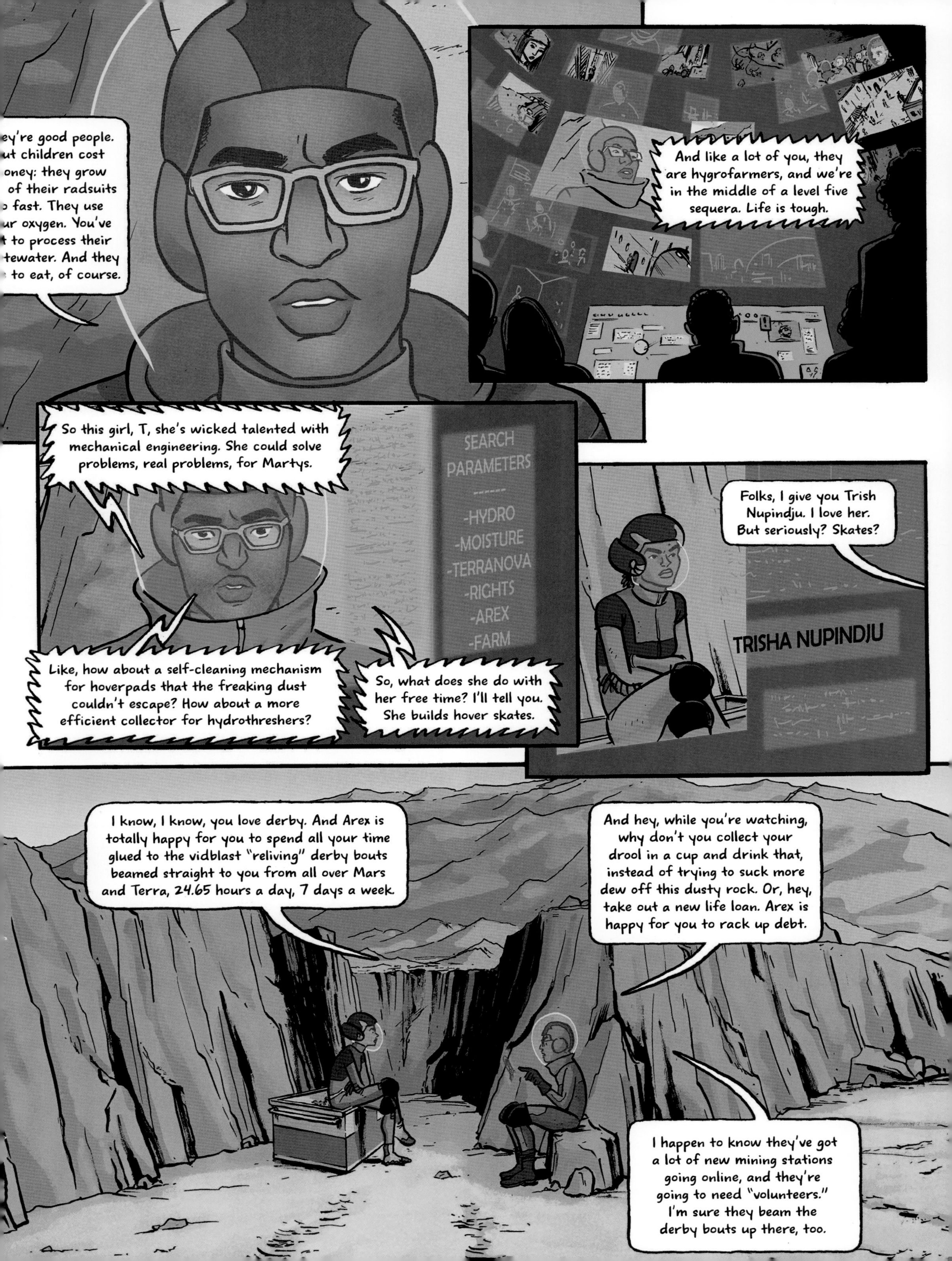

ey're good people. ut children cost oney: they grow of their radsuits fast. They use ur oxygen. You've t to process their tewater. And they to eat, of course.
And like a lot of you, they are hygrofarmers, and we're in the middle of a level five sequera. Life is tough.
So this girl, T, she's wicked talented with mechanical engineering. She could solve problems, real problems, for Martys.
SEARCH PARAMETERS
-HYDRO
-MOISTURE
-TERRANOVA
-RIGHTS
-AREX
-FARM
Like, how about a self-cleaning mechanism for hoverpads that the freaking dust couldn't escape? How about a more efficient collector for hydrothreshers?
So, what does she do with her free time? I'll tell you. She builds hover skates.
Folks, I give you Trish Nupindju. I love her. But seriously? Skates?
TRISHA NUPINDJU
I know, I know, you love derby. And Arex is totally happy for you to spend all your time glued to the vidblast "reliving" derby bouts beamed straight to you from all over Mars and Terra, 24.65 hours a day, 7 days a week.
And hey, while you're watching, why don't you collect your drool in a cup and drink that, instead of trying to suck more dew off this dusty rock. Or, hey, take out a new life loan. Arex is happy for you to rack up debt.
I happen to know they've got a lot of new mining stations going online, and they're going to need "volunteers." I'm sure they beam the derby bouts up there, too.

Or, how about this? Maybe it's time to do something Arex won't like: Shut off the vidblast. Shut off the flow of new debt. Your life is hard enough without wasting all your time watching a bunch of women skate in a circle.

Marq! Seriously? Shut up!

This is the Angry Red Planet. Until next time.

IMAGE SEARCH: VEHICLE ALTERATION 2 HIGH VALUE SEARCH PARAMETERS. ADD TO QUEUE.

All right, kiddos. Now we're really sucking dew!

Hi, Seli.

I never thought I would be this happy to go to school in my life.

WWWWHIRR

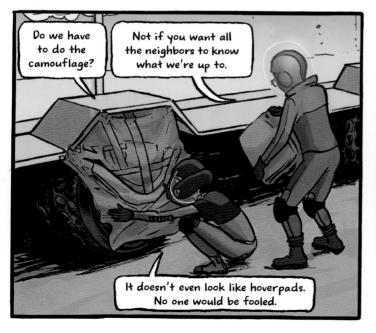

Do we have to do the camouflage?

Not if you want all the neighbors to know what we're up to.

It doesn't even look like hoverpads. No one would be fooled.

Clud. New rip in my radsuit.

Patch kit in the cubby.

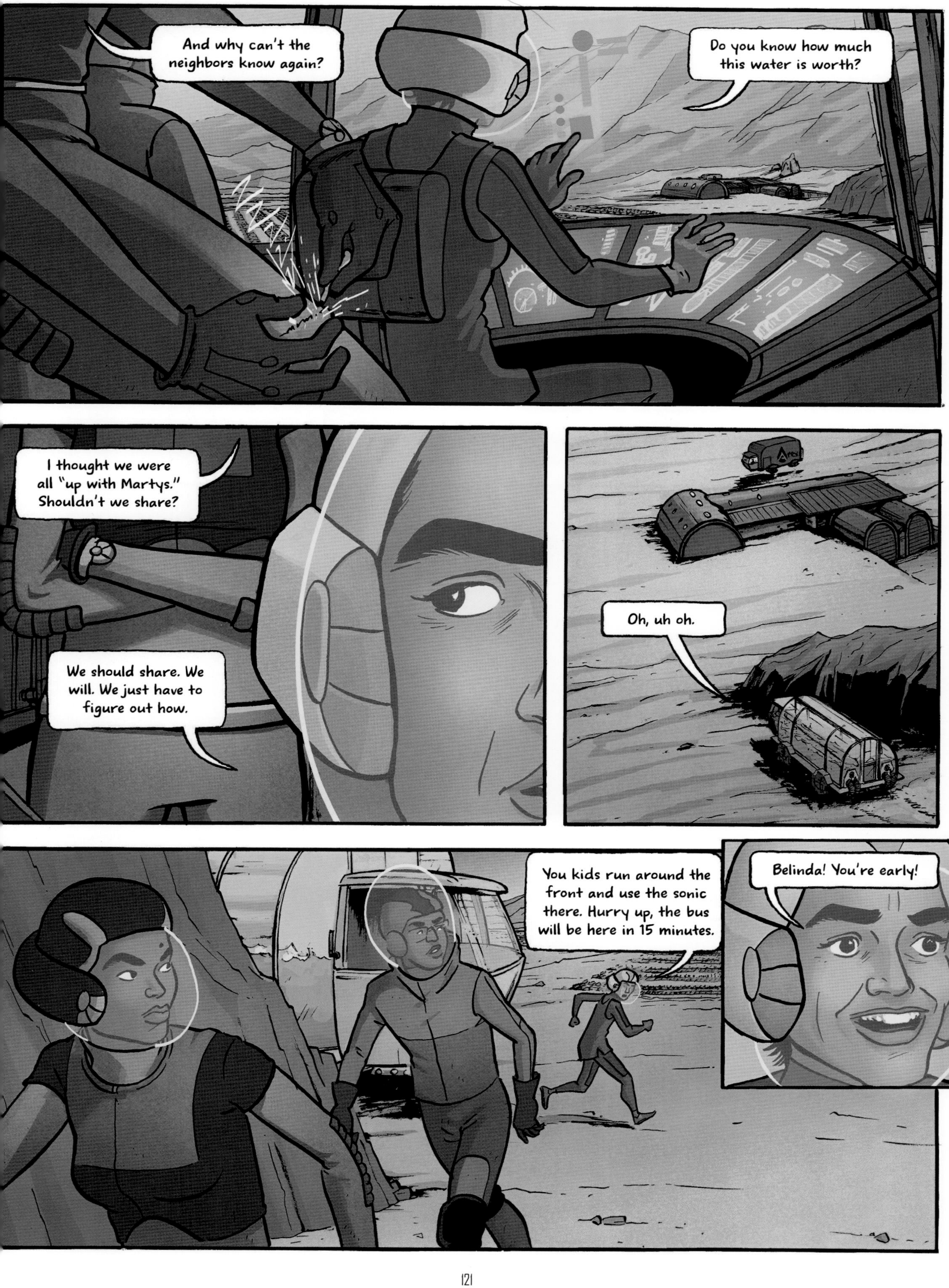
And why can't the neighbors know again?
Do you know how much this water is worth?
I thought we were all "up with Martys." Shouldn't we share?
We should share. We will. We just have to figure out how.
Oh, uh oh.
You kids run around the front and use the sonic there. Hurry up, the bus will be here in 15 minutes.
Belinda! You're early!

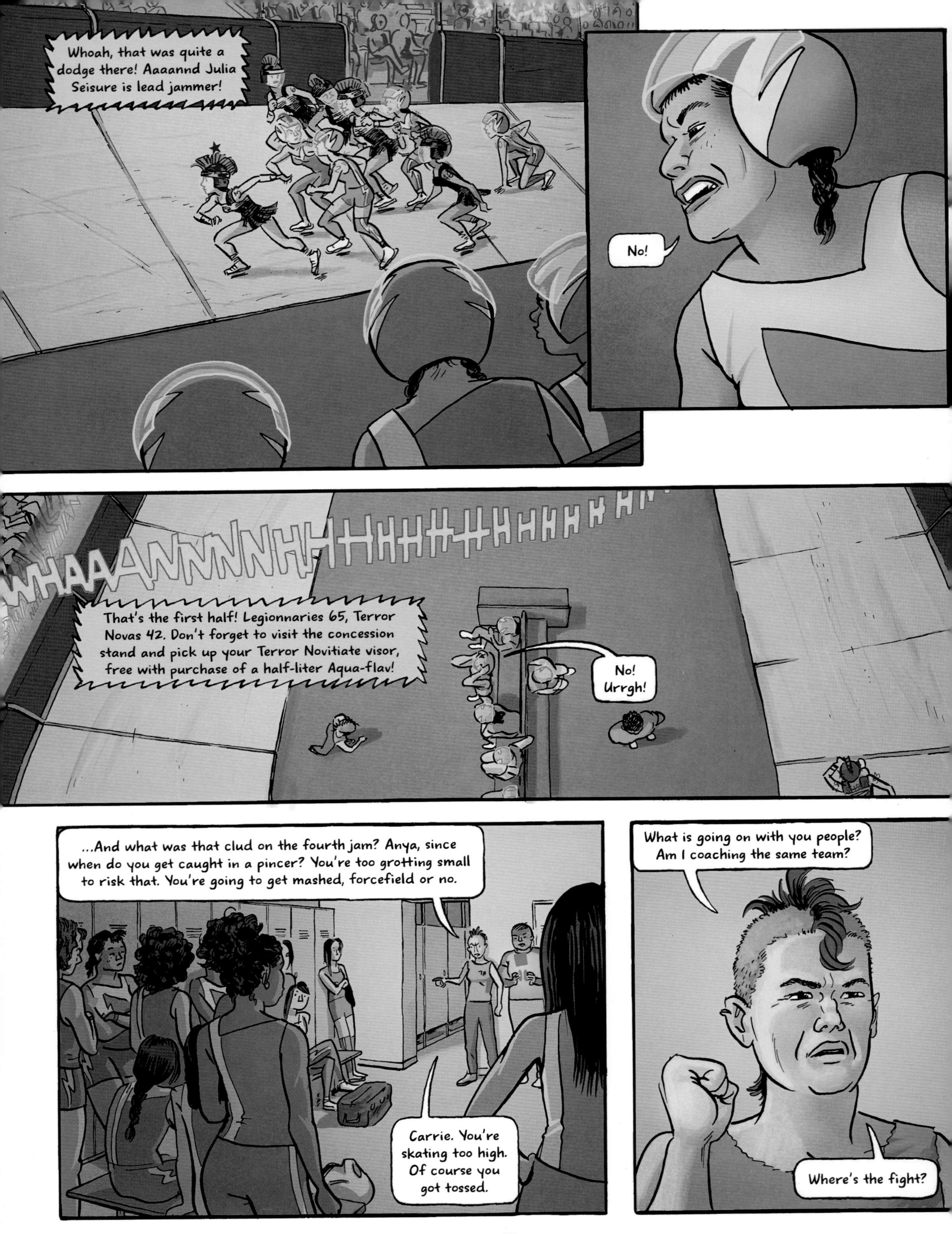

Whoah, that was quite a dodge there! Aaaannd Julia Seisure is lead jammer!
No!
WHAAANNNNHHHHHHHHHHHHH
That's the first half! Legionnaries 65, Terror Novas 42. Don't forget to visit the concession stand and pick up your Terror Novitiate visor, free with purchase of a half-liter Aqua-flav!
No! Urrgh!
...And what was that clud on the fourth jam? Anya, since when do you get caught in a pincer? You're too grotting small to risk that. You're going to get mashed, forcefield or no.
Carrie. You're skating too high. Of course you got tossed.
What is going on with you people? Am I coaching the same team?
Where's the fight?

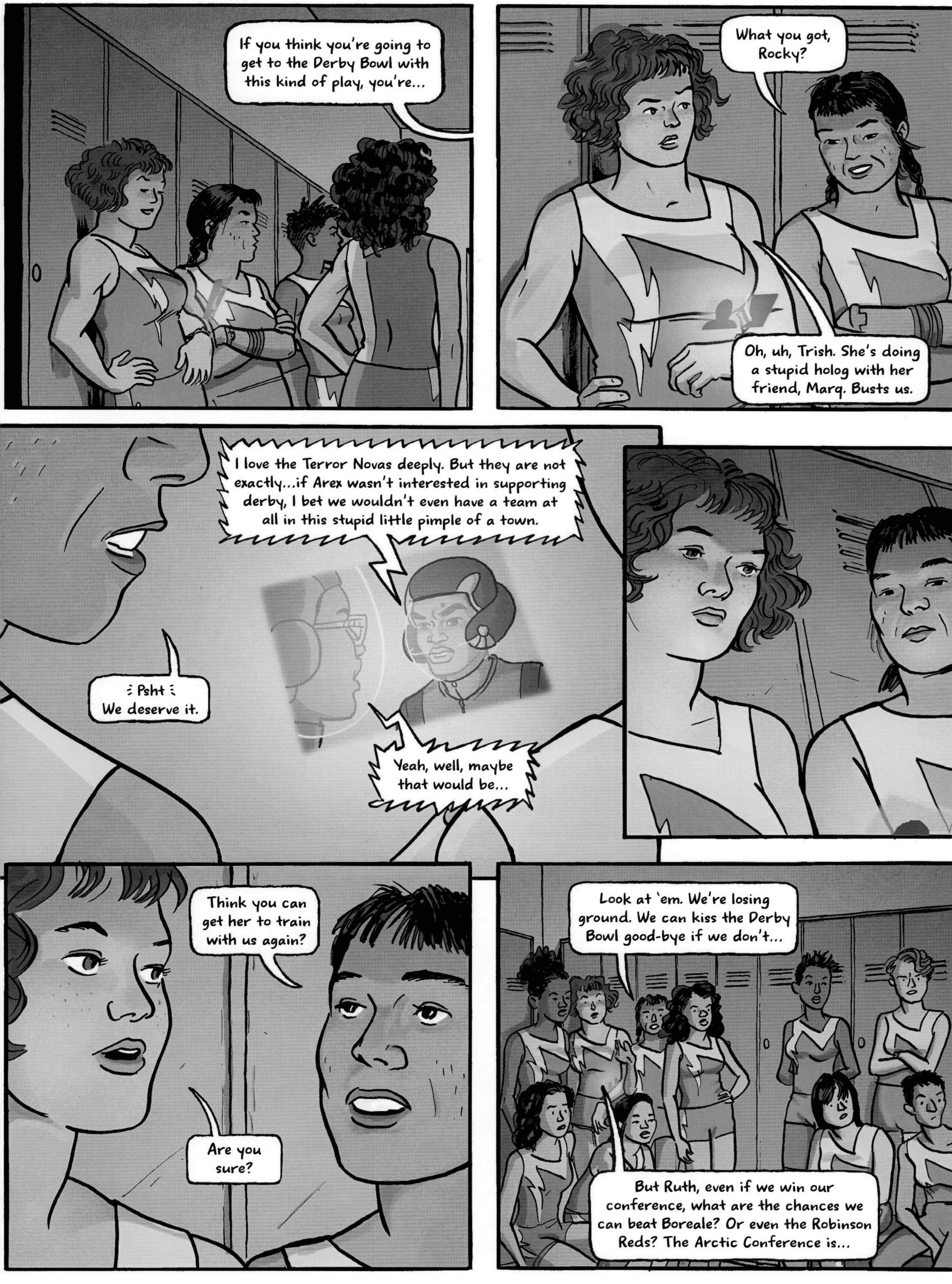

If you think you're going to get to the Derby Bowl with this kind of play, you're...
What you got, Rocky?
Oh, uh, Trish. She's doing a stupid holog with her friend, Marq. Busts us.
I love the Terror Novas deeply. But they are not exactly...if Arex wasn't interested in supporting derby, I bet we wouldn't even have a team at all in this stupid little pimple of a town.
Psht
We deserve it.
Yeah, well, maybe that would be...
Think you can get her to train with us again?
Are you sure?
Look at 'em. We're losing ground. We can kiss the Derby Bowl good-bye if we don't...
But Ruth, even if we win our conference, what are the chances we can beat Boreale? Or even the Robinson Reds? The Arctic Conference is...

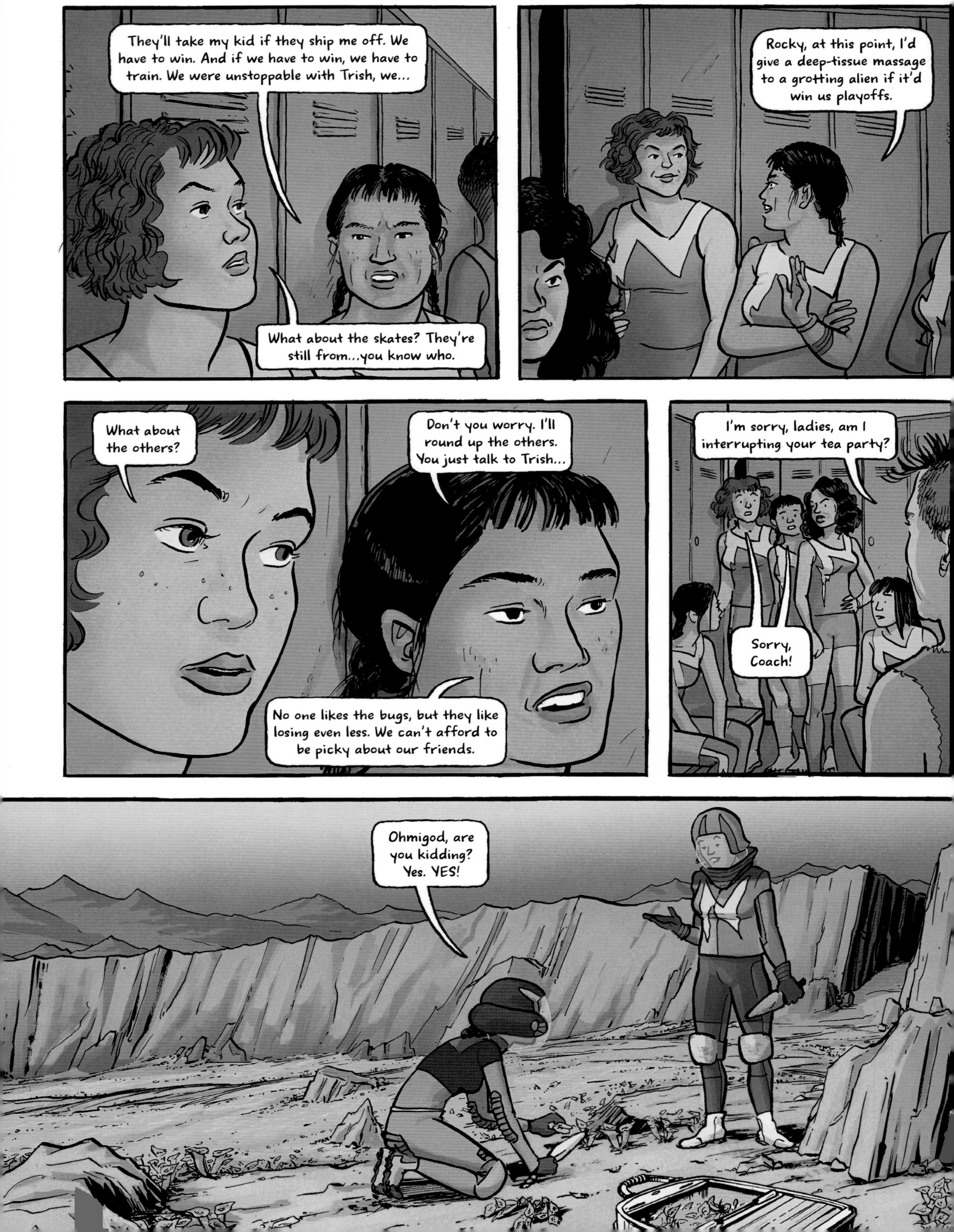
They'll take my kid if they ship me off. We have to win. And if we have to win, we have to train. We were unstoppable with Trish, we...
What about the skates? They're still from...you know who.
Rocky, at this point, I'd give a deep-tissue massage to a grotting alien if it'd win us playoffs.
What about the others?
Don't you worry. I'll round up the others. You just talk to Trish...
No one likes the bugs, but they like losing even less. We can't afford to be picky about our friends.
I'm sorry, ladies, am I interrupting your tea party?
Sorry, Coach!
Ohmigod, are you kidding? Yes. YES!

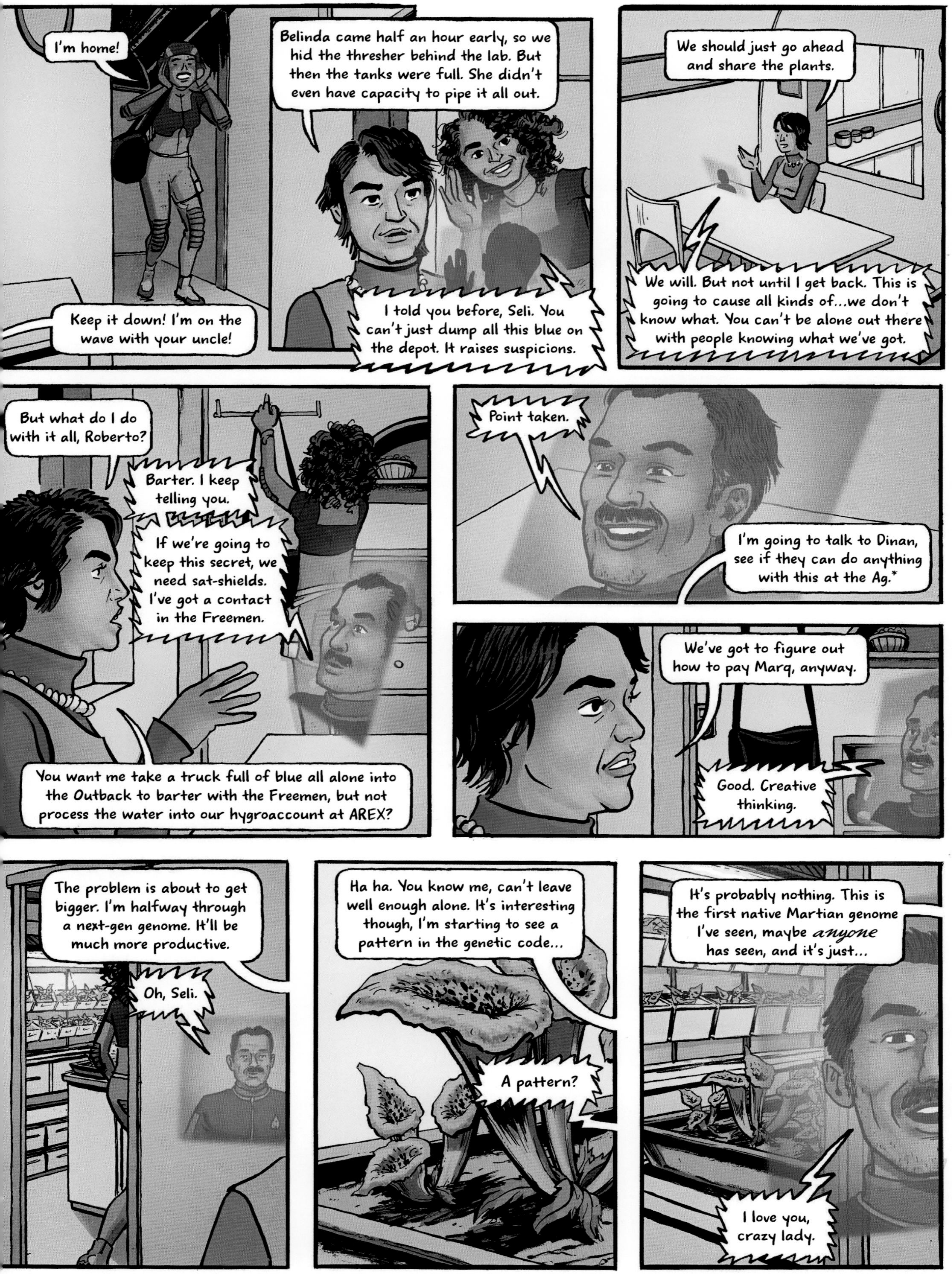
I'm home!
Keep it down! I'm on the wave with your uncle!
Belinda came half an hour early, so we hid the thresher behind the lab. But then the tanks were full. She didn't even have capacity to pipe it all out.
I told you before, Seli. You can't just dump all this blue on the depot. It raises suspicions.
We should just go ahead and share the plants.
We will. But not until I get back. This is going to cause all kinds of...we don't know what. You can't be alone out there with people knowing what we've got.
But what do I do with it all, Roberto?
Barter. I keep telling you.
If we're going to keep this secret, we need sat-shields. I've got a contact in the Freemen.
You want me take a truck full of blue all alone into the Outback to barter with the Freemen, but not process the water into our hygroaccount at AREX?
Point taken.
I'm going to talk to Dinan, see if they can do anything with this at the Ag.*
We've got to figure out how to pay Marq, anyway.
Good. Creative thinking.
The problem is about to get bigger. I'm halfway through a next-gen genome. It'll be much more productive.
Oh, Seli.
Ha ha. You know me, can't leave well enough alone. It's interesting though, I'm starting to see a pattern in the genetic code...
A pattern?
It's probably nothing. This is the first native Martian genome I've seen, maybe *anyone* has seen, and it's just...
I love you, crazy lady.

*The agricultural school at Terra Nova Community College

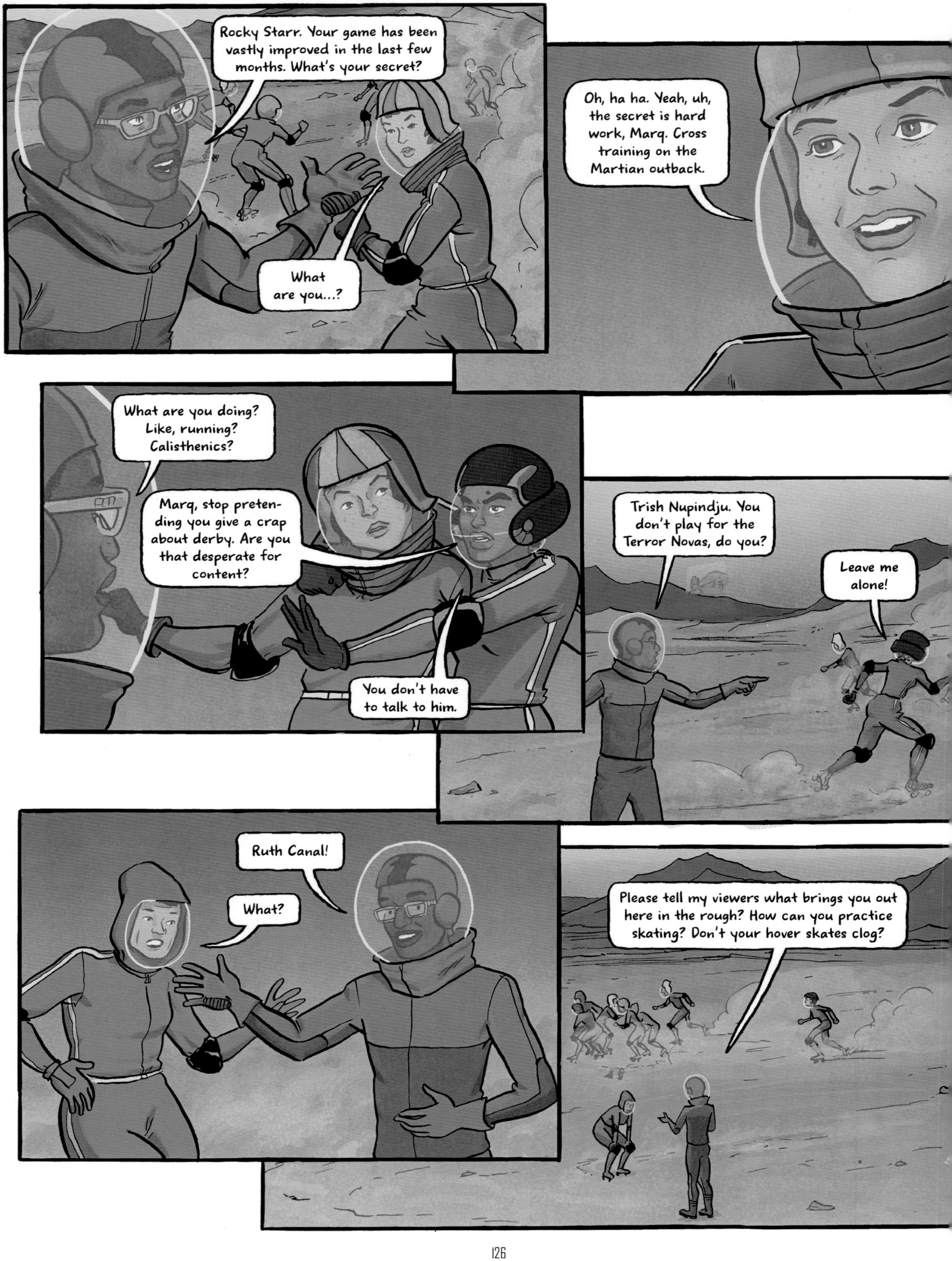
Rocky Starr. Your game has been vastly improved in the last few months. What's your secret?
What are you...?
Oh, ha ha. Yeah, uh, the secret is hard work, Marq. Cross training on the Martian outback.
What are you doing? Like, running? Calisthenics?
Marq, stop pretending you give a crap about derby. Are you that desperate for content?
You don't have to talk to him.
Trish Nupindju. You don't play for the Terror Novas, do you?
Leave me alone!
Ruth Canal!
What?
Please tell my viewers what brings you out here in the rough? How can you practice skating? Don't your hover skates clog?

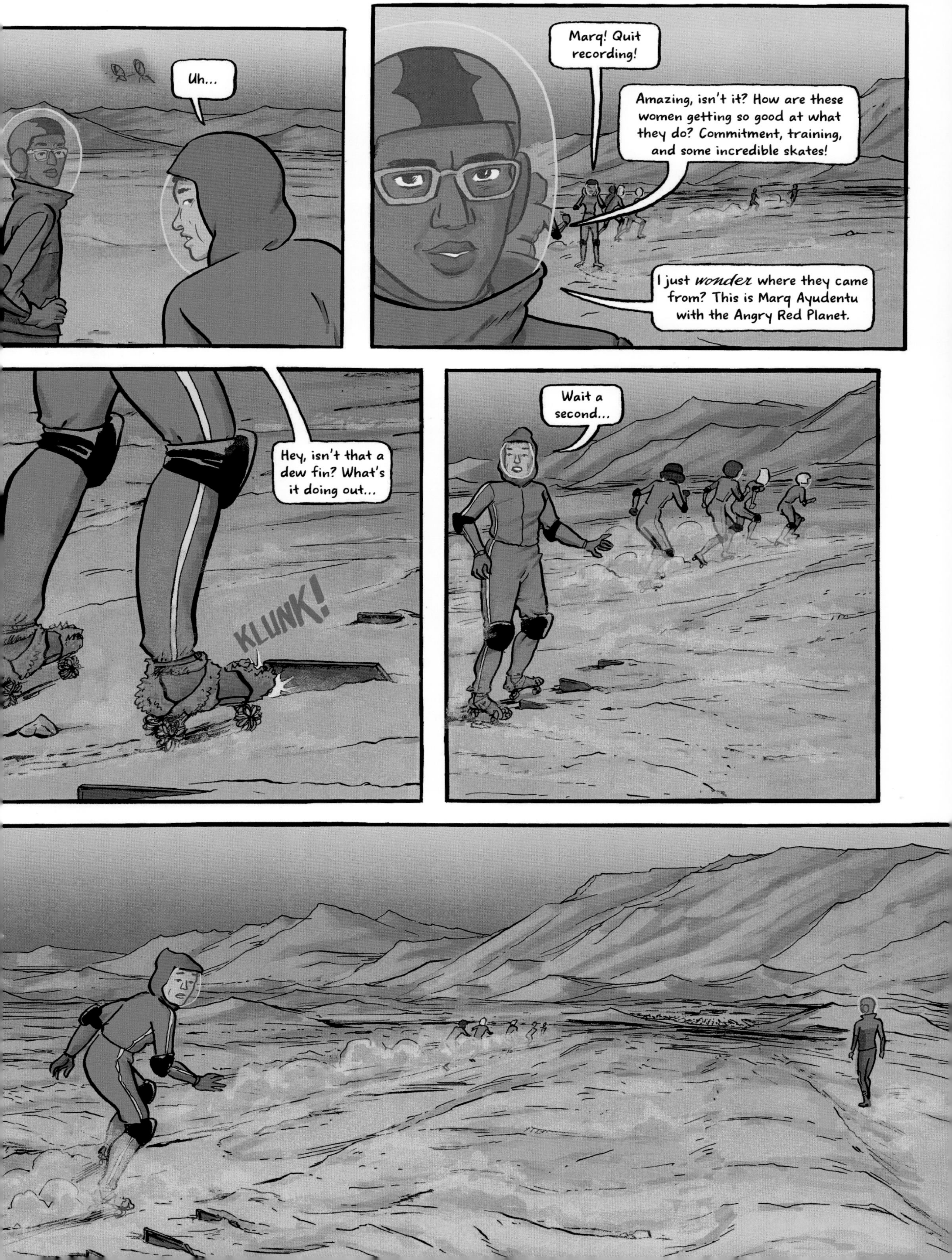

Uh...
Marq! Quit recording!
Amazing, isn't it? How are these women getting so good at what they do? Commitment, training, and some incredible skates!
I just *wonder* where they came from? This is Marq Ayudentu with the Angry Red Planet.
Hey, isn't that a dew fin? What's it doing out...
KLUNK!
Wait a second...

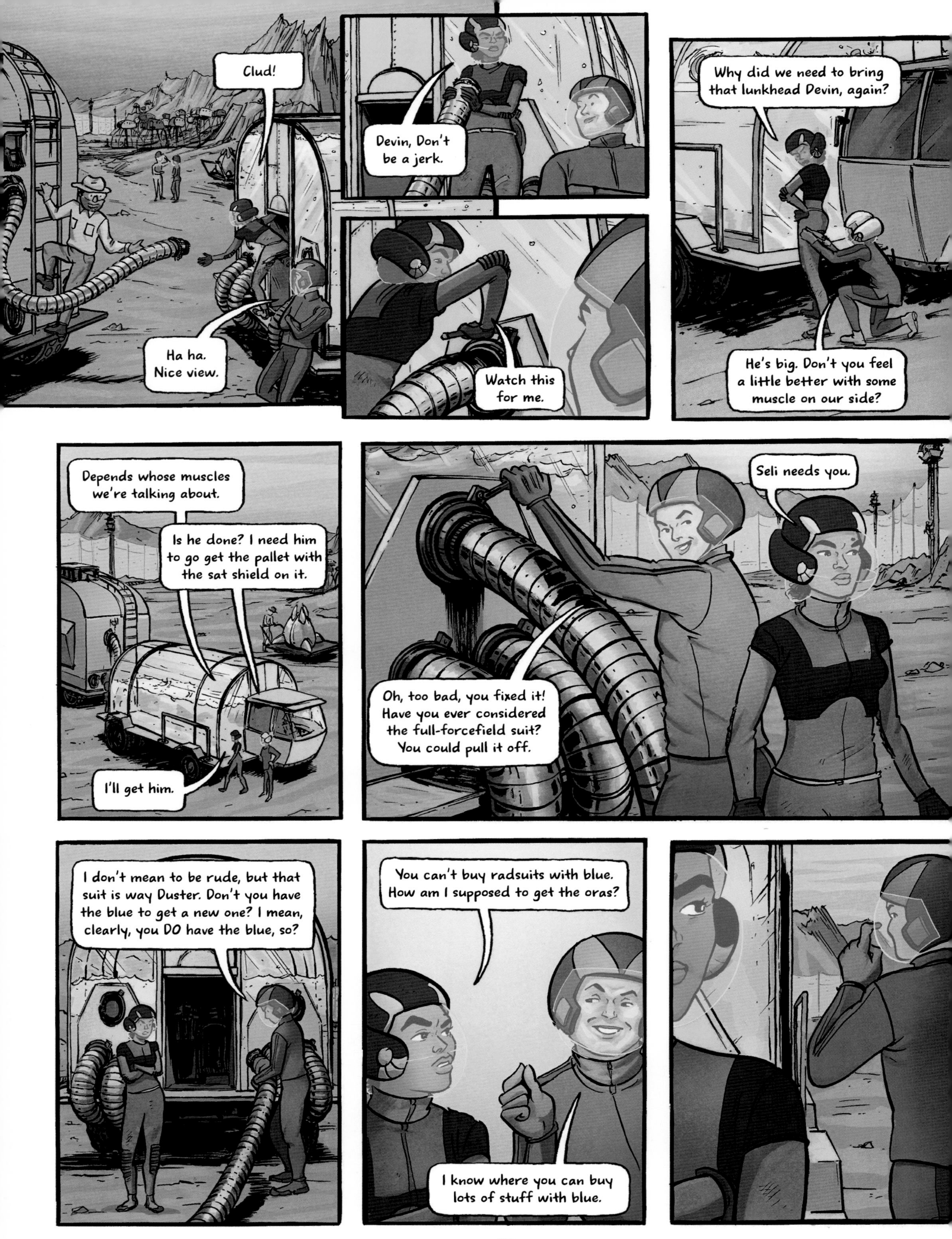
Clud!
Ha ha. Nice view.
Devin, Don't be a jerk.
Watch this for me.
Why did we need to bring that lunkhead Devin, again?
He's big. Don't you feel a little better with some muscle on our side?
Depends whose muscles we're talking about.
Is he done? I need him to go get the pallet with the sat shield on it.
I'll get him.
Seli needs you.
Oh, too bad, you fixed it! Have you ever considered the full-forcefield suit? You could pull it off.
I don't mean to be rude, but that suit is way Duster. Don't you have the blue to get a new one? I mean, clearly, you DO have the blue, so?
You can't buy radsuits with blue. How am I supposed to get the oras?
I know where you can buy lots of stuff with blue.

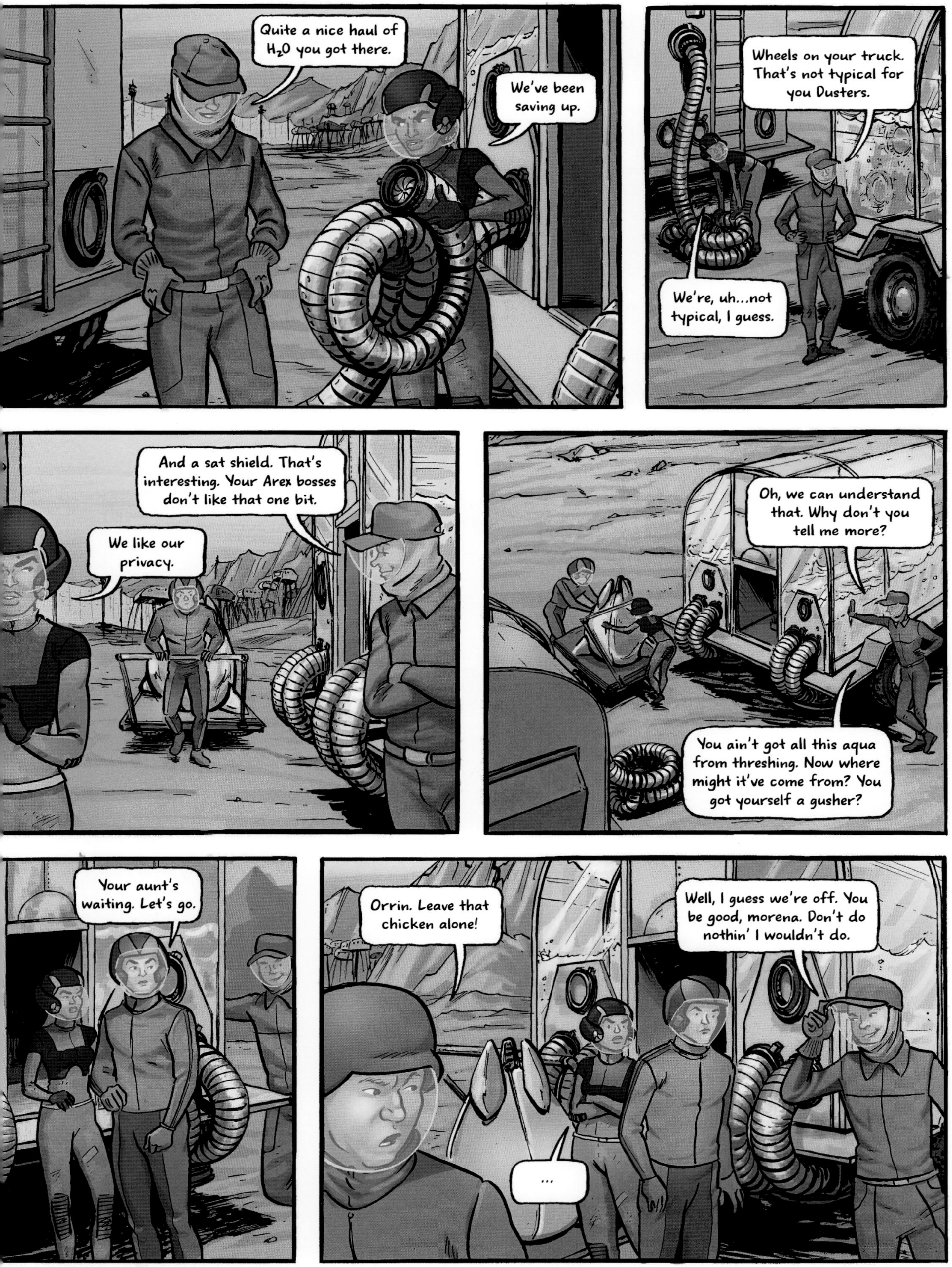
Quite a nice haul of H_2O you got there.
We've been saving up.
Wheels on your truck. That's not typical for you Dusters.
We're, uh...not typical, I guess.
And a sat shield. That's interesting. Your Arex bosses don't like that one bit.
We like our privacy.
Oh, we can understand that. Why don't you tell me more?
You ain't got all this aqua from threshing. Now where might it've come from? You got yourself a gusher?
Your aunt's waiting. Let's go.
Orrin. Leave that chicken alone!
Well, I guess we're off. You be good, morena. Don't do nothin' I wouldn't do.
...

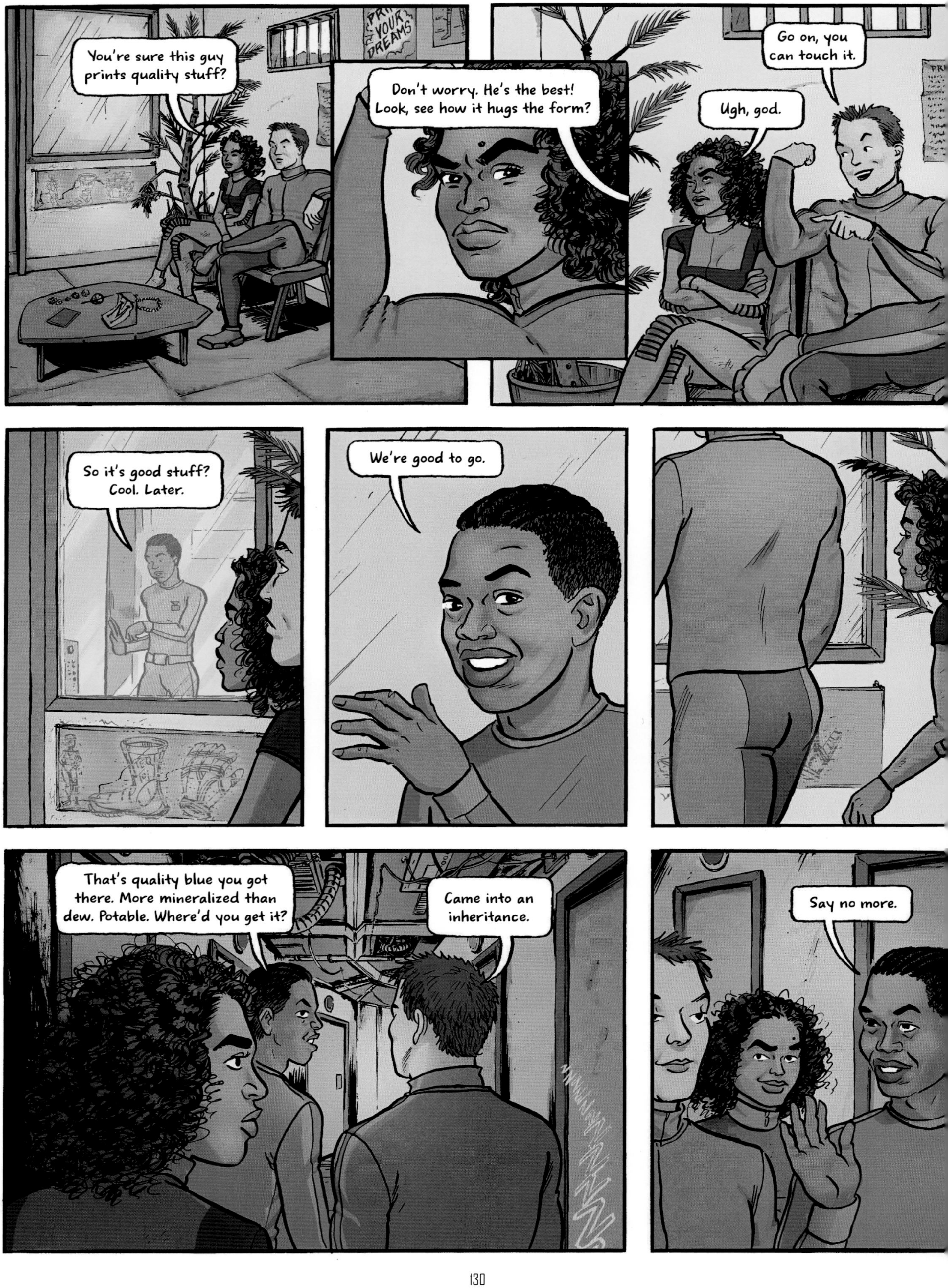

PRINT YOUR DREAMS
You're sure this guy prints quality stuff?
Don't worry. He's the best! Look, see how it hugs the form?
Go on, you can touch it.
Ugh, god.
So it's good stuff? Cool. Later.
We're good to go.
That's quality blue you got there. More mineralized than dew. Potable. Where'd you get it?
Came into an inheritance.
Say no more.

You've got credit for a level X suit. You looking for a spare?

No, it's for my friend here.

Well! You're very kind to your friends. Get in the booth, sweetie.

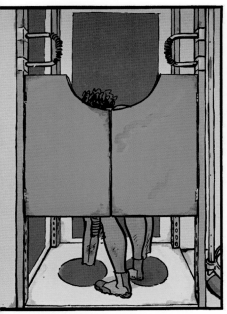

No looking!

We're not looking!

RESCAN   PRIVACY

Aw!

Come on, Dev. You've seen that before.

He has not!

OK, get dressed. Let's build something awesome!

PING!

SONAR SCAN COMPLETE

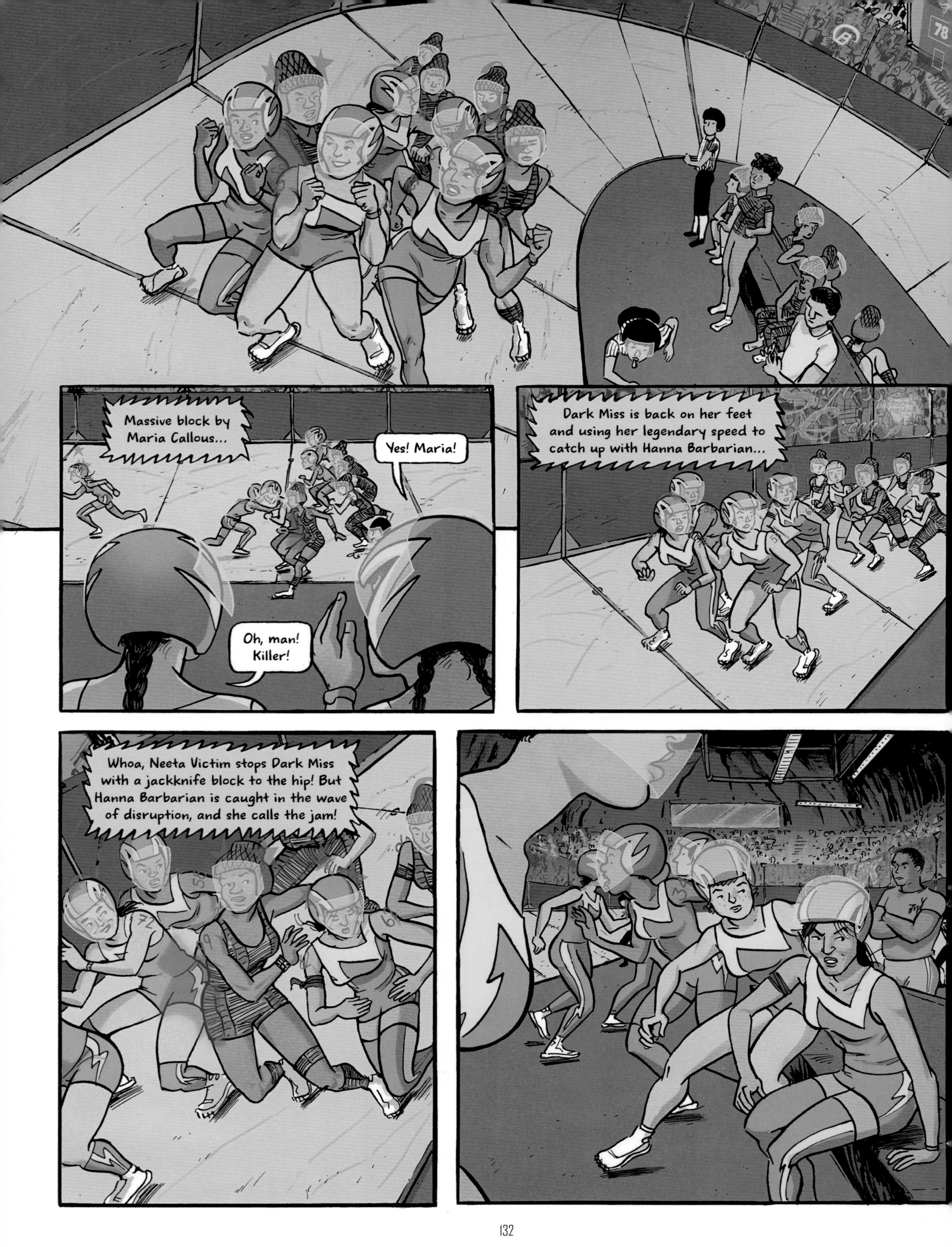

Massive block by Maria Callous...
Yes! Maria!
Oh, man! Killer!
Dark Miss is back on her feet and using her legendary speed to catch up with Hanna Barbarian...
Whoa, Neeta Victim stops Dark Miss with a jackknife block to the hip! But Hanna Barbarian is caught in the wave of disruption, and she calls the jam!

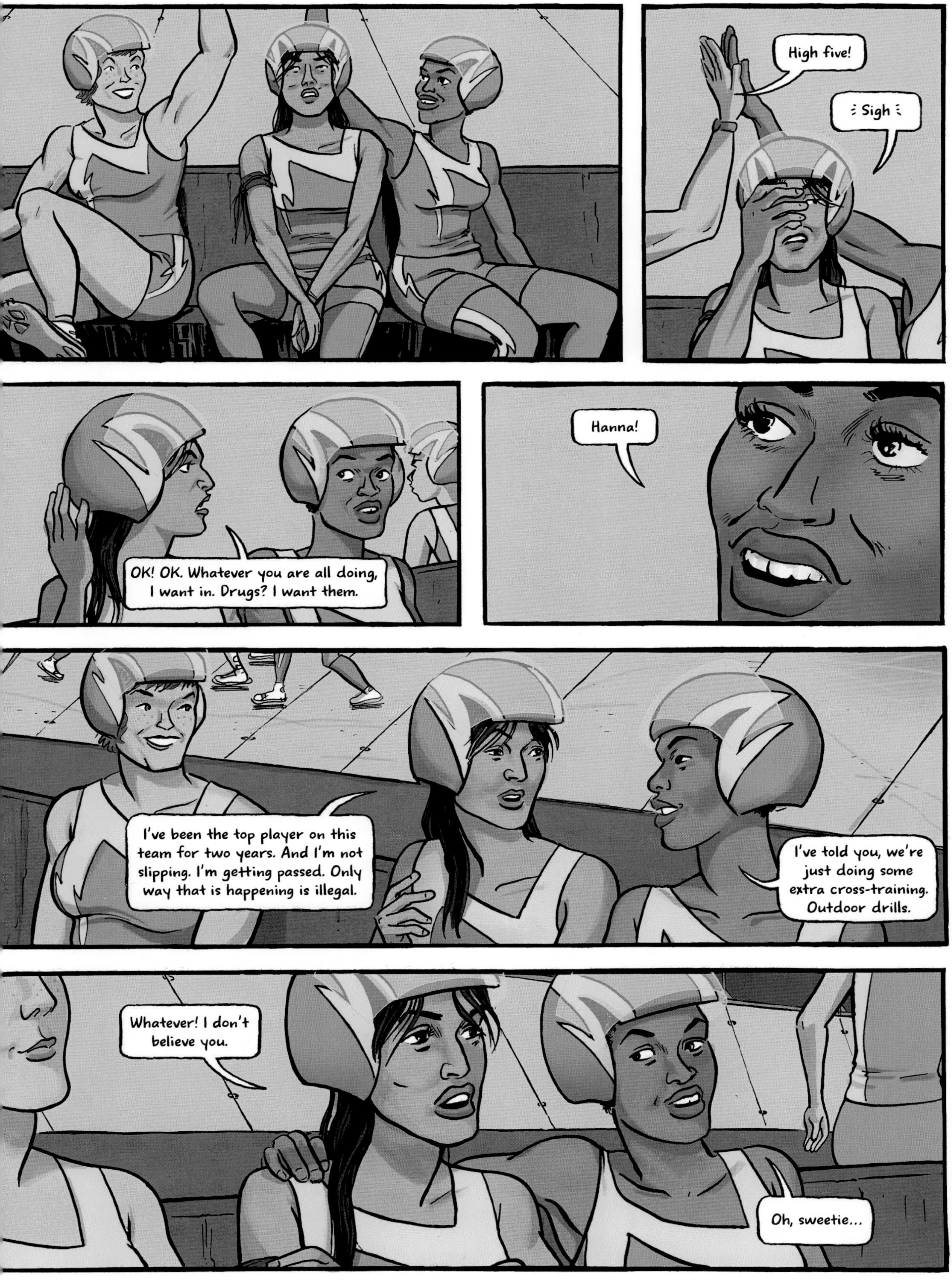
High five!
Sigh
OK! OK. Whatever you are all doing, I want in. Drugs? I want them.
Hanna!
I've been the top player on this team for two years. And I'm not slipping. I'm getting passed. Only way that is happening is illegal.
I've told you, we're just doing some extra cross-training. Outdoor drills.
Whatever! I don't believe you.
Oh, sweetie...

Don't "oh, sweetie" me.

Put me on the list. I plan to win the Derby Bowl this year.

Sure, Hanna. When we pass out the illegal performance-enhancing rocks, you're on the list.

You're so full of grot.

You're leaving in two days. Your little crew of supercharged players is getting smaller. Get me in.

We'll talk.

Right, Rocky? We'll talk.

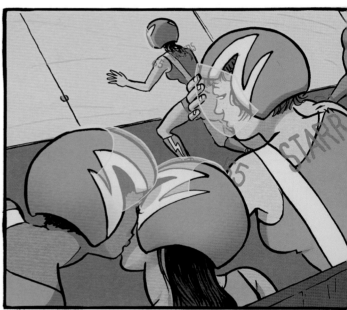

I can't believe you're with her.

Ha ha! Yeah, well. She's a handful.

With under two minutes on the clock, the Chaos leads at 92 to 89! This is a pivotal moment, folks.

Whoever wins today will play the Marineris Conference champion Minotaurs next week for a trip to the Derby Bowl!

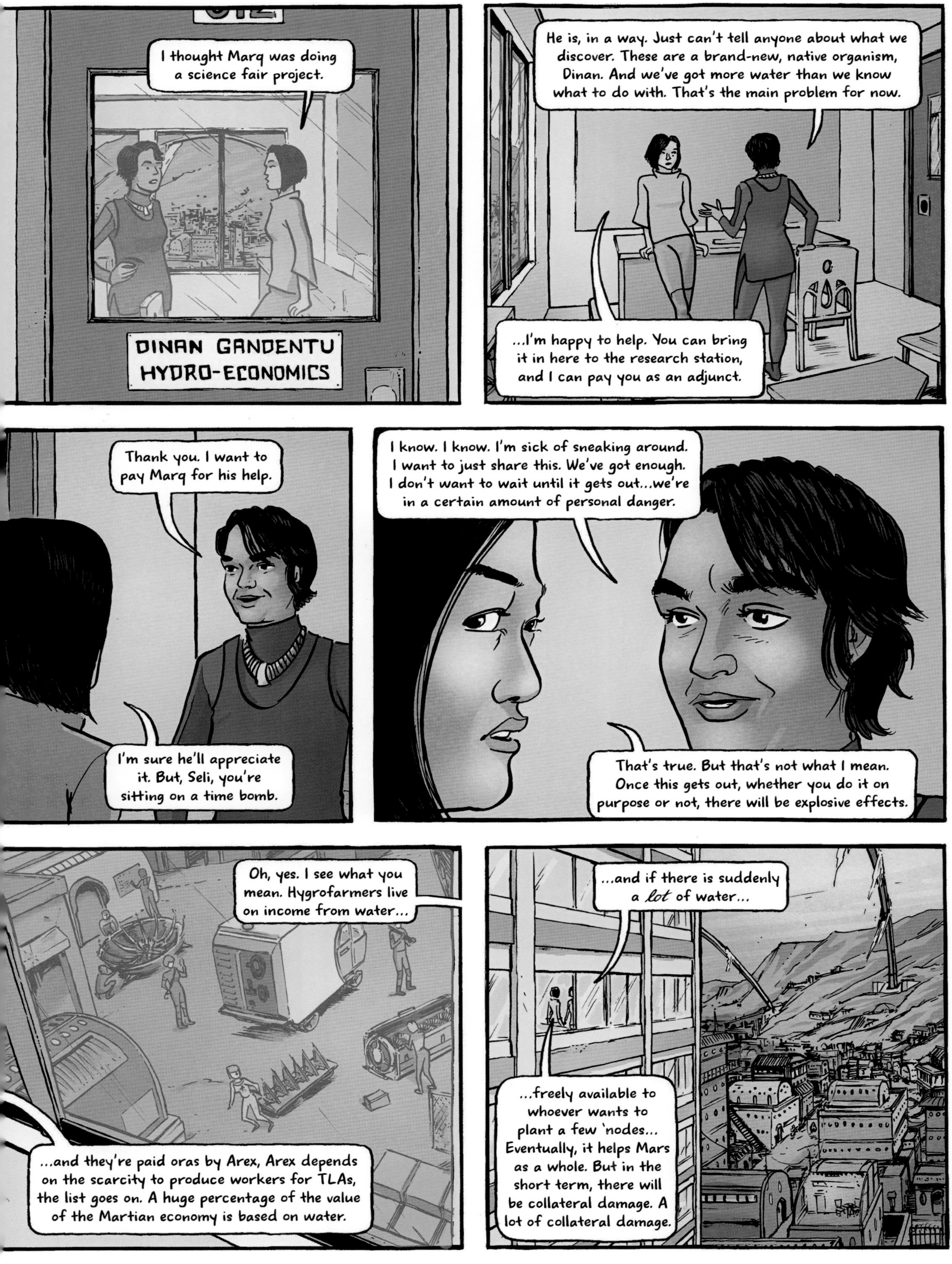

I thought Marq was doing a science fair project.
DINAN GANDENTU
HYDRO-ECONOMICS
He is, in a way. Just can't tell anyone about what we discover. These are a brand-new, native organism, Dinan. And we've got more water than we know what to do with. That's the main problem for now.
...I'm happy to help. You can bring it in here to the research station, and I can pay you as an adjunct.
Thank you. I want to pay Marq for his help.
I'm sure he'll appreciate it. But, Seli, you're sitting on a time bomb.
I know. I know. I'm sick of sneaking around. I want to just share this. We've got enough. I don't want to wait until it gets out...we're in a certain amount of personal danger.
That's true. But that's not what I mean. Once this gets out, whether you do it on purpose or not, there will be explosive effects.
Oh, yes. I see what you mean. Hygrofarmers live on income from water...
...and they're paid oras by Arex, Arex depends on the scarcity to produce workers for TLAs, the list goes on. A huge percentage of the value of the Martian economy is based on water.
...and if there is suddenly a *lot* of water...
...freely available to whoever wants to plant a few 'nodes... Eventually, it helps Mars as a whole. But in the short term, there will be collateral damage. A lot of collateral damage.

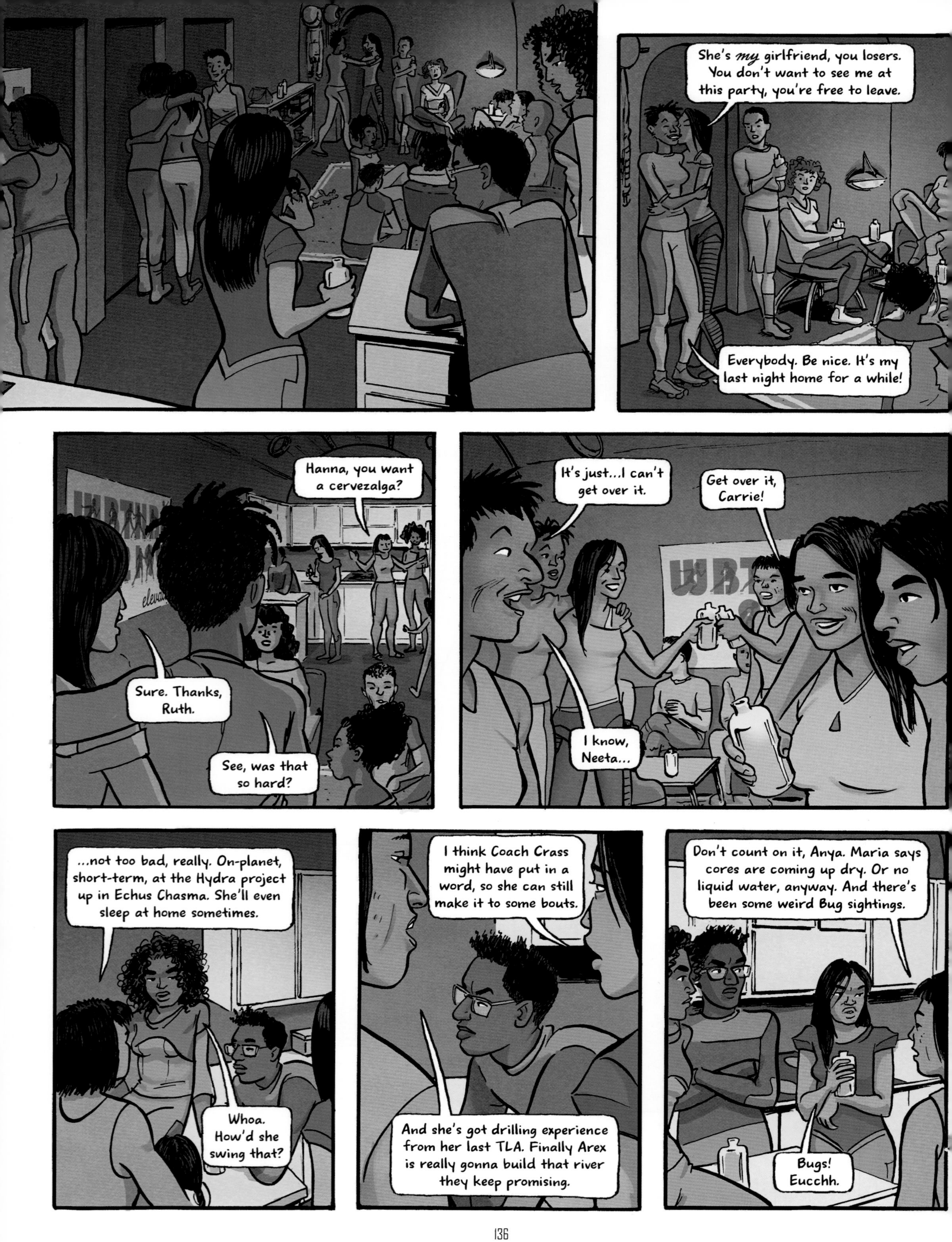
She's *my* girlfriend, you losers. You don't want to see me at this party, you're free to leave.
Everybody. Be nice. It's my last night home for a while!
Hanna, you want a cervezalga?
Sure. Thanks, Ruth.
See, was that so hard?
It's just...I can't get over it.
Get over it, Carrie!
I know, Neeta...
...not too bad, really. On-planet, short-term, at the Hydra project up in Echus Chasma. She'll even sleep at home sometimes.
Whoa. How'd she swing that?
I think Coach Crass might have put in a word, so she can still make it to some bouts.
And she's got drilling experience from her last TLA. Finally Arex is really gonna build that river they keep promising.
Don't count on it, Anya. Maria says cores are coming up dry. Or no liquid water, anyway. And there's been some weird Bug sightings.
Bugs! Eucchh.

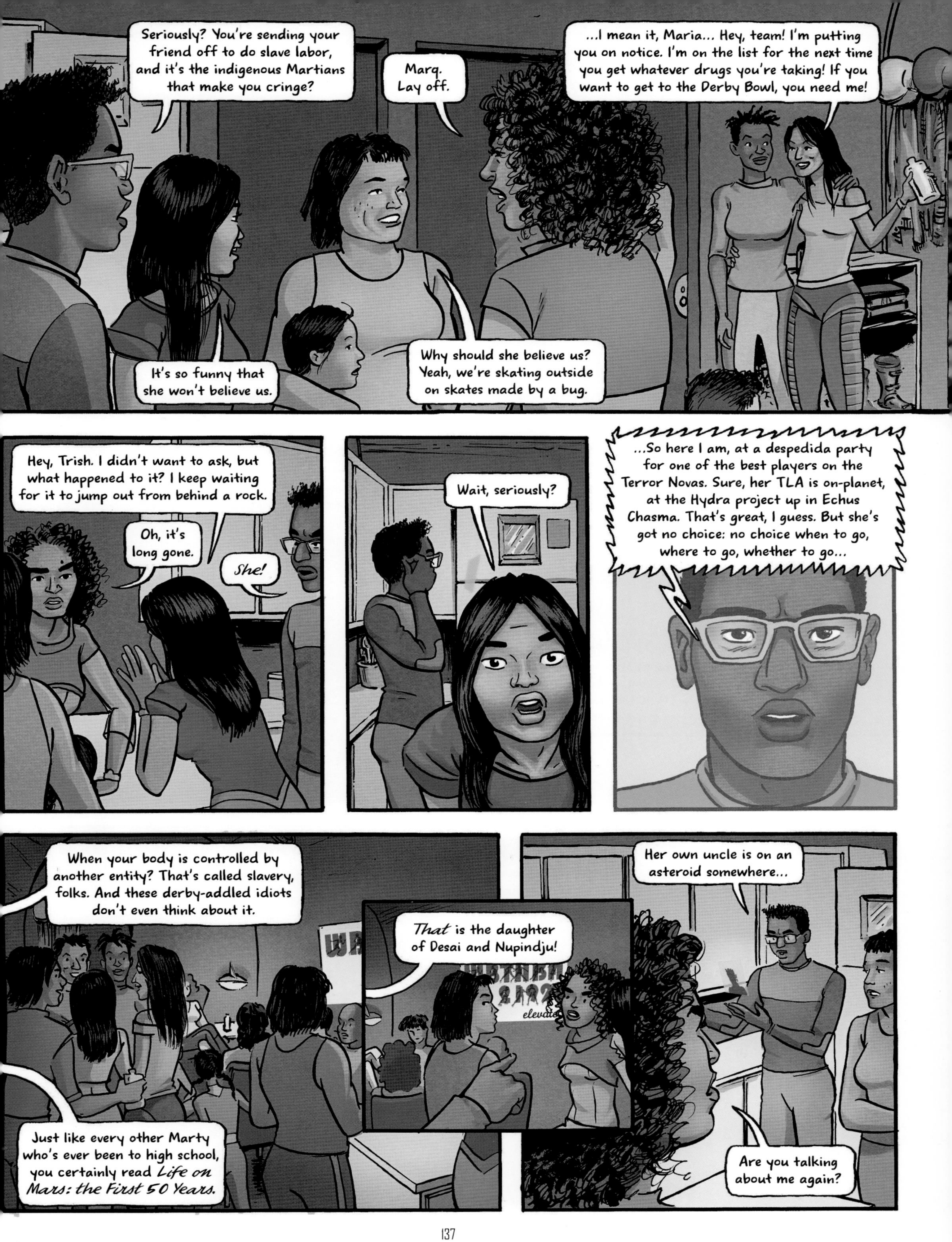

Seriously? You're sending your friend off to do slave labor, and it's the indigenous Martians that make you cringe?
Marq. Lay off.
...I mean it, Maria... Hey, team! I'm putting you on notice. I'm on the list for the next time you get whatever drugs you're taking! If you want to get to the Derby Bowl, you need me!
It's so funny that she won't believe us.
Why should she believe us? Yeah, we're skating outside on skates made by a bug.
Hey, Trish. I didn't want to ask, but what happened to it? I keep waiting for it to jump out from behind a rock.
Oh, it's long gone.
She!
Wait, seriously?
...So here I am, at a despedida party for one of the best players on the Terror Novas. Sure, her TLA is on-planet, at the Hydra project up in Echus Chasma. That's great, I guess. But she's got no choice: no choice when to go, where to go, whether to go...
When your body is controlled by another entity? That's called slavery, folks. And these derby-addled idiots don't even think about it.
Just like every other Marty who's ever been to high school, you certainly read *Life on Mars: the First 50 Years.*
That is the daughter of Desai and Nupindju!
Her own uncle is on an asteroid somewhere...
Are you talking about me again?

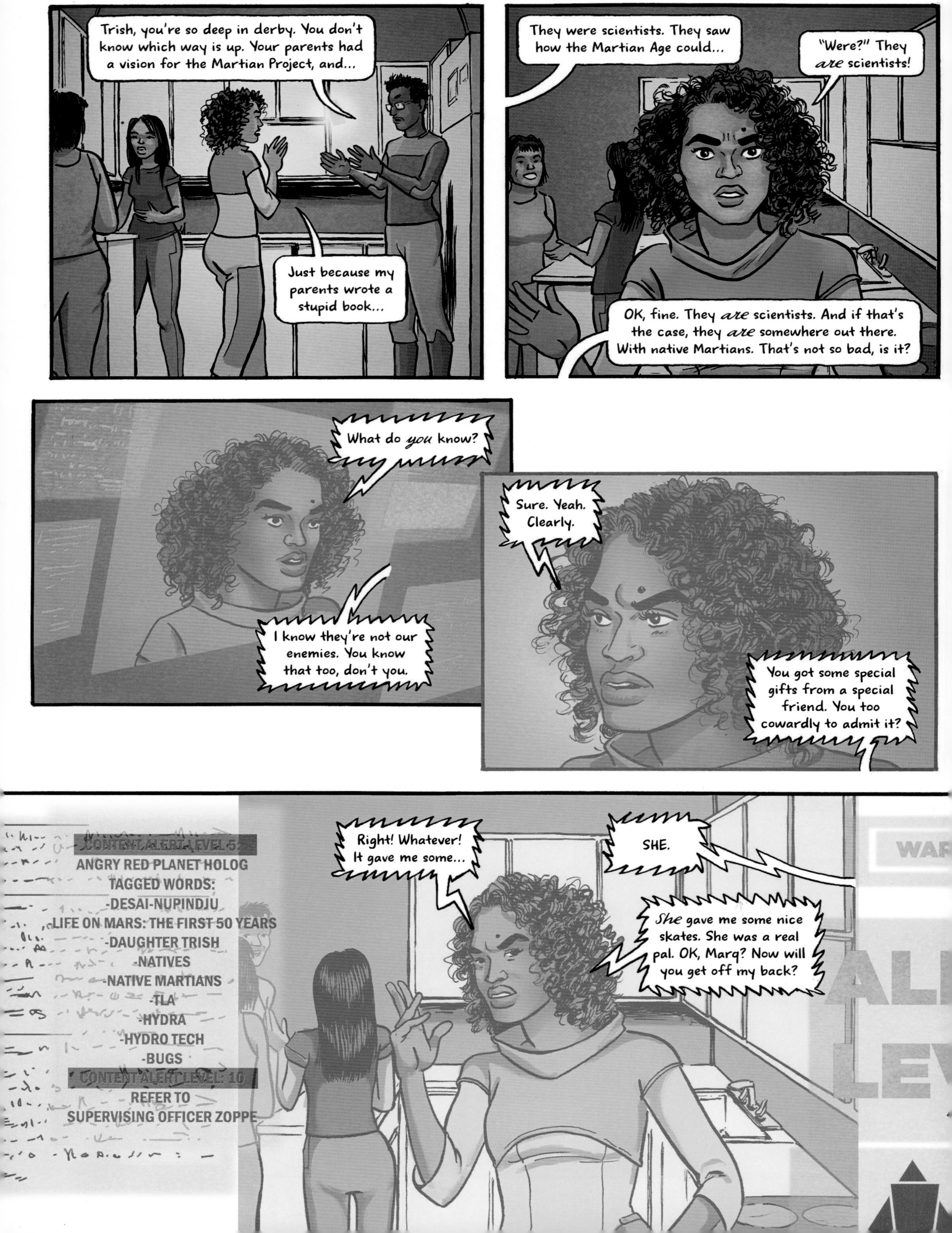

Trish, you're so deep in derby. You don't know which way is up. Your parents had a vision for the Martian Project, and...
Just because my parents wrote a stupid book...
They were scientists. They saw how the Martian Age could...
"Were?" They *are* scientists!
OK, fine. They *are* scientists. And if that's the case, they *are* somewhere out there. With native Martians. That's not so bad, is it?
What do *you* know?
I know they're not our enemies. You know that too, don't you.
Sure. Yeah. Clearly.
You got some special gifts from a special friend. You too cowardly to admit it?
CONTENT ALERT LEVEL 5:
ANGRY RED PLANET HOLOG
TAGGED WORDS:
-DESAI-NUPINDJU
-LIFE ON MARS: THE FIRST 50 YEARS
-DAUGHTER TRISH
-NATIVES
-NATIVE MARTIANS
-TLA
-HYDRA
-HYDRO TECH
-BUGS
CONTENT ALERT LEVEL: 10
REFER TO
SUPERVISING OFFICER ZOPPE
Right! Whatever! It gave me some...
SHE.
She gave me some nice skates. She was a real pal. OK, Marq? Now will you get off my back?

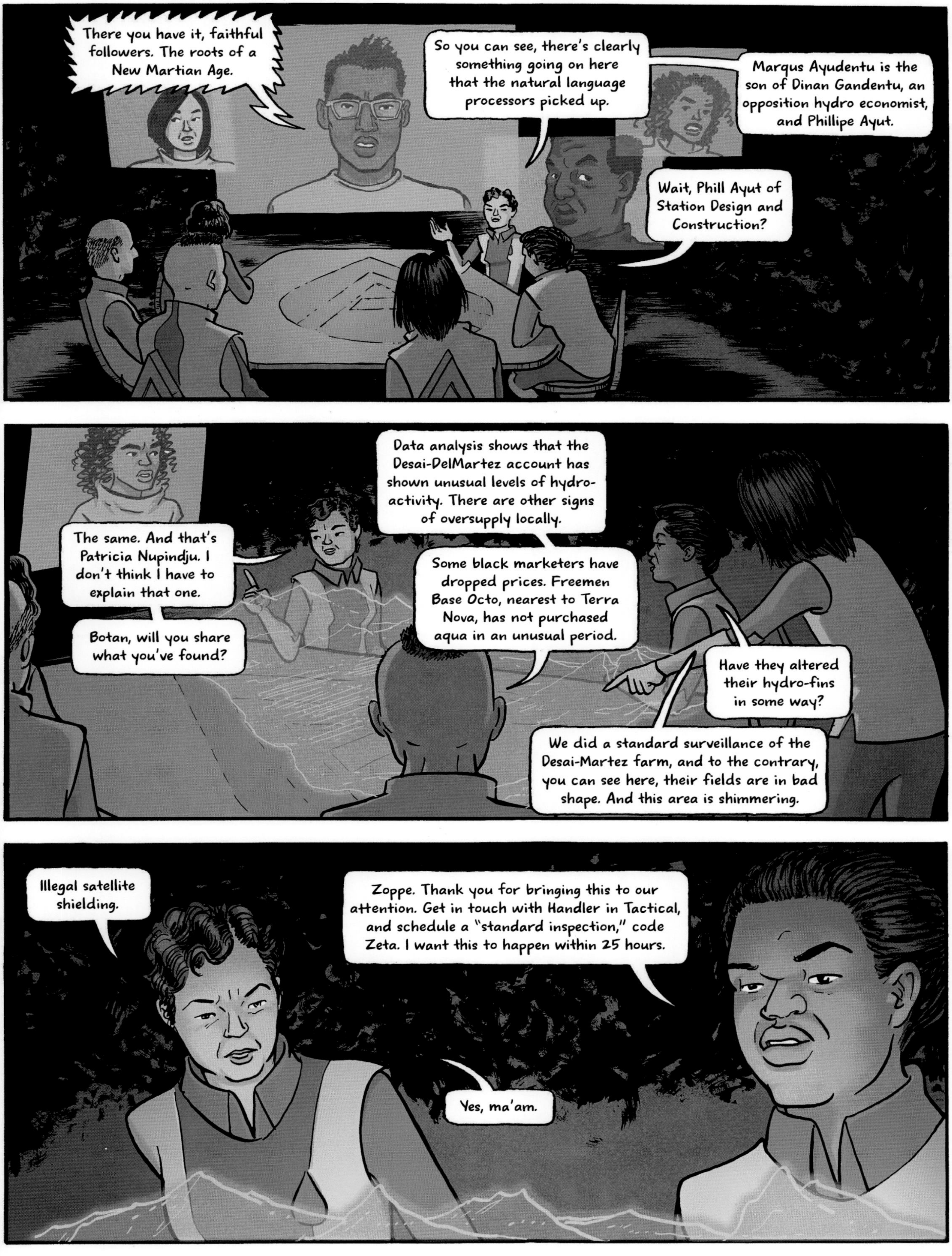
There you have it, faithful followers. The roots of a New Martian Age.
So you can see, there's clearly something going on here that the natural language processors picked up.
Marqus Ayudentu is the son of Dinan Gandentu, an opposition hydro economist, and Phillipe Ayut.
Wait, Phill Ayut of Station Design and Construction?
The same. And that's Patricia Nupindju. I don't think I have to explain that one.
Botan, will you share what you've found?
Data analysis shows that the Desai-DelMartez account has shown unusual levels of hydro-activity. There are other signs of oversupply locally.
Some black marketers have dropped prices. Freemen Base Octo, nearest to Terra Nova, has not purchased aqua in an unusual period.
Have they altered their hydro-fins in some way?
We did a standard surveillance of the Desai-Martez farm, and to the contrary, you can see here, their fields are in bad shape. And this area is shimmering.
Illegal satellite shielding.
Zoppe. Thank you for bringing this to our attention. Get in touch with Handler in Tactical, and schedule a "standard inspection," code Zeta. I want this to happen within 25 hours.
Yes, ma'am.

...As previously established, the lichens in their natural state are genetic clones. Which is interesting. Clearly, the way we hand-propagate, those nodes are clones; they're broken out of the same organism.

But why should the original field be genetic identicals, if they are naturally occurring? It's possible that there was one individual that eventually populated the site, or...

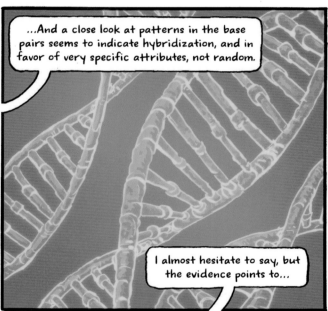

...And a close look at patterns in the base pairs seems to indicate hybridization, and in favor of very specific attributes, not random.

I almost hesitate to say, but the evidence points to...

BUZZZZZZZ

Grot! Arex?!

Lab secured.

WHUMP!

Can I help you?

I am supervisor Nicolette Zoppe. We are here to conduct a standard spot inspection of the premises and Arex-leased equipment.

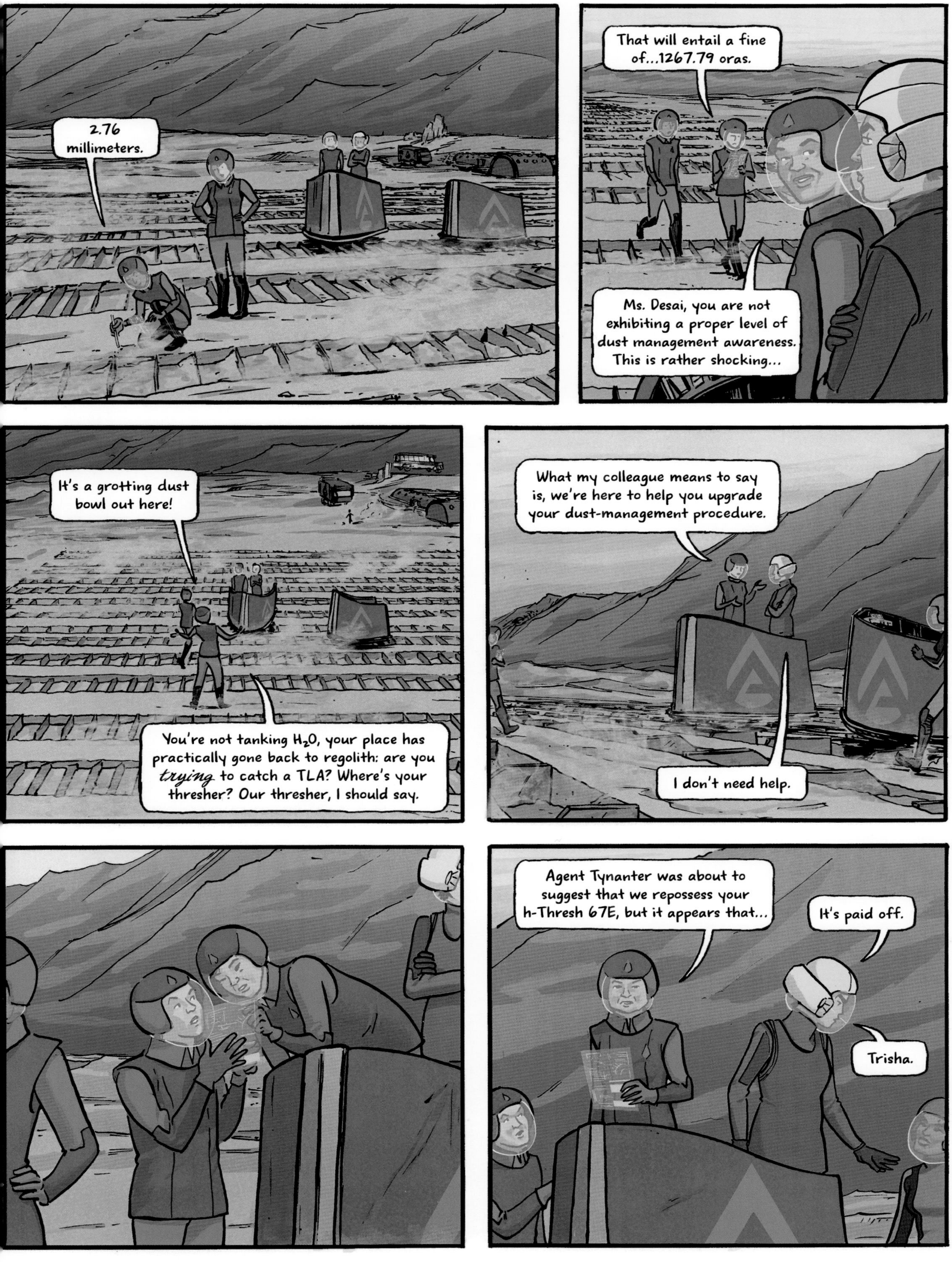
2.76 millimeters.
That will entail a fine of...1267.79 oras.
Ms. Desai, you are not exhibiting a proper level of dust management awareness. This is rather shocking...
It's a grotting dust bowl out here!
You're not tanking H_2O, your place has practically gone back to regolith: are you *trying* to catch a TLA? Where's your thresher? Our thresher, I should say.
What my colleague means to say is, we're here to help you upgrade your dust-management procedure.
I don't need help.
Agent Tynanter was about to suggest that we repossess your h-Thresh 67E, but it appears that...
It's paid off.
Trisha.

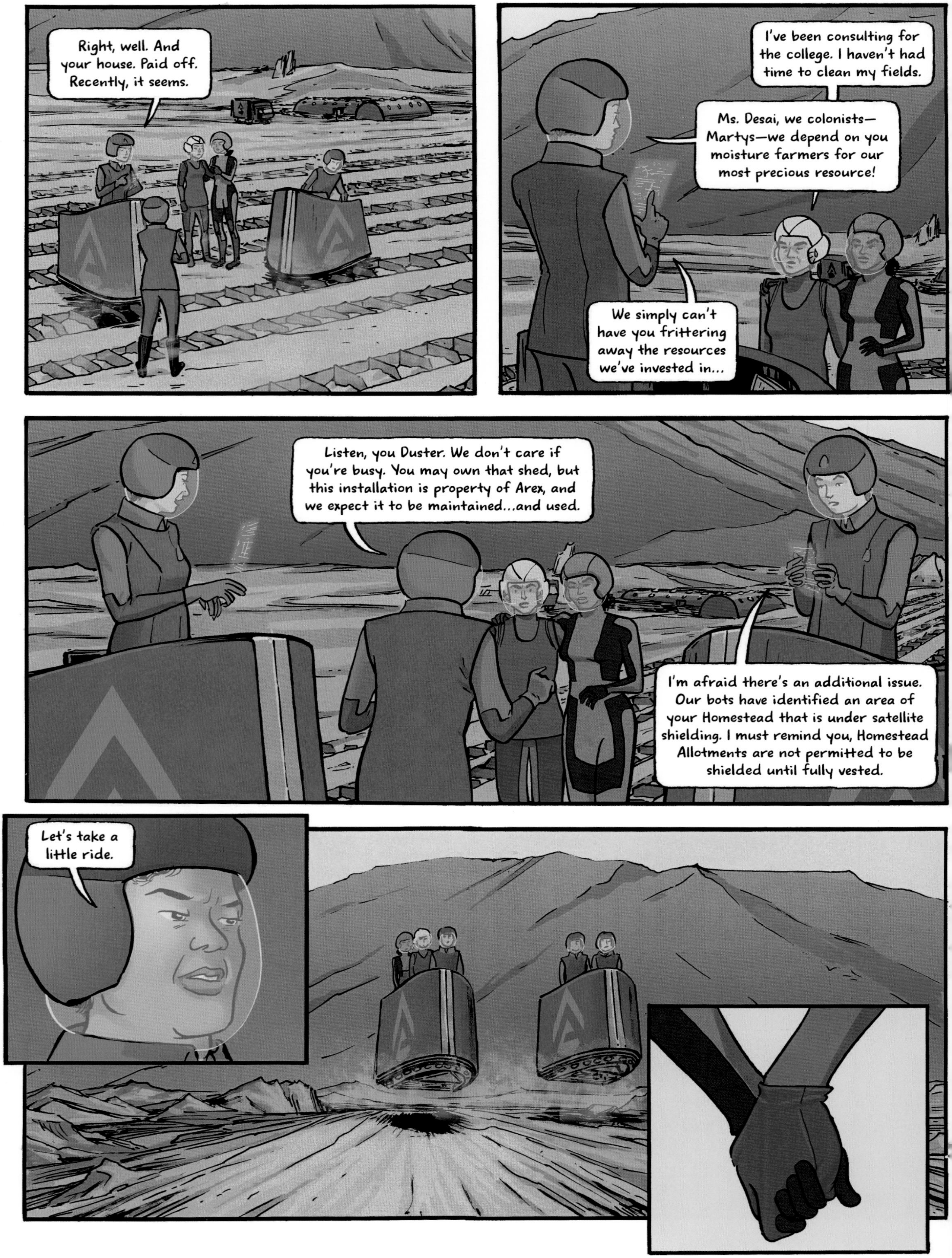

Right, well. And your house. Paid off. Recently, it seems.
I've been consulting for the college. I haven't had time to clean my fields.
Ms. Desai, we colonists—Martys—we depend on you moisture farmers for our most precious resource!
We simply can't have you frittering away the resources we've invested in...
Listen, you Duster. We don't care if you're busy. You may own that shed, but this installation is property of Arex, and we expect it to be maintained...and used.
I'm afraid there's an additional issue. Our bots have identified an area of your Homestead that is under satellite shielding. I must remind you, Homestead Allotments are not permitted to be shielded until fully vested.
Let's take a little ride.

This is the location. Over that lip.

The grotting skimmers won't mount that!

We'll walk.

What the clud? Is this some kind of a joke?

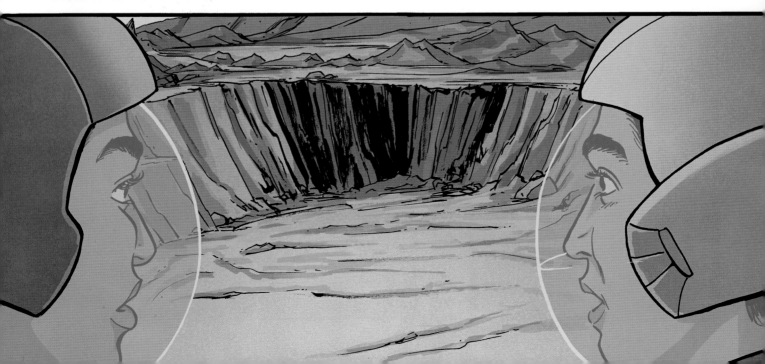

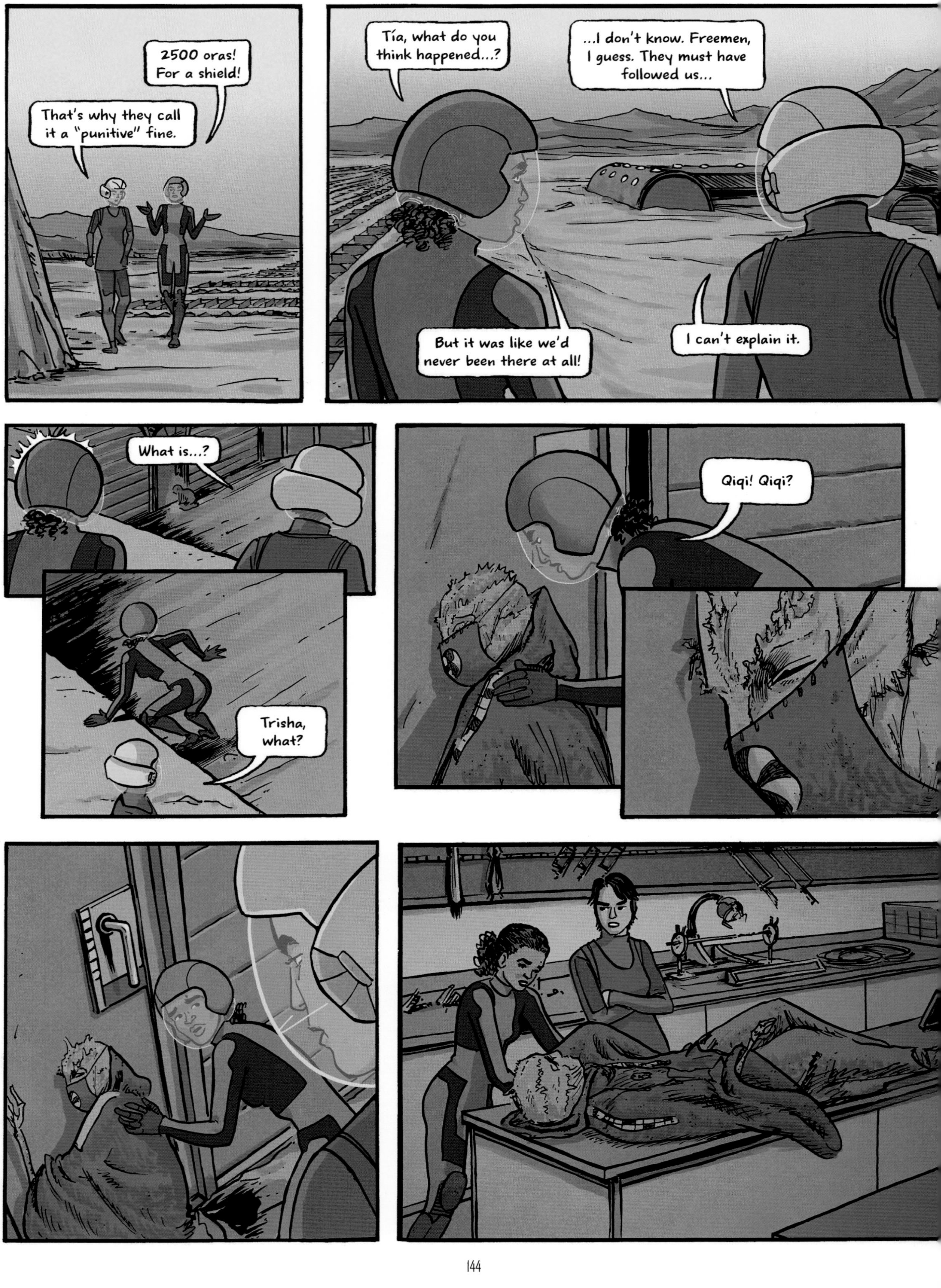
2500 oras! For a shield!
That's why they call it a "punitive" fine.
Tía, what do you think happened...?
...I don't know. Freemen, I guess. They must have followed us...
But it was like we'd never been there at all!
I can't explain it.
What is...?
Trisha, what?
Qiqi! Qiqi?

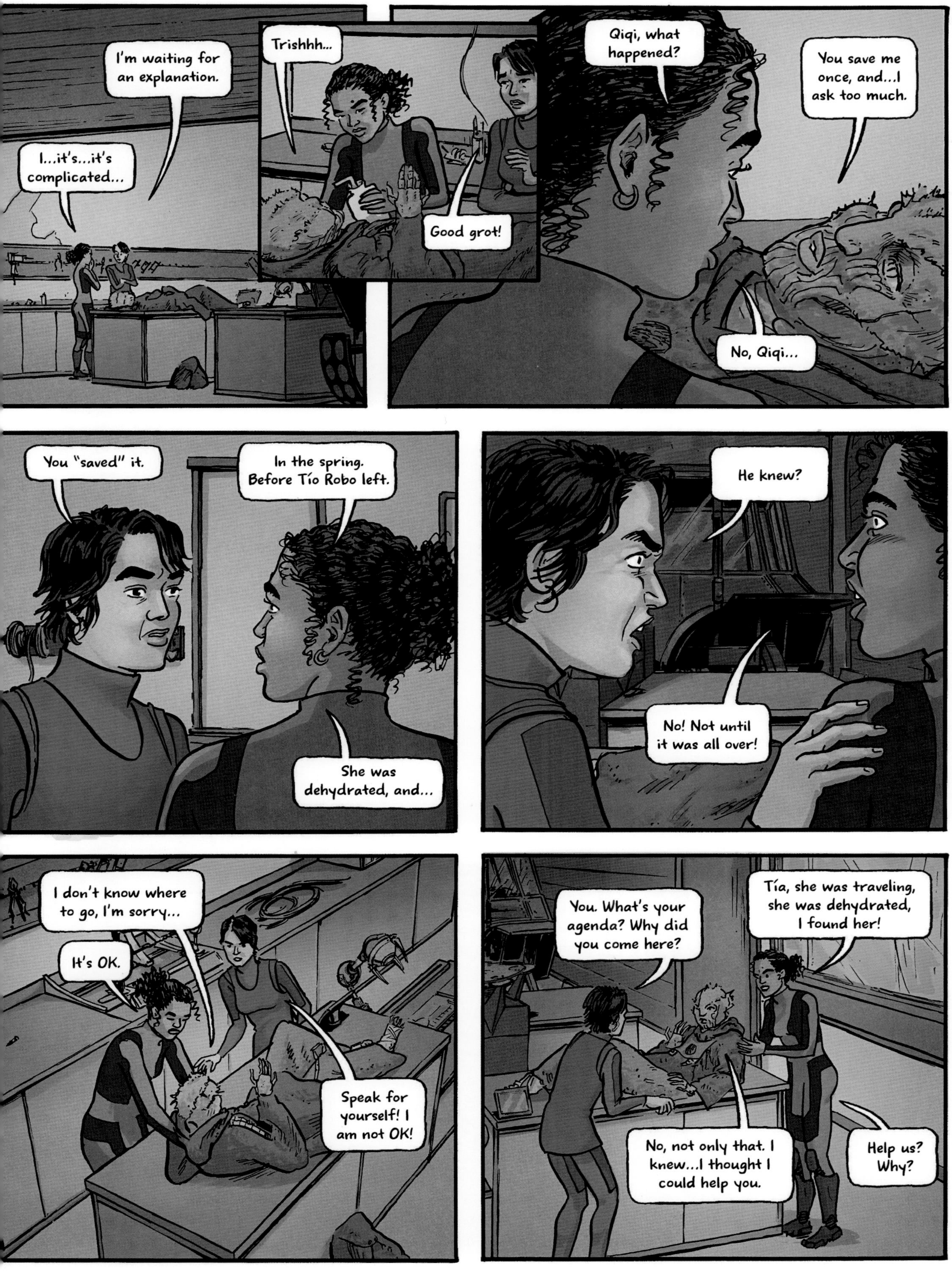
I'm waiting for an explanation.
I...it's...it's complicated...
Trishhh...
Good grot!
Qiqi, what happened?
You save me once, and...I ask too much.
No, Qiqi...
You "saved" it.
In the spring. Before Tío Robo left.
She was dehydrated, and...
He knew?
No! Not until it was all over!
I don't know where to go, I'm sorry...
It's OK.
Speak for yourself! I am not OK!
You. What's your agenda? Why did you come here?
Tía, she was traveling, she was dehydrated, I found her!
No, not only that. I knew...I thought I could help you.
Help us? Why?

I wanted to tell you but it wasn't safe. I bring lich-khen because I know you need water. I know from...

You brought the... that explains their hybridized DNA...

Roberto knew?

He told me not to say, that you'd be freaked out...

Your parents...

Right, exactly, because...

Hell yes, I'm freaked out! You and Roberto have been hiding this...

Now my people cast me out. They discover that I give lich-khen. They say I am malformed.

Wait, what?

I am...not like-kt them. No one tells me to do, I *decide* for me. I have...ideazz. I am born wrong.

Your people don't make decisions?

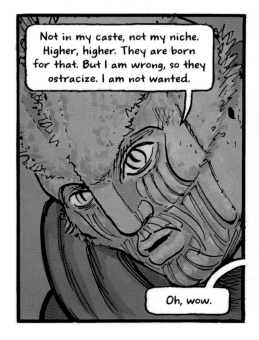

Not in my caste, not my niche. Higher, higher. They are born for that. But I am wrong, so they ostracize. I am not wanted.

Oh, wow.

...And now, I do not-tk know where to go. My clan drop me here, take lich-khen from field...

Take lichen? You mean they took the nodes?

They clean the land.

146

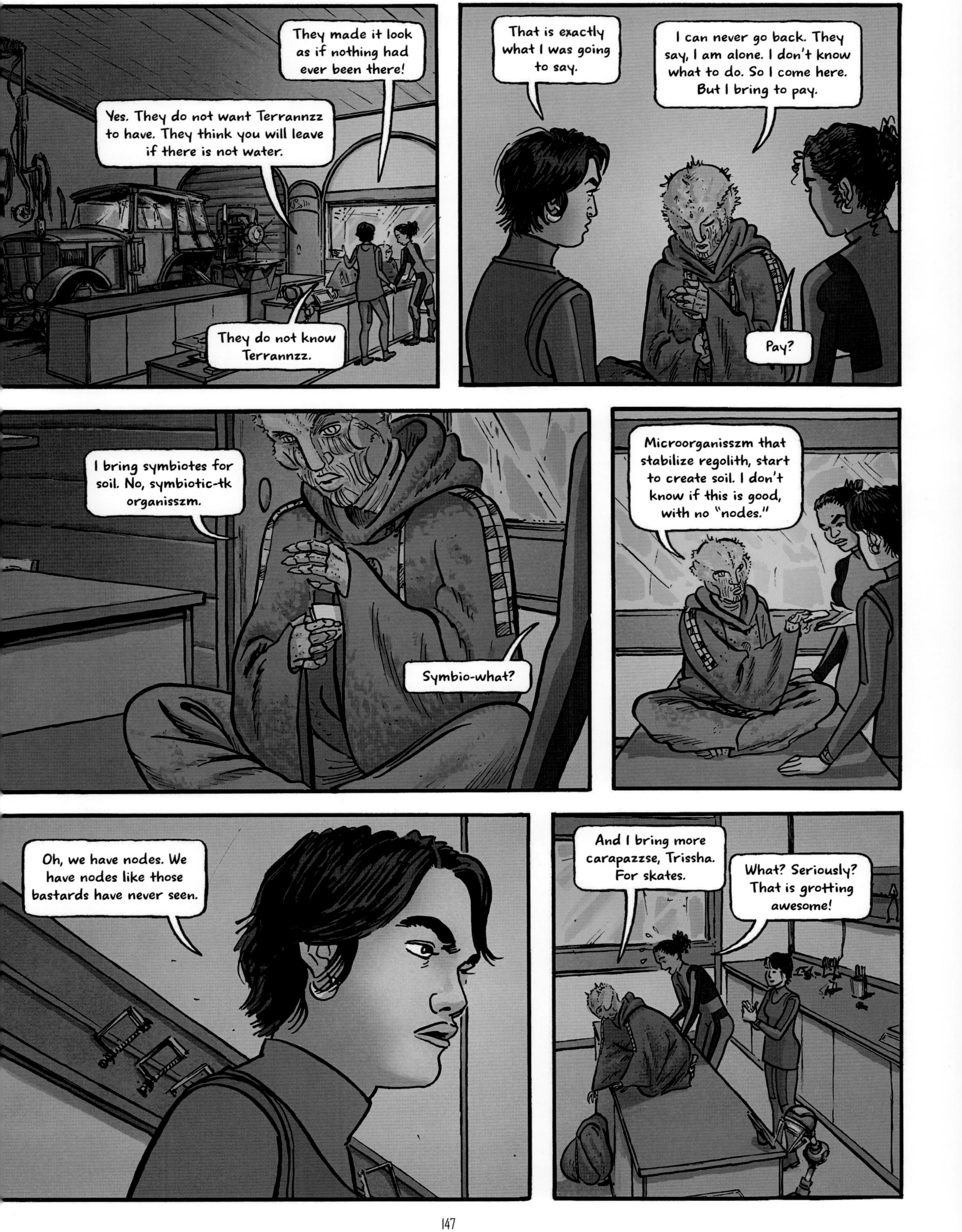
They made it look as if nothing had ever been there!
Yes. They do not want Terrannzz to have. They think you will leave if there is not water.
They do not know Terrannzz.
That is exactly what I was going to say.
I can never go back. They say, I am alone. I don't know what to do. So I come here. But I bring to pay.
Pay?
I bring symbiotes for soil. No, symbiotic-tk organisszm.
Symbio-what?
Microorganisszm that stabilize regolith, start to create soil. I don't know if this is good, with no "nodes."
Oh, we have nodes. We have nodes like those bastards have never seen.
And I bring more carapazzse, Trissha. For skates.
What? Seriously? That is grotting awesome!

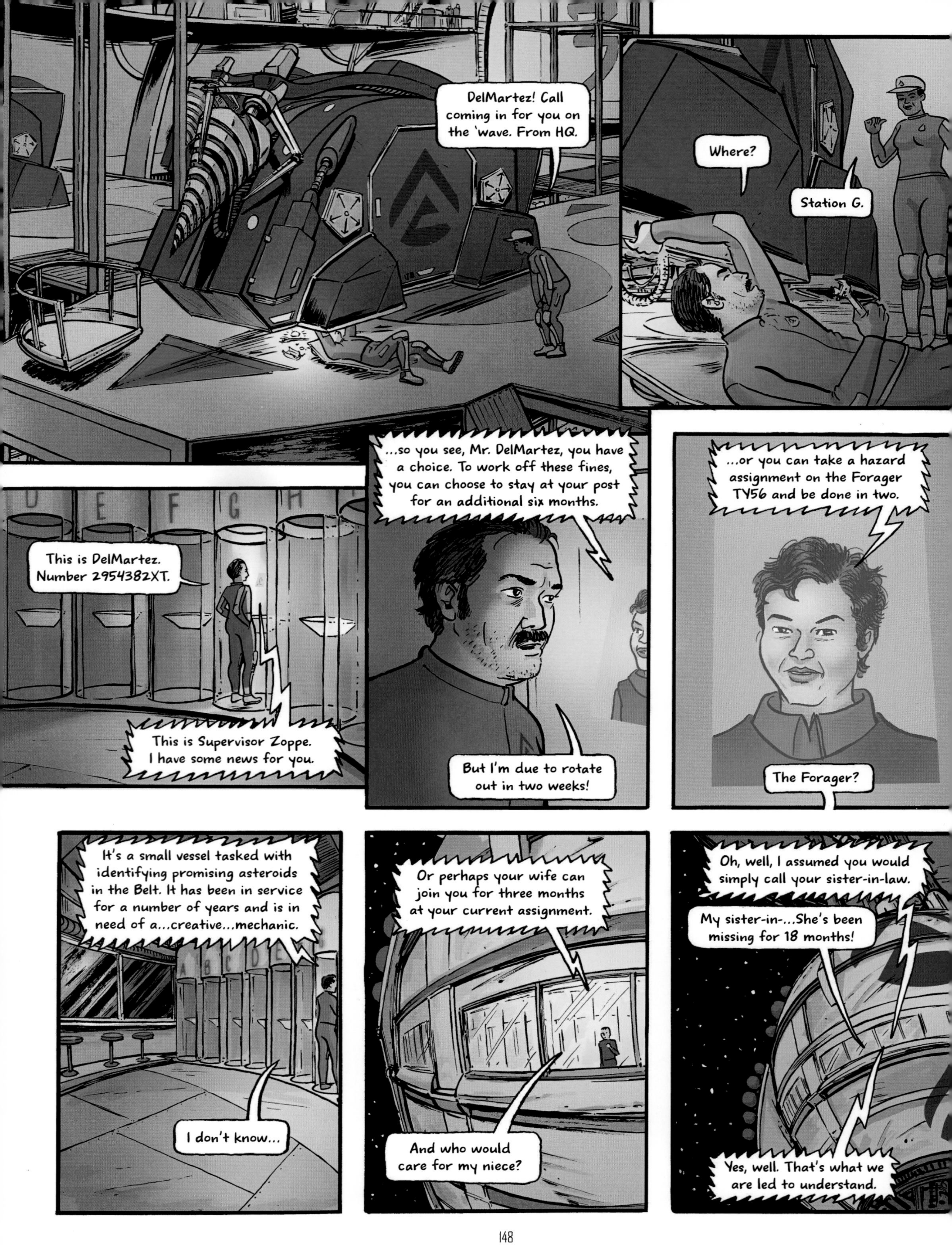
DelMartez! Call coming in for you on the 'wave. From HQ.
Where?
Station G.
This is DelMartez. Number 2954382XT.
This is Supervisor Zoppe. I have some news for you.
...so you see, Mr. DelMartez, you have a choice. To work off these fines, you can choose to stay at your post for an additional six months.
But I'm due to rotate out in two weeks!
...or you can take a hazard assignment on the Forager TY56 and be done in two.
The Forager?
It's a small vessel tasked with identifying promising asteroids in the Belt. It has been in service for a number of years and is in need of a...creative...mechanic.
I don't know...
Or perhaps your wife can join you for three months at your current assignment.
And who would care for my niece?
Oh, well, I assumed you would simply call your sister-in-law.
My sister-in-...She's been missing for 18 months!
Yes, well. That's what we are led to understand.

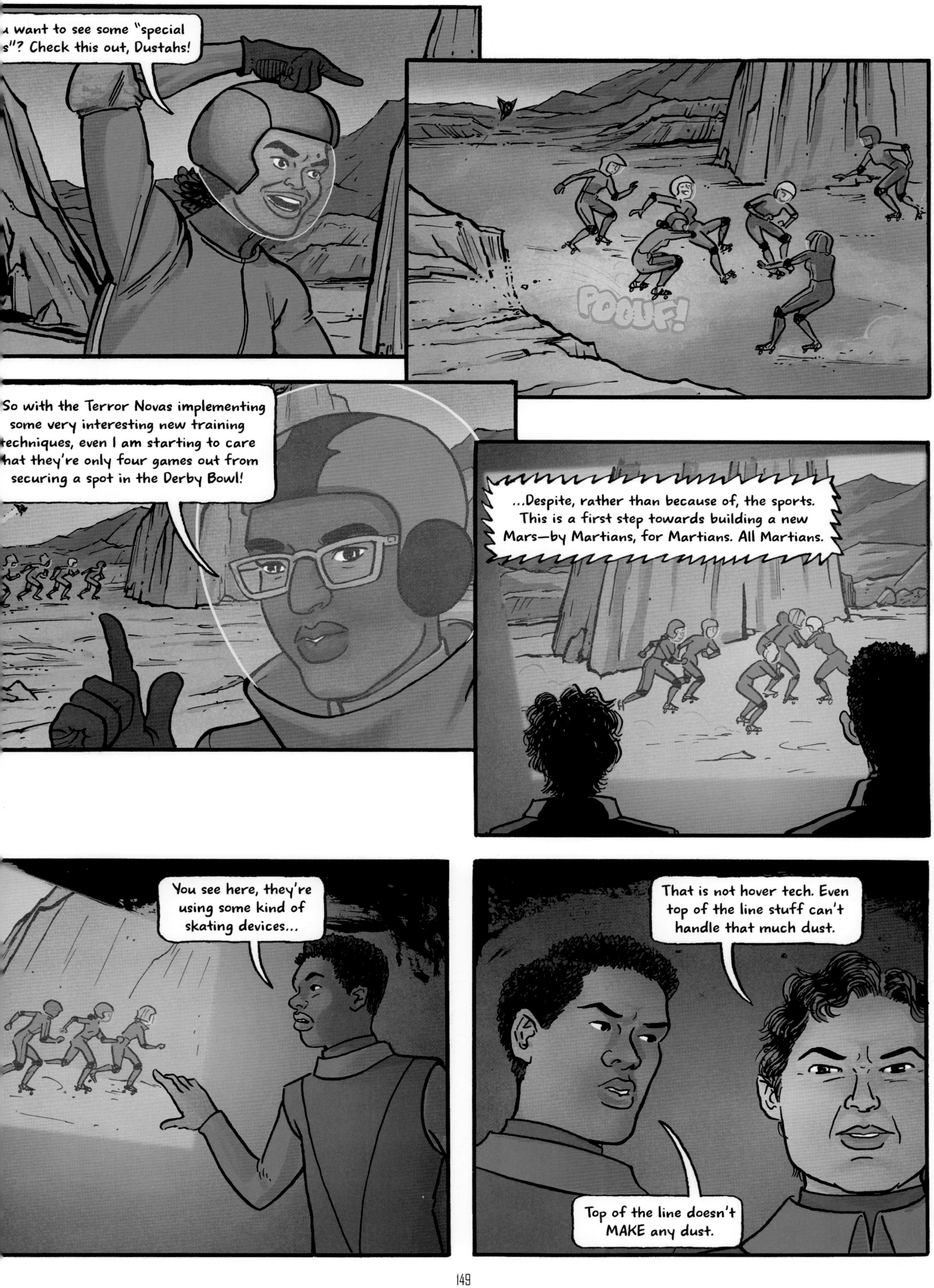
u want to see some "special s"? Check this out, Dustahs!
FOOUF!
So with the Terror Novas implementing some very interesting new training techniques, even I am starting to care hat they're only four games out from securing a spot in the Derby Bowl!
...Despite, rather than because of, the sports. This is a first step towards building a new Mars—by Martians, for Martians. All Martians.
You see here, they're using some kind of skating devices...
That is not hover tech. Even top of the line stuff can't handle that much dust.
Top of the line doesn't MAKE any dust.

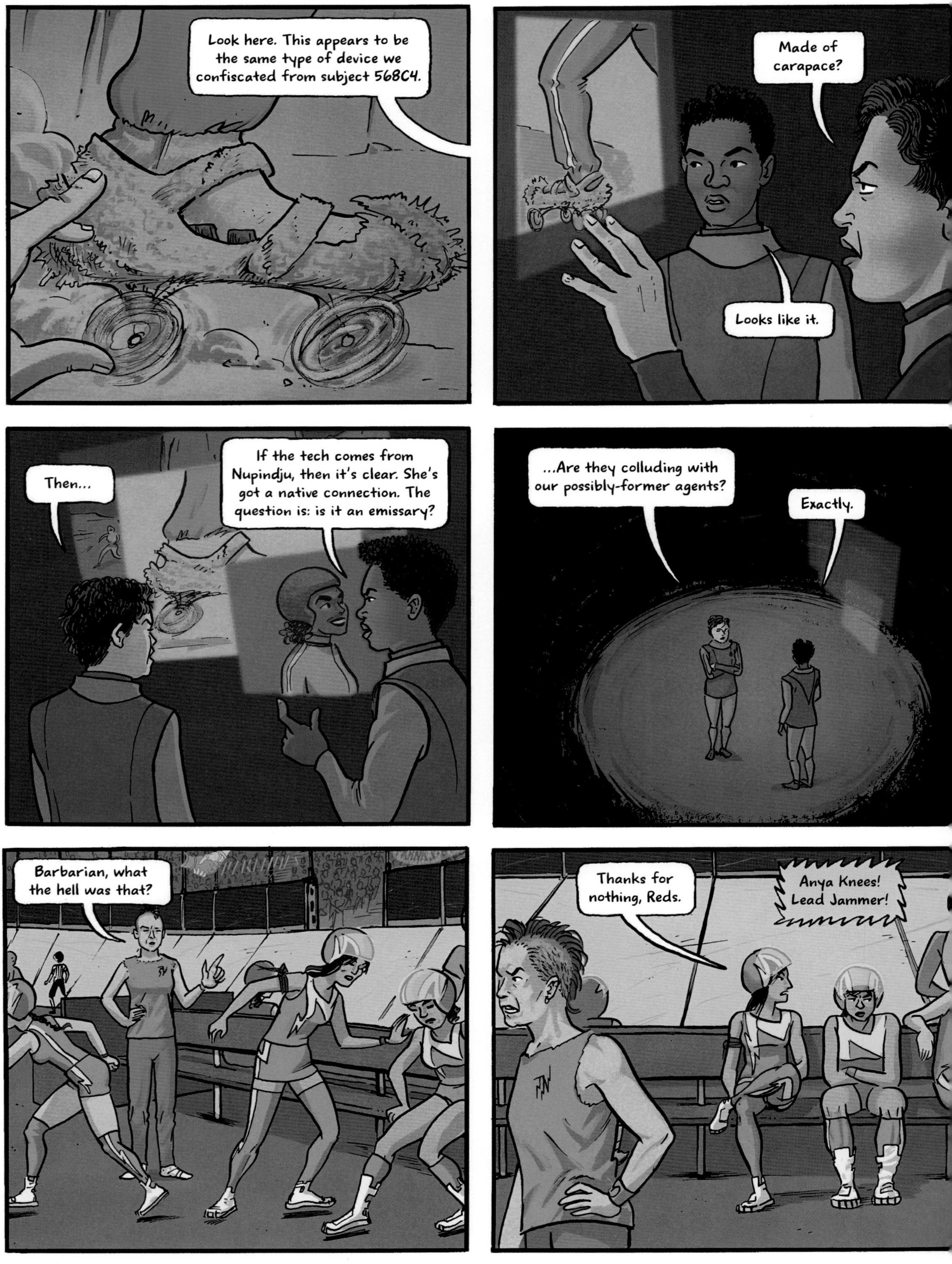
Look here. This appears to be the same type of device we confiscated from subject 568C4.
Made of carapace?
Looks like it.
Then...
If the tech comes from Nupindju, then it's clear. She's got a native connection. The question is: is it an emissary?
...Are they colluding with our possibly-former agents?
Exactly.
Barbarian, what the hell was that?
Thanks for nothing, Reds.
Anya Knees! Lead Jammer!

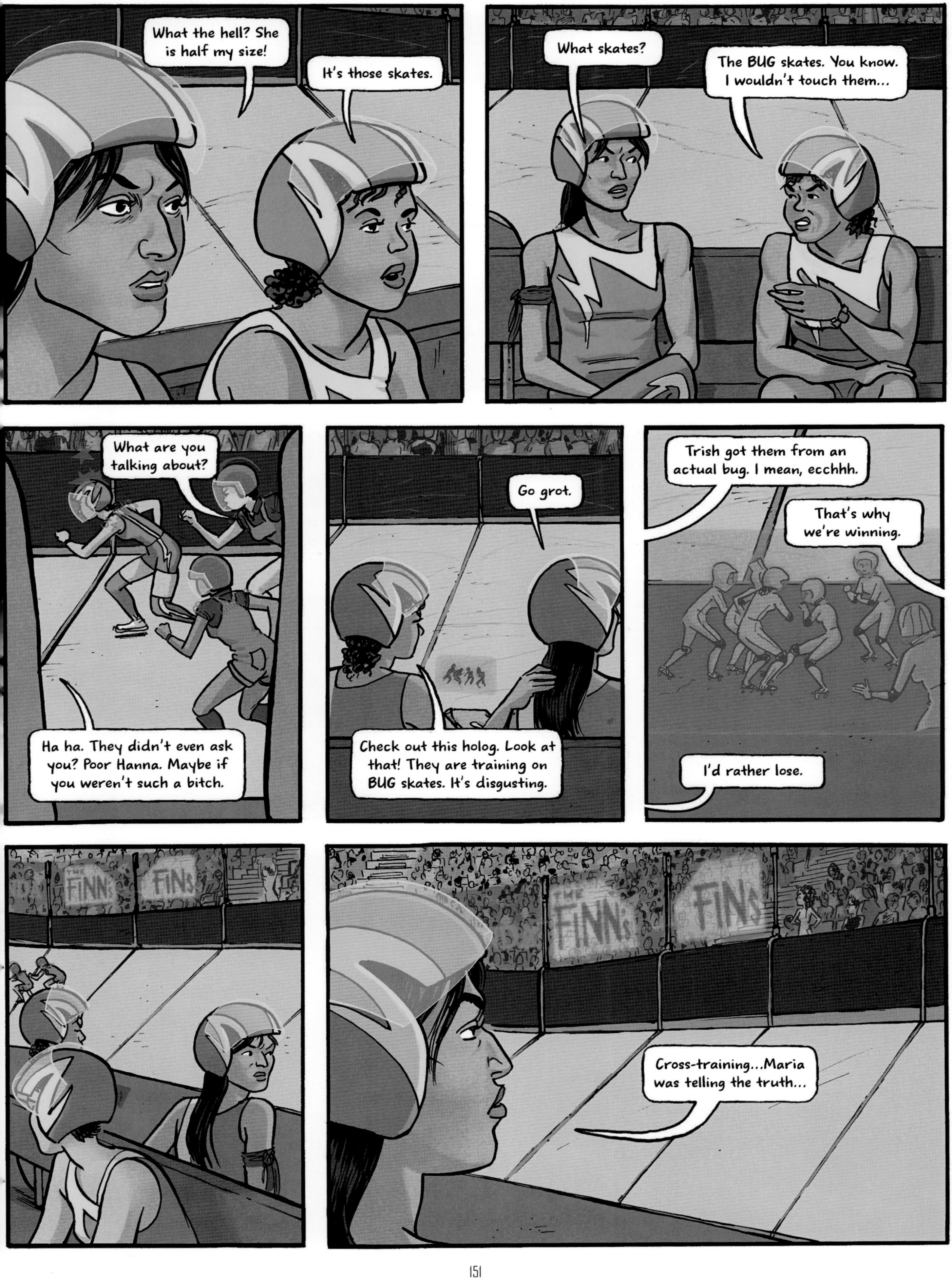
What the hell? She is half my size!
It's those skates.
What skates?
The BUG skates. You know. I wouldn't touch them...
What are you talking about?
Ha ha. They didn't even ask you? Poor Hanna. Maybe if you weren't such a bitch.
Go grot.
Check out this holog. Look at that! They are training on BUG skates. It's disgusting.
Trish got them from an actual bug. I mean, ecchhh.
That's why we're winning.
I'd rather lose.
THE FINNs
FINs
THE FINNs
FINs
Cross-training...Maria was telling the truth...

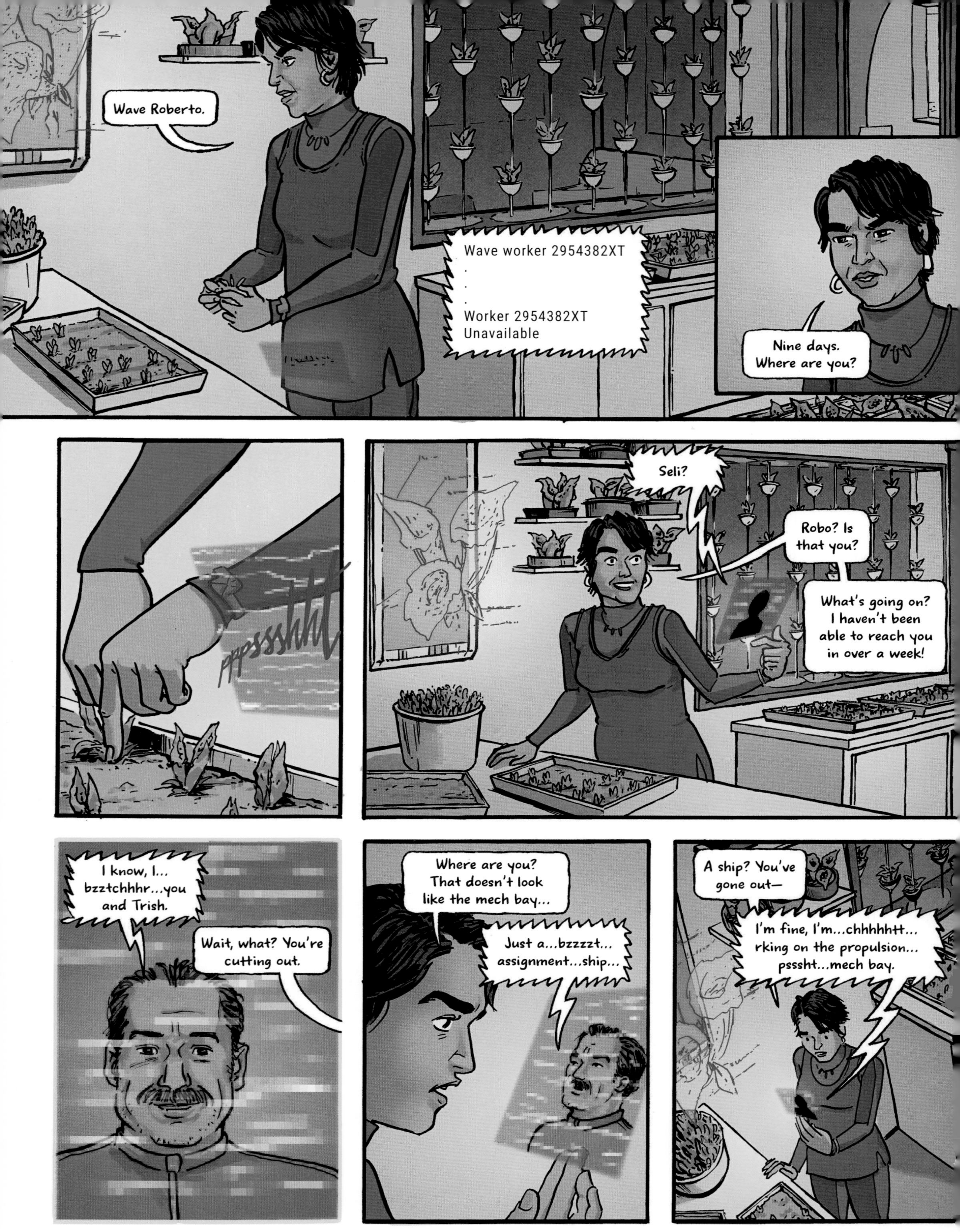
Wave Roberto.
Wave worker 2954382XT
.
.
.
Worker 2954382XT
Unavailable
Nine days. Where are you?
pppsssshht
Seli?
Robo? Is that you?
What's going on? I haven't been able to reach you in over a week!
I know, I... bzztchhhr...you and Trish.
Wait, what? You're cutting out.
Where are you? That doesn't look like the mech bay...
Just a...bzzzzt... assignment...ship...
A ship? You've gone out—
I'm fine, I'm...chhhhhtt... rking on the propulsion... psssht...mech bay.

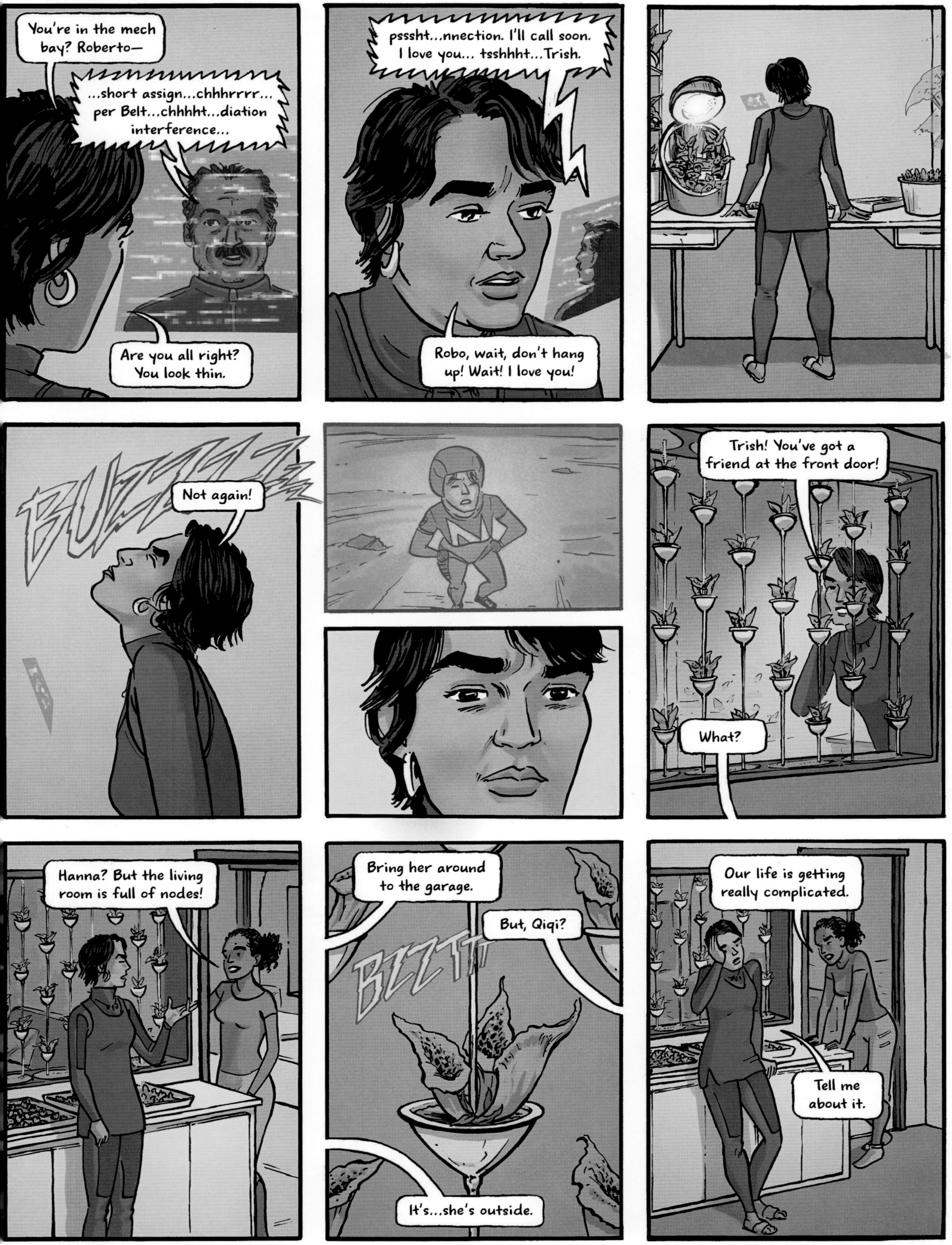
You're in the mech bay? Roberto—
...short assign...chhhrrrr... per Belt...chhhht...diation interference...
Are you all right? You look thin.
pssssht...nnection. I'll call soon. I love you... tsshhht...Trish.
Robo, wait, don't hang up! Wait! I love you!
BUZZZZZ
Not again!
Trish! You've got a friend at the front door!
What?
Hanna? But the living room is full of nodes!
Bring her around to the garage.
But, Qiqi?
BZZTTT
It's...she's outside.
Our life is getting really complicated.
Tell me about it.

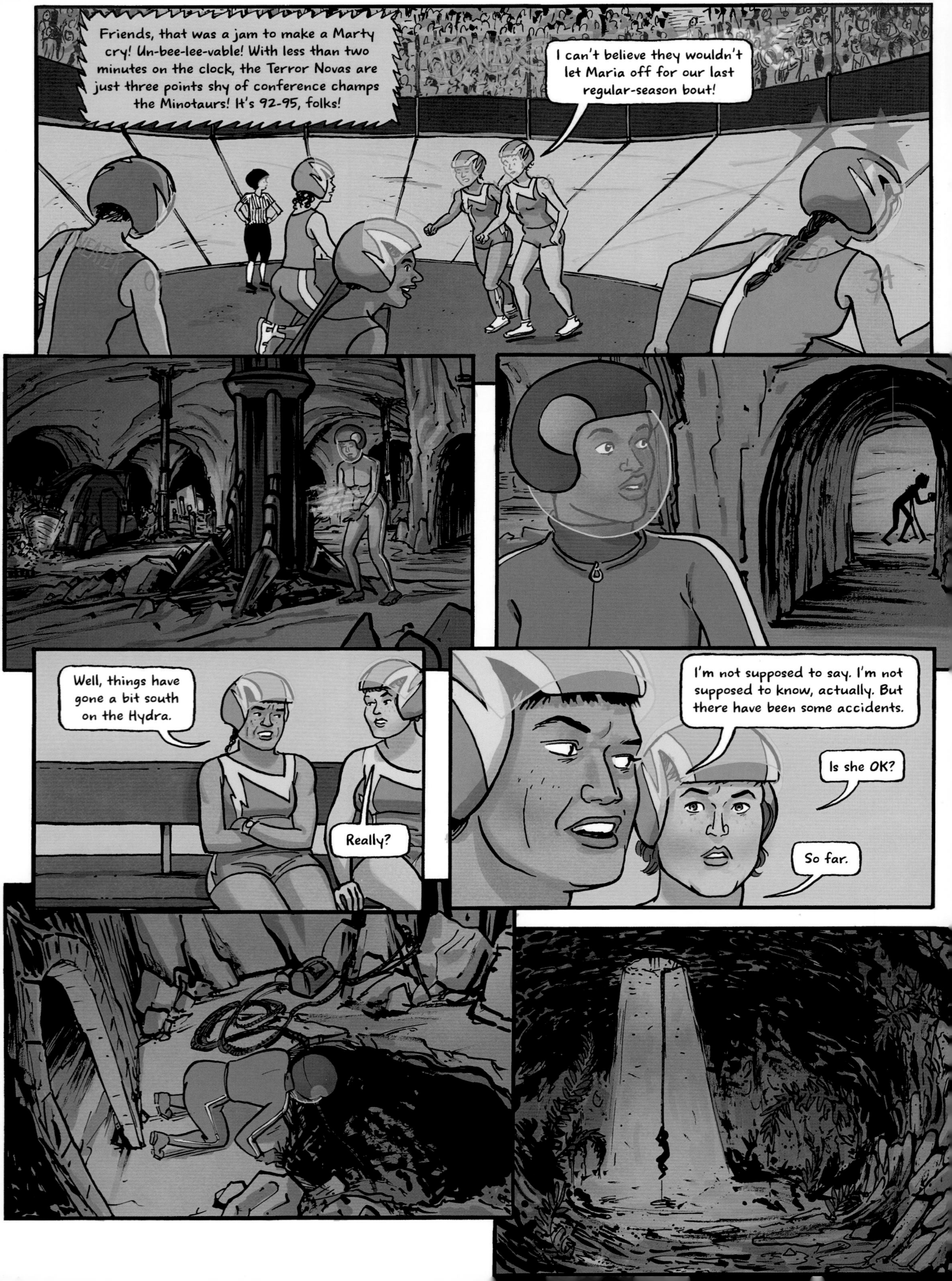

Friends, that was a jam to make a Marty cry! Un-bee-lee-vable! With less than two minutes on the clock, the Terror Novas are just three points shy of conference champs the Minotaurs! It's 92-95, folks!
I can't believe they wouldn't let Maria off for our last regular-season bout!
Well, things have gone a bit south on the Hydra.
Really?
I'm not supposed to say. I'm not supposed to know, actually. But there have been some accidents.
Is she OK?
So far.

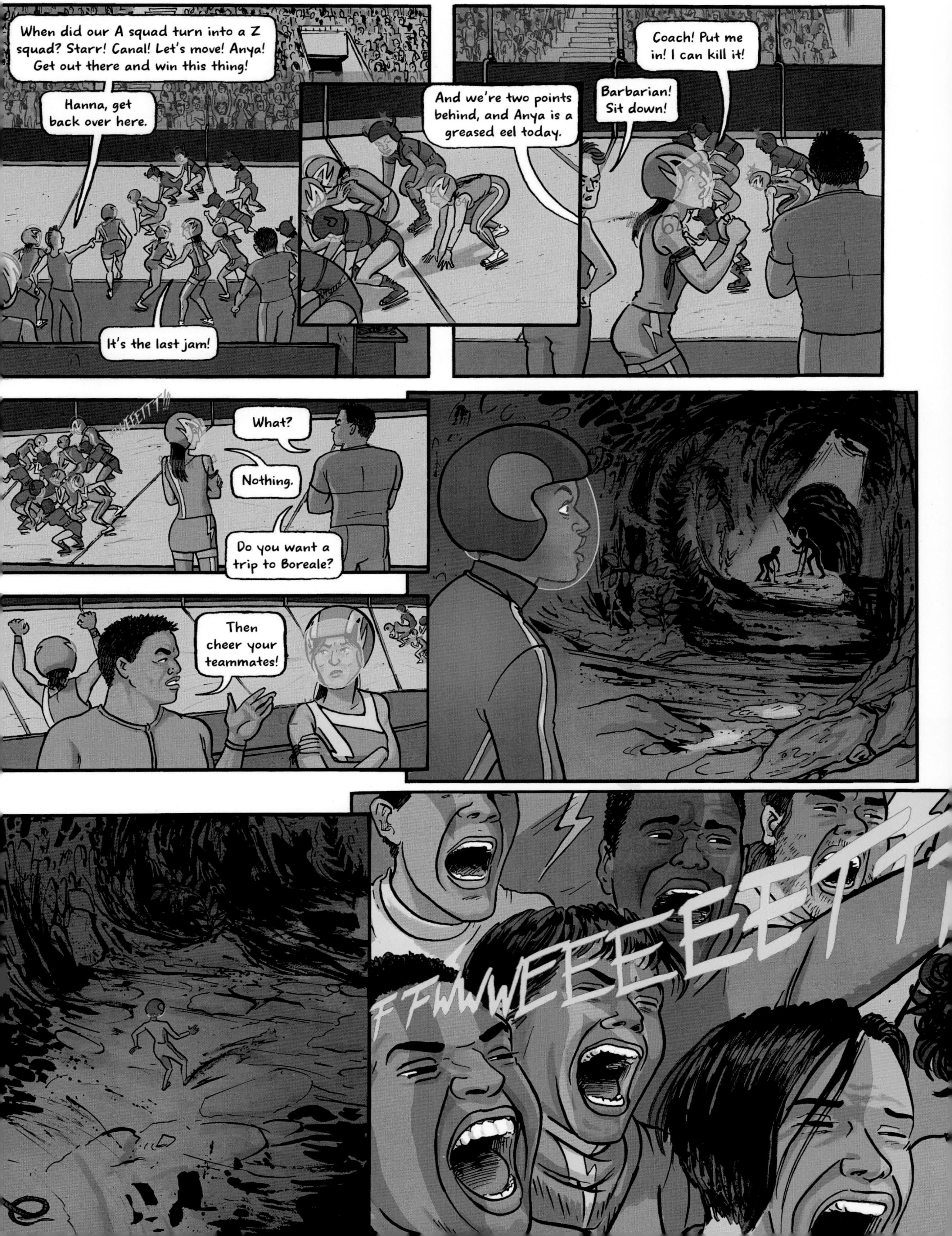
When did our A squad turn into a Z squad? Starr! Canal! Let's move! Anya! Get out there and win this thing!
Hanna, get back over here.
It's the last jam!
And we're two points behind, and Anya is a greased eel today.
Coach! Put me in! I can kill it!
Barbarian! Sit down!
What?
Nothing.
Do you want a trip to Boreale?
Then cheer your teammates!
FFWWWEEEEEETTT

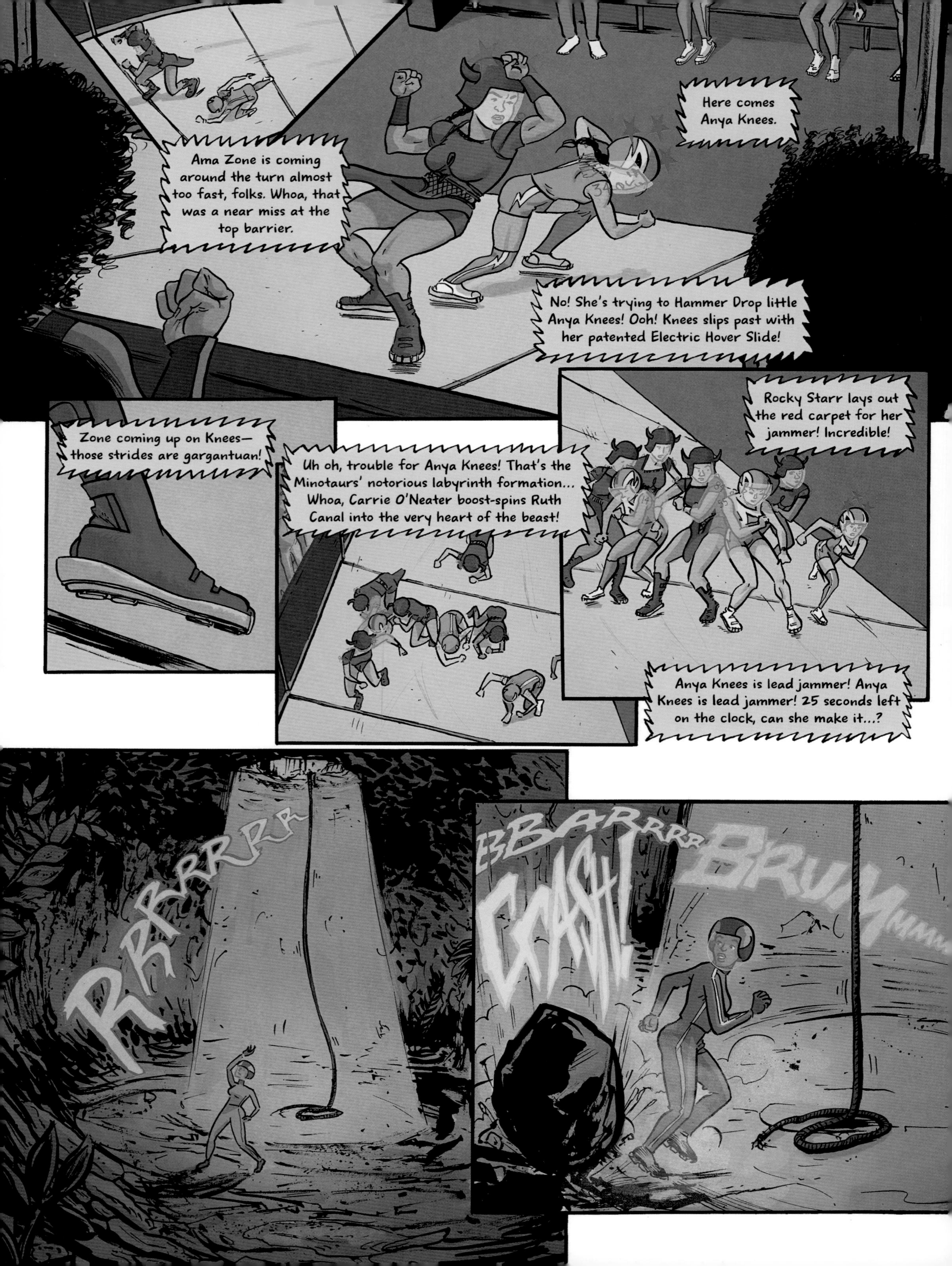
Here comes Anya Knees.
Ama Zone is coming around the turn almost too fast, folks. Whoa, that was a near miss at the top barrier.
No! She's trying to Hammer Drop little Anya Knees! Ooh! Knees slips past with her patented Electric Hover Slide!
Zone coming up on Knees—those strides are gargantuan!
Uh oh, trouble for Anya Knees! That's the Minotaurs' notorious labyrinth formation... Whoa, Carrie O'Neater boost-spins Ruth Canal into the very heart of the beast!
Rocky Starr lays out the red carpet for her jammer! Incredible!
Anya Knees is lead jammer! Anya Knees is lead jammer! 25 seconds left on the clock, can she make it...?
RRRRRRR
BARRRRR
CRASH!
BRUM

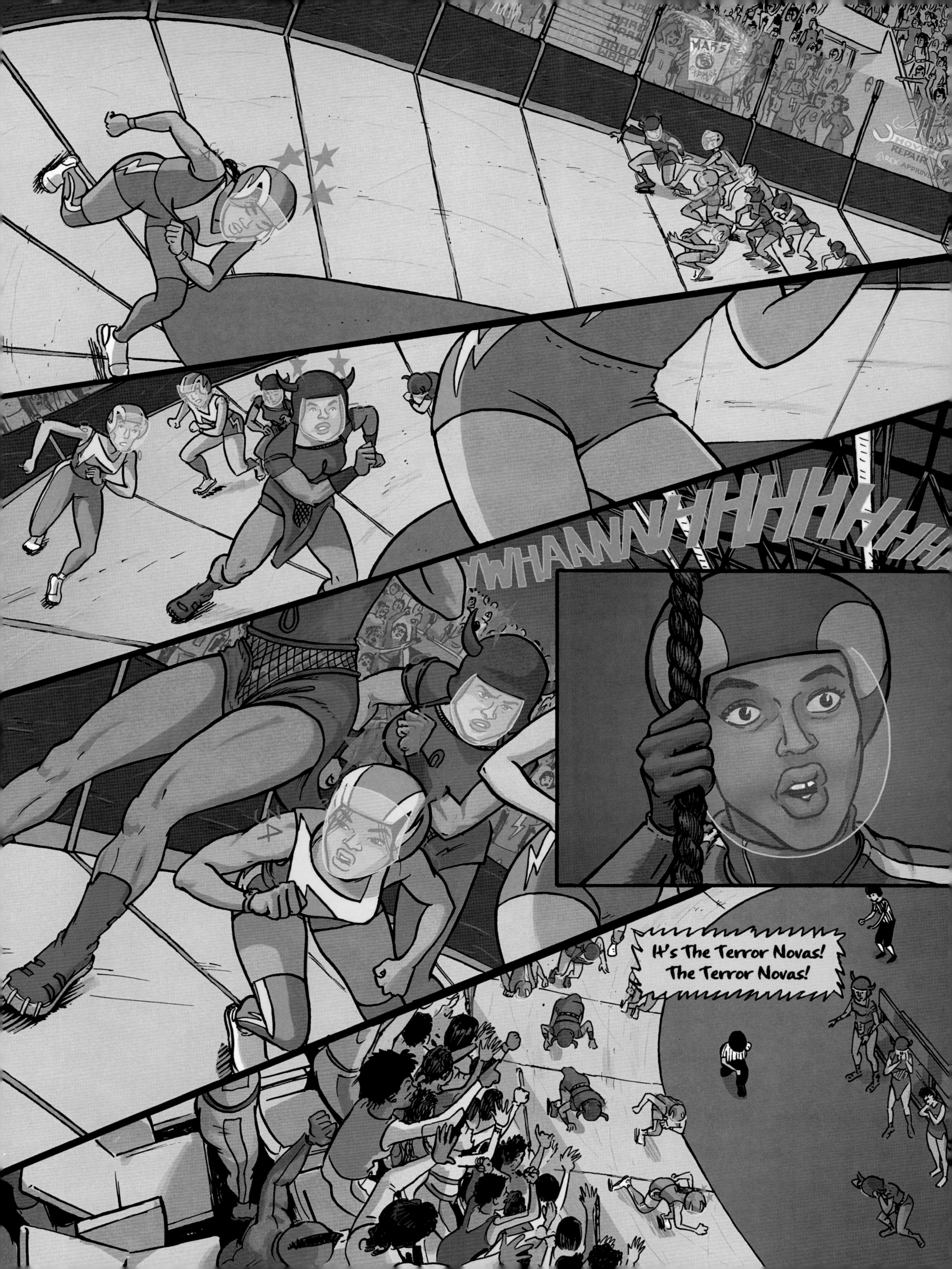
WHAANNHHHHHHHHH
It's The Terror Novas! The Terror Novas!

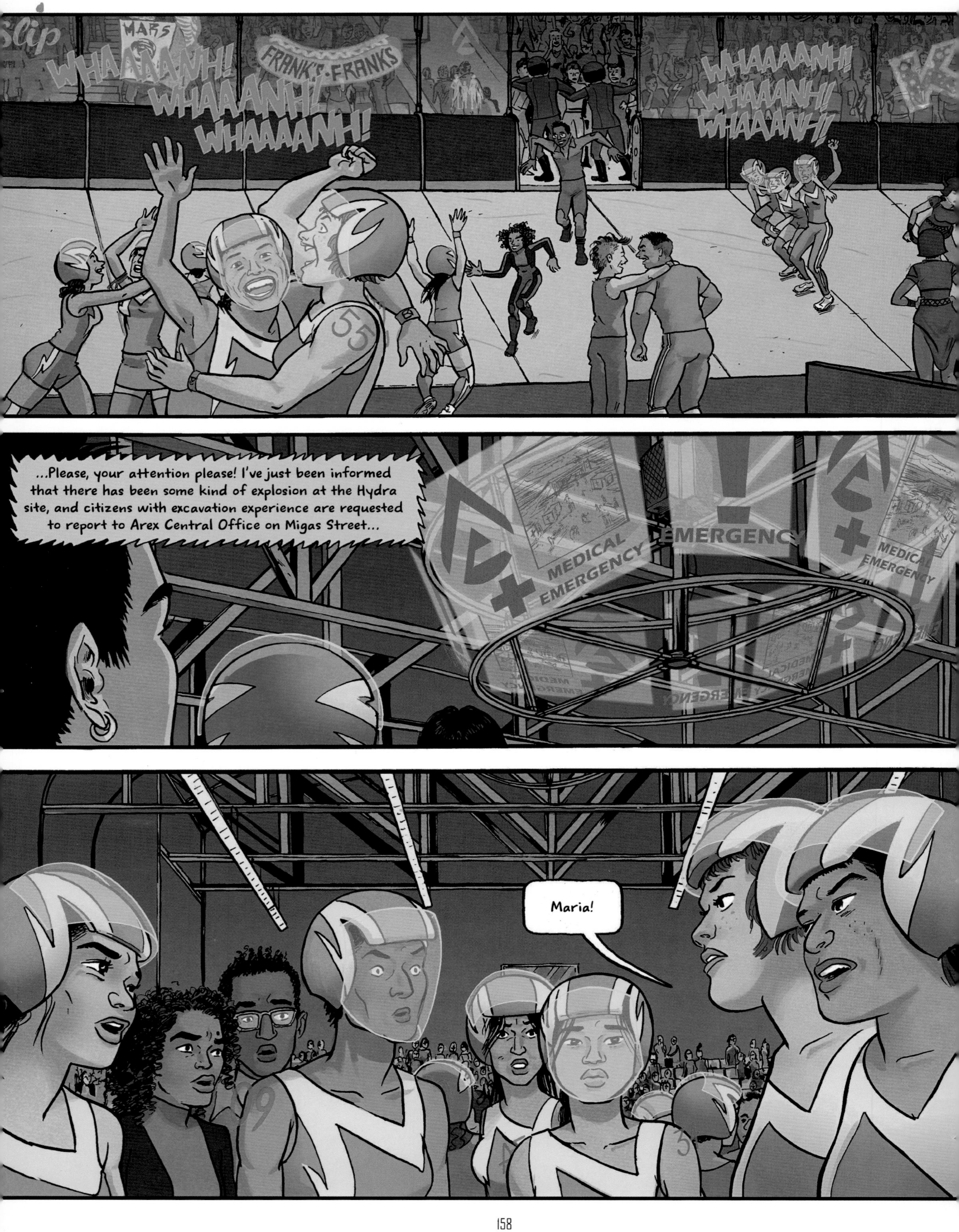

MARS
FRANK'S FRANKS
WHAAAANH! WHAAANH! WHAAAANH!
WHAAAANH! WHAAAANH! WHAAAANH!
...Please, your attention please! I've just been informed that there has been some kind of explosion at the Hydra site, and citizens with excavation experience are requested to report to Arex Central Office on Migas Street...
MEDICAL EMERGENCY
EMERGENCY
MEDICAL EMERGENCY
Maria!

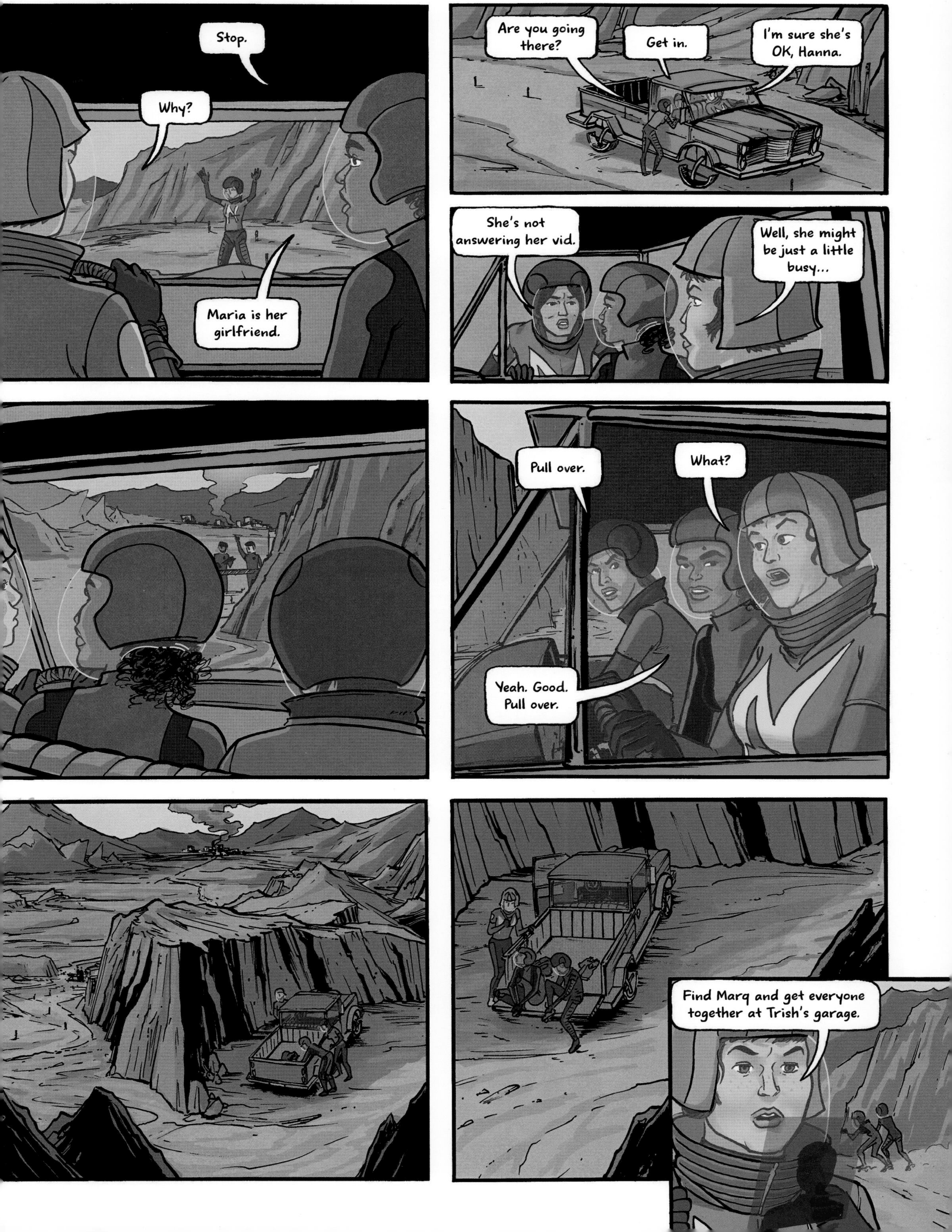
Stop.
Why?
Maria is her girlfriend.
Are you going there?
Get in.
I'm sure she's OK, Hanna.
She's not answering her vid.
Well, she might be just a little busy...
Pull over.
What?
Yeah. Good. Pull over.
Find Marq and get everyone together at Trish's garage.

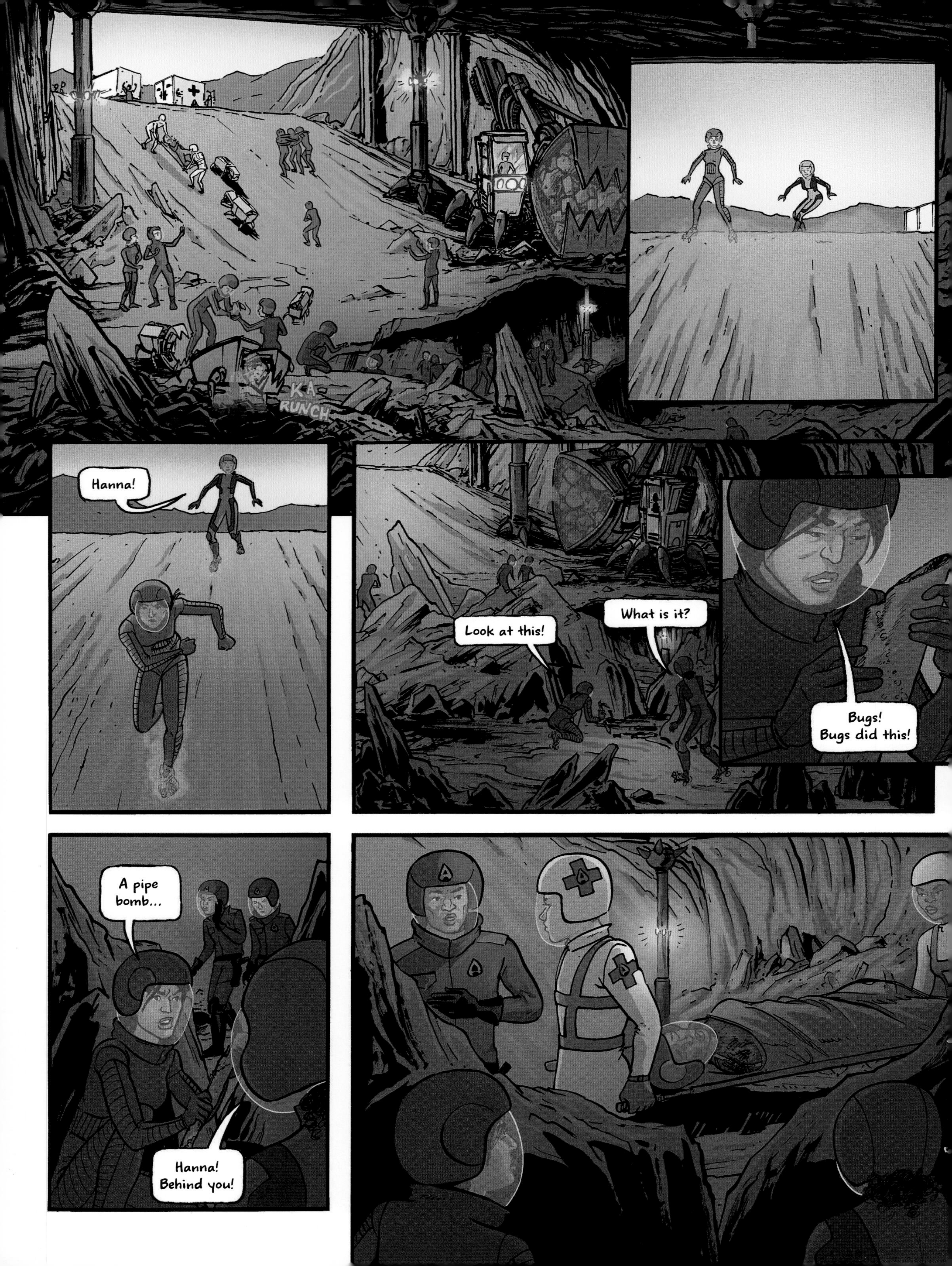
KA RUNCH
Hanna!
Look at this!
What is it?
Bugs!
Bugs did this!
A pipe bomb...
Hanna!
Behind you!

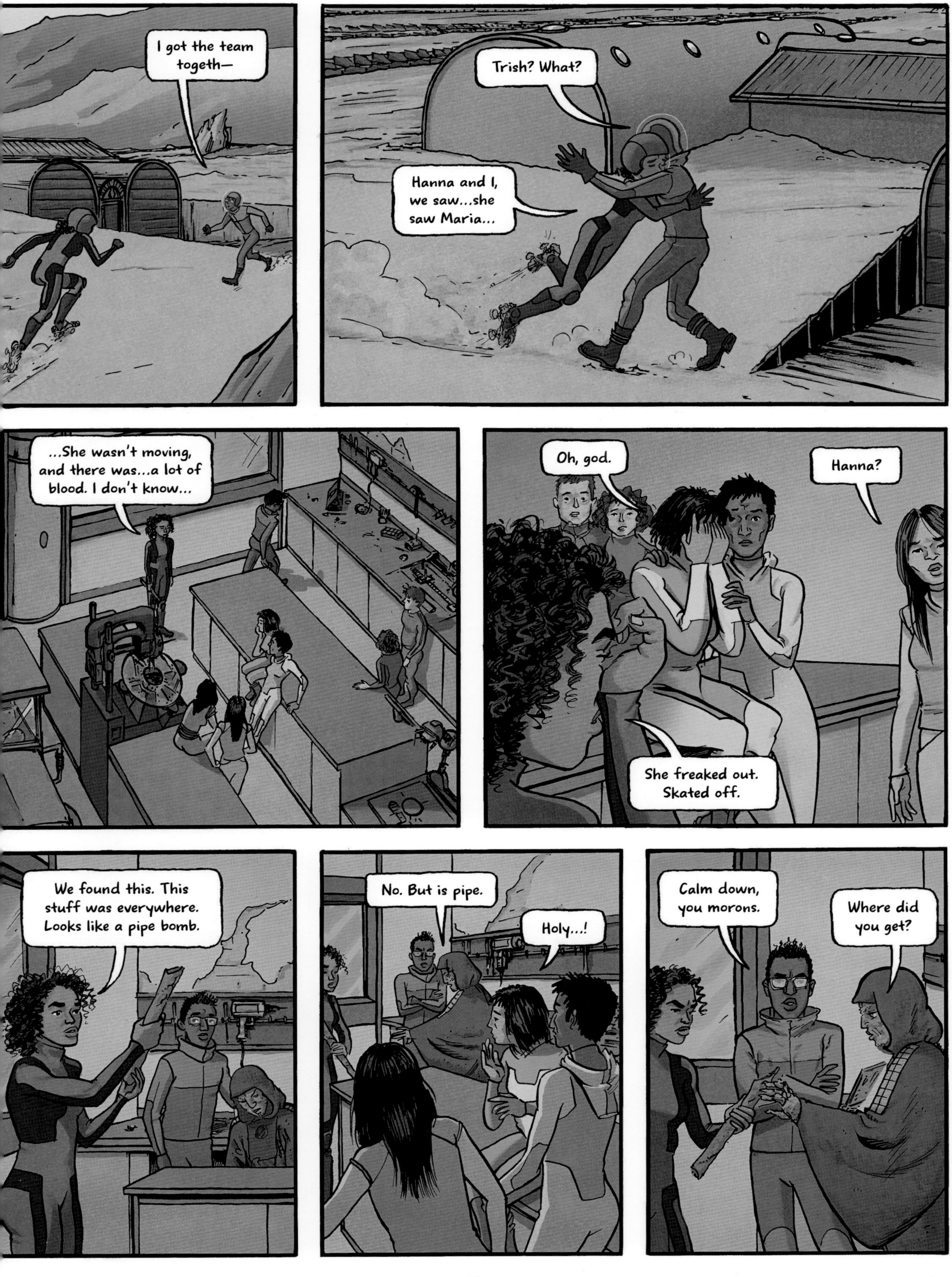

I got the team togeth—
Trish? What?
Hanna and I, we saw...she saw Maria...
...She wasn't moving, and there was...a lot of blood. I don't know...
Oh, god.
Hanna?
She freaked out. Skated off.
We found this. This stuff was everywhere. Looks like a pipe bomb.
No. But is pipe.
Holy...!
Calm down, you morons.
Where did you get?

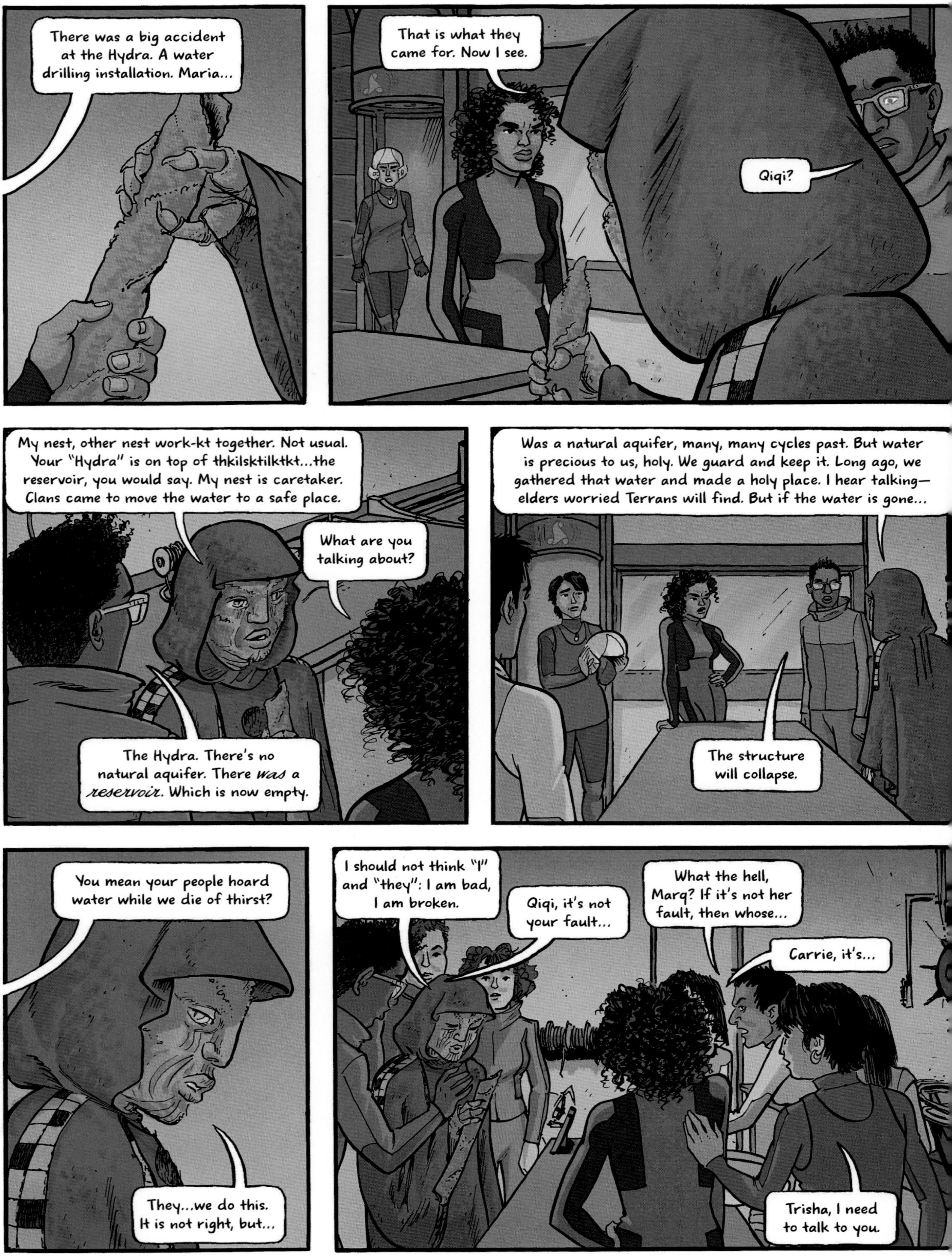
There was a big accident at the Hydra. A water drilling installation. Maria...
That is what they came for. Now I see.
Qiqi?
My nest, other nest work-kt together. Not usual. Your "Hydra" is on top of thkilsktilktkt...the reservoir, you would say. My nest is caretaker. Clans came to move the water to a safe place.
What are you talking about?
The Hydra. There's no natural aquifer. There *was* a *reservoir*. Which is now empty.
Was a natural aquifer, many, many cycles past. But water is precious to us, holy. We guard and keep it. Long ago, we gathered that water and made a holy place. I hear talking—elders worried Terrans will find. But if the water is gone...
The structure will collapse.
You mean your people hoard water while we die of thirst?
They...we do this. It is not right, but...
I should not think "I" and "they": I am bad, I am broken.
Qiqi, it's not your fault...
What the hell, Marq? If it's not her fault, then whose...
Carrie, it's...
Trisha, I need to talk to you.

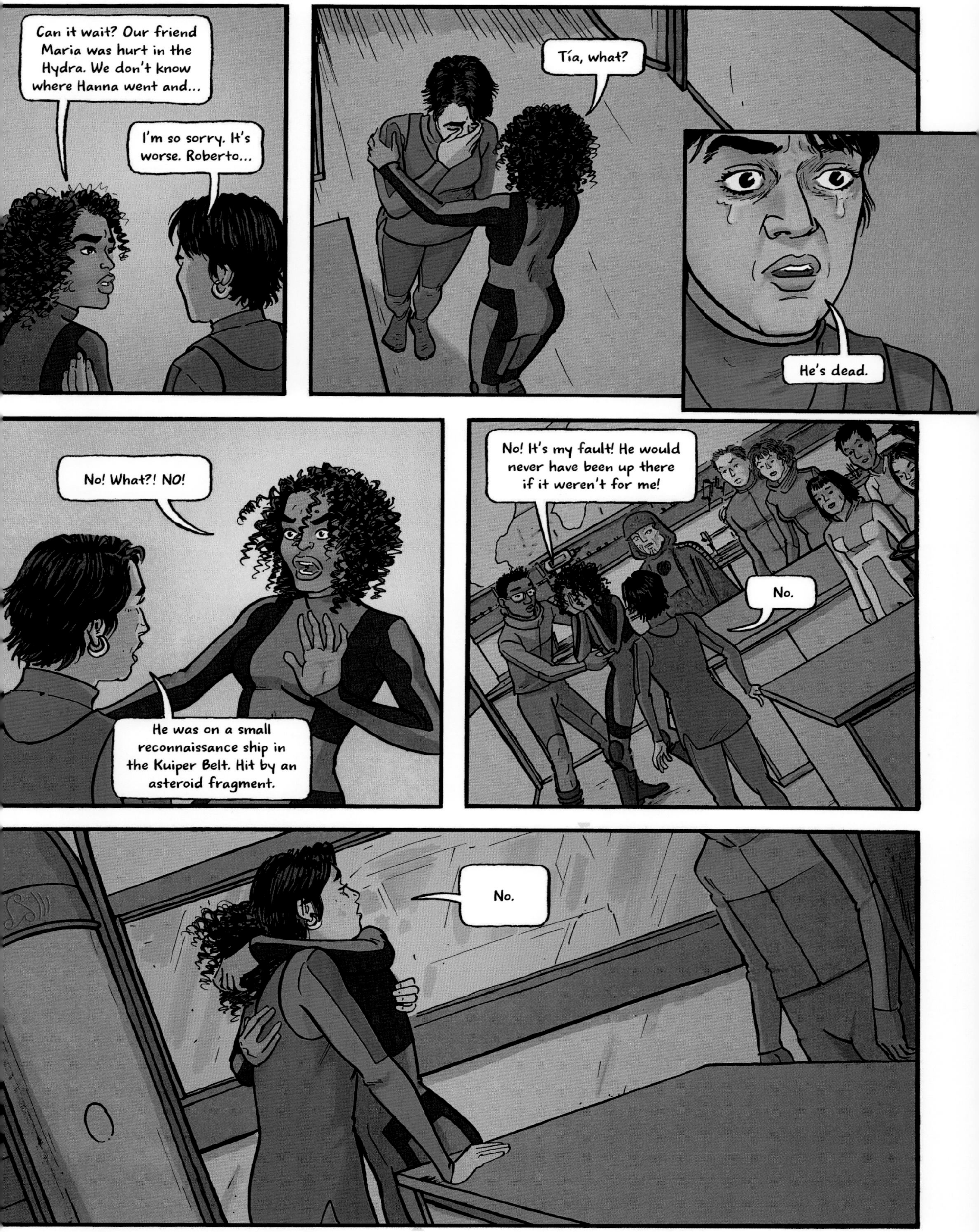
Can it wait? Our friend Maria was hurt in the Hydra. We don't know where Hanna went and...
I'm so sorry. It's worse. Roberto...
Tía, what?
He's dead.
No! What?! NO!
He was on a small reconnaissance ship in the Kuiper Belt. Hit by an asteroid fragment.
No! It's my fault! He would never have been up there if it weren't for me!
No.
No.

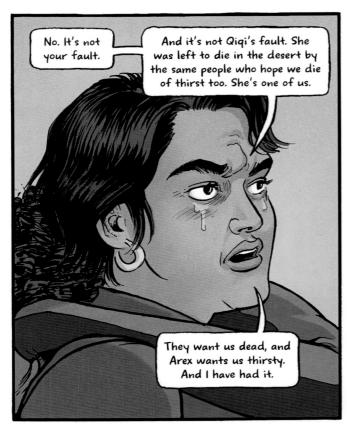

No. It's not your fault.

And it's not Qiqi's fault. She was left to die in the desert by the same people who hope we die of thirst too. She's one of us.

They want us dead, and Arex wants us thirsty. And I have had it.

We know who is responsible.

Girls, I need your help. We are going to *destroy* this system. Tonight.

Strap on your skates.

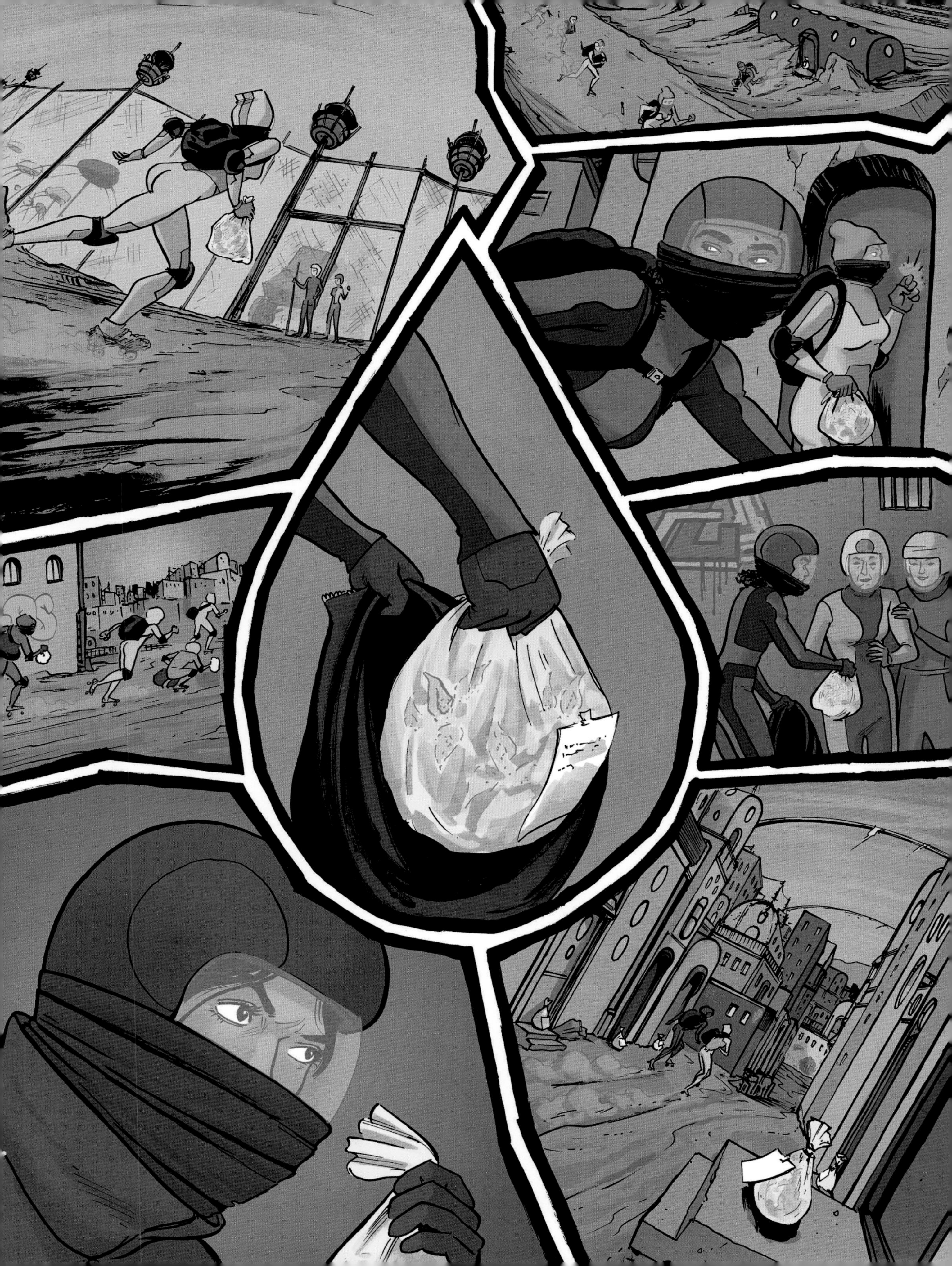

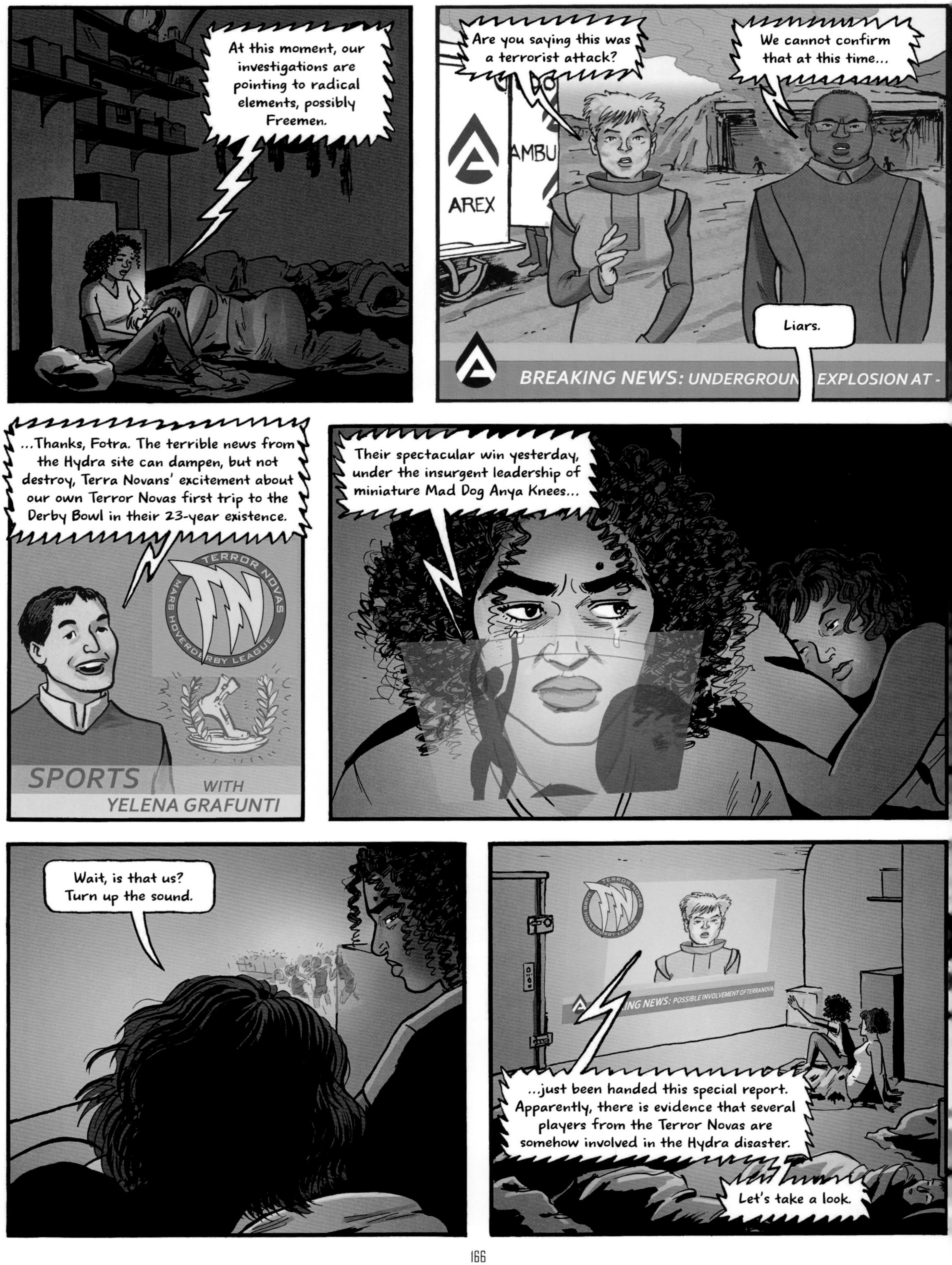
At this moment, our investigations are pointing to radical elements, possibly Freemen.
Are you saying this was a terrorist attack?
We cannot confirm that at this time...
AMBU
AREX
Liars.
BREAKING NEWS: UNDERGROUN EXPLOSION AT -
...Thanks, Fotra. The terrible news from the Hydra site can dampen, but not destroy, Terra Novans' excitement about our own Terror Novas first trip to the Derby Bowl in their 23-year existence.
TERROR NOVAS
MARS HOVERDERBY LEAGUE
SPORTS
WITH
YELENA GRAFUNTI
Their spectacular win yesterday, under the insurgent leadership of miniature Mad Dog Anya Knees...
Wait, is that us? Turn up the sound.
ING NEWS: POSSIBLE INVOLVEMENT OF TERRANOVA
...just been handed this special report. Apparently, there is evidence that several players from the Terror Novas are somehow involved in the Hydra disaster.
Let's take a look.

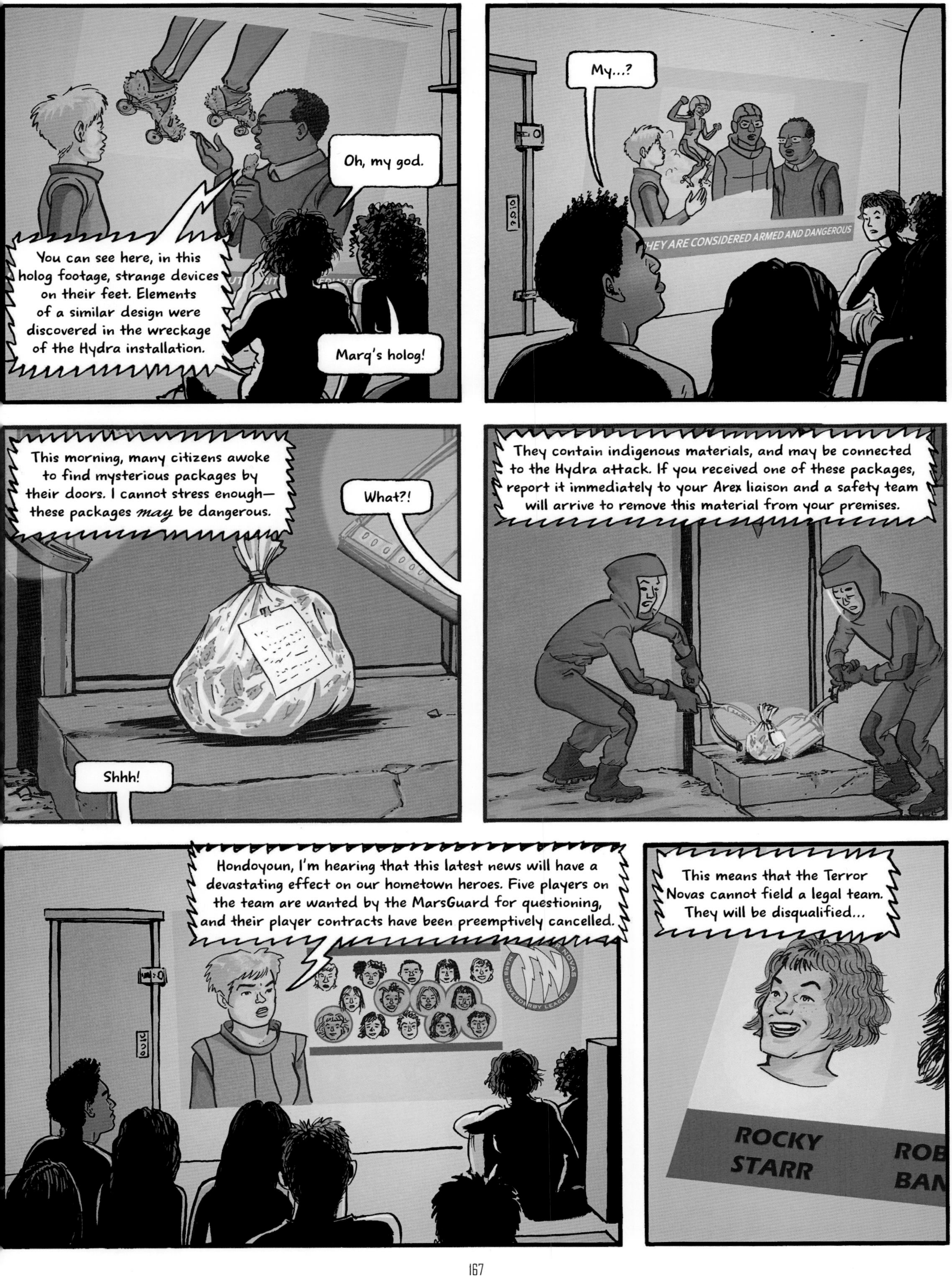
Oh, my god.
You can see here, in this holog footage, strange devices on their feet. Elements of a similar design were discovered in the wreckage of the Hydra installation.
Marq's holog!
My...?
THEY ARE CONSIDERED ARMED AND DANGEROUS
This morning, many citizens awoke to find mysterious packages by their doors. I cannot stress enough—these packages *may* be dangerous.
What?!
Shhh!
They contain indigenous materials, and may be connected to the Hydra attack. If you received one of these packages, report it immediately to your Arex liaison and a safety team will arrive to remove this material from your premises.
Hondoyoun, I'm hearing that this latest news will have a devastating effect on our hometown heroes. Five players on the team are wanted by the MarsGuard for questioning, and their player contracts have been preemptively cancelled.
This means that the Terror Novas cannot field a legal team. They will be disqualified...
ROCKY STARR

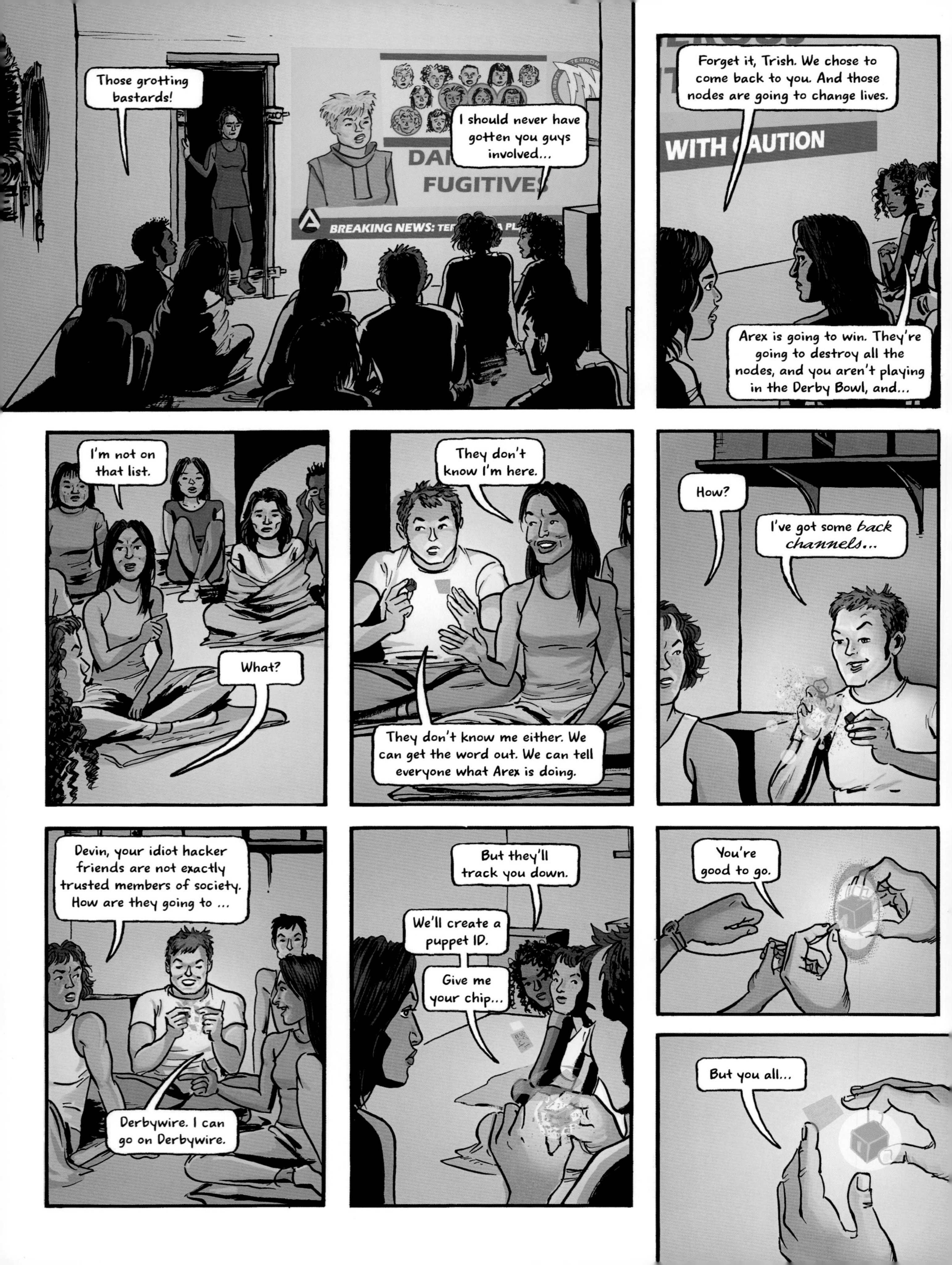
Those grotting bastards!
DAN... FUGITIVES
BREAKING NEWS:
I should never have gotten you guys involved...
WITH CAUTION
Forget it, Trish. We chose to come back to you. And those nodes are going to change lives.
Arex is going to win. They're going to destroy all the nodes, and you aren't playing in the Derby Bowl, and...
I'm not on that list.
What?
They don't know I'm here.
They don't know me either. We can get the word out. We can tell everyone what Arex is doing.
How?
I've got some *back channels*...
Devin, your idiot hacker friends are not exactly trusted members of society. How are they going to ...
Derbywire. I can go on Derbywire.
But they'll track you down.
We'll create a puppet ID.
Give me your chip...
You're good to go.
But you all...

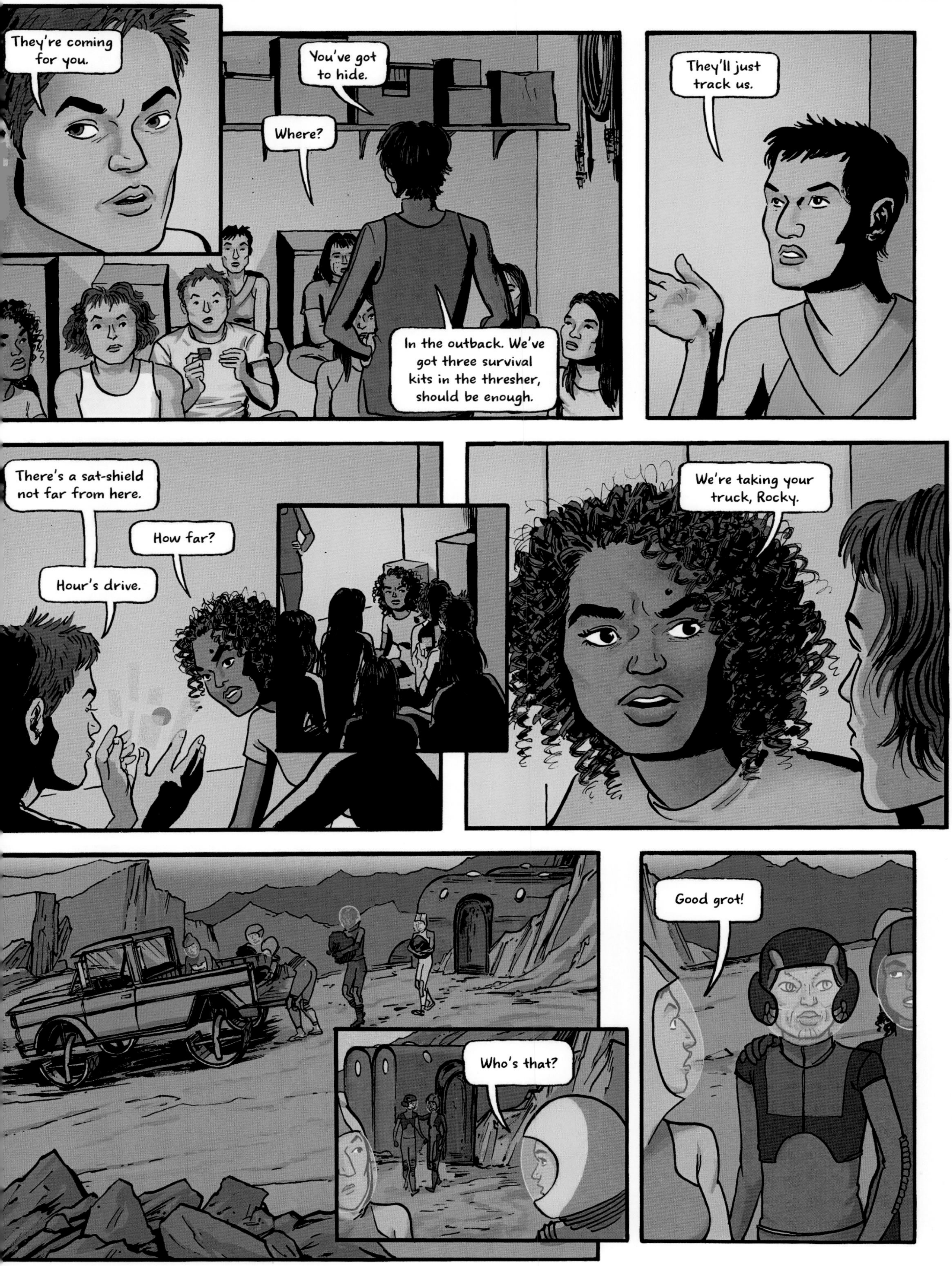
They're coming for you.
You've got to hide.
Where?
In the outback. We've got three survival kits in the thresher, should be enough.
They'll just track us.
There's a sat-shield not far from here.
How far?
Hour's drive.
We're taking your truck, Rocky.
Who's that?
Good grot!

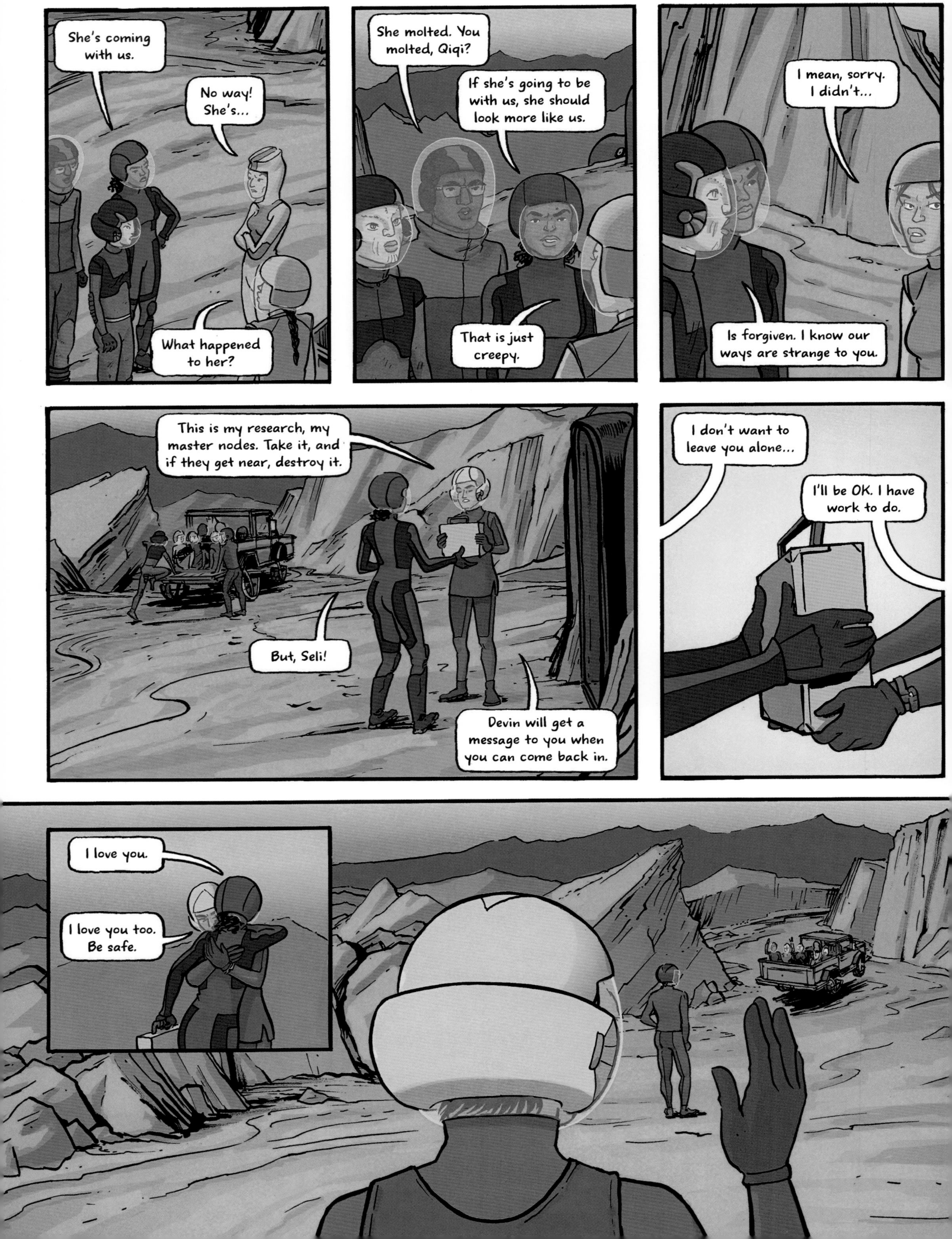
She's coming with us.
No way! She's...
What happened to her?
She molted. You molted, Qiqi?
If she's going to be with us, she should look more like us.
That is just creepy.
I mean, sorry. I didn't...
Is forgiven. I know our ways are strange to you.
This is my research, my master nodes. Take it, and if they get near, destroy it.
But, Seli!
Devin will get a message to you when you can come back in.
I don't want to leave you alone...
I'll be OK. I have work to do.
I love you.
I love you too. Be safe.

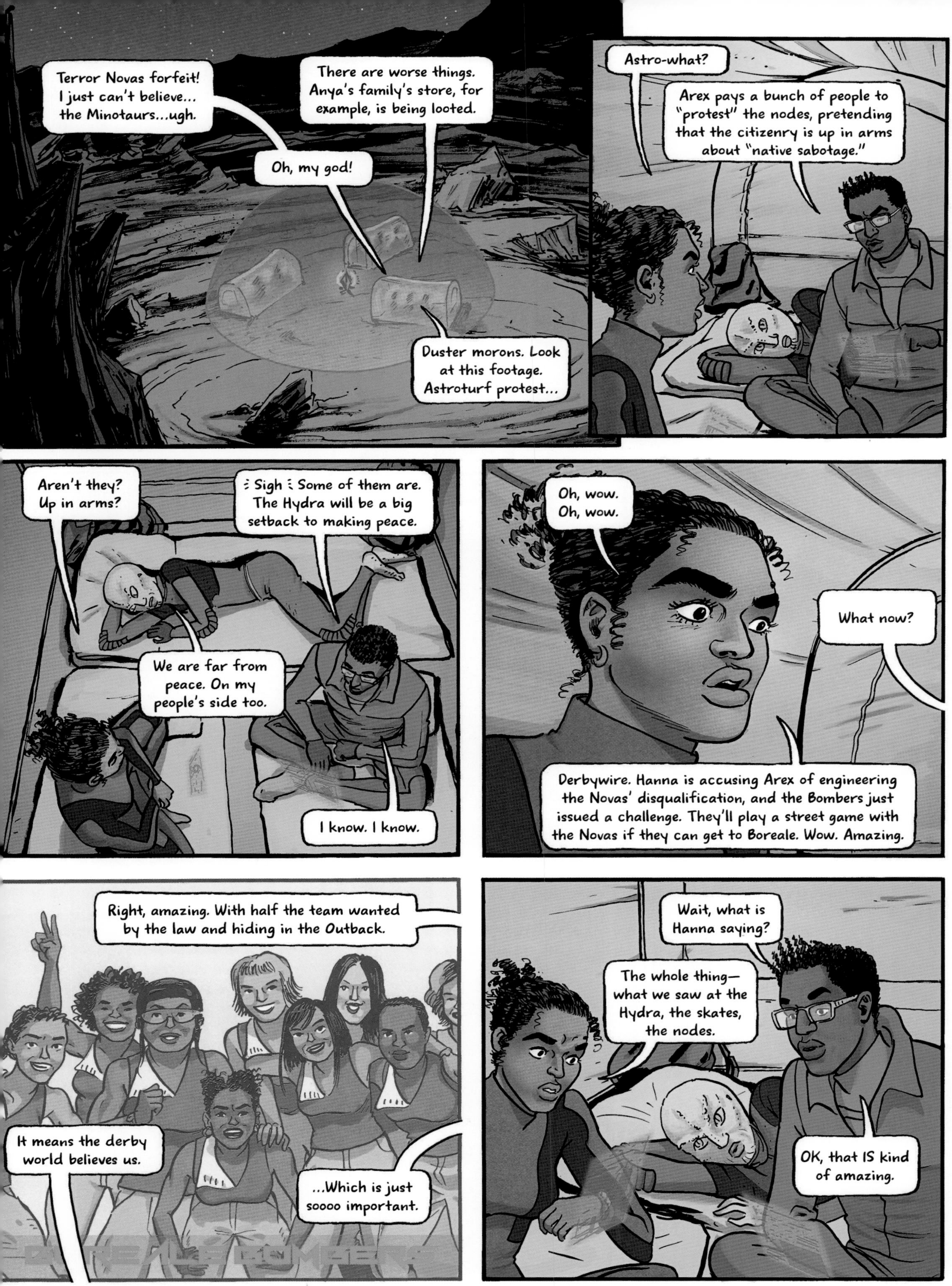

Terror Novas forfeit! I just can't believe... the Minotaurs...ugh.
Oh, my god!
There are worse things. Anya's family's store, for example, is being looted.
Duster morons. Look at this footage. Astroturf protest...
Astro-what?
Arex pays a bunch of people to "protest" the nodes, pretending that the citizenry is up in arms about "native sabotage."
Aren't they? Up in arms?
⁝ Sigh ⁝ Some of them are. The Hydra will be a big setback to making peace.
We are far from peace. On my people's side too.
I know. I know.
Oh, wow. Oh, wow.
What now?
Derbywire. Hanna is accusing Arex of engineering the Novas' disqualification, and the Bombers just issued a challenge. They'll play a street game with the Novas if they can get to Boreale. Wow. Amazing.
Right, amazing. With half the team wanted by the law and hiding in the Outback.
It means the derby world believes us.
...Which is just soooo important.
Wait, what is Hanna saying?
The whole thing— what we saw at the Hydra, the skates, the nodes.
OK, that IS kind of amazing.

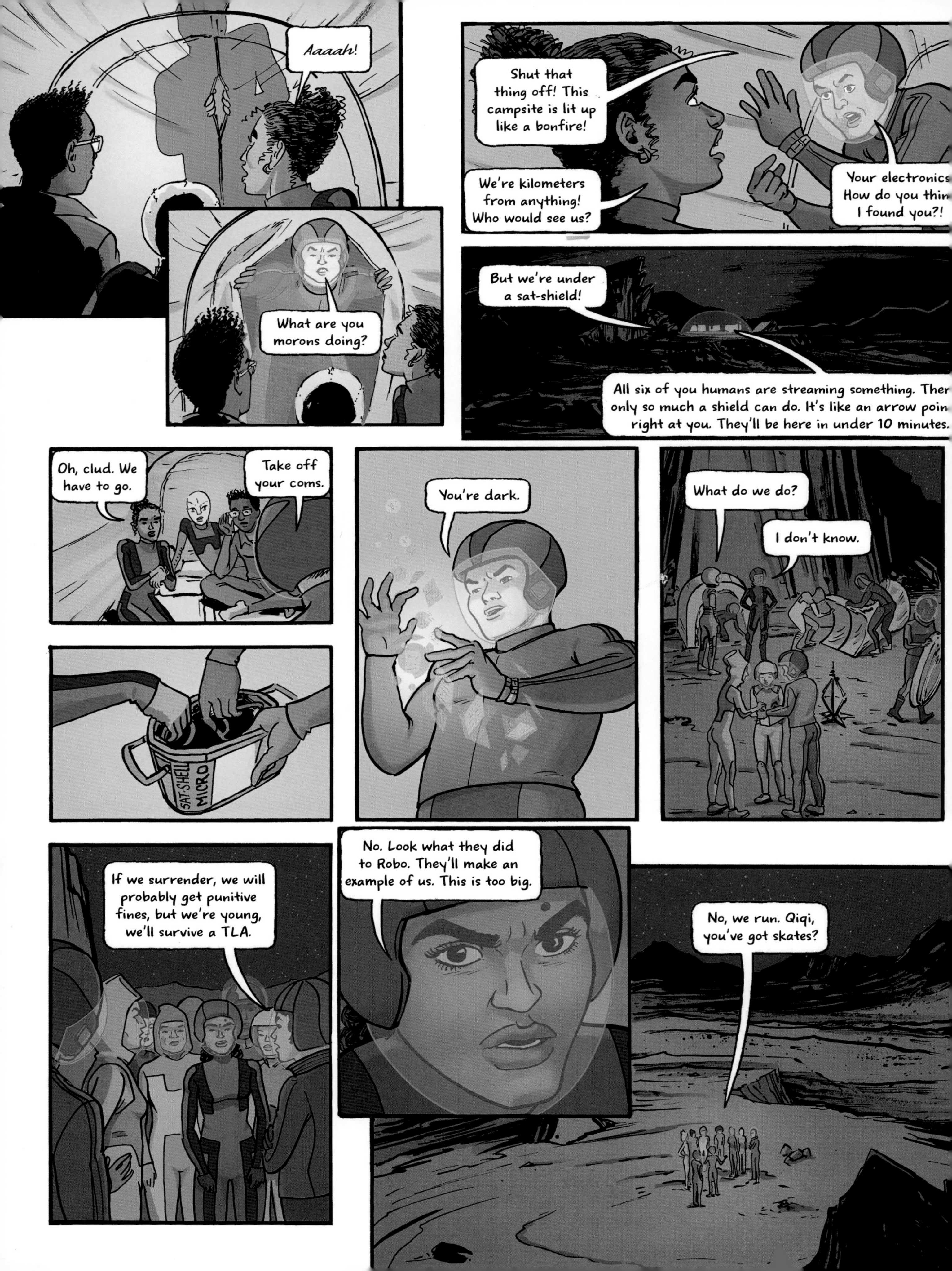
Aaaah!
What are you morons doing?
Shut that thing off! This campsite is lit up like a bonfire!
We're kilometers from anything! Who would see us?
Your electronics How do you thin I found you?!
But we're under a sat-shield!
All six of you humans are streaming something. Ther only so much a shield can do. It's like an arrow poin right at you. They'll be here in under 10 minutes.
Oh, clud. We have to go.
Take off your coms.
SAT-SHELL MICRO
You're dark.
What do we do?
I don't know.
If we surrender, we will probably get punitive fines, but we're young, we'll survive a TLA.
No. Look what they did to Robo. They'll make an example of us. This is too big.
No, we run. Qiqi, you've got skates?

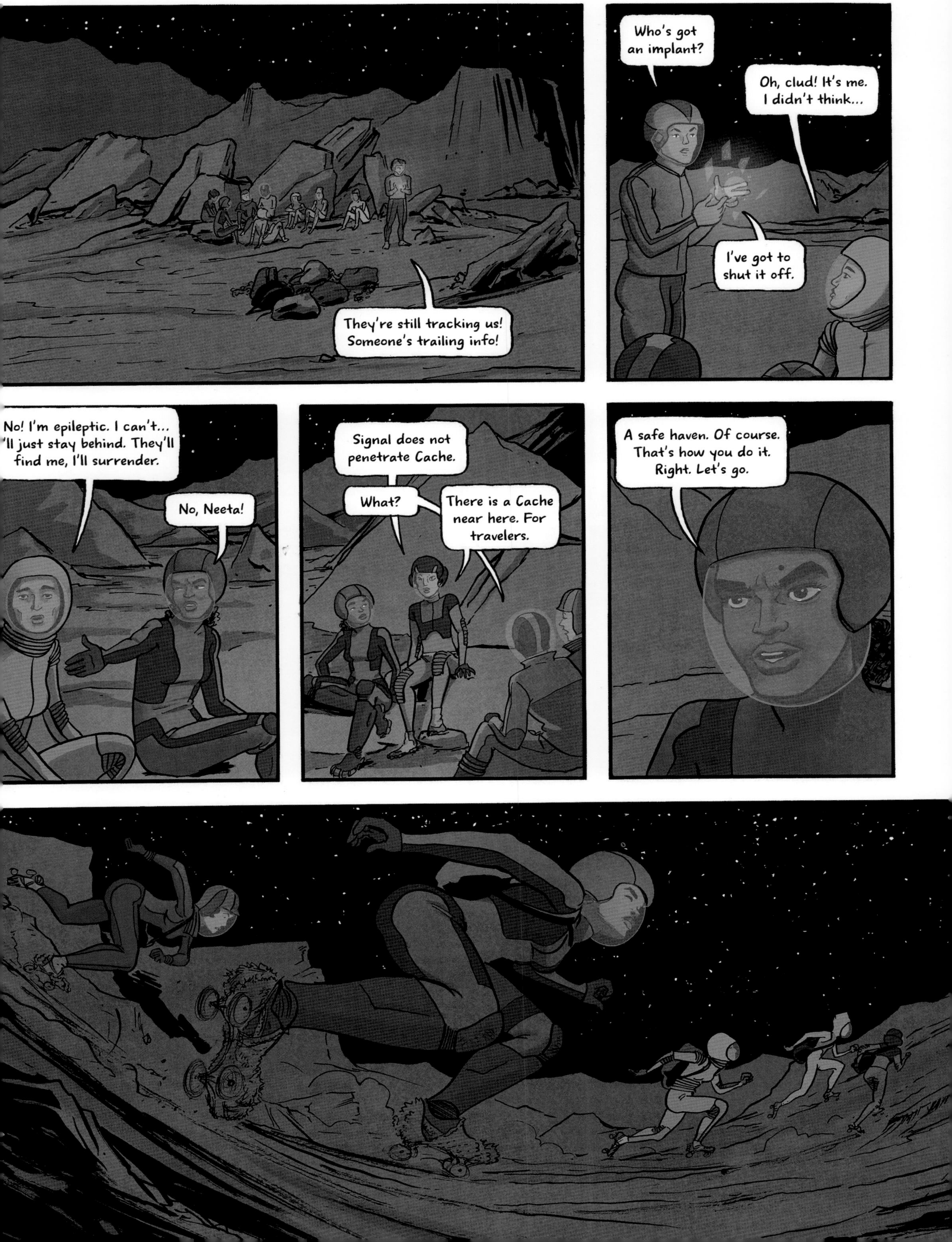
They're still tracking us! Someone's trailing info!
Who's got an implant?
Oh, clud! It's me. I didn't think...
I've got to shut it off.
No! I'm epileptic. I can't... 'll just stay behind. They'll find me, I'll surrender.
No, Neeta!
Signal does not penetrate Cache.
What?
There is a Cache near here. For travelers.
A safe haven. Of course. That's how you do it. Right. Let's go.

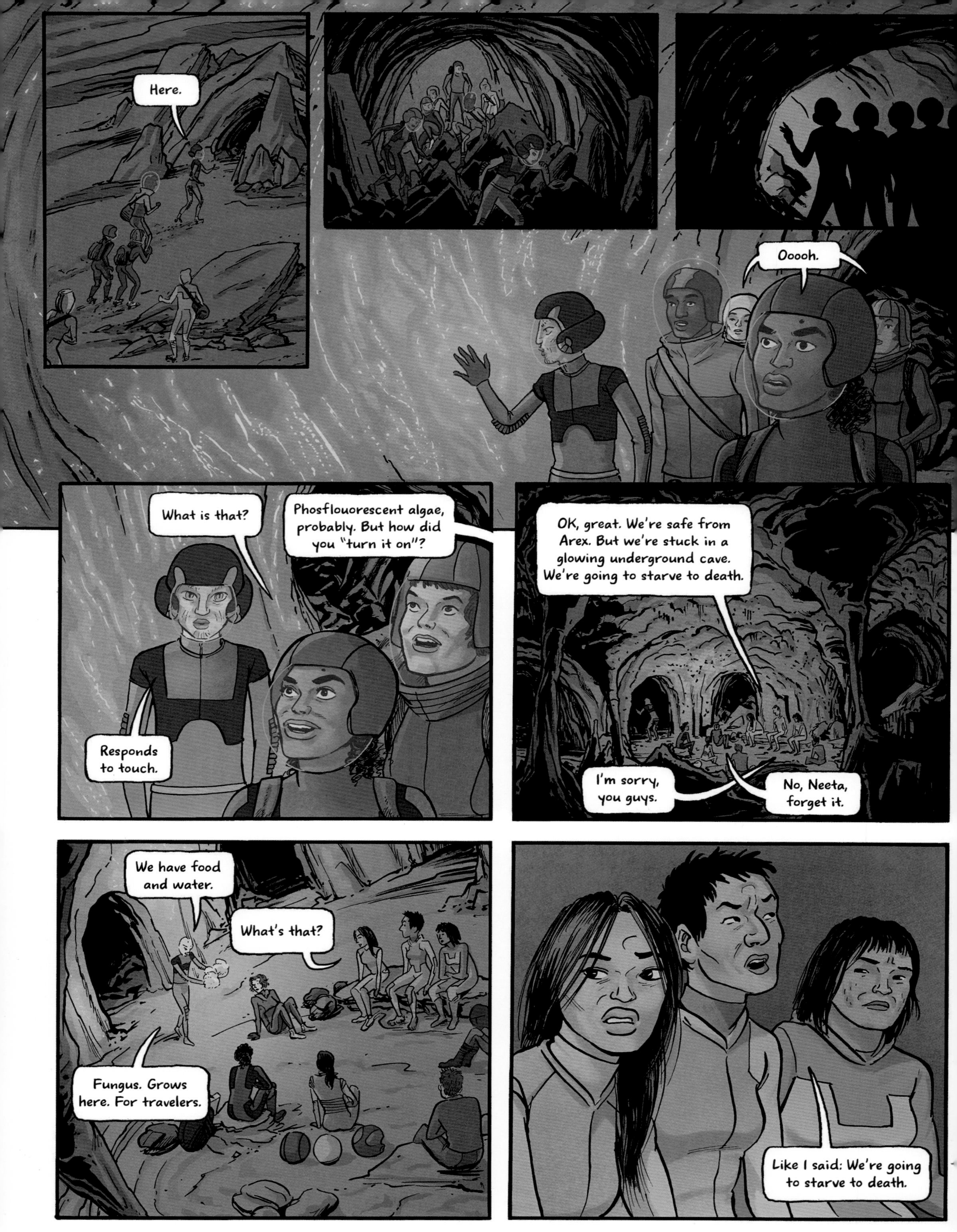
Here.
Ooooh.
What is that?
Phosflouorescent algae, probably. But how did you "turn it on"?
Responds to touch.
OK, great. We're safe from Arex. But we're stuck in a glowing underground cave. We're going to starve to death.
I'm sorry, you guys.
No, Neeta, forget it.
We have food and water.
What's that?
Fungus. Grows here. For travelers.
Like I said: We're going to starve to death.

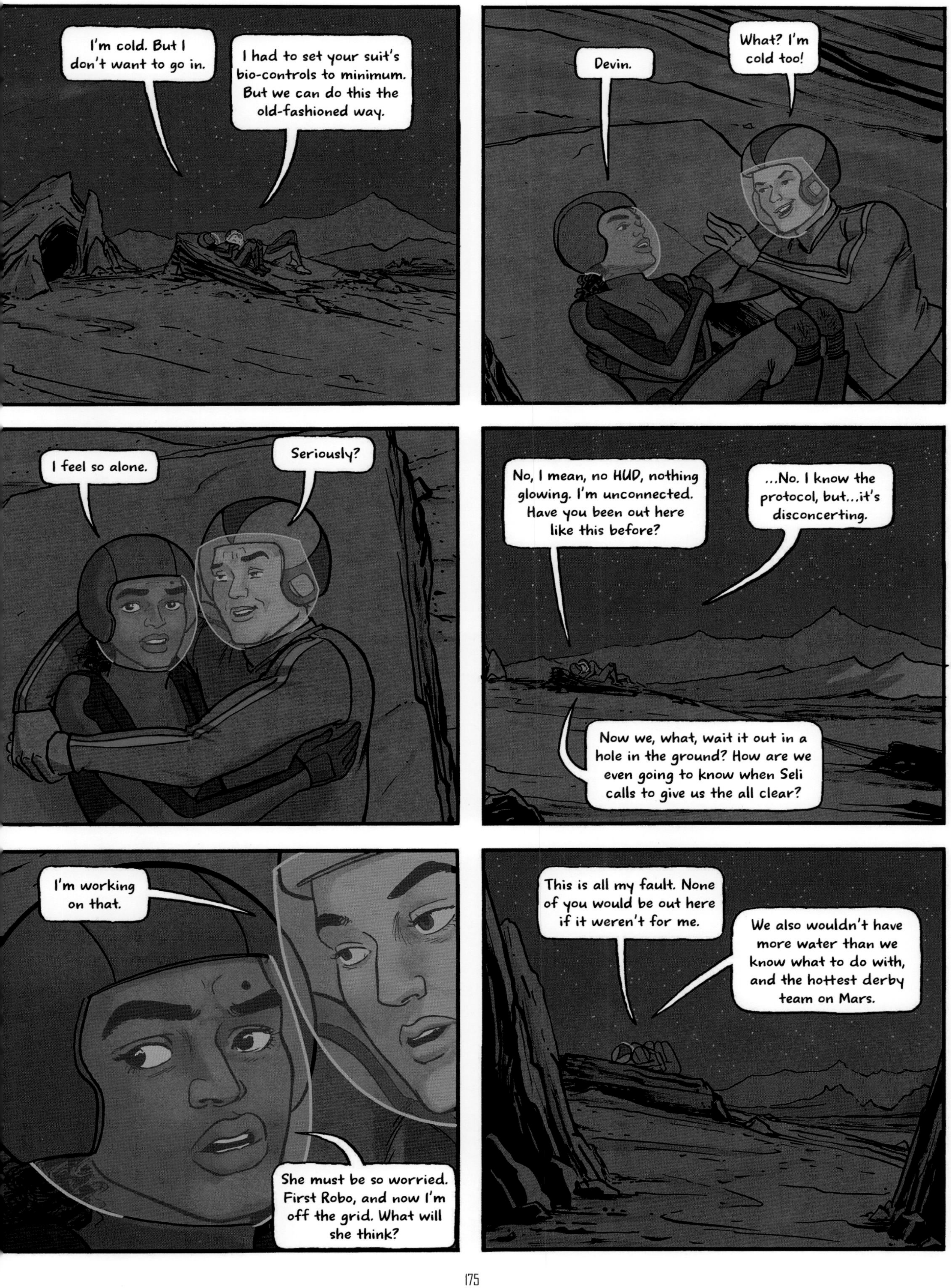
I'm cold. But I don't want to go in.
I had to set your suit's bio-controls to minimum. But we can do this the old-fashioned way.
Devin.
What? I'm cold too!
I feel so alone.
Seriously?
No, I mean, no HUD, nothing glowing. I'm unconnected. Have you been out here like this before?
...No. I know the protocol, but...it's disconcerting.
Now we, what, wait it out in a hole in the ground? How are we even going to know when Seli calls to give us the all clear?
I'm working on that.
She must be so worried. First Robo, and now I'm off the grid. What will she think?
This is all my fault. None of you would be out here if it weren't for me.
We also wouldn't have more water than we know what to do with, and the hottest derby team on Mars.

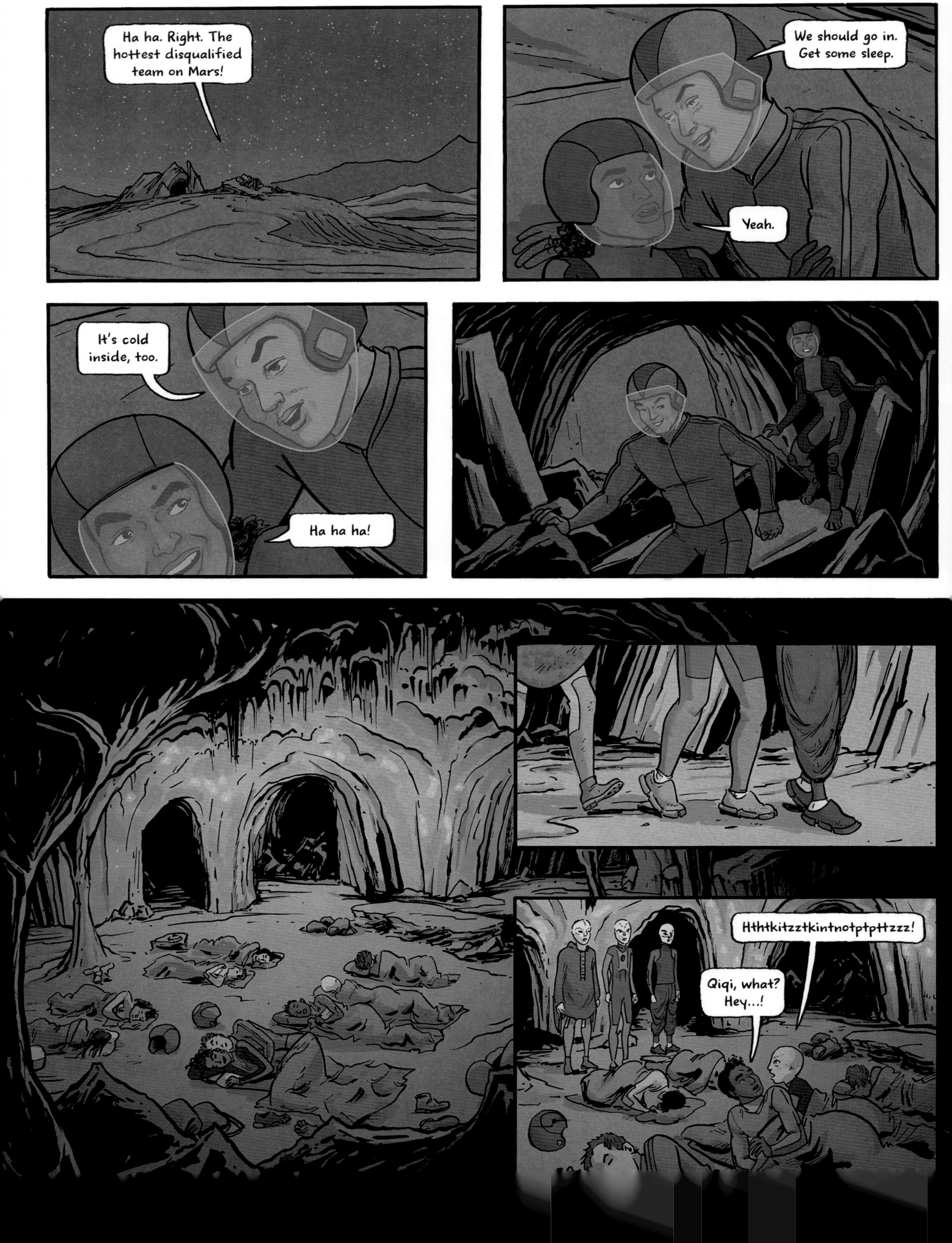
Ha ha. Right. The hottest disqualified team on Mars!
We should go in. Get some sleep.
Yeah.
It's cold inside, too.
Ha ha ha!
Hthtkitzztkintnotptptzzz!
Qiqi, what? Hey...!

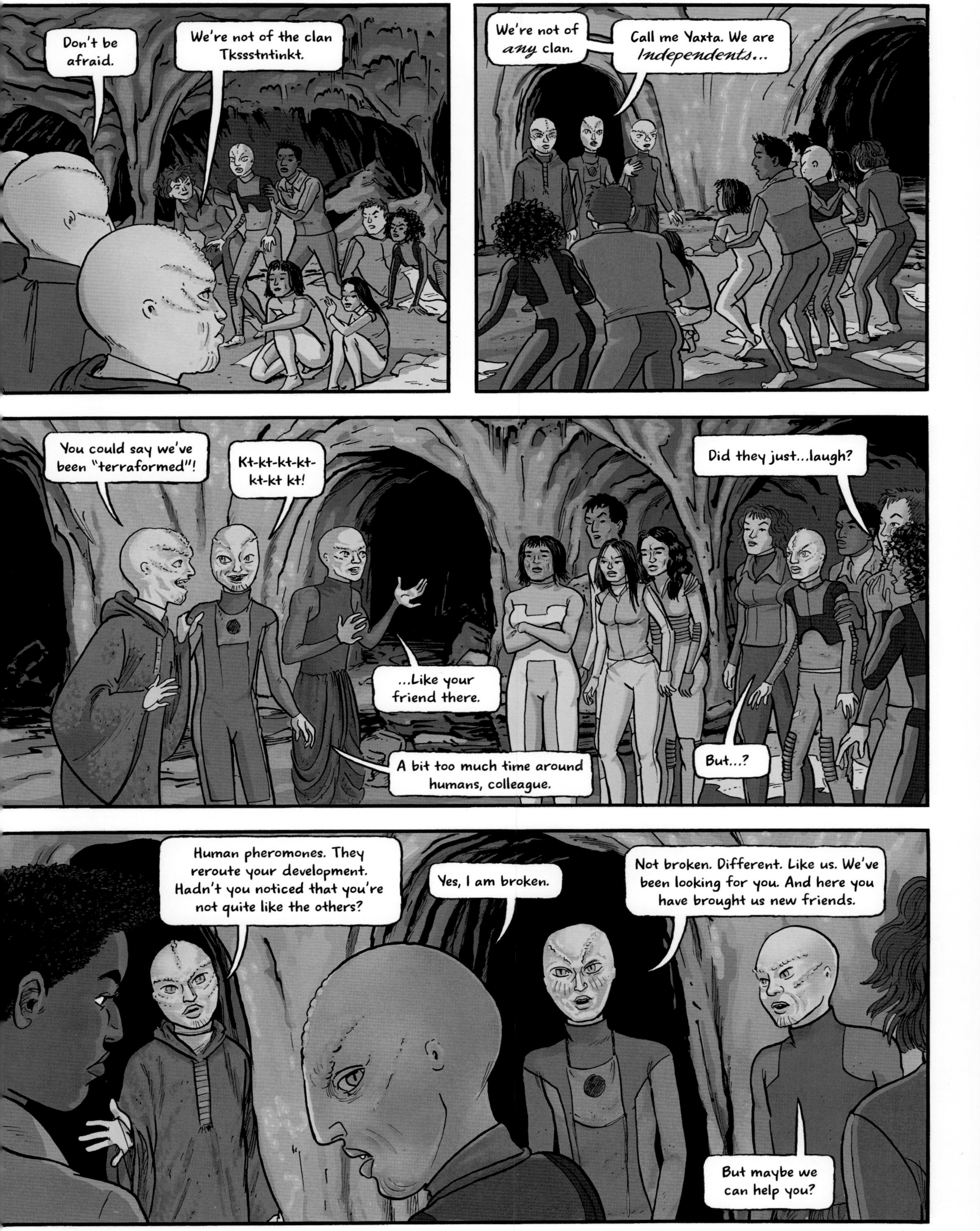
Don't be afraid.
We're not of the clan Tksssntntinkt.
We're not of *any* clan.
Call me Yaxta. We are *Independents...*
You could say we've been "terraformed"!
Kt-kt-kt-kt-kt-kt-kt kt!
...Like your friend there.
A bit too much time around humans, colleague.
Did they just...laugh?
But...?
Human pheromones. They reroute your development. Hadn't you noticed that you're not quite like the others?
Yes, I am broken.
Not broken. Different. Like us. We've been looking for you. And here you have brought us new friends.
But maybe we can help you?

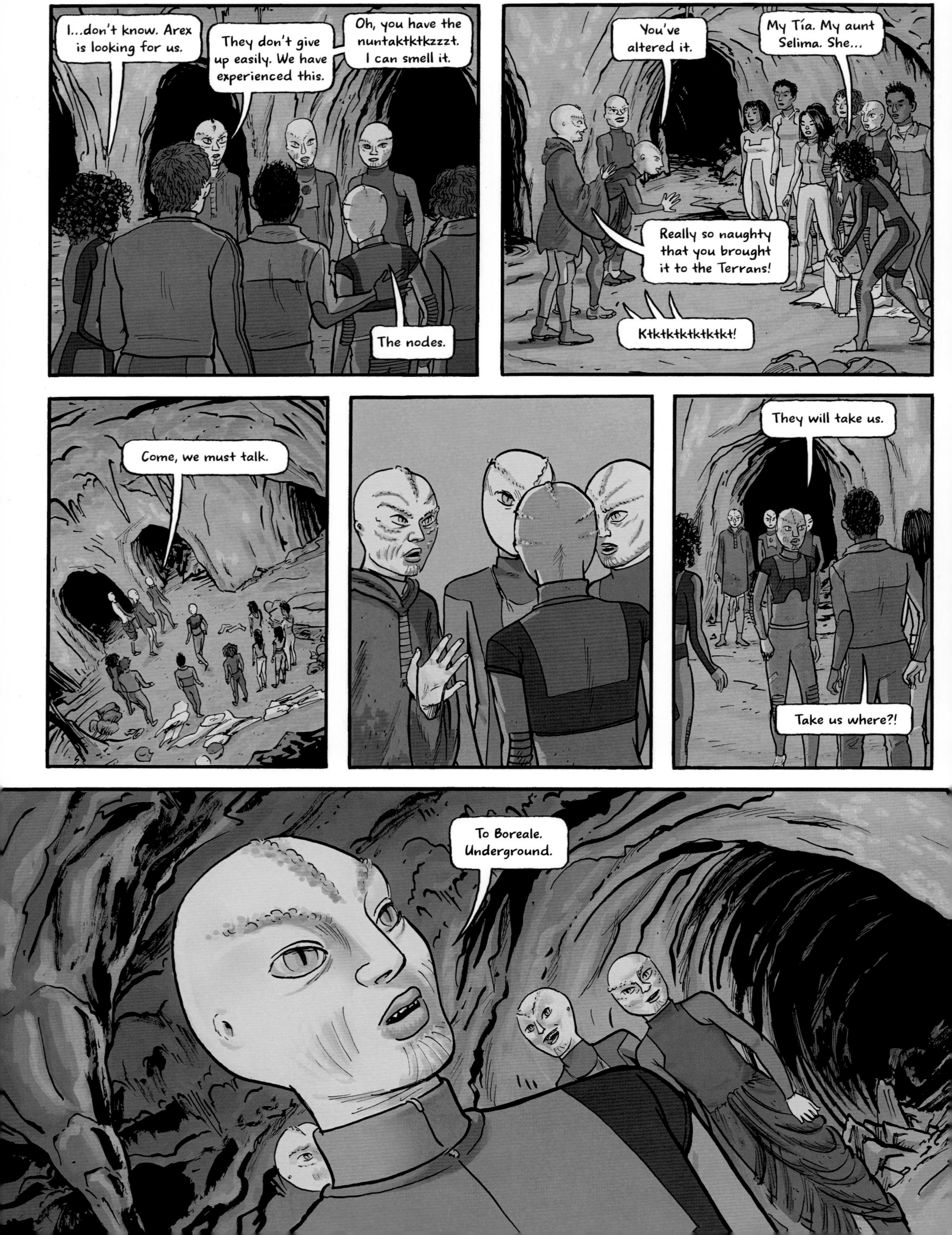
I...don't know. Arex is looking for us.
They don't give up easily. We have experienced this.
Oh, you have the nuntaktktkzzzt. I can smell it.
The nodes.
You've altered it.
My Tía. My aunt Selima. She...
Really so naughty that you brought it to the Terrans!
Ktktktktktktkt!
Come, we must talk.
They will take us.
Take us where?!
To Boreale. Underground.

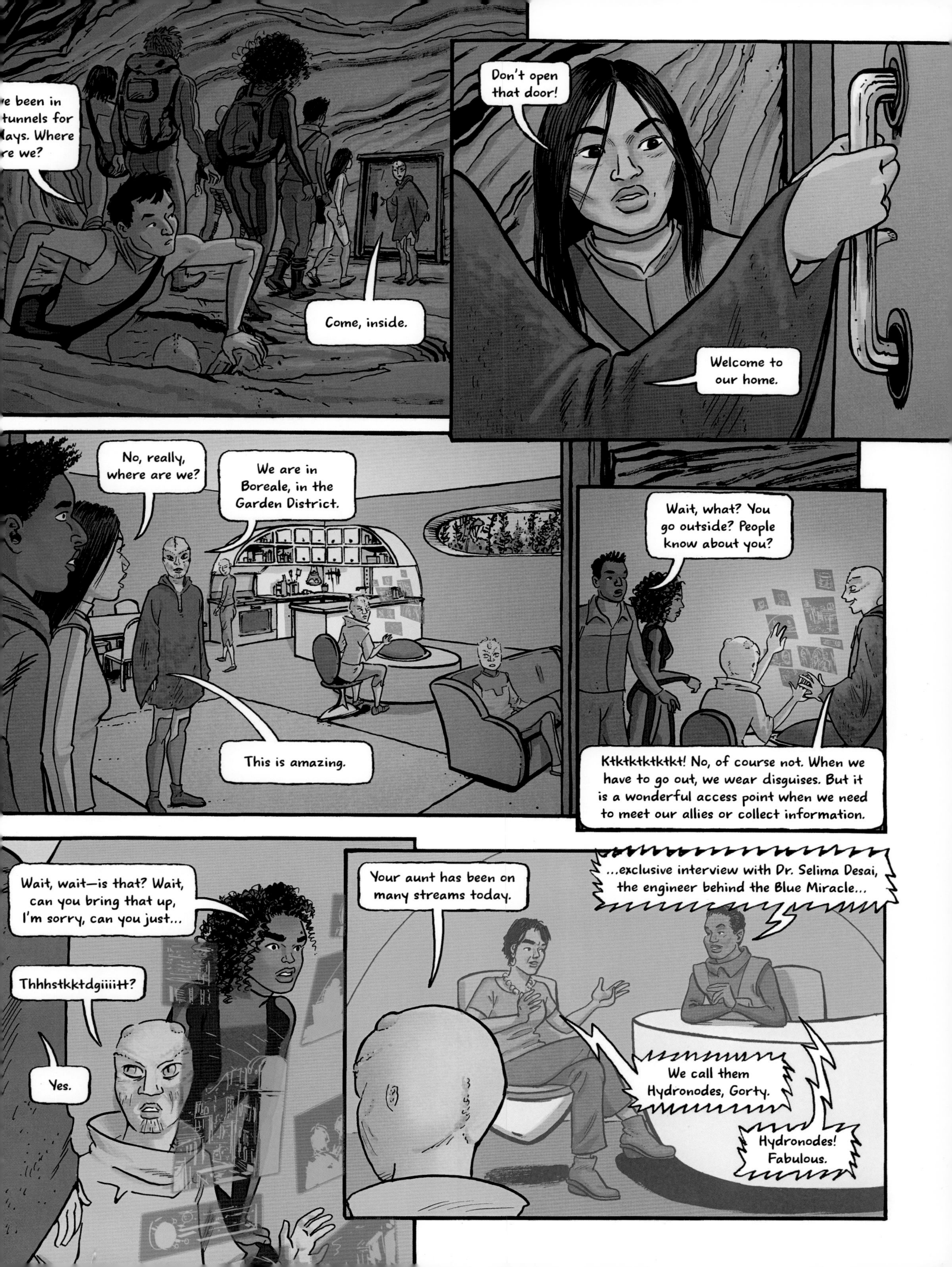

've been in
tunnels for
days. Where
are we?
Come, inside.
Don't open
that door!
Welcome to
our home.
No, really,
where are we?
We are in
Boreale, in the
Garden District.
This is amazing.
Wait, what? You
go outside? People
know about you?
Ktktktktktkt! No, of course not. When we have to go out, we wear disguises. But it is a wonderful access point when we need to meet our allies or collect information.
Wait, wait—is that? Wait, can you bring that up, I'm sorry, can you just...
Thhhstkktdgiiiitt?
Yes.
Your aunt has been on many streams today.
...exclusive interview with Dr. Selima Desai, the engineer behind the Blue Miracle...
We call them Hydronodes, Gorty.
Hydronodes! Fabulous.

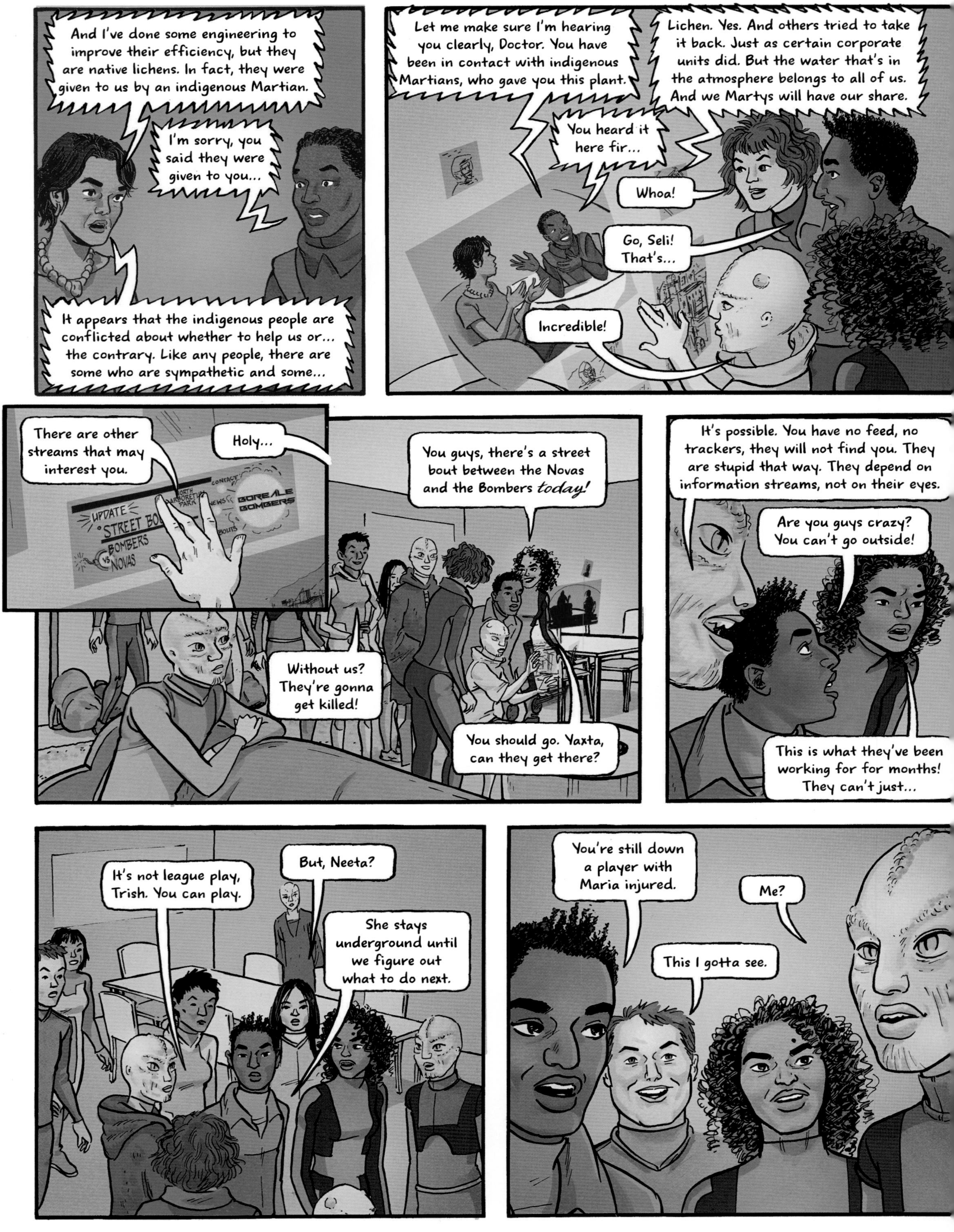
And I've done some engineering to improve their efficiency, but they are native lichens. In fact, they were given to us by an indigenous Martian.
I'm sorry, you said they were given to you...
It appears that the indigenous people are conflicted about whether to help us or... the contrary. Like any people, there are some who are sympathetic and some...
Let me make sure I'm hearing you clearly, Doctor. You have been in contact with indigenous Martians, who gave you this plant.
You heard it here fir...
Lichen. Yes. And others tried to take it back. Just as certain corporate units did. But the water that's in the atmosphere belongs to all of us. And we Martys will have our share.
Whoa!
Go, Seli! That's...
Incredible!
There are other streams that may interest you.
Holy...
UPDATE
BOMBERS
VS
NOVAS
CONTACT
NEWS
BOREALE BOMBERS
You guys, there's a street bout between the Novas and the Bombers *today*!
Without us? They're gonna get killed!
You should go. Yaxta, can they get there?
It's possible. You have no feed, no trackers, they will not find you. They are stupid that way. They depend on information streams, not on their eyes.
Are you guys crazy? You can't go outside!
This is what they've been working for for months! They can't just...
It's not league play, Trish. You can play.
But, Neeta?
She stays underground until we figure out what to do next.
You're still down a player with Maria injured.
Me?
This I gotta see.

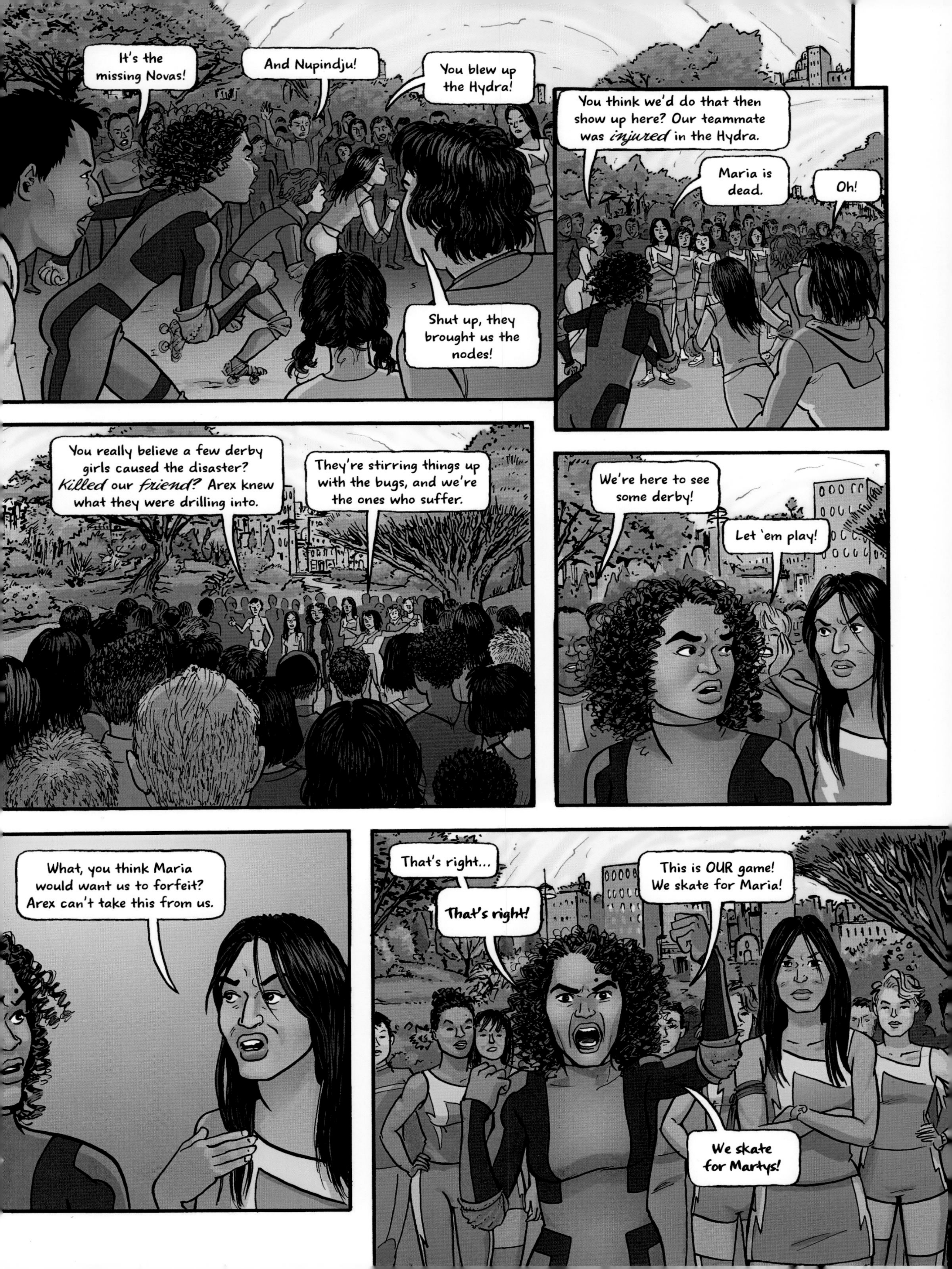
It's the missing Novas!
And Nupindju!
You blew up the Hydra!
Shut up, they brought us the nodes!
You think we'd do that then show up here? Our teammate was *injured* in the Hydra.
Maria is dead.
Oh!
You really believe a few derby girls caused the disaster? *Killed* our *friend?* Arex knew what they were drilling into.
They're stirring things up with the bugs, and we're the ones who suffer.
We're here to see some derby!
Let 'em play!
What, you think Maria would want us to forfeit? Arex can't take this from us.
That's right...
That's right!
This is OUR game! We skate for Maria!
We skate for Martys!

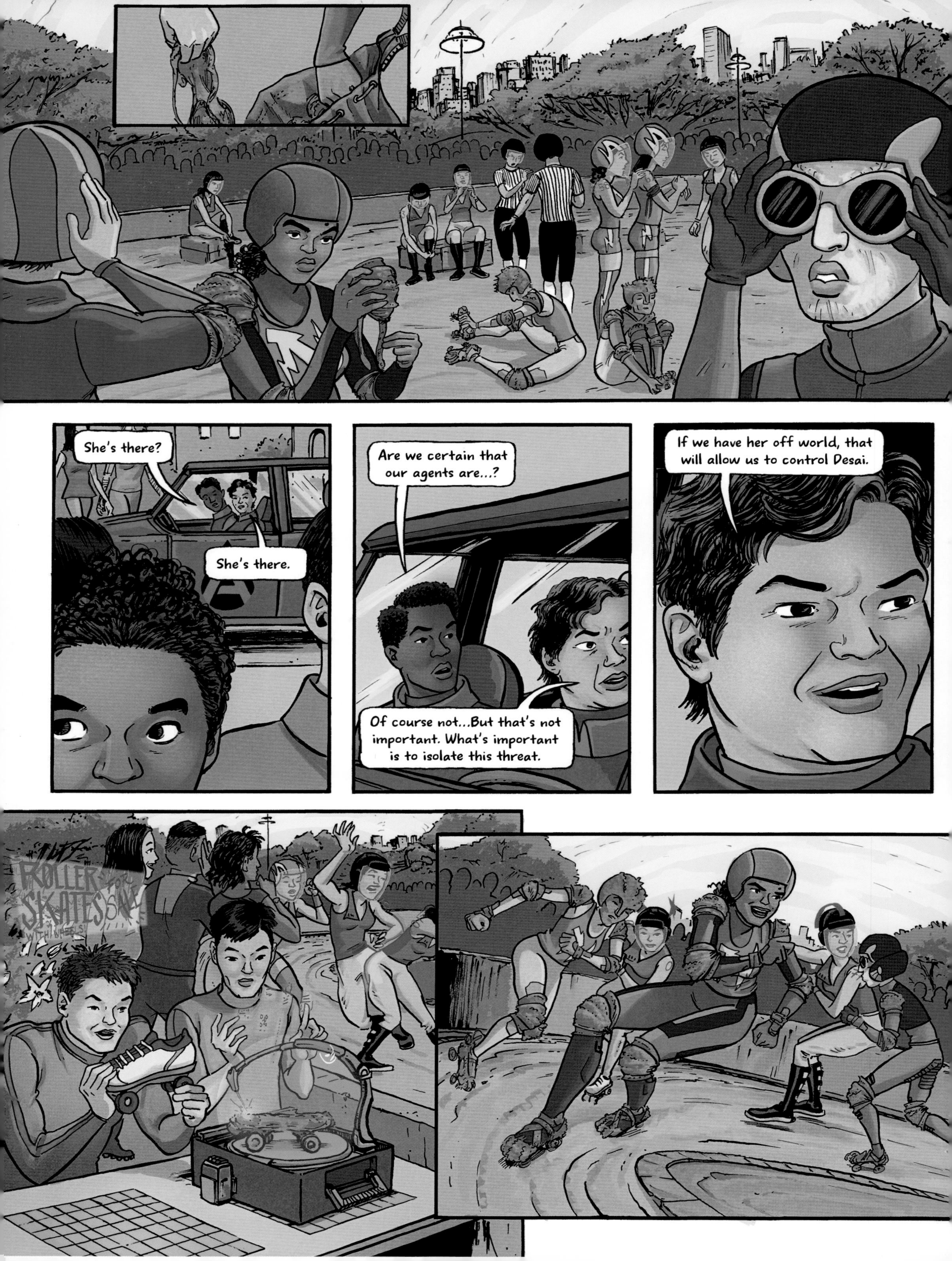
She's there?
She's there.
Are we certain that our agents are...?
Of course not...But that's not important. What's important is to isolate this threat.
If we have her off world, that will allow us to control Desai.
ROLLER SKATES FOR SALE
WITH WHEELS!

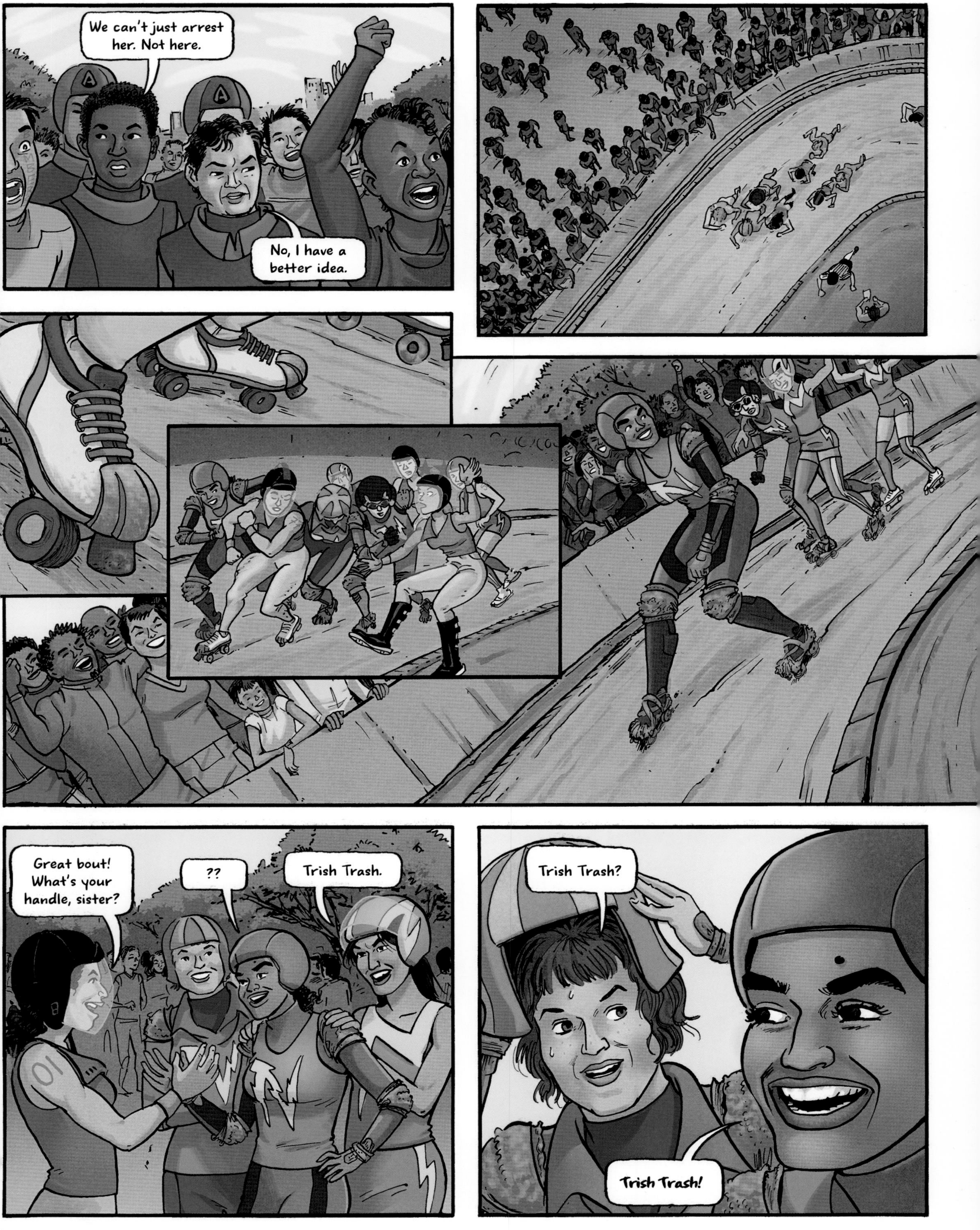
We can't just arrest her. Not here.
No, I have a better idea.
Great bout! What's your handle, sister?
??
Trish Trash.
Trish Trash?
Trish Trash!

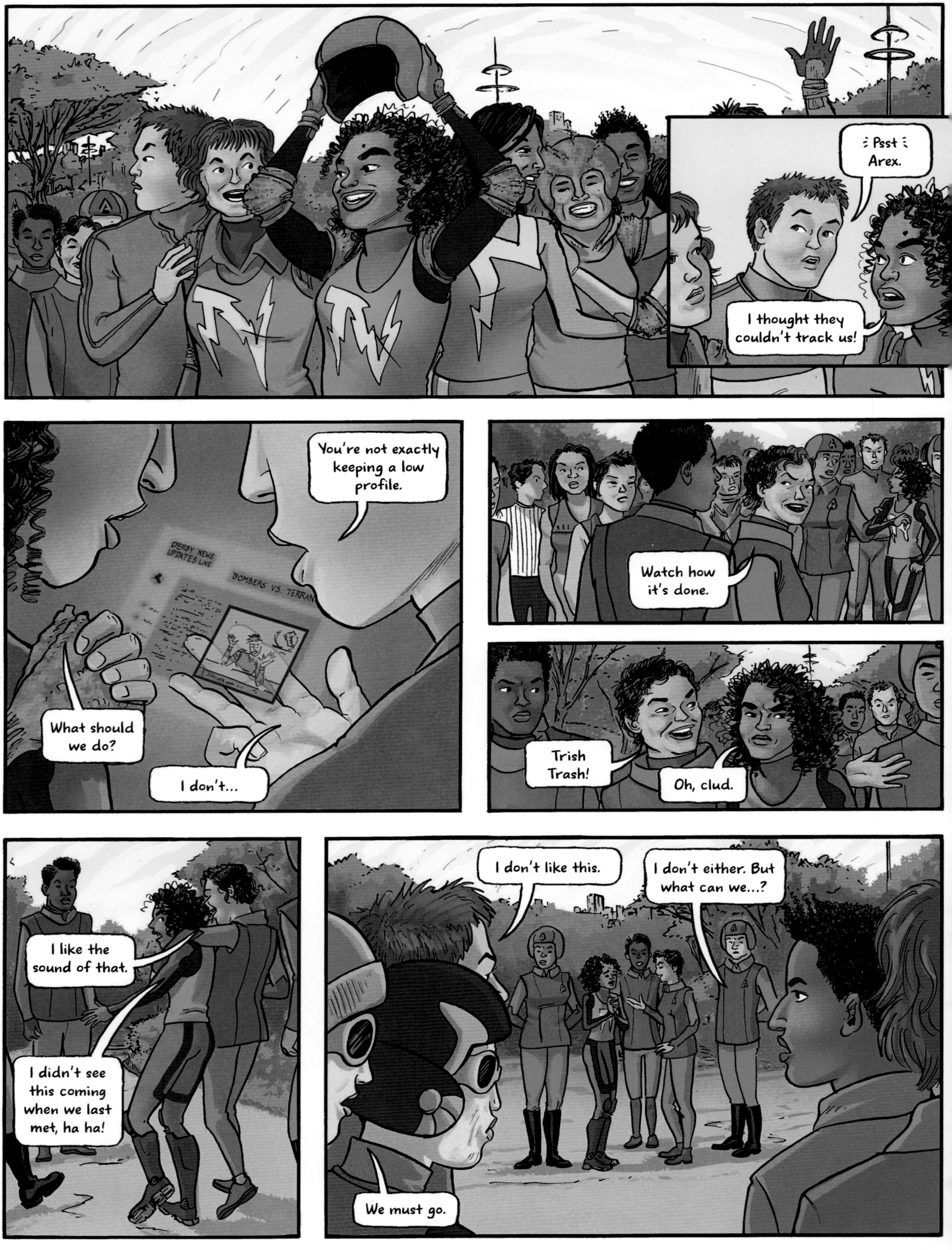

Psst Arex.
I thought they couldn't track us!
You're not exactly keeping a low profile.
DERBY NEWS UPDATES LIVE
BOMBERS VS. TERRAN
What should we do?
I don't...
Watch how it's done.
Trish Trash!
Oh, clud.
I like the sound of that.
I didn't see this coming when we last met, ha ha!
I don't like this.
I don't either. But what can we...?
We must go.

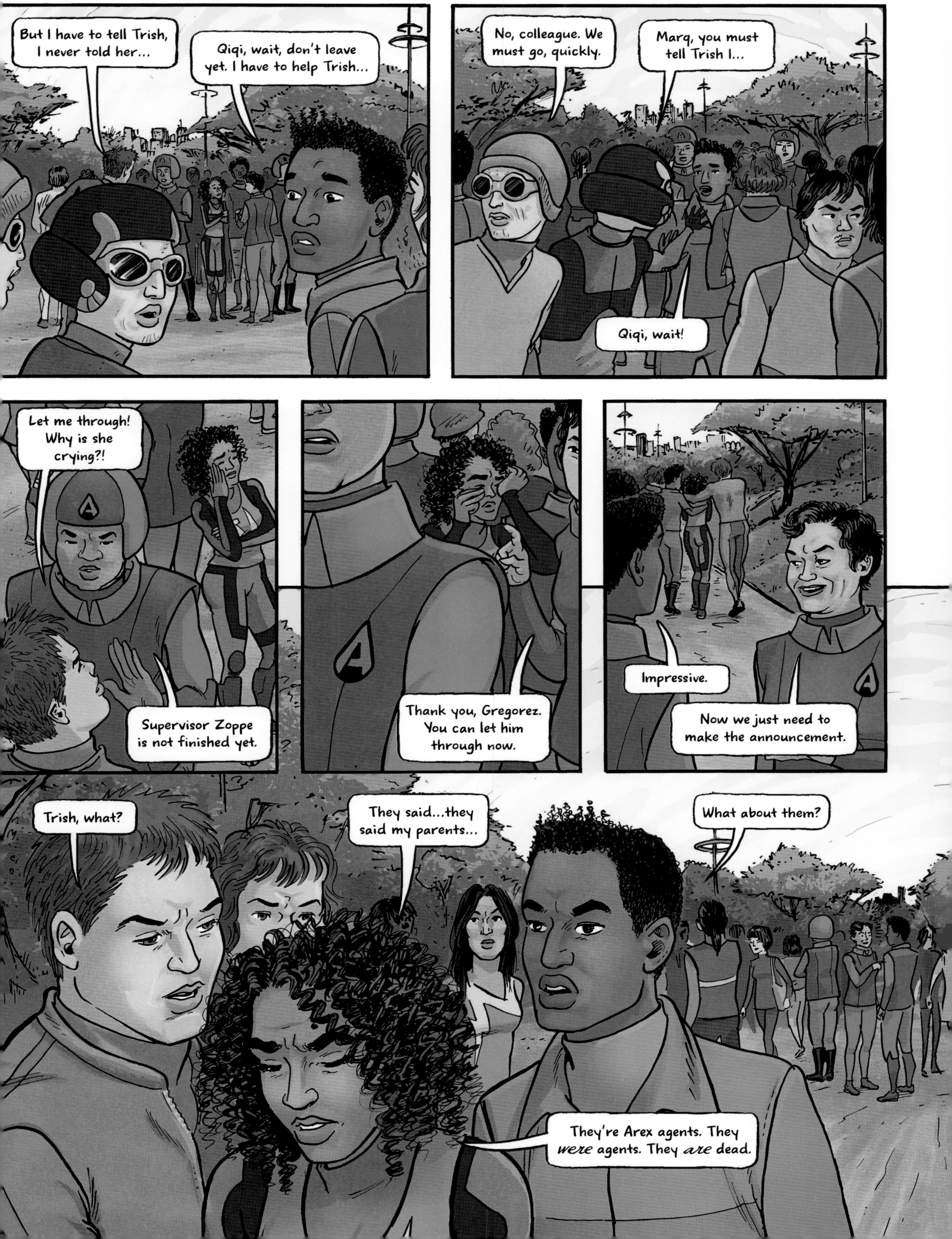

But I have to tell Trish, I never told her...
Qiqi, wait, don't leave yet. I have to help Trish...
No, colleague. We must go, quickly.
Marq, you must tell Trish I...
Qiqi, wait!
Let me through! Why is she crying?!
Supervisor Zoppe is not finished yet.
Thank you, Gregorez. You can let him through now.
Impressive.
Now we just need to make the announcement.
Trish, what?
They said...they said my parents...
What about them?
They're Arex agents. They *were* agents. They *are* dead.

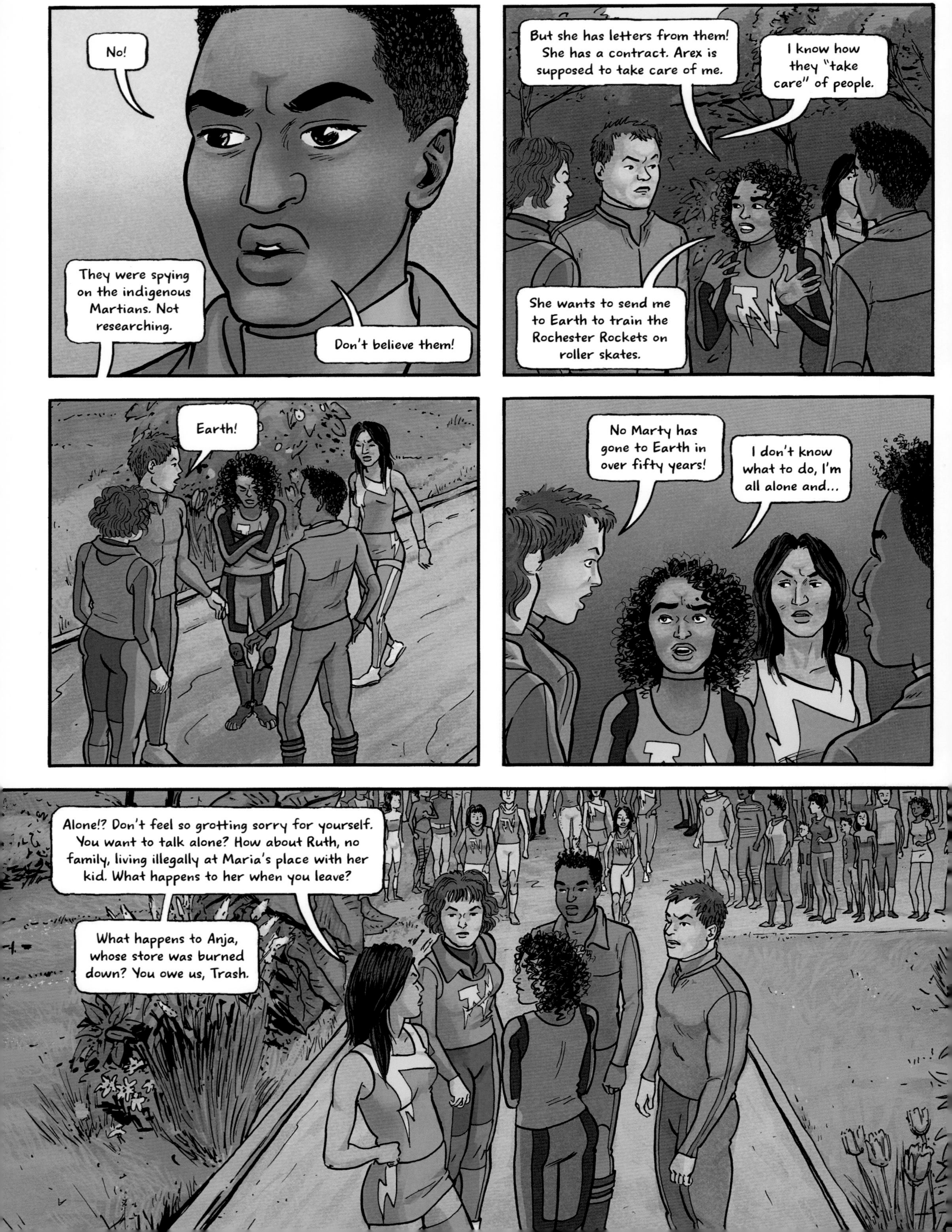
No!
They were spying on the indigenous Martians. Not researching.
Don't believe them!
But she has letters from them! She has a contract. Arex is supposed to take care of me.
I know how they "take care" of people.
She wants to send me to Earth to train the Rochester Rockets on roller skates.
Earth!
No Marty has gone to Earth in over fifty years!
I don't know what to do, I'm all alone and...
Alone!? Don't feel so grotting sorry for yourself. You want to talk alone? How about Ruth, no family, living illegally at Maria's place with her kid. What happens to her when you leave?
What happens to Anja, whose store was burned down? You owe us, Trash.

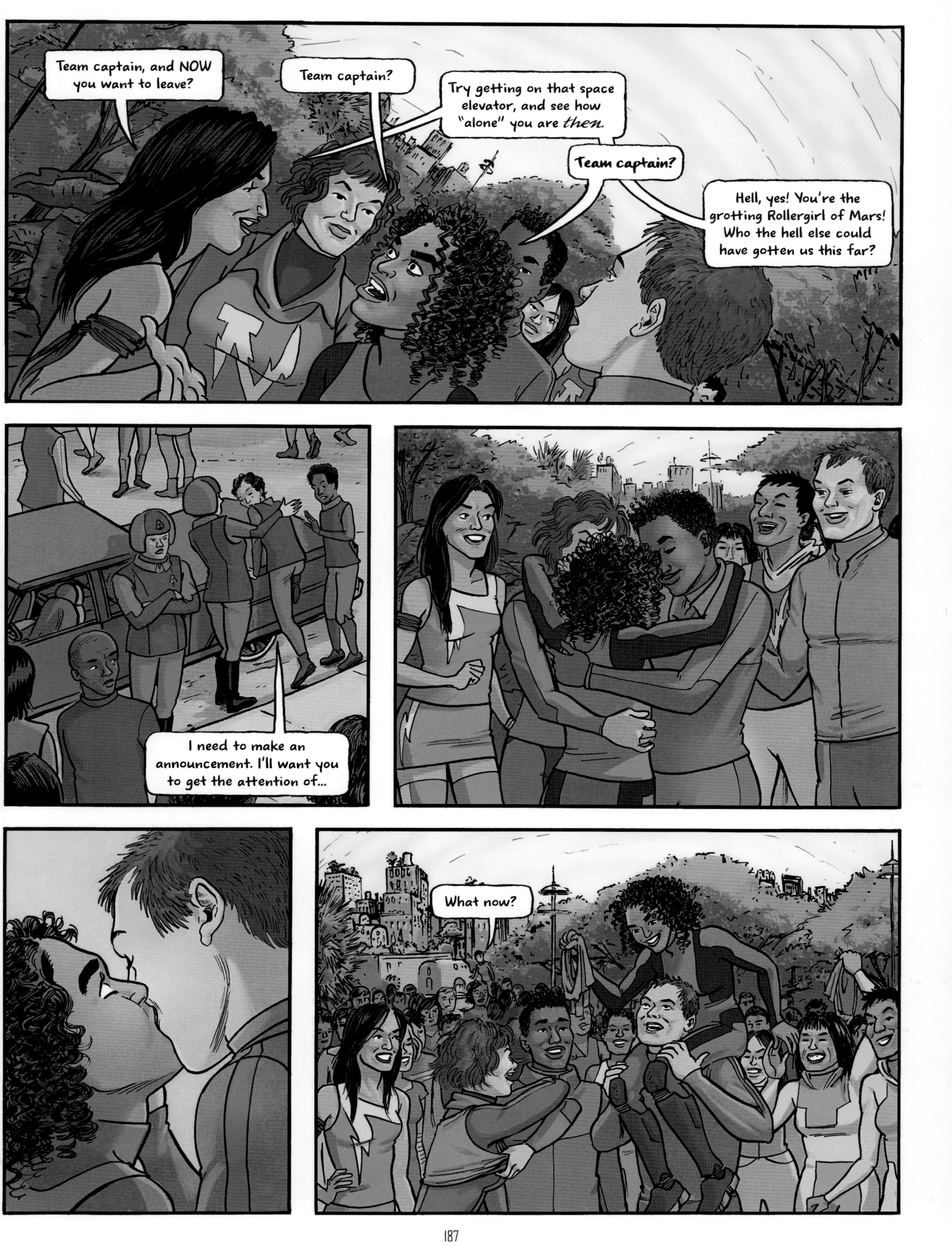
Team captain, and NOW you want to leave?
Team captain?
Try getting on that space elevator, and see how "alone" you are *then*.
Team captain?
Hell, yes! You're the grotting Rollergirl of Mars! Who the hell else could have gotten us this far?
I need to make an announcement. I'll want you to get the attention of...
What now?

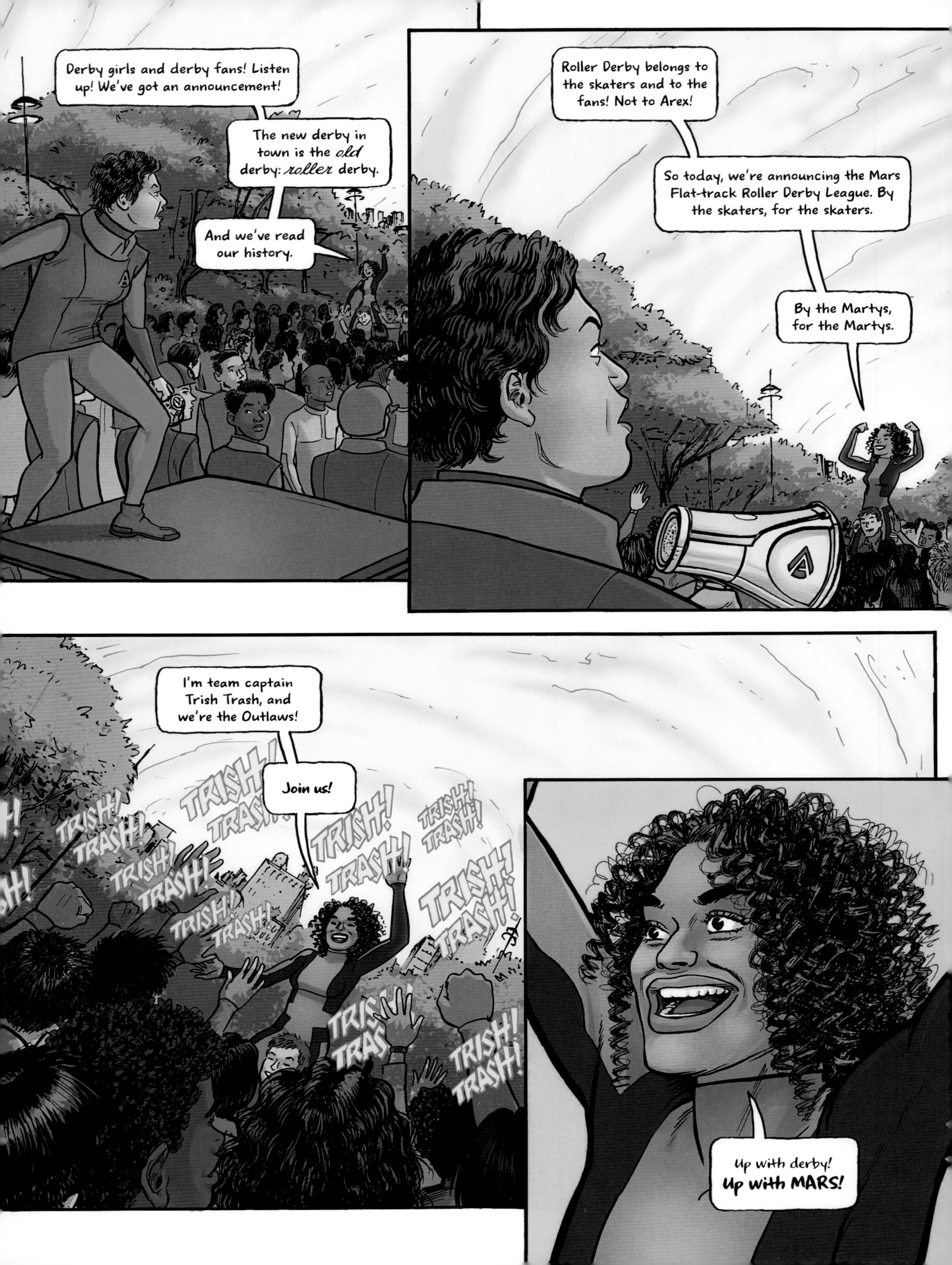

Derby girls and derby fans! Listen up! We've got an announcement!
The new derby in town is the *old* derby: *roller* derby.
And we've read our history.
Roller Derby belongs to the skaters and to the fans! Not to Arex!
So today, we're announcing the Mars Flat-track Roller Derby League. By the skaters, for the skaters.
By the Martys, for the Martys.
I'm team captain Trish Trash, and we're the Outlaws!
Join us!
TRISH! TRASH!
TRISH! TRASH!
TRISH! TRASH!
TRISH! TRASH!
TRISH! TRASH!
TRISH! TRASH!
TRISH! TRASH!
TRISH! TRASH!
Up with derby!
Up with MARS!

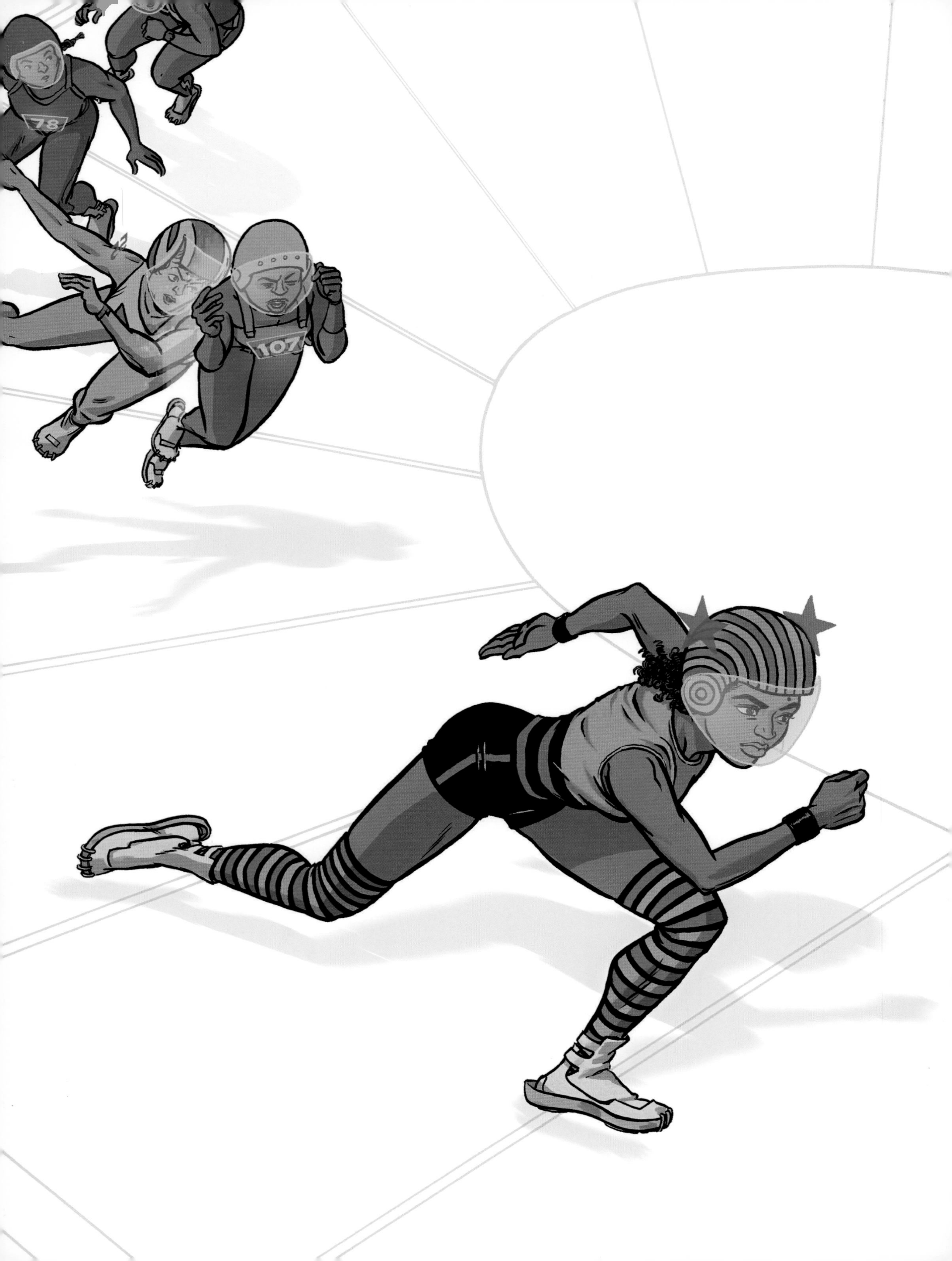
78
107

Hoverderby

Hoverderby is a contact sport played by two teams of five players each, hoverskating in a counter-clockwise direction on a banked track. One player on each team is able to score points (a "jammer"), by passing players on the other team. Non-scoring players ("blockers" and "pivots") must try to assist their team's jammer while impeding the jammer of the other team.

Basics of play [edit]

This section consists of a brief overview of hoverderby rules and play. It must not be construed as a complete or definitive description of such rules. For legal and complete rules, please consult sections 11326.8890 through 12870.3345 of the Log of WBTHDA.[1]

Games, known as "bouts," consist of short "jams," periods of play of up to two minutes. A bout lasts one hour of play, divided into two half-hour periods.

Jammers, indicated by two holographic stars on either side of their helmets, line up on the start line behind pivots (with a holographic stripe on their helmets), and blockers (no indication on helmets). At the whistle, players' hover skates are released from the track, and they must begin forward motion or they will slide into the infield, earning a penalty.

Jammers must complete a full non-scoring pass of all opposing players before they may begin scoring points. The first jammer to pass all opposing players is named the "lead jammer" and acquires a third holographic star above her helmet. The lead jammer has the ability to end the jam at any time by patting her hips with both hands. The pivot and the other blockers, may attempt to block any player on the opposing team using any legal blocking zone, and may contact any legal target zone. These zones consist of, essentially, the torso, hips, and upper arms (see section 12129.1120 of the Log for specifics). Hits and contact in other areas are penalties.

A team may field a roster of up to 14 players per game, five of whom will play in any one jam.

Required safety gear includes helmets with four-quadrant forcefields installed, and derbydromes must be equipped with forcefield barriers to protect audiences from players, who may be moving at up to 75 kph.

[1] Women's Banked Track Hoverderby Association

History [edit]

Hoverderby has its roots in the 20th century, in two distinct phases. The first of these emerged from endurance roller skating races. In the mid 1930s, under the direction of sports promoter Leo Seltzer, What was then known as "Roller Derby" morphed into a professional contact sport played between two teams of five players each, on a banked track.

DERBY GEAR: THEN AND NOW

PLAYER POSITION
HELMET "PANTY" COVER

HELMET

WAR PAINT

MOUTH GUARD

PLAYER NUMBER

ELBOW PADS

WRIST GUARDS

KNEE PADS

QUAD SKATES

LEATHER BODY

SPEED STRAP

PLATE

TRUCKS

WHEELS

TOE STOP

ALGA-FLEX BODY

MECH FRAME

HOVER PADS

HOVER TOESTOP

SHOCK HELMET

PLAYER POSITION HOLOGRAM

CONTROLS

PLAYER NUMBER

WRISTCOM/ NAV UNIT

HELMET-GENERATED FORCE FIELD

HOVER SKATES

2016

2192

Back matter art and colors by Lydia Roberts

Photo Credit: L. Roberts

At that time, skaters wore "quad roller skates," boots with four wheels attached in a rectangular configuration, as hover tech was not developed until 2078.

This phase of development saw some of the basic rules of the sport develop, but it was also marked by exploitative violence and fictional storylines akin to what spectators would have expected from professional wrestling at the time (this is well before the lo-EarthOrbit FullContact BattleSphere was developed). This iteration of the sport was designed to appeal to spectators of television, the two-dimensional video medium prevalent at the time.

This early era of derby was over by the end of that century. In 2002, however, the sport was unexpectedly revived by a group of women in Austin, Texas, who founded an all-female amateur league. (At that time, Texas, a region of the southwest part of the then-United States, still had a livable climate. See entry on pre-desertification southwest North America/major cities.) Though it was played on quad roller skates, and usually on a flat track, this version of derby is the true predecessor of today's hoverderby. The rules teams play by today were developed and refined in the first few decades of the 21st century. By 2014, there were over 1200 amateur leagues, most of them

Avocado Pitts

Photo Credit: L. Roberts

exclusively female, playing all around the world. Male and co-ed teams began picking up steam as well, and by 2050, it was unusual to find any medium-sized town almost anywhere in the world without its own amateur league. As the world approached the Meltdown, derby proved to be a durable and attractive pastime for a humanity on the brink.

When hovertech was commercialized in 2073-2078, one of the first applications was to derby. Immediately, however, it became clear that the canonical flat-track and flat-track rules would not work for hoverskating. The gory impalement and death of Avocado Pitts of the Manitoba Mamas as she skidded off the flat track during the Playoffs of 2078 on the vidblast in every fan's living room was the tipping point for the world, already reeling from billions suffering and dying from the Meltdown's floods and droughts that year. The outcry led the WFTDA (Women's Flat Track Derby Association) management to a long and very public soul searching, from which they emerged as the WBTHDA.

Banked tracks were built wherever hoverskates were in use, to contain the enormous speed and inertia of the radical (at the time) new technology. Nonetheless, the 2080s and 2090s saw many serious injuries. As soon as forcefields became commonly available, they were mandated in all hoverderbydromes in barrier walls, and in 2114, by the time virtually all derby was hoverderby, personal forcefields were required in all derby helmets.

The steeply-banked track of today's derby necessitates speedy play and allows for dramatic action, and it's widely thought that these developments have contributed to the enormous popularity of derby, which has held its position as humanity's number one sport for the last 38 years.

Hoverderby on Mars [edit]

Derby was exported to Mars with the Pioneers. It's well known that Mars' first settlers were derby fans, but they also improvised a flat track in the midst of their first rough scientific settlement, at Robinson Crater. Unfortunately, it soon became apparent that the dust kicked up by all that skating and falling would gum up every hoverpad and intake in the vicinity, so they abandoned the recreation league within three months.

2016 Conferences

1 Arcadia Conference, based in the Vastitas Borealis, home of Mars's number one team, the Boreale Bombers.

2 Southern Conference, based in Hellas.

3 Utopia Conference, based in Utopia Planitia.

4 Marineris Conference (AKA the Duster League) based in the Marineris Chasma.

Full list of Martian WBTHDA teams

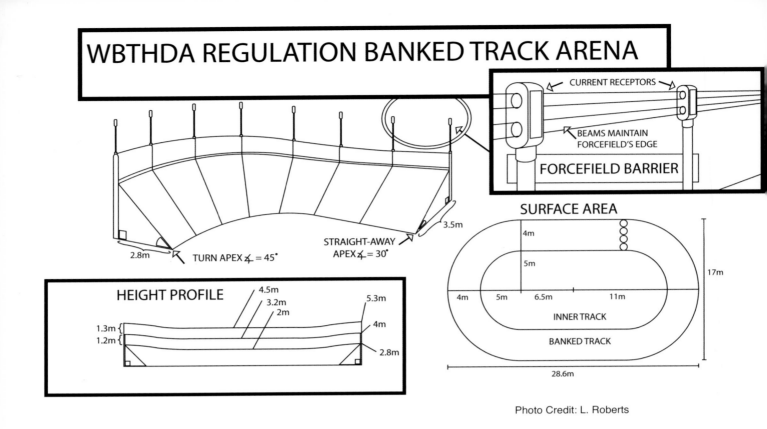

WBTHDA REGULATION BANKED TRACK ARENA

CURRENT RECEPTORS

BEAMS MAINTAIN FORCEFIELD'S EDGE

FORCEFIELD BARRIER

3.5m

STRAIGHT-AWAY APEX ∡ = 30°

2.8m

TURN APEX ∡ = 45°

SURFACE AREA

4m

5m

4m   5m   6.5m   11m

INNER TRACK

BANKED TRACK

17m

28.6m

HEIGHT PROFILE

4.5m
3.2m
2m
5.3m
1.3m {
1.2m {
4m
2.8m

Photo Credit: L. Roberts

Third wave settlers build the first crude derbydrome in Zubrinsville. Amateur teams played in this drome for 25 years, before it fell into disrepair. Today it can be visited as the Museum of Derby and Hoversport on Mars.

Derby became a professional sport on Mars in 2128 (39ME[1]), and there are today four conferences of teams.

[1] Mars Era year 39, which spans 2128-2129 CE

Radsuits

The sleek and powerful radsuit of today is evolved from bulky compression suits of the first Mars Pioneers. The Martian atmosphere at the time of the Pioneers' arrival was extremely thin, and average ambient outdoor temperature was –55°C, lower during the frequent dust storms. Habitats and work modules were pressurized and built under the surface, and any surface walks required pressure suits and oxygen supplies.

As terraforming efforts took hold in the beginning of the 22nd century, gradually various features of the pressure suits were rendered unnecessary, and the modern radsuit evolved. In 2113 (31ME),

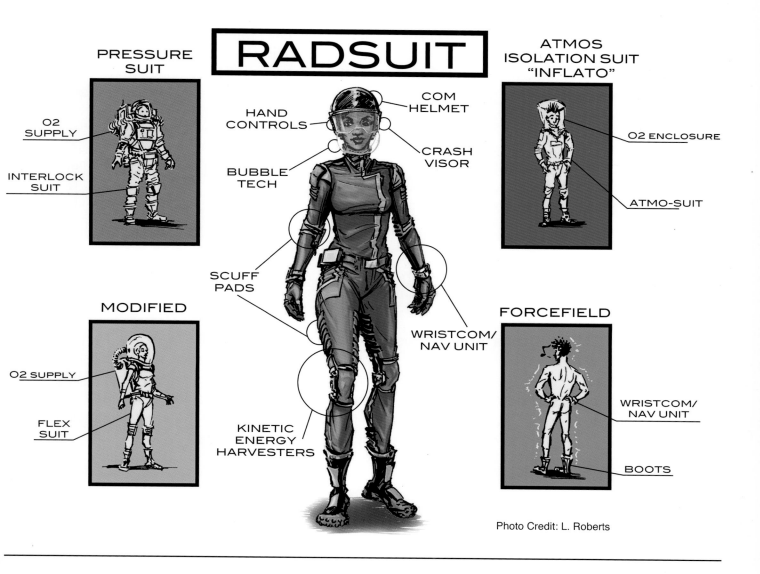

RADSUIT

PRESSURE SUIT
- O2 SUPPLY
- INTERLOCK SUIT

MODIFIED
- O2 SUPPLY
- FLEX SUIT

ATMOS ISOLATION SUIT "INFLATO"
- O2 ENCLOSURE
- ATMO-SUIT

FORCEFIELD
- WRISTCOM/ NAV UNIT
- BOOTS

- HAND CONTROLS
- COM HELMET
- CRASH VISOR
- BUBBLE TECH
- SCUFF PADS
- WRISTCOM/ NAV UNIT
- KINETIC ENERGY HARVESTERS

Photo Credit: L. Roberts

atmospheric pressure was deemed sufficient for comfortable non-pressurized surface walks. By 2138 (44ME), global temperatures had stabilized to the point that there is rarely life-threatening cold weather (except during dust storms). Atmospheric concentration of CO_2 remains poisonous to humans, and O_2 levels too low to breathe without supplementation and/or filtration, but masks to do this job are small and lightweight, and under normal circumstances, supplemental O_2 is not required. Kinetic energy pumps power the HUD, gas exchange, water conservation, and temperature controls of a modern radsuit.

Of course, cosmic radiation remains a threat, but radiation shielding was crude in those early suits, contributing to high levels of DNA damage and disease. Terraformation researchers continue to work on methods to create the magnetosphere that Mars still lacks, and drug treatments for radiation exposure are very effective. Nonetheless, one of the most important functions of a radsuit is the shielding it offers the wearer. This shielding is also required to be installed in all buildings.

Despite the obvious utility of radiation shielding, the Planetary Council of Mars has felt it necessary to issue a series of regulations in the last few years having to do with radsuits. Many Mars citizens have taken to wearing Atmos Isolation Suits (popularly known as "inflatos"), partial radsuits, and even flimsy rebreathers with goggles, all of which will assist with making the atmosphere breathable, but will not protect the wearer from radiation. Wearing nothing but a forcefield is quite dangerous and has produced outraged pundits on the vidblast, but regulation has not yet been issued regarding this fashion among the young and trendy.

Arex has issued rules for those with an ACSOD[1] of –20K per individual (in other words, an individual eligible for a TLA[2]), requiring full radsuit use at all times for the protection of Arex's investment and the individual's family ACSOD. Violators may be prosecuted.

[1] Ares Collective Statement of Debt

[2] Temporary Labor Assignment

The Homestead Debate

By 2062, Earth was locked into a warming feedback loop, headed for the Meltdown. Tac Nontilor, the visionary founder of Arex, then known as Ares Exploration Corporation, had sent several missions to Mars already, including the Mayflower, one of nine ships carrying the settlers now thought of as the Pioneers. Rapid desertification in central Africa, Australia, and in the south of the United States of America threatened to spark a world war, as it did in fact in 2076. This was the scene when Nontilor delivered his electrifying talk at TED 2062 proposing a Homesteading effort on Mars.

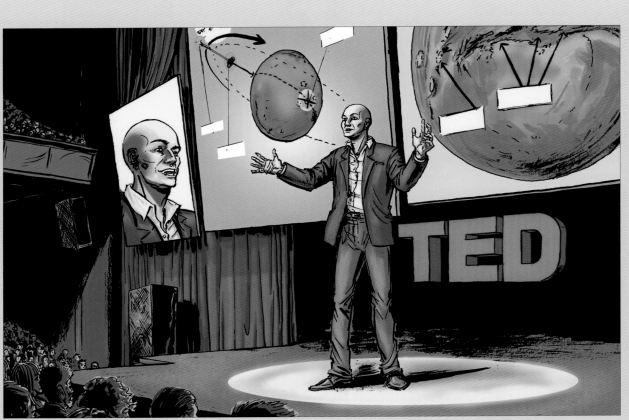

Tac Nontilor at TED 2062

Photo Credit: L. Roberts

Homesteading citizens arrive on the first Arex transport 2072.

Photo Credit: L. Roberts

Nontilor suggested that the United Nations (precursor to the Planetary Council of Mars) offer land to colonists on Mars in exchange for developing that land. Arex would provide transport to Mars and materials that the colonists would need to begin life there (habitats, farm equipment, pressure suits, even food and water), in exchange for a percentage of their products, or for a percentage of their work hours to be spent on Arex development projects. Nontilor's proposal was akin to a National Guard contract, and was proposed in a spirit of helping those whose lives were coming apart due to the environment's collapse. Nonetheless, it was immediately attacked by pundits as a kind of "slavery," which argument was completely undermined by the voluntary nature of the contracts.

The UN, unable to muster sufficient troops to control the unrest in the most severely affected areas of Earth, immediately embraced the idea, which then provided a much-needed safety valve that postponed the worst violence until the war in 2076-2081. No colonist was forced to emigrate, and in fact, despite the dangers and unknowns, demand was immediately very high. Arex's shuttles began delivering settlers with Civic Labor Agreements to Mars in 2072 (11ME), and, as the space elevators on Mars and Earth were completed, continued on an increasingly rapid schedule for the next 15 years, peaking in 2087.

Criticism in the media by Terrans opposed to the program changed in character over time from accusations of a new style of slavery to the accusation that Arex could take more people to Mars if it tried. Conditions on Earth deteriorated and attacks on the shuttles, particularly from the increasingly lawless Habitats [1], increased until the last shuttle arrived in 2110 (30ME).

A total of nearly one million humans were saved by the Homestead program from almost certain destruction in the Meltdown.

[1] "Piracy Aboard the Habitats: the Decline of Humanity's Life-Saving Space Stations in the aftermath of the Meltdown". Balthazar Commission Hearings, Volume XI. Habitat Archives and Research Center. March 22, 2141. Sections IV.3245.29 to IV.5678.01

Native Martians

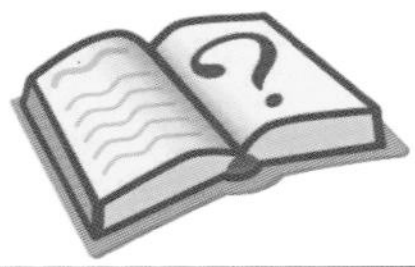

This page makes controversial statements, and needs to cite research as justification. Please help wiki.marsred improve this article.

(disambiguation)

- *Native martians,* non-human beings evolved on Mars (indigenous Martians)
- *Native martians,* humans born on Mars (commonly known as Martys)

Main article: Human colonization of Mars

In the last 25 years, there have been numerous but as yet unconfirmed reports of sightings of humanoid [needs citation] creatures in the Martian outback. These beings, known as "Bugs", for their insect-like [needs citation] appearance, live in caves [needs citation] and prey on humans [needs citation] living in isolated areas, such as moisture farmers in the midlands.

Arex and the PCM[1] has known about native Martians since the pioneers, but has kept that knowledge from settlers in an effort to prevent terror and panic [needs citation].

Knowledgable sources report that the natives' attacks are increasing in frequency [needs citation], and humans should gird for battle [needs citation].

[1] Planetary Council of Mars

THE MARTIAN MENACE

Native martian (artist's conception)

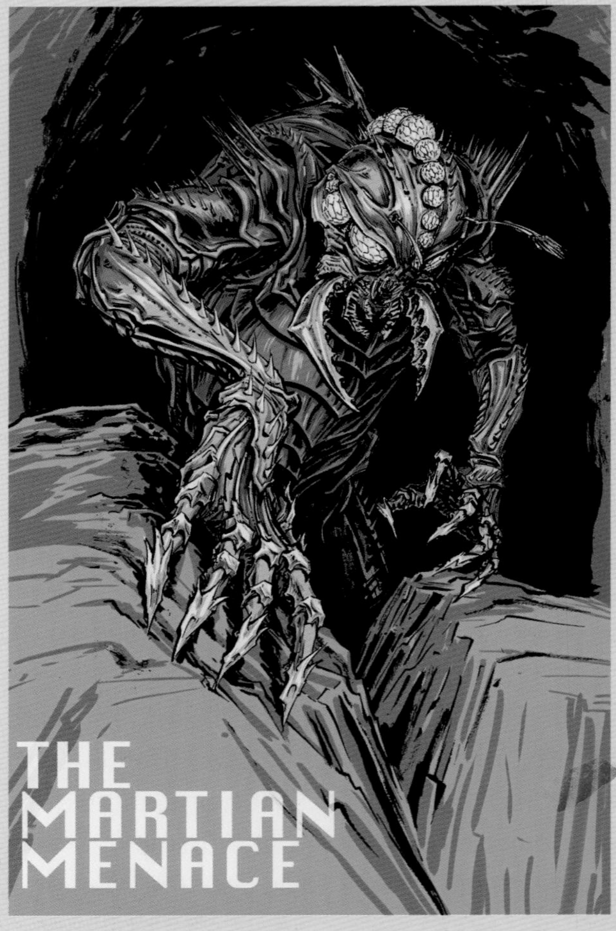
THE
MARTIAN
MENACE

Photo Credit: L. Roberts

Ares Collective Statement of Debt (ACSOD) [edit]

The Ares Collective Statement of Debt (ACSOD) is a report run each micro-second on all human Martian residents deriving from their legally-binding contractual obligations with Governmental and Quasi-Governmental Bodies on Mars (GQGBM).

The ACSOD was implemented in ME20 when large numbers of First Wave settlers (Homesteaders) who had signed indenturement contracts for their passage and equipment began to fail and face bankruptcy. Initially, TLAs (Temporary Labor Assignments) were assigned haphazardly and came without warning. The ACSOD was an attempt to standardize application of the TLA Rule and give settlers predictability as to when they might expect to be asked to participate in Civic Labor for the greater good.

The ACSOD can be used to determine eligibility for goods and services provided by the GQGBM, but it is illegal to discriminate based on ACSOD. An individual's ACSOD is instantly accessible to any official of the GQGBM via wristcom, or failing that, retinal scan.

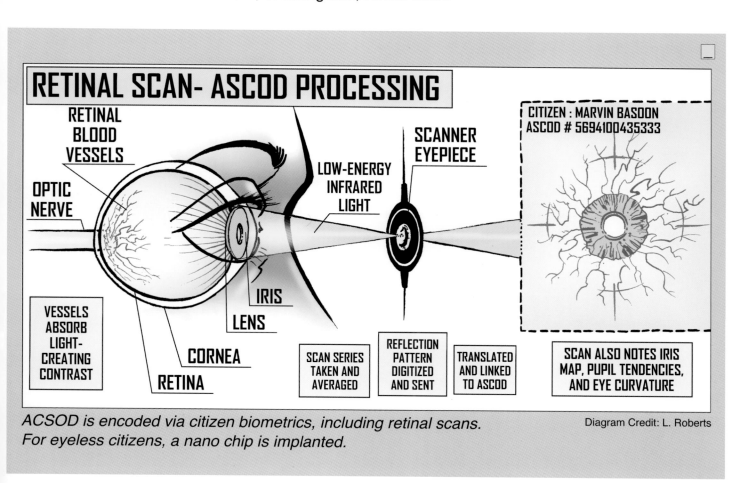

RETINAL SCAN- ASCOD PROCESSING

RETINAL BLOOD VESSELS

OPTIC NERVE

LOW-ENERGY INFRARED LIGHT

SCANNER EYEPIECE

CITIZEN : MARVIN BASDON
ASCOD # 5694100435333

IRIS

LENS

CORNEA

RETINA

VESSELS ABSORB LIGHT-CREATING CONTRAST

SCAN SERIES TAKEN AND AVERAGED

REFLECTION PATTERN DIGITIZED AND SENT

TRANSLATED AND LINKED TO ASCOD

SCAN ALSO NOTES IRIS MAP, PUPIL TENDENCIES, AND EYE CURVATURE

ACSOD is encoded via citizen biometrics, including retinal scans. For eyeless citizens, a nano chip is implanted.

Diagram Credit: L. Roberts

Temporary Labor Assignment (TLA) [edit]

When Terrans made the choice to emigrate to Mars during the Meltdown, more often than not, they escaped extremely dire situations in their home regions, including war, drought, and famine. In deciding to take the radical step of emigrating, these humans took action to assure the future for their families. But they were in many cases without resources, unable to pay for their passage, nor the substantial costs of setting up a Homestead to begin hygrofarming or algae tanking.

Arex's founder, Tac Nontilor, foresaw this problem when he first proposed the Homestead program. His revolutionary solution was to allow these first-wave Homesteaders to pay for their passage and equipment by becoming better Martian citizens, and contributing a portion of their labor, or the fruits of their labor, to developing Mars. He called these contracts Civic Labor Agreements. The labor of early settlers had a major impact on the human habitability of Mars.

Opponents of the practice misleadingly took to calling the Civic Laborers, "Indents," after the indenturement contracts enforced during the brutal colonizations by European Terrans of various Terran landmasses such as those later known as Australia and the United States of America (see article on Pre-Meltdown Geopolitical Boundaries and Nation-States).

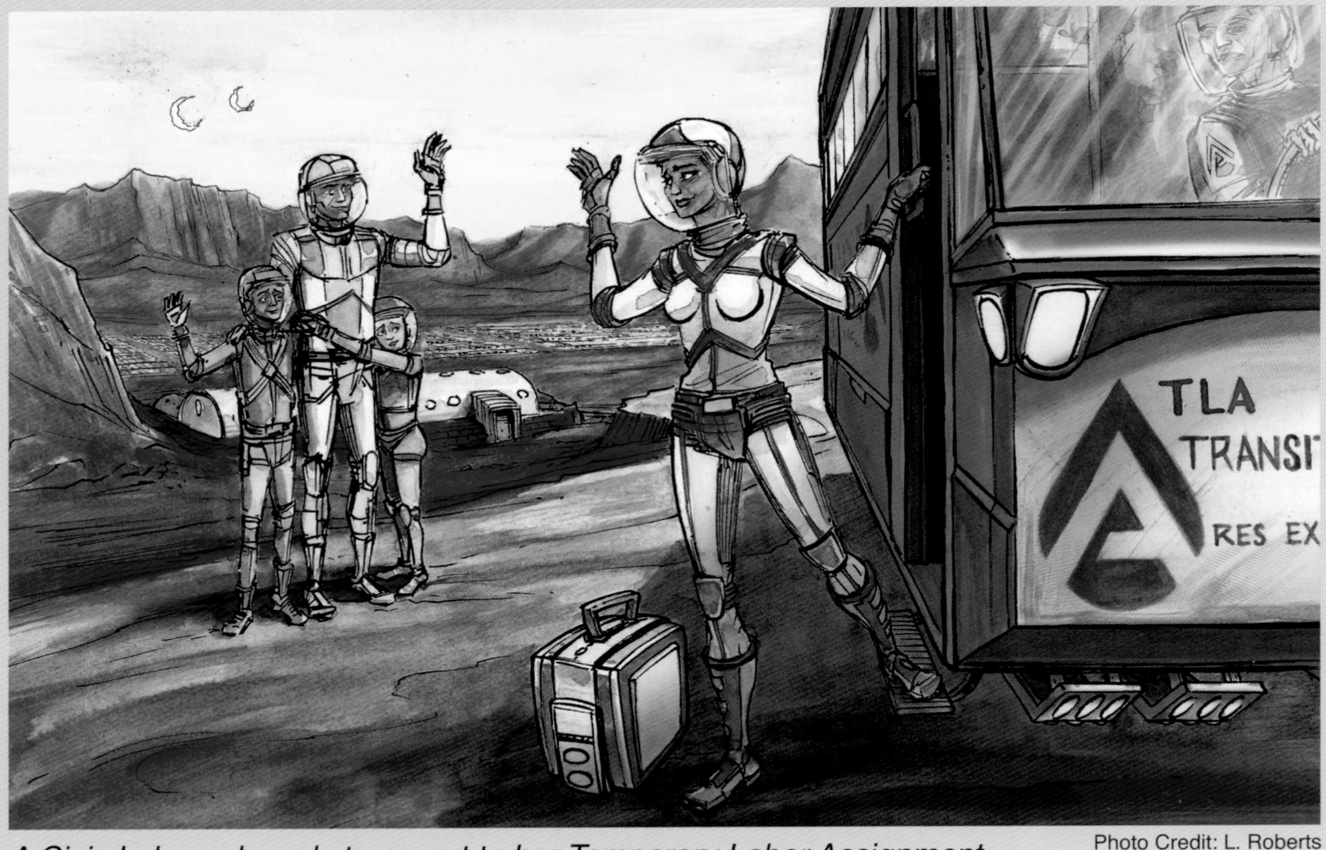

TLA
TRANSI
RES EX

A Civic Laborer boards transport to her Temporary Labor Assignment.

Photo Credit: L. Roberts

Unfortunately, due to unexpectedly adverse conditions, many Civic Laborers overreached their ability to produce sufficient quantities of water or whatever other agricultural products they had agreed to contribute, and Arex (Then known as Ares Exploration Company) was left with a difficult dilemma: how to maintain fairness among settlers, yet support the growth of the colony. Thus was born a revolutionary concept: the Temporary Labor Assignment (TLA). The TLA, though involuntary in the sense that implementation would be triggered based on the status of an individual or family's ACSOD, proved an extremely efficient vehicle both to develop new resources for the planet (in particular via asteroid mining) as well as to erase large amounts of family debt, as Arex pays generous hazard bonuses for off-world assignments, and decease in the service of a TLA triggers automatic full debt forgiveness for the immediate family members (up to 4 individuals) of the defunct worker.

Asteroid Mining [edit]

Early attempts at asteroid mining involved altering asteroids' orbits until they could be captured into near Earth orbit. This approach has obvious dangers, but the increasingly dire environmental conditions coming to bear on Earth during the 2040s made exporting mining activities off world too attractive to resist. The first two asteroids captured (2007AJAM8 and 2010JRMA6) provided much-needed rocket fuel used by Ares Exploration Company (later Arex) for its initial colonization forays to Mars with the Pioneers. In addition, the gold and platinum mined was so plentiful that it caused a short-lived global economic panic in 2047 as the price of gold fell precipitously, and many of the forebears of those who later became Third Wave Martian settlers, popularly known as Freemen, lost the majority of their wealth. This incident is memorialized in the lore of the Freemen as the End of the Yellow Brick Road and marks the beginning of their fixation as a group on "Blue," or water. (See article on Freemen (Martian Survivalist Colonies)).

Asteroid 2023QVC6, AKA "Black Sky"

Photo Credit: L. Roberts

The third asteroid dragged into Earth orbit, 2023QVC6, popularly known as, "Black Sky," missed its target and collided with Earth near Boca Raton, United States of America, in 2052. The resulting destruction was massive, with an estimated 65,000 immediate casualties, and another 1,086,000 over the next few months. Ironically, this terrible disaster may have postponed the demise of the rest of Florida (see article on Pre-Meltdown Geographical Land Masses) for a bit longer, as the dust in the atmosphere postponed the Meltdown by an estimated 5 years.

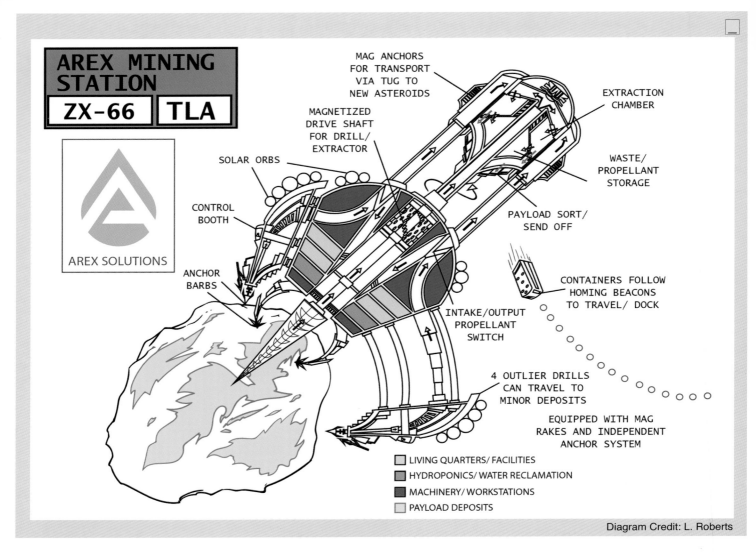

AREX MINING STATION

ZX-66 | **TLA**

AREX SOLUTIONS

MAG ANCHORS FOR TRANSPORT VIA TUG TO NEW ASTEROIDS

EXTRACTION CHAMBER

MAGNETIZED DRIVE SHAFT FOR DRILL/ EXTRACTOR

WASTE/ PROPELLANT STORAGE

SOLAR ORBS

PAYLOAD SORT/ SEND OFF

CONTROL BOOTH

CONTAINERS FOLLOW HOMING BEACONS TO TRAVEL/ DOCK

ANCHOR BARBS

INTAKE/OUTPUT PROPELLANT SWITCH

4 OUTLIER DRILLS CAN TRAVEL TO MINOR DEPOSITS

EQUIPPED WITH MAG RAKES AND INDEPENDENT ANCHOR SYSTEM

☐ LIVING QUARTERS/ FACILITIES
☐ HYDROPONICS/ WATER RECLAMATION
☐ MACHINERY/ WORKSTATIONS
☐ PAYLOAD DEPOSITS

Diagram Credit: L. Roberts

After the Black Sky disaster, asteroid mining companies abandoned the near-Earth-orbit strategy and began mining asteroids more or less in situ. (Although two large icy asteroids were intentionally crashed into Mars in 2054 and 2057 to generate atmosphere, heat, and humidity as part of a terraformation stage later criticized as "extreme" and "dangerous." (See article on Mars Terraformation Strategies.)

As a result of the more-dangerous deep space work conditions, however, the Worker Failure rate went up, and incidences of SPTSD (Space Post-Traumatic Stress Disorder) were on the rise, which raised the mining companies' insurance premiums to the point where many of these companies were faced with bankruptcy. Fortunately, this rise in Worker Failure coincided with an influx of available workers due to the inception of the TLA system on Mars, which stabilized worker population.

Asteroid mining is today the main source of processed ore for all Human colonies as well as Terra, where mining has been completely outlawed since 2085. It also plays a crucial role in providing water to Mars during the ongoing sequera[1]. While space labor remains dangerous, particularly in Asteroid Belt and Kuiper Belt assignments, annual casualty rates have come down quite a bit in recent years [needs citation], in contrast to the early history of asteroid mining.

[1]Sequera: severe drought conditions that show signs of having become baseline expectations. See articles on Mars Meteorological Conditions, Equatorial Earth post-Meltdown Sequera.

Ismail Khan [edit]

Ismail Khan was a water prospector, pilot, and engineer who arrived on Mars in 2073 (11ME) early in the second wave of settlements. Handsome and charismatic, he was also an early reality-vidblast star on the popular Pioneers series, seasons 4-13.

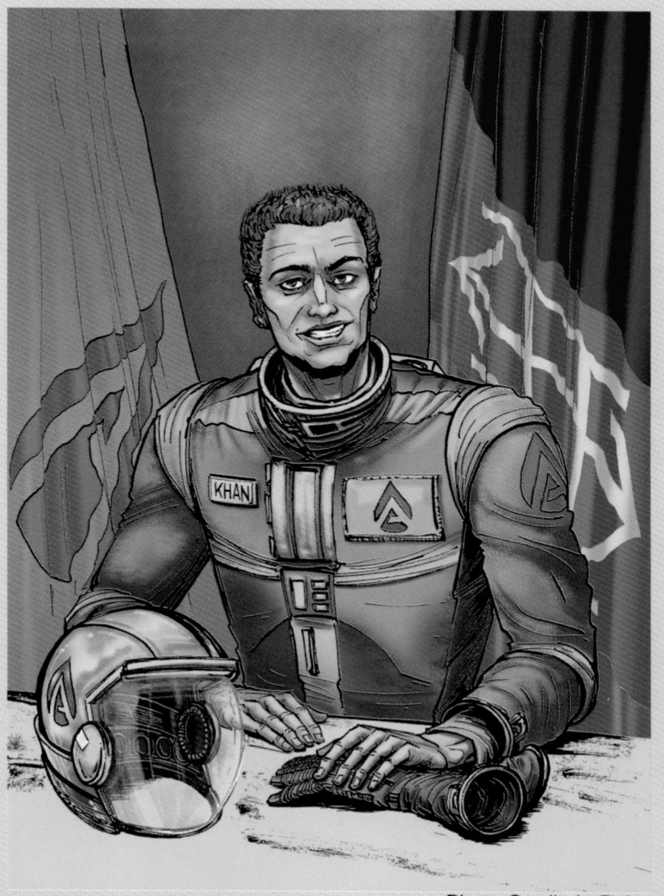
KHAN

Photo Credit: L. Roberts

Commander Ismail Khan in 2072.

As an employee of Arex, Khan, in conjunction with his partner, Nadia Vodyanova, developed the first prototype hydrosails today used by moisture farmers across Mars.

During the period 2075-2079 (13-14ME) Khan and Vodyanova prospected for water extensively in Vastitis. They discovered several important water sources that have since run dry due to over-utilization, or to some other unknown factor [needs citation].

During their last trip together, Aprilbis 11 of 14ME, Vodyanova reported that she had detected elevated levels of humidity in a cavern in Mawrth Vallis [needs citation]. She and Khan entered the cavern, and saw what she described as "tracks" in the dust, at which point she proposed leaving the cavern. Khan demurred, and descended deeper into the cavern. He was not seen again.

Vodyanova contended that he was abducted by indigenous Martians, a suggestion for which she was ridiculed until her death in 48ME. Sightings of what appear to be some kind of native species of Martian [needs citation] in the last 11 years have rehabilitated her reputation to an extent.

A recent run of the popular retro "comic strip" *Tales of the Early Colonists* contains several factual inaccuracies.

- Ismail Khan and Nadia Vodyanova wore full pressure suits when taking surface walks.
- Third Wave settlers known as the Freemen did not arrive on Mars until 2090 (20ME), and have never been documented as having engaged in open firefights with other settlers.
- Cyrus Khan, nephew of Ismail Khan, and later the founder of the controversial New Order of Green Men, was never taken along on water prospecting or hydro-drilling missions. At the time of Ismail Khan's disappearance, he was four years old.

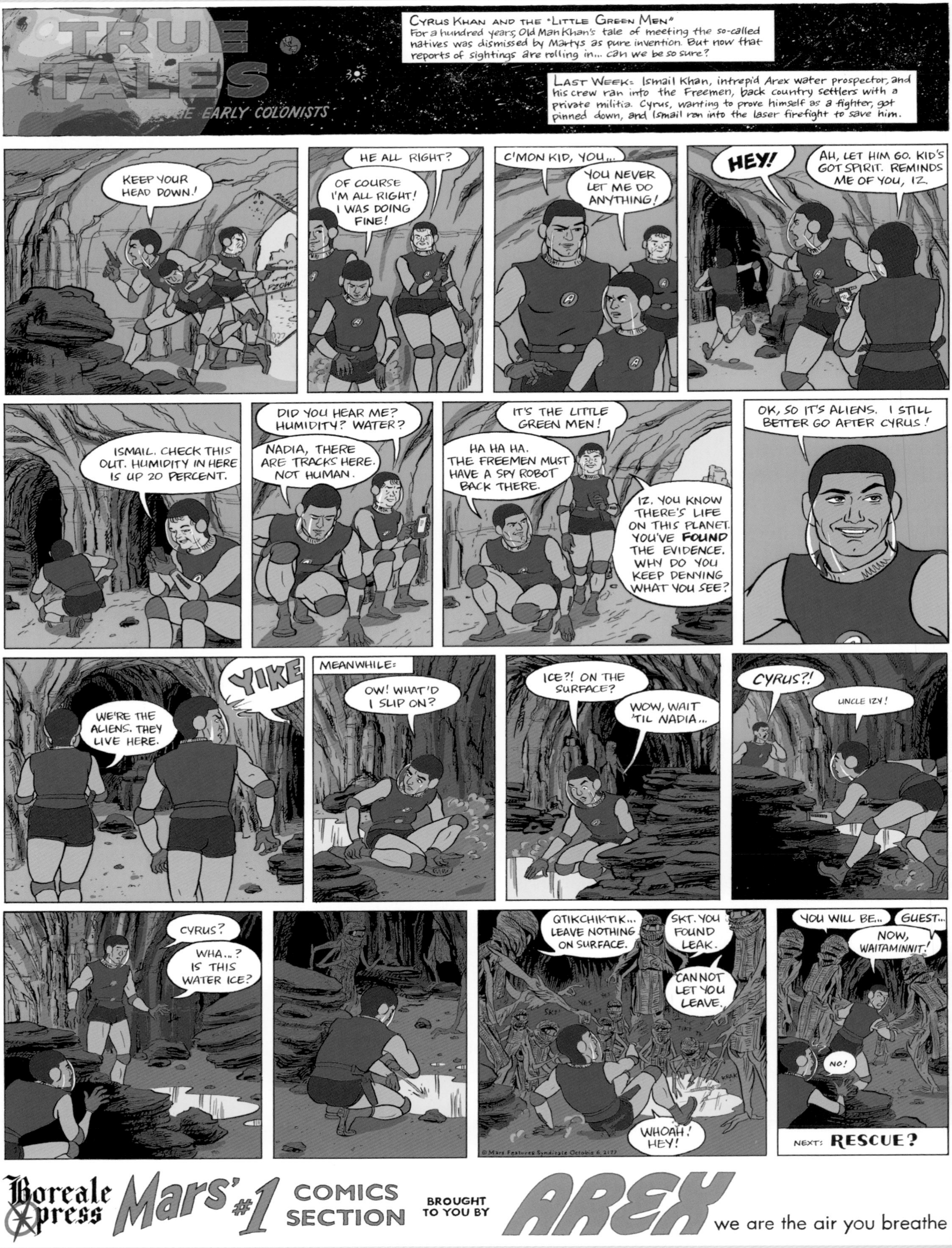

TRUE TALES
EARLY COLONISTS
CYRUS KHAN AND THE "LITTLE GREEN MEN"
For a hundred years, Old Man Khan's tale of meeting the so-called natives was dismissed by Martys as pure invention. But now that reports of sightings are rolling in... can we be so sure?
LAST WEEK: Ismail Khan, intrepid Arex water prospector, and his crew ran into the Freemen, back country settlers with a private militia. Cyrus, wanting to prove himself as a fighter, got pinned down, and Ismail ran into the laser firefight to save him.
KEEP YOUR HEAD DOWN!
PZOW!
HE ALL RIGHT?
OF COURSE I'M ALL RIGHT! I WAS DOING FINE!
C'MON KID, YOU...
YOU NEVER LET ME DO ANYTHING!
HEY!
AH, LET HIM GO. KID'S GOT SPIRIT. REMINDS ME OF YOU, IZ.
ISMAIL. CHECK THIS OUT. HUMIDITY IN HERE IS UP 20 PERCENT.
DID YOU HEAR ME? HUMIDITY? WATER?
NADIA, THERE ARE TRACKS HERE. NOT HUMAN.
IT'S THE LITTLE GREEN MEN!
HA HA HA. THE FREEMEN MUST HAVE A SPY ROBOT BACK THERE.
IZ. YOU KNOW THERE'S LIFE ON THIS PLANET. YOU'VE **FOUND** THE EVIDENCE. WHY DO YOU KEEP DENYING WHAT YOU SEE?
OK, SO IT'S ALIENS. I STILL BETTER GO AFTER CYRUS!
WE'RE THE ALIENS. THEY LIVE HERE.
YIKE
MEANWHILE:
OW! WHAT'D I SLIP ON?
ICE?! ON THE SURFACE?
WOW, WAIT 'TIL NADIA...
CYRUS?!
UNCLE IZY!
CYRUS?
WHA...? IS THIS WATER ICE?
QTIKCHIKTIK... LEAVE NOTHING ON SURFACE.
SKT. YOU FOUND LEAK.
CANNOT LET YOU LEAVE.
WHOAH! HEY!
© Mars Features Syndicate Octobis 6, 2177
YOU WILL BE...
GUEST...
NOW, WAITAMINNIT!
NO!
NEXT: RESCUE?
Boreale Press
Mars' #1 COMICS SECTION
BROUGHT TO YOU BY
AREX
we are the air you breathe

Mars Features Syndicate Octobis 6 2177.

Photo Credit: J. Abel

Timeline of Mars Colonization [edit]

2050-2055 (0 - 2ME) The first wave of Martian settlers, known now as the "Pioneers" due to the reality vidblast series of the same name that documented the period and funded 78.95% [2] of the cost of the journey, arrived on Mars. The Pioneers arrived in a series of 9 ships owned by Ares Exploratory Corporation (later Arex) with international cooperation. Co-sponsoring nations included United States of America, the Russian Union, the European Alliance, Ghana, China, Japan, Indiastan, and United South American States, along with either 23 or 36 other countries and corporate units (up to 13 contributors remain in dispute, despite 17 cases brought and settled at the International Space Court).

The Pioneers were chosen in a very public sorting on the basis of their training and abilities, alongside personality traits and lack of immediate family members. Despite this process, attrition rate was high, due to accident, self-inflicted injury, as well as disease, as medicine had not yet developed Genetic Print technology. There were also a total of 20 seats reserved on the ships for private passengers who paid their own way.

2055-2070 (2 - 10ME) First generation Martians born, more ships arrived. Human population rose to 1000. Terraformation efforts managed to create a minimal atmosphere, and build a small amount of organic material in (carefully isolated) soil.

2060 (5ME) Bombardment with asteroids added water to atmosphere, and also resulted in the deaths of up to 236 Martians.

2065 (7ME) Arex built space elevators on Earth and Mars.

2072 (11ME) The Homestead program began shipping large numbers of settlers to Mars. Initially, many settlers self-funded the trip, or were sponsored by governments, but once the Hot War began (2076 - 2081) the majority of the settlers arrived under Civic Labor Agreements/ indenturement contracts with Arex. The Homestead program spanned the years 2072 - 2110 (30ME), peaking in 2087. Approximately 912,345 [3] human settlers arrived on Mars in this program, largely from the equatorial region of Earth, the area most brutally affected by the Meltdown.

2075-85 (12 - 17ME) An unknown number of ships (estimated 7) carrying members of an extremist Prepper cult left their private Habitat-style orbitenvironment and arrived on Mars. It's thought that at least one ship was lost in transit, and that in the range of 1300 undocumented settlers arrived in this wave. These are the ancestors of the Martians now known as Freemen, who tend to live in large self-sufficient mobile habitats in the outback of Mars, protected from surveillance by satellite shielding and powerful armaments. Despite the fact that these settlements are illegal, the MarsGuard has thus far proven unequal to the task of eradicating them.

Martians known as Freemen are thought to live in large mobile habitats protected from surveillance by satellite shielding and powerful armaments. [Artist's Rendition]

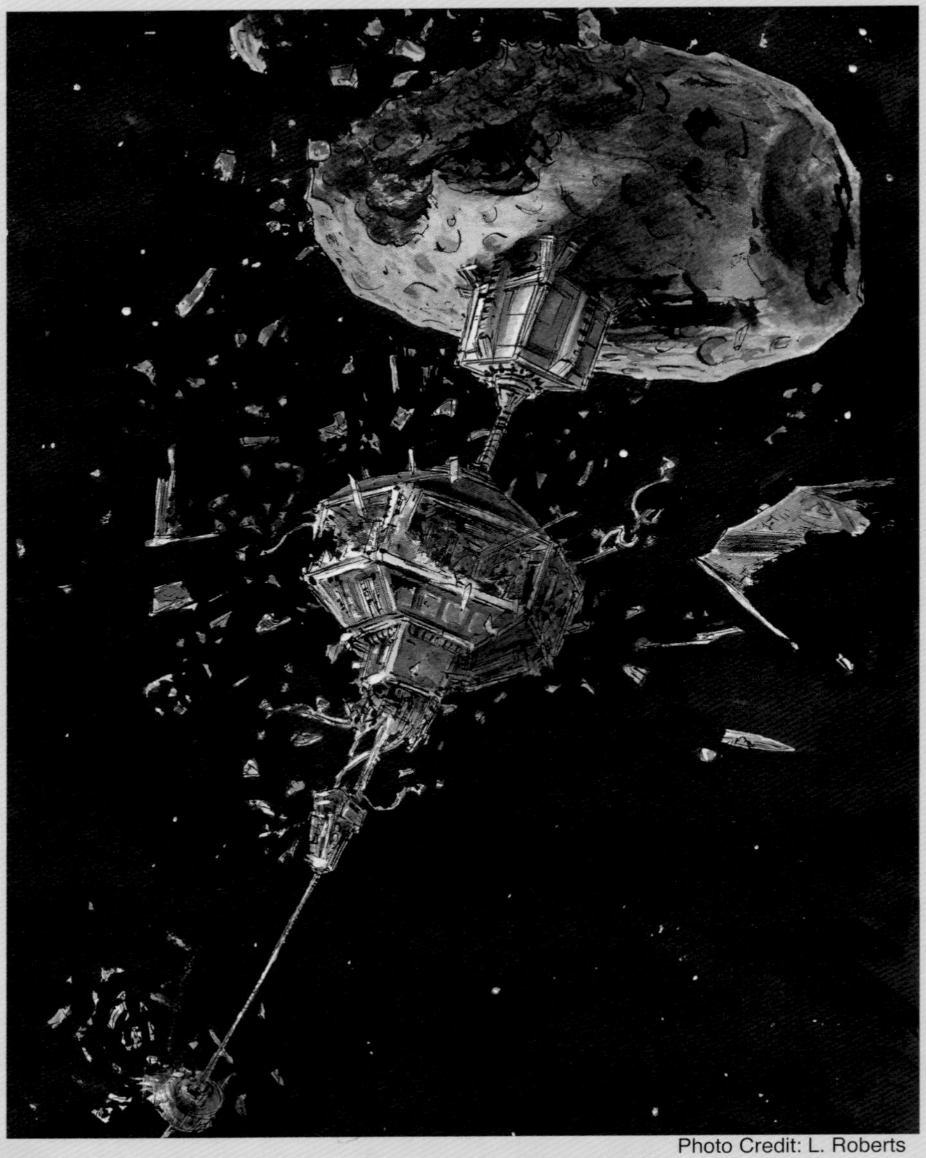

Photo Credit: L. Roberts

Martian partisan terrorists destroy the Homestead carrier Laura Ingalls Wilder in 2111 (30ME).

2080-82 (15 - 16ME) The Meltdown: Earth suffered catastrophic environmental collapse.

2083 (16ME) Earth ceased sending financial support to Mars. This year also marks Earth's complete ban on any kind of carbon-generating activity, creating a robust market for industrial and mining products from Mars and nearby asteroids.

2084 (17ME) Earth passed the Secure Our World Act (SOW), effectively banning any off-world settlers, whether originating on Mars, Europa, asteroids, or the orbiting Habitats, from returning to the surface.

2111 (30ME) The last of the Homestead ships arrived at the Martian space elevator, and was destroyed by Martian partisan terrorists before it could return to Earth, destroying 1.3 billion oras of cargo, killing three crew members, and causing massive damage to the space elevator itself. This is generally thought to mark the end of the Colonization phase of Martian history.

Living with Trish Trash for the last ten years has changed my life. I've become a roller derby fan, a Mars-colonization aficionado, and a lot better at drawing people of color. Collaborating closely with a talented cartoonist such as Lydia Roberts caused me to rethink how I approach panel layouts, perspective, and pacing. Building an entire world, instead of the smaller job of "only" figuring out the web of relationships among a group of people (though I had to do that too...) stretched my writing abilities and my perspective. Thinking about, and depicting how political awareness grows sneakily, and is then sometimes thrust upon us, is maybe entirely too a propos at the current moment.

Trish's Mars is boiling under the surface, poised on the verge of breaking the Terran colonial grip. And Trish is just a kid; what could she possibly do that could have any effect on the outcome of her unstable moment? I've also got kids. They're also living in a time of incredible upheaval that could turn out fine, or turn into bloody disaster. I'm grateful to Trish for helping me imagine a way out.

—Jessica Abel

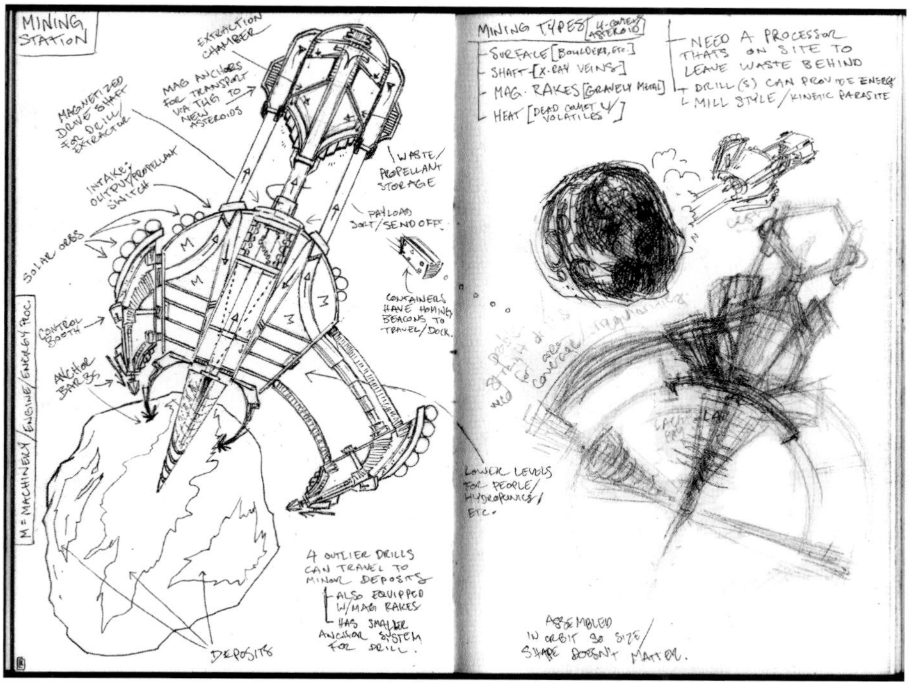

MINING STATION
EXTRACTION CHAMBER
MAGNETIZED DRIVE SHAFT FOR DRILL/EXTRACTOR
WASTE/PROPELLANT STORAGE
PAYLOAD SORT/SEND OFF
SOLAR ORBS
CONTAINERS HAVE HOMING BEACONS TO TRAVEL/DOCK.
CONTROL BOOTH
ANCHOR BARBS
M=MACHINERY/ENGINE/ENERGY PROC.
LOWER LEVELS FOR PEOPLE/HYDROPONICS/ETC.
4 OUTLIER DRILLS CAN TRAVEL TO MINOR DEPOSITS
ALSO EQUIPPED W/MAG RAKES
HAS SMALLER ANCHOR SYSTEM FOR DRILL.
DEPOSITS
MINING TYPES
SURFACE [BOULDERS, ETC.]
SHAFT [X-RAY VEINS]
HEAT [DEAD COMET VOLATILES]
NEED A PROCESSOR THATS ON SITE TO LEAVE WASTE BEHIND
DRILL(S) CAN PROVIDE ENERGY
MILL STYLE/KINETIC PARASITE
ASSEMBLED IN ORBIT SO SIZE/SHAPE DOESN'T MATTER.

Sketches by Lydia Roberts

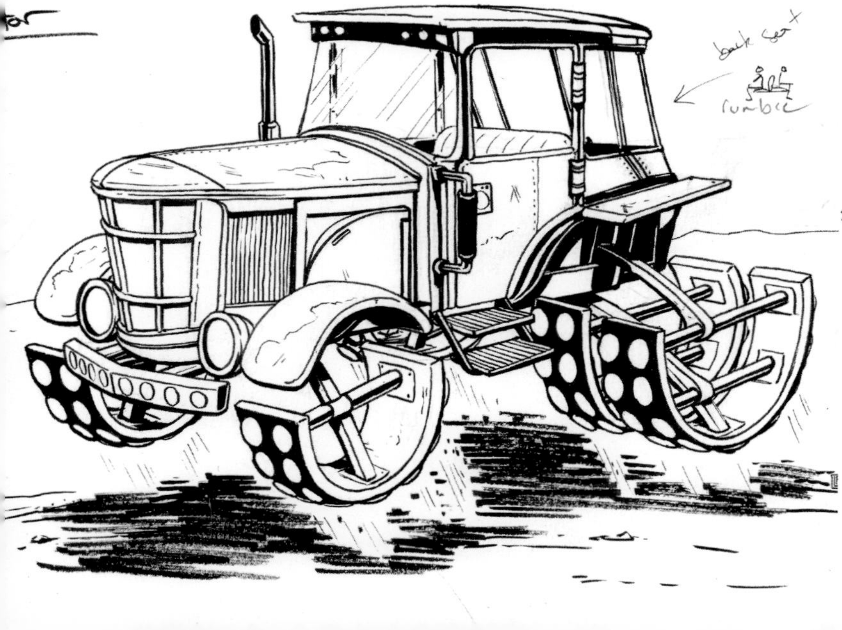

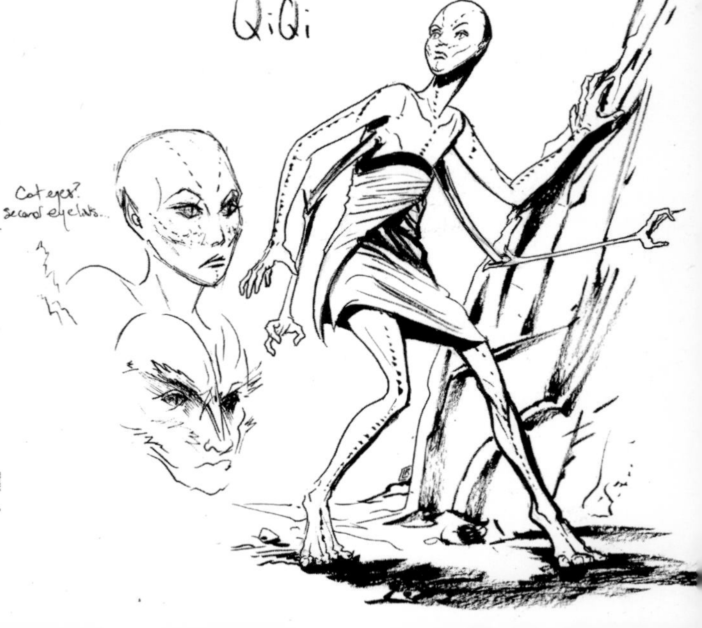

QiQi
Cat eyes? second eyelids...

Cartoonist and writer Jessica Abel is the author of *Growing Gills: How to Find Creative Focus When You're Drowning in Your Daily Life*, the graphic novel *La Perdida* (winner of the the 2002 "Best New Series" Harvey Award), as well as two collections of stories from her 1990s comic book *Artbabe*. She co-authored the graphic novel *Life Sucks*, and is the author of the graphic documentary (and podcast), *Out on the Wire*, about how the best radio producers in the world use story to keep us listening.
Abel and her husband, the cartoonist Matt Madden, were series editors for *The Best American Comics from 2007 to 2013*. Together they created two textbooks about making comics, *Drawing Words & Writing Pictures* and *Mastering Comics*. The Eisner-award nominated *Trish Trash: Rollergirl of Mars*, debuted in November 2016. Abel is chair of the Illustration Program at the Pennsylvania Academy of Fine Arts.
She lives with her family in Philadelphia, Pennsylvania.

Lydia Roberts lives and works in Brooklyn, New York. She creates comics, paintings, drawings, and other art paraphernalia and loves her Kawasaki dirt-bike. Born in Westchester, PA; raised in Atlanta, GA ; grew up in Albuquerque, NM. Lydia holds a BFA Cartooning and Illustration - SVA.

Walter Pezzali (known professionally as "Walter") is one of the most accomplished colorists working in French-language comics today. He was among the very first colorists to introduce digital coloring to the *bandes dessinées* industry and he's been a fixture in French comics for nearly two decades. The list of cartoonists Walter has worked with is a who's-who of the very best contemporary French cartoonists: Lewis Trondheim, Joann Sfar, Killoffer, Manu Larcenet, Christophe Blain, and many more.

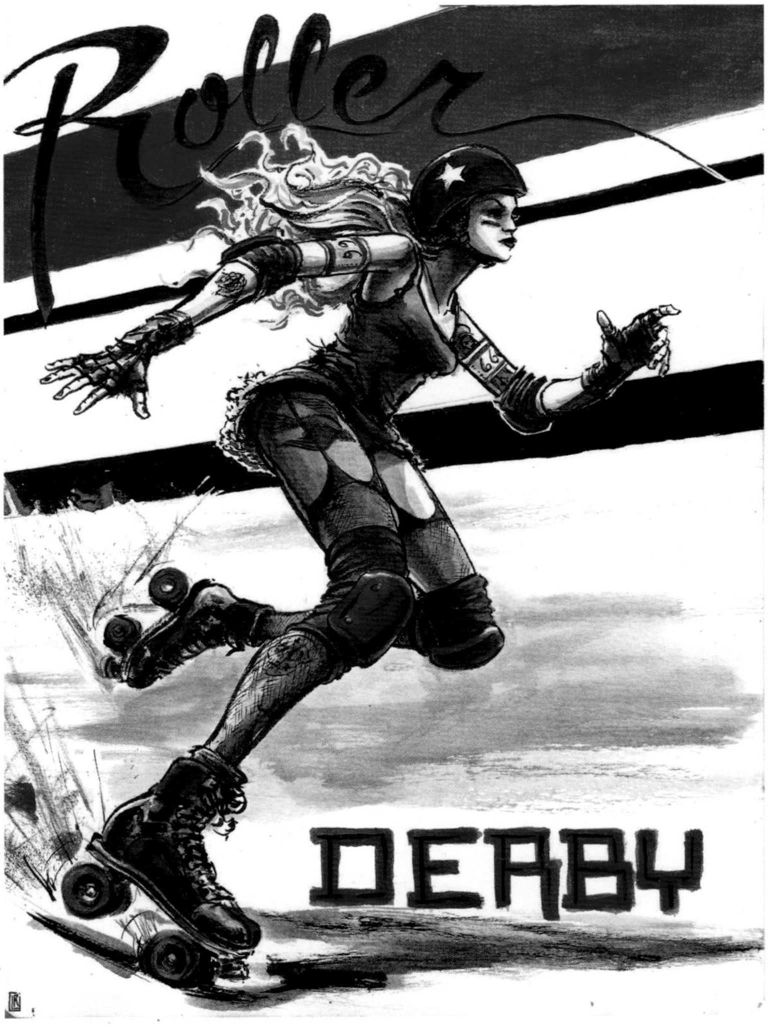
Roller
DERBY

Illustration by Lydia Roberts